Library of Congress Cataloging-in-Publication Data

Language development.
  (Meaning and choice in language; v. 1)
  (Advances in discourse process; v. 27)
  Bibliography: p.
  Includes index.
  1. Language acquisition. 2. Language and languages—
Study and teaching. I. Hasan, Ruqaiya. II. Martin,
J. R. III. Series. IV. Series: Advances in discourse
processes; v. 27
P26.H29M4   vol. 1 410 s [418' .007] 87-33274
[P118]
ISBN 0-89391-443-6

Ablex Publishing Corporation
355 Chestnut Street
Norwood, New Jersey 07648

TABLE OF CONTENTS

PREFACE TO THE SERIES

Roy O. Freedle

Series Editor

This series of volumes provides a forum for the cross-fertilization of ideas from a diverse number of disciplines, all of which share a common interest in discourse—be it prose comprehension and recall, dialogue analysis, text grammar construction, computer simulation of natural language, cross-cultural comparisons of communicative competence, or other related topics. The problems posed by multisentence contexts and the methods required to investigate them, while not always unique to discourse, are still sufficiently distinct as to benefit from the organized mode of scientific interaction made possible by this series.

Scholars working in the discourse area from the perspective of sociolinguistics, psycholinguistics, ethnomethodology and the sociology of language, educational psychology (e.g., teacher-student interaction), the philosophy of language, computational linguistics, and related subareas are invited to submit manuscripts of monograph or book length to the series editor. Edited collections of original papers resulting from conferences will also be considered.

Volumes in the Series

FOREWORD

This is the first volume in the series entitled Meaning and Choice in Language: Studies for Michael Halliday. Volume Two on meaning and form will be edited by Margaret Berry, Christopher Butler, and Robin Fawcett, while Volume Three on discourse, meaning and society is to be edited by Peter Fries and Michael Gregory.

In the preparation of this volume, our thanks are due to Linda Gerot and Carmel Cloran for their editorial assistance.

J R M
R H

INTRODUCTION

1. HALLIDAY: A BIOGRAPHICAL SKETCH

Michael Alexander Kirkwood Halliday was born in Leeds, England, in 1925. He first become interested in the complexities of language as a young student attempting to understand how language functioned in literature. In 1942, he joined the National Services Programme. He was selected to study Chinese, his preferred choice. After a period of war service in India, he was called back to London to teach Chinese to army personnel. These classes were held at the School of Oriental and African Studies of London University, where he was also able to continue with his own study of Chinese.

The experience of first learning a foreign language and then teaching it further quickened his interest in the study of language. In 1947 Halliday traveled to China to study at Peking University, where he took his first degree as an external student from London University. He stayed in China and worked as a volunteer in the Chinese Industrial Cooperatives for several months. It was during this period that he received the news that he had been awarded a postgraduate scholarship, tenable in China for the first two years. As a postgraduate student, he worked first with Professor Luo Zhuanpei at Peking University, studying Chinese phonology, lexicography, and comparative historical linguistics. However, his own interests were more in the direction of synchronic linguistics, especially the area of grammatical variation in modern Chinese dialects. This lead Luo Zhuanpei to recommend him to Professor Wang Li, who was conducting a survey of modern Chinese dialects in Canton. Halliday worked with Wang Li on this survey during 1949, and devised his own methods for collecting data on grammatical variation in Chinese dialects. At the same time, he was able to pursue his growing interest in grammar and sociolinguistics. He read widely, becoming familiar with the current Russian debates on language as well as with the sociologically oriented approaches of the Prague School.

In 1949 Halliday returned to London with the dialect data he had collected in Canton, which he was planning to use as the basis for his

Ph.D. research. However, his plans had to be set aside when he found himself enrolled at Cambridge for this degree (the department there was not prepared to supervise research in modern Chinese). It is a matter for speculation how much sociolinguistics lost by this decision, as grammatical variation across dialects still remains but a nascent field. For his Ph.D. research Halliday worked on the Chinese *Secret History of the Mongols*. Professor J.R. Firth (S.O.A.S.) acted as his supervisor by special arrangement. Halliday's association with Firth proved formative: Over the years that followed he was to develop and articulate many well-known Firthian themes on the nature of language and its relation to social context.

Halliday lectured in Chinese at Cambridge before moving to Edinburgh in 1956, where he taught linguistics. In 1963 he moved to University College, London; he became professor of linguistics in 1965, and remained there until 1970. Between 1970 and 1976 he took up positions at many centers of learning including Brown University, Center for Advanced Studies in the Behavioral Sciences (at Stanford), the University of Illinois, and the University of Essex. Since 1976 he has been professor of linguistics at the University of Sydney, from which position he will retire at the end of 1987.

2.   HALLIDAY'S MODEL

2.1   Linguistics as Action

One of the most important things to keep in mind when interpreting Halliday's work is that for him linguistics is a form of political action. This commitment stems directly from his active involvement in linguistic research and leftist politics while a graduate student in the early fifties. During that period he made two observations. One was that there were probably more people around who were good at making speeches and organizing people than there were people who were good at studying language. The second was that if a truly Marxist linguistics were to be developed, then a kind of distance was required—a kind of distance that is not possible if one is too involved in short term political expediency. So instead of making a simple choice between the two Halliday dedicated himself to developing a linguistics that was socially accountable [85].

From this commitment stem many of the central features of Halliday's work. Perhaps the easiest to recognize is his involvement with educational concerns, particularly with the teaching of English, both as a second language and as a mother tongue. It is no accident that his first major publication, which introduced scale and category grammar to a wide audience, was in the then still developing field of ESL: *The Linguistic Sciences and Language Teaching* [13]. And the publication of his long-awaited *Introduction to Functional Grammar* [91] was in large part a response to the need for a grammar suitable to analyzing spoken and written texts in educational contexts.

Halliday's stance during the entire period of his involvement in educational linguistics is very revealing when we come to consider what exactly is meant by linguistics as "doing." He quite consistently made a point of never telling teachers what to do. Instead he concentrated on imparting relevant understandings about language [19, 27, 28, 35, 41, 50, 61, 64, 70, 72, 80, 97]. In other words, the distance referred to above was maintained. It was not that Halliday couldn't have told teachers what to do—he had been a language teacher himself for many years. But this was not the task he had set himself: His role was that of developing a relevant linguistics.

Something that struck Halliday on a number of occasions during his discussions with teachers was that for linguistics to be relevant it would have to provide understanding about language development, and eventually a language-based theory of learning. Fortunately, the opportunity to study early language development arose with the birth of his son Nigel in 1969. Halliday's social perspective on language learning contrasted sharply with the then dominant rationalist views inspired by Chomsky. In place of an innate language-acquisition device he posited an active interacting dyad; and in place of a purportedly impoverished and often ill-formed linguistic environment he focused on a rich and fluent array of meaning-making acts, clearly developed to suit both child and caretaker needs. In a sense he took the "mystery" out of language learning, showing the care, concern, effort, and mutual support that go into learning how to mean [42, 46, 51, 57, 63, 67, 69, 76, 83].

The significance of Halliday's work on language development as far as educational linguistics is concerned cannot be overestimated. It made linguistics relevant not just in terms of what language is and what needs to be learned, but also in terms of how language is learned. This means that educators can look to linguistics for answers to questions concerning methodology as well as syllabus design. It is no longer simply a question of what to teach, but how to teach as well. The chapters in this volume draw on Halliday's work in both ways and illustrate the kind of social accountability his model enables linguistics to achieve.

Taken as a whole, these chapters can be seen to treat the distance Halliday insisted on in developing his model as a kind of scale. Painter and Cloran operate at the typical Hallidayan end of the scale, making relevant observations about language development. Butt operates in part in this way, but as well, like Christie, focuses on classroom interaction itself as a site for language learning. Rothery, and Drury and her colleagues address teaching practice directly, making suggestions about teaching and syllabus design. And Thornton and his colleagues look back on the first major project in mother-tongue education to span this scale. It is this ranging across theory and practice without dualizing the two that Halliday's model has inspired. Perhaps more clearly than any other aspect of his work it illustrates his concern with linguistics as a form of social action—his thinking is for doing.

2.2 Grammar as Meaning

Fundamentally Halliday is a grammarian—certainly the most original English grammarian of his generation and without doubt the one who looked farthest outside of grammar in order to understand grammar itself. His major achievement has been to develop a grammar of English with a dual focus: on meaning, which is the raison d'être for grammar; and on grammar, without which there can be no meaning. It is a functional grammar of this kind that underpins the relevance of his linguistics as a whole.

In developing a grammar based on meaning, Halliday drew principally on the work of Firth, Hjelmslev, and Whorf [44, 55, 89]. His grammar has a number of distinctive and interacting characteristics, which we will briefly review here.

First, there is the notion of choice [8, 15]. Grammar for Halliday is a resource which is most naturally modeled as a network of interdependent choices. These choices Halliday views for the most part as choices in meaning. The paradigmatic organization of Halliday's grammar contrasts sharply with the syntagmatic organization of most competing models and is the reason that Halliday's work is normally referred to as *systemic linguistics*.

Grammatical systems were organized by Halliday in two ways, reflecting the degree and nature of their interdependence. Most basically they are organized by rank, with clause, group/phrase, and word acting as the points of origin of distinct networks of choice [5, 16, 79]. Rank in other words organizes system networks with respect to constituency. The second major organizing principle is metafunction [25, 30, 39, 40, 45]. Clause-rank systems (and some group/phrase-rank systems as well) tend to fall into distinctive groupings. At clause rank these are referred to as *transitivity*, *mood*, and *theme* [23, 31]. Looking across ranks and searching for a semantic interpretation of this patterning, Halliday proposed that grammar was in general organized with respect to three major types of meaning. Functional components in the grammar in other words reflect the more general metafunctions: ideational, interpersonal, and textual, with ideational subdivided into experiential and logical [40, 59, 65].

Grammatical systems represent part of a language's meaning potential. In actual text the choices selected are realized in structures. These structures themselves reflect metafunctional diversity, with experiential systems realized by particulate structures, interpersonal systems through prosodic patterns, textual systems in a culminative wavelike rhythm, and logical systems through iterative dependency [71]. In order to map these different simultaneous structures onto each other, Halliday made use of function (or relational) labels as well as class (or category) ones. By conflating these grammatical functions onto each other, the structural output of different functional components in the grammar could be integrated [25, 79]. At the same time this functional labeling meant that meaningful choices in the potential were modeled in the actual output of these systems. This has tremendous advantages for text analysis, where meaning has to be kept clearly in view at all times [59].

By organizing choice with respect to both rank and metafunction and through conflating the various functional structures realizing these systems, Halliday engineered an extravagant framework within which to pursue his description of English. In contrast to grammarians intent on parsimony and formal representations, he sought to incorporate as much meaning as possible in his grammatical analysis. His model, in other words, is an importing one [91].

The limitations of an enterprise of this kind are not obvious. The relationship between grammar and semantics is natural, not arbitrary. And so there is no obvious dividing line between meaning and form as there is between phonology and grammar [91]. In general Halliday has treated semantics and grammar as a scale, not seeking to draw any sharp boundary between the two levels. But there are four boundary areas that deserve special comment here: *lexis, taxis, intonation,* and *cohesion.*

First, lexis. In the early sixties Halliday adopted a Firthian perspective on lexis, approaching it from the point of view of collocation and accepting descriptive responsibility for admitting *powerful/strong arguments* but excluding *powerful cups of tea* [5, 17]. Later, as scale and category grammar was systemicized, Halliday was drawn toward ''the grammarian's dream,'' as he had referred to it in ''Categories of the Theory of Grammar'' [5]—namely, treating the relationship between grammar and lexis as a question of delicacy. Grammar, in other words, was concerned with general meanings, lexis with specific ones. The two could be formally related in system networks with the more general grammatical features subclassified by more delicate lexical ones. The aim here was to integrate grammar and lexis in such a way that lexicogrammar as a whole could be conceived as a meaning-making resource, thus avoiding the more traditional bricks (lexicon)—mortar (syntax) view. This move went a long way to breaking down one commonly accepted limitation on grammatical description, although it remains to be reconciled with the earlier and still valuable collocational perspective.

A second limitation Halliday faced had to do with what could be considered the highest-ranking unit in the grammar. In scale and category grammar this was the sentence, which itself consisted of one or more clauses. Considered paradigmatically, however, and with logical meaning taken into account, the sentence seemed better defined as a clause complex. The relationship between clauses in a sentence was thus reconceived in terms of dependency rather than constituency, with the sentence abandoned as a rank in its own right [79]. By the time he wrote *An Introduction to Functional Grammar* [91], Halliday had developed a well-articulated description of the way clauses could depend on each other in a clause complex, recognizing both type of dependency (paratactic or hypotactic) and type of logico-semantic relation (expansion or projection). But by this point his descriptions of dependency structure had pushed beyond the power of his realization apparatus to generate them. He could describe the intricate clause patterns of spontaneous spoken monologue, but he could not yet derive them. It is quite typical of Halliday's work on grammar that he did not allow the absence of generative formalisms for dynamic patterns to stand in the way of grammatical analysis. For him computability makes way for testing grammars; it does not stand in the way of developing them.

Third, intonation. It was originally David Abercrombie who pushed Halliday to this frontier. Familiar with Halliday's work on Chinese [1, 4, 77, 86], he assigned him the task of teaching intonation during an ESL summer school. Halliday's analysis of tone and information structure was as usual semantic in orientation. And he took the novel step of arguing, as with lexis above, that intonation was best conceived as most delicate *mood* [9, 10, 21,29]. This in a sense blurs the traditional and well-recognized boundary between grammar and phonology. It is again typical of Halliday to extend the grammar in quest of meaning and to treat realization wherever possible as a scale, even where it means crossing stratal boundaries.

Finally, cohesion. There is one area, in fact, where grammar did run out. And that has to do with relations between clause complexes or cohesion [12]. Although fundamentally a grammarian, Halliday has always accepted descriptive responsibility for describing text in context. Functional grammar has a crucial role to play in this enterprise; but it cannot do all the work. To overcome this limitation, Halliday worked with Hasan on non-structural relations. Their *Cohesion in English* [54] remains the principal reference text on intersentential relations to date. People talk and write texts, not sentences. It was obvious to Halliday that a relevant model of language would have to go beyond the sentence, as it were. Thus he developed cohesion to complement lexicogrammar and pave the way for comprehensive descriptions of text as semantic choice in social context [59].

The picture of Halliday's model presented to this point can perhaps best be tied together as follows. If one treats linguistics as a form of social action then one's model of language must be useful and relevant. As far as grammar was concerned this meant developing a description of English that gave access to statements of meaning. Halliday's most original contribution lies in having developed a functional grammar of English that can be used to analyze spoken and written texts from the point of view of the meanings they realize [91].

2.3 Language as Culture

Analyzing meaning in text means more than describing clauses and their co-text. Texts arise in social contexts; they are one mode—and perhaps the most pervasive one—of manifesting culture. So a relevant model of language needs to go beyond lexicogrammar and cohesion and examine relations between texts and the social factors that shape their meanings.

Halliday of course inherited from Firth a strong contextual orientation. Working with others of the so-called neo-Firthians in the early sixties, he proposed a tripartite framework for dealing with context— the now familiar trilogy of field, mode, and tenor [13, 24]. Put simply, field was oriented to social activity, mode to channel, and tenor to social relations between participants. Closely related frameworks were developed by Gregory, Ure, and Ellis. All proved useful for categorizing situational factors.

It was not until the later sixties, when more comprehensive system networks had been developed for English clauses, that a natural relation between systems in the grammar and these contextual categories could be observed. This natural relationship involved associating metafunction and context as follows: ideational meaning with field, interpersonal meaning with tenor, and textual meaning with mode [40, 65].

Halliday's suggestion was that a grammar built up around the idea of choice needed to be seen as probabilistic [1, 4]. The correlation between context and metafunction could then be interpreted in terms of reweighted probabilities. Tenor, for example, would tend to affect the way in which speakers selected interpersonal options; similarly, field would tend to skew ideational choices; and mode would influence textual features. In this way Halliday was able to project the organization of his grammar back onto context and motivate nonlinguistic categories with linguistic ones.

Projecting the grammar back onto context took Halliday as far as what we might characterize as context of situation. There remains the question of the context of culture—the social system and social structures that in turn give rise to field, mode, and tenor. For a Marxist linguistics to be viable, this step is an absolutely crucial one. Halliday's strategy was to cooperate on an interdisciplinary basis, taking Bernstein's sociology as the most relevant social theory to make a place for language in its interpretation of society and culture.

Bernstein's interest in socialization and its educational consequences made this association especially appropriate. The two worked together while Halliday was professor of linguistics at University College in London. Halliday was one of the few linguists to appreciate the significance of Bernstein's work [38, 39, 65] throughout an enduring period of profound misunderstandings of Bernstein's work in the academic community as a whole. The development and integration of Halliday's linguistics with Bernstein's sociology remains a challenging and worthwhile goal. It is hard to imagine a more powerful interpretation of language and culture than such a marriage would afford.

It remains to comment on Whorf and realization. One of the major problems with the discussion of language and context undertaken above is its tendency to treat context as determining language, when in fact, as Halliday has often argued, text affects context even as choices determined by context are realized in text. Once again Halliday's model at present falls short of his goals. Realization as usually modeled makes language subservient to context—directed from above. What one really wants is a model in which realizing a text feeds back into the system, with accumulated feedback leading or not leading to systemic change. Whorf gave language a more deterministic role in this process than most linguists. For Whorf language symbolized reality. This is a perspective Halliday would share [22, 60, 90].

One final comment is perhaps in order here. Halliday, as we have seen, developed a highly distinctive interpretation of English grammar by enriching it with a strong orientation to meaning and culture. He looked farther outside of grammar than any other English grammarian, precisely in order to understand grammar itself. For Halliday, literary studies, for example, are a source of insight into the linguistic system [11, 12, 32, 82, 87]: Foregrounding highlights grammar.

Once a grammar is enriched in this way, it becomes a useful tool for analyzing the contexts in which it is used. We have already noted the way in which Halliday used its metafunctional organization to ground register analysis. But the work of deploying Halliday's grammar to analyze our culture has barely begun [85, 93, 94, 96]. Whorf once remarked that in the end science will turn to linguistics to find out what it means (at that point we might hope that humanities and social science would already have done so). It could be argued that it takes a very arrogant linguist even to dream this possible. Hjelmslevian transcendence is offensive to some. So it is somewhat chastening to keep in mind that while by nature Halliday is a very humble man, he has almost certainly developed the grammar and the linguistics to do the job.

M.A.K. HALLIDAY—PUBLICATIONS

Books and Articles

1. Grammatical categories in Modern Chinese. *Transactions of the Philological Society,* 1956, 177–244. (See no. 55 below).
2. The linguistic basis of a mechanical thesaurus. *Mechanical Translation,* 3(3), 1956, 81–88.
3. Some aspects of systematic description and comparison in grammatical analysis. *Studies in Linguistic Analysis* (Special Volume of the Philological Society). Oxford: Blackwell, 1957, 54–67.
4. *The Language of the Chinese* Secret History of the Mongols (Publications of the Philological Society 17). Oxford: Blackwell, 1959.
5. Categories of the theory of grammar. *Word, 17*(3), 1961, 241–292. (Reprinted as Bobbs-Merrill Reprint Series No. Language-36) (See no. 55 below.)
6. Linguistique générale et linguistique appliquée à l'enseignement des langues. *Études de Linguistique Appliquée, 1,* 1961, 5–42. (English version in no. 18 below)
7. Linguistics and machine translation. *Zeitschrift für Phonetik, Sprachwissenschaft und Kommunikationsforschung,* 15(½), 1962, 145–158. (See no. 18 below.)
8. Class in relation to the axes of chain and choice in language. *Linguistics, 2,* 1963, 5–15. (See no. 55 below.)
9. The tones of English. *Archivum Linguisticum, 15*(1), 1963, 1–28. (See no. 21 below.)
10. Intonation in English grammar. *Transactions of the Philological Society,* 1963, 143–169. (See no. 21 below.)
11. Descriptive linguistics in literary studies. In Alah Duthie (ed.), *English Studies Today (3rd series).* Edinburgh: Edinburgh University Press, 1964; 25–39. (Reprinted in Donald C. Freeman (ed.), *Linguistics and Literary Style,* New York: Holt, Rinehart & Winston, 1970, 57–72)

12. The linguistic study of literary texts. In Horace Lunt (ed.), *Proceedings of the Ninth International Congress of Linguists*. The Hague: Mouton, 1964, 302–307. (Revised version reprinted in Seymour Chatman & Samuel R. Levin (eds.), *Essays on the Language of Literature*. Boston: Houghton Mifflin, 1967, 217–223)

13. (with Angus McIntosh & Peter Strevens) *The Linguistic Sciences and Language Teaching*. London: Longman (Longmans Linguistics Library), 1964; Bloomington, IN: Indiana University Press, 1966; English Language Book Society (The Teacher's Bookshelf), 1970. (Chap. 4 reprinted in Joshua A. Fishman (ed.), *Readings in the Sociology of Language*. The Hague: Mouton, 1968, 139–169)

14 Syntax and the consumer. In C.I.J.M. Stuart (ed.), *Report on the Fifteenth Annual (First International) Round Table Meeting on Linguistics and Language Study*. (Monograph Series in Language & Linguistics 17). Washington, DC: Georgetown University Press, 1964, 11–24. (See no. 79 below.)

15. Some notes on "deep" grammar. *Journal of Linguistics*, 2(1), 1966, 57–67. (See no. 55 below.)

16. The concept of rank: a reply. *Journal of Linguistics*, 2(1), 1966. 110–118.

17. Lexis as a linguistic level. In C. E. Bazell, J. C. Catford, M. A. K. Halliday, & R. H. Robins (eds.), *In Memory of J. R. Firth*. London: Longmans Linguistics Library, 1966, 148–162. (See no. 55 below.)

18. (with Angus McIntosh) *Patterns of Language: Papers in General, Descriptive and Applied Linguistics*. London: Longman (Longmans Linguistics Library), 1966; Bloomington, IN: Indiana University Press, 1966. (includes English version of no. 6 and reprint of no. 7 above)

19. Linguistics and the teaching of English. In James N. Britton (ed.), *Talking and Writing: A Handbook for English Teachers*. London: Methuen, 1967, 80–90.

20. *Some Aspects of the Thematic Organization of the English Clause* (Memorandum RM-5224-PR), Santa Monica, California: The Rand Corporation, 1967. (See no. 55 below.)

21. *Intonation and Grammar in British English* (Janua Linguarum Series Practica 48). The Hague: Mouton, 1967. (Revised reprint of nos. 9, 10 above)

22. *Grammar, Society and the Noun*. London: H. K. Lewis for University College London, 1967. (See no. 60 below.)

23. Notes on transitivity and theme in English (Parts 1–3). *Journal of Linguistics*, 3(1), 1967, 37–81; 3(2), 1967, 199–244; 4(2), 1968; 179–215.

24. Language and experience. *The Place of Language. Educational Review*, 20(2), University of Birmingham, 1968, 95–106.

25. Options and functions in the English clause. *Brno Studies in English*, 8, 1969, 81–88. (See no. 79 below.)

26. Systemic grammar. *La Grammatica; La Lessicologia (Atti del I e Del II Convegno di Studi, Società di Linguistica Italiana)*. Rome: Bulzoni, 1969. (See no. 55 below.)

27. Linguistics and the language learner (in Chinese). *Bulletin of the Teachers' Training College, Singapore*, November 1969.

28. Relevant models of language. *The State of Language. Educational Review*, University of Birmingham, 22(1), 1969, 26–37. (See no. 40 below.)

29. *A Course in Spoken English: Intonation* (Part 2 of Ronald Mackin, M. A. K. Halliday, & J. M. Sinclair, *A Course in Spoken English*). London: Oxford University Press, 1970. (See no. 55 below.)

30. Language structure and language function. In John Lyons (ed.), *New Horizons in Linguistics*. Harmondsworth: Penguin, 1970, 140–165.

31. Functional diversity in language, as seen from a consideration of modality and mood in English. *Foundations of Language*, 6(3), 1970, 322–361. (See no. 55 below.)

32. Linguistic function and literary style: an enquiry into the language of William Golding's *The Inheritors*. In Seymour Chatman (ed.), *Literary Style: A Symposium* New York: Oxford University Press, 1971, 362–400. (See no. 40 below.)

33. Language in a social perspective. *The Context of Language. Educational Review*, University of Birmingham, 23(3), 1971, 165–188. (See no. 40 below.)

34. A "linguistic approach" to the teaching of the mother tongue? *The English Quarterly* (Canadian Council of Teachers of English), 4(2), 1971, 13–24.

35. Language acquisition and initial literacy. In Malcom P. Douglass (ed.), *Claremont Reading Conference 35th Yearbook*, 1971, 63–68.

36. *Towards a Sociological Semantics* (Working Papers and Prepublications C-14). Urbino: Centro Interazionale di Semiotica e di Linguistica, Università di Urbino, 1972. (See no. 40 below.)

37. National language and language planning in a multilingual society. *East African Journal*, November 1972.

38. Foreword to Basil Bernstein (ed.), *Class, Codes and Control: Vol. II. Applied Studies Towards a Sociology of Language*. London: Routledge & Kegan Paul (Primary Socialization, Language and Education), 1973, ix–xvi.

39. The functional basis of language. In Basil Bernstein (ed.), *Class, Codes and Control: Vol. II* (same volume as no. 38), 343–366.

40. *Explorations in the Functions of Language.* London: Edward Arnold (Explorations in Language Study), 1973; New York: Elsevier, 1975. (Reprint, with revision, of nos. 28, 32, 33, 36, 39 above)

41. Foreword to David Mackay, Brian Thompson & Pamela Schaub, *Breakthrough to Literacy: Teachers' Resource Book.* Glendale, CA: Bowmar, 1973, iii–x.

42. A sociosemiotic perspective on language development. *Bulletin of the School of Oriental and Africal Studies,* 37(1) (W. H. Whiteley Memorial Volume), 1974, 98–118. (See no. 46 below.)

43. *Language and Social Man.* (Schools Council Programme in Linguistics and English Teaching: Papers, Series II, Vol. 3). London: Longman 1974, (See no. 65 below.)

44. Discussion with M. A. K. Halliday. In Herman Parret, *Discussing Language.* The Hague: Mouton, 1974, 81–120. (See no. 65 below.)

45. The place of "functional sentence perspective" in the system of linguistic description. In Frantisek Danes (ed.), *Papers on Functional Sentence Perspective.* Prague: Academia (Czechoslovak Academy of Sciences), 1974.

46. *Learning How to Mean: Explorations in the Development of Language.* London: Edward Arnold (Explorations in Language Study), 1975; New York: Elsevier, 1977. (Includes reprint of nos. 42, 51, 57)

47. Language as social semiotic: towards a general sociolinguistic theory. In Adam Makkai & Valerie Becker Makkai (eds.), *The First LACUS Forum.* Columbia, SC: Hornbeam Press, 1975, 17–46. Also in Adam Makkai, Valerie Becker Makkai, & Luigi Heilmann (eds.), *Linguistics at the Crossroads.* Padua: Liviana; Lake Bluff, IL: Jupiter Press, 1977, 13–41. (See no. 65 below.)

48. Sociological aspects of semantic change. In Luigi Heilmann (ed.), *Proceedings of the Eleventh International Congress of Linguists.* Bologna: Il Mulino, 1975, 853–879. (See no. 65 below.)

49. The context of linguistics. In Francis P. Dineen (ed.), *Report of the Twenty-fifth Annual Round Table Meeting on Linguistics and Language Study* (Monograph Series in Languages & Linguistics 27). Washington, DC: Georgetown University Press, 1975. (See no. 60 below.)

50. Talking one's way in: A sociolinguistic perspective on language and learning. In Alan Davies (ed.), *Problems of Language and Learning.* London: Heinemann, 1975, 8–26.

51. Learning how to mean. In Eric Lenneberg & Elizabeth Lenneberg (eds.), *Foundations of Language Development: A Multidisciplinary Perspective.* New York: Academic Press; Paris: UNESCO Press,

1975, vol. I (pt. 3, "Ontogeny," chap. 14), 239–265. (See no. 46 above.)

52. Some aspects of sociolinguistics and Aspects of sociolinguistic research. *Interactions Between Linguistics and Mathematical Education* (Report on a Symposium sponsored by UNESCO - CEDO - ICMI, Nairobi, September 1974). Paris: UNESCO (Ed-74/CONF. 808 (64–73) and 808/7), 1975. (See no. 65 below.)

53. "The teacher taught the student English": An essay in applied linguistics. In Peter A. Reich (ed.), *The Second LACUS Forum*. Columbia, SC: Hornbeam Press, 1976. 344–349. Also in Mohammad Ali Jazayery, Edgar C. Polomé, & Werner Winter (eds.), *Linguistic and Literary Studies in Honor of Archibald A. Hill: Vol. 4. Linguistics and Literature/Sociolinguistics and Applied Linguistics*. (Trends in Linguistics Studies & Monographs 10). The Hague: Mouton 1979, 233–242.

54. (with Ruqaiya Hasan) *Cohesion in English* (English Language Series 9). London: Longman, 1976.

55. *System and Function in Language: Selected Papers Edited by G. R. Kress*. London: Oxford University Press, 1976. (Includes reprints of extracts from nos. 1, 5, 8, 15, 17, 20, 26, 29, 31, 45 above)

56. Anti-languages. *American Anthropologist*, 78(3), 1976, 570–584. (See no. 65 below.)

57. Early language learning: a sociolinguistic approach. In William C. McCormack & Stephen A. Wurm (eds.), *Language and Man, Anthropological Issues*. The Hague: Mouton (World Anthropology Series), 1976, 97–124. (See no. 46 above.)

58. How children learn language. In K. D. Watson & R. D. Eagleson (eds.), *English in Secondary Schools: Today and Tomorrow*. Ashfield, N.S.W., Australia: English Teachers' Association of New South Wales, 1977, 20–37.

59. Text as semantic choice in social contexts. In Teun A. van Dijk & Janos Petofi (eds.), *Grammars and Descriptions* (Research in Text Theory 1). Berlin & New York: de Gruyter, 1977, 176–225. (See no. 65 below.)

60. *Aims and Perspectives in Linguistics* (Applied Linguistics Association of Australia Occasional Papers 1), 1977. (Includes reprint of nos. 22, 49 above)

61. Some thoughts on language in the middle school years. *English in Australia*, 42, November 1977, 3–16.

62. Eine Interpretation der funktionalen Beziehung zwischen Sprache und Sozialstruktur (An interpretation of the functional relationship between language and social structure). In Uta Quasthoff (ed.), *Sprachstruktur—Sozialstruktur: Zur Linguistischen Theorienbil-*

dung. Konigstein: Scriptor, 1978, 3–42. (English version in no. 65 below)

63. Meaning and the construction of reality in early childhood. In Herbert L., Pick, Jr., & Elliot Saltzman (eds.), *Modes of Perceiving and Processing of information.* Hillsdale, NJ: Erlbaum, 1978, 67–96 (chap. 5).

64. Is learning a second language like learning a first language all over again? In D. E. Ingram & T. J. Quinn (eds.), *Language Learning in Australian Society: Proceedings of the 1976 Congress of the Applied Linguistics Association of Australia.* Melbourne: Australian International Press & Publications, 1978, 3–19.

65. *Language as Social Semiotic: The Social Interpretation of Language and Meaning.* London: Edward Arnold, 1978; Baltimore, MD: University Park Press, 1979. (Includes reprints of extracts from nos. 43, 44, 47, 48, 52, 56, 59, 62 above)

66. *Notes on Talking Shop: Demands on Language* (for use with the Film Australia production). Lindfield, N.S.W.: Film Australia (Australian Film Commission), 1978, 4–41.

67. One child's protolanguage. In Margaret Bullowa (ed.), *Before Speech: The Beginnings of Interpersonal Communication.* Cambridge, England: Cambridge University Press, 1976, 171–190.

68. Development of texture in child language. In Terry Myers (ed.), *The Development of Conversation and Discourse.* Edinburgh: Edinburgh University Press, 1979, 72–87.

69. The ontogenesis of dialogue. In Wolfgang U. Dressler (ed.), *Pro ceedings of the Twelfth International Congress of Linguists* (Innsbrücker Beitrage zur Sprachwissenchaft, Special Volume), 1979, 539–544.

70. Some reflections on language education in multilingual societies, as seen from the standpoint of linguistics. In Madge Claxton (ed.), *Report of the 1977 Seminar on Language Education in Multilingual Societies.* Singapore: Regional Language Centre (RELC), 1979.

71. Modes of meaning and modes of expression: Types of grammatical structure, and their determination by different semantic functions. In D. J. Allerton, Edward Carney, & David Holdcroft (eds.), *Function and Context in Linguistic Analysis: Essays Offered to William Haas.* Cambridge, England: Cambridge University Press, 1979, 57–79.

72. Linguistics in teacher education. In Jillian Maling-Keepes & Bruce D. Keepes (eds.), *Language in Education: The Language Development Project, Phase I.* Canberra: Curriculum Development Centre, 1979, 279–286.

73. Differences between spoken and written language: Some impli-

cations for literacy teaching. In Glenda Page, John Elkins, & Barrie O'Connor (eds.), *Communication Through Reading: Proceedings of the Fourth Australian Reading Conference*. Adelaide, South Australia: Australian Reading Association, 1979, vol. 2, 37–52.

74. On being teaching. In Sidney Greenbaum, Geoffrey Leech, & Jan Svartivk (eds.), *Studies in English Linguistics: For Randolph Quirk*. London: Longman, 1980, 61–64.

75. (with Ruqaiya Hasan) *Text and Context: Aspects of Language in a Social-Semiotic Perspective (Sophia Linguistica, 6)*. Tokyo: Sophia University, Linguistic Institute for International Communication, 1980, 4–91.

76. The contribution of developmental linguistics to the interpretation of language as a system. In Even Hovdhaugen (ed.), *The Nordic Languages and Modern Linguistics: Proceedings of the Fourth International Conference of Nordic and General Linguistics, Oslo 1980*. Oslo: Universitetsforlaget, 1980, 1–18.

77. The origin and early development of Chinese phonological theory. In R. E. Asher & Eugénie J. A. Henderson (eds.), *Towards a History of Phonetics*. Edinburgh: Edinburgh University Press, 1981, 123–139.

78. Text semantics and clause grammar: Some patterns of realization. In James E. Copeland & Philip W. Davis (eds.), *The Seventh LACUS Forum*. Columbia, SC: Hornbeam, Press, 1981, 31–59.

79. (with J. R. Martin) (eds.) *Readings in Systemic Linguistics*. London: Batsford Academic and Educational, 1981. (Includes reprints of nos. 14, 25 above; also "Types of Structure," Working Paper, 1965, and "Structure," Working Paper, 1969)

80. Three aspects of children's language development: Learning language, learning through language, learning about language. In Yetta M. Goodman, Myna M. Haussler, & Dorothy S. Strickland (eds.), *Oral and Written Language Development: Impact on Schools* (International Reading Association & National Council of Teachers of English: Proceedings from the 1979 and 1980 IMPACT Conferences). n.p., no.d, 7–19.

81. How is a text like a clause? In Sture Allen (ed.), *Text Processing: Text Analysis and Generation, Text Typology and Attribution* (Proceedings of Nobel Symposium 51). Stockholm: Almqvist & Wiksell International, 1982, 209–247.

82. The de-automatization of grammar: From Priestley's *An Inspector Calls*. In John M. Anderson (ed.), *Language Form and Linguistic Variation: Papers Dedicated to Angus McIntosh* (Current Issues in Linguistic Theory 15). Amsterdam: John Benjamins, 1982, 129–159.

83. On the transition from child tongue to mother tongue. *Australian Journal of Linguistics*, 3(2), 1983, 201–216.

84. Linguistics in theory and practice. *Waiyu Jiaoxue yu Yanjiu* (Foreign Language Teaching and Research), 56, 1983, 24–32.

85. Linguistics in the university: The question of social accountability. In James E. Copeland (ed.), *New Directions in Linguistics and Semiotics*. Houston, TX: Rice University Studies (New Series 2), 1984, 51–67.

86. Grammatical metaphor in English and Chinese. In Beverly Hong (ed.), *New Papers in Chinese Language Use* (Contemporary China Papers 18). Canberra: Contemporary China Centre, Australian National University, 1984, 9–18.

87. Foreword to Michael Cummings & Robert Simmons, *The Language of Literature: A Stylistic Introduction to the Study of Literature*. Oxford: Pergamon Press (Pergamon Institute of English), 1983, vii–xiv.

88. Language as code and language as behaviour: A systemic-functional interpretation of the nature and ontogenesis of dialogue. In Robin Fawcett et al. (eds.), *The Semiotics of Culture and Language*. London: Frances Pinter (Open Linguistics Series), 1984, vol. 1, 3–35.

89. Systemic background. In James D. Benson & William S. Greaves (eds.), *Systemic Perspectives on Discourse; Vol. 1. Selected Theoretical Papers from the Ninth International Systemic Workshop* (Advances in Discourse Processes XV). Norwood, NJ: Ablex, 1985, 1–15.

90. On the ineffability of grammatical categories. In Alan Manning, Pierre Martin, & Kim McCalla (eds.), *The Tenth LACUS Forum 1983*. Columbia, SC: Hornbeam Press, 1984, 3–18.

91. *An Introduction to Functional Grammar*. London, Baltimore, Melbourne: Edward Arnold, 1985.

92. Dimensions of discourse analysis: Grammar. In Teun A. van Dijk (ed.), *Handbook of Discourse Analysis: Vol. 2. Dimensions of Discourse*. London: Academic Press, 1985, 29–56.

93. (with Ruqaiya Hasan) *Language, Context and Text: A Social-Semiotic Perspective* (Language and Learning, ECS 805). Geelong, Victoria, Australia: Deakin University Press, 1985.

94. Language across the culture. In Makhan L. Tickoo (ed.), *Language Across the Curriculum: Papers from the 1985 Regional Seminar*. Singapore: Regional Language Centre, 1985.

95. It's a fixed word order language is English. *ITL Review of Applied Linguistics*, 67-68, 1985, 91–116.

96. *Spoken and Written Language* (Language and Learning, ECS 805). Geelong, Australia: Deakin University Press, 1985.

97. *Learning Asian Languages.* Sydney: Centre for Asian Studies, University of Sydney (in press).

98. ''So you say 'pass' . . . Thank you three muchly': How conversation means: contexts and functions.'' In A.D. Grimshaw (ed.), *Interdisciplinary Perspective on Discourse: Parallel Studies of a Naturally Occurring Conversation.* Norwood: Ablex (in press).

99. ''Language and the order of nature.'' In D. Attridge, A. Durant, N. Fabb & C. MacCabe (eds.), *The Linguistics of Writing.* Manchester University Press (in press).

100. Poetry as scientific discourse: the nuclear sections of *In Memoriam.* In L. M. O'Toole & D. Birch (eds.), *Functions of Style.* London: Frances Pinter (in press).

CHAPTER 1

LEARNING LANGUAGE: A FUNCTIONAL VIEW OF LANGUAGE DEVELOPMENT

Clare Painter

University of Sydney
New South Wales, Australia

1. Introduction

M. A. K. Halliday's work on language development (see especially Halliday, 1975, 1978c, 1979a, 1979b, 1983, 1984a) provides us with a coherent functional interpretation in which language is seen as evolving ontogenetically in response to the child's changing needs. This perspective allows us to consider both *how* and *why* a child comes to learn language in the first few years. My concern in this chapter will be to suggest that an understanding of these two questions is a necessary foundation for determining teaching practice in the language classrooms (whether it be mother tongue, or second or foreign language), since it is there that we attempt to intervene to help learners develop their language further.

However, we can hardly address the matter of language development, either in the home or the school, without also considering closely what it is we are calling "language." I propose therefore to open with an outline of relevant aspects of Halliday's functional view of language as a prelude to a closer look at the nature of language development as he conceives it.

The body of the chapter will comprise an account of first language development illustrated from two case studies—my study of my son, Hal, and Halliday's study of his son, Nigel (Halliday, 1975; Painter, 1984, for a detailed account). In this account my focus will be simultaneously on the how and why of development and the what of language. This in turn will provide the basis for a closing discussion of some of the implications Halliday's view of language development holds for educational practice.

1.1 Halliday's View of Language in Relation to Other Approaches: A Meaning-Oriented View

Halliday's view of language is in contrast to some approaches currently popular in educational writing. For example, Halliday has always focused on the nature of language as a symbolic system—a resource for making meanings. This contrasts with one familiar approach within education where language is seen in terms of user "skills." To view language primarily as a set of skills, whether of "refining and combining sentence constituents" (Anglin, 1980, p. 111) or of managing modes of expression (reading, writing, listening, talking), is to deemphasize its character as a symbolic resource, with certain inevitable consequences for the classroom. For example, teaching may focus on decontextualized sentence construction exercises which ignore language as a meaning-making system; or the focus may be on training the eye and ear to perceive and relate graphic and phonic shapes and on training the hand and the tongue to make them. And certainly, in the teaching of English as mother tongue in Australia, these foci are prominent throughout the early years of school. However I would suggest that mastery of such skills would not take the learner very far since it ignores the issue of meaning.

Taking language as a symbolic system implies that, whether reading or speaking, listening or writing, the individual is engaged in making meanings in some particular context. To understand how this is done, and how we can help the child to do it more effectively, we need to appreciate how the language system is organized to make meanings. Further, we need to have a clear view of what is meant by context and how the language system is organized to respond to context.

Halliday's systemic-functional framework addresses these issues, and so it avoids the simplistic view of language learning as skills training. At the same time, it distinguishes itself from those approaches to language which assume a sharp dichotomy between form and meaning, where the system of language is seen simply as a formal algorithm, leaving us with the problem of how such a formal system comes to be used for meaning. In the early 1960s, such a view of language became dominant with Chomsky's work, and since our ideas of what language is like inevitably affect our ideas about how language is learned, the Chomskyan approach heralded a view of language development in sharp contrast to that of Halliday's. Since Chomsky and his followers conceived of language as a set of rules for generating syntactic structures, and since the rules for generating these structures appeared highly complex, it seemed reasonable to hypothesize that each child is born with an innate knowledge of an abstract linguistic structure which underlies all languages

(Chomsky, 1968; McNeill, 1970). So the child in infancy was seen as having the task of matching his innate knowledge of this abstract "universal grammar" with its local manifestation in the particular language of his community (Richards, 1982, p. 368). From this perspective, all the child needs for language learning is "exposure" to some language. If such exposure was forthcoming, the child—it was maintained—"acquired" his mother tongue in the short time between 18 months and 4 years of age.

Such a view of language would seem to have certain implications for learning in general, and for learning (more of) language in particular. One unavoidable implication is that all individuals come to school, equipped with language, ready to learn other things—for which language would be simply a means of expression. However, it is a well-known fact that not all children are equally successful at learning these "other things." A theory of language development that maintains that the process of development is completed by age 4 is unlikely to see failure at school as a linguistic matter at all: Indeed, it can see neither failure nor success in terms of control of language. Some other reason(s) must be found. Could it be due to differences in intelligence? If so, intelligence must be seen as unaffected by language. Butt (1985; and Chapter 2 in this volume) presents convincing arguments, based on current research, against holding this position.

Perhaps then we could take the view that while all children have an equal knowledge of the syntactic rules of their language by this age, they still have to be taught how to use their language—that their competence has to be turned into performance. This at times seems to be Bruner's position (Bruner, 1977, p. 273): "Whilst language in its formal sense is mastered swiftly . . . its semantic meanings and pragmatic uses for 'getting things done with words' comes much more slowly."

Teaching practices based on these assumptions will see forms and uses as quite distinct matters for attention, an assumption to be questioned in this chapter. Moreover, although a view that focuses on the learning or teaching of rules of use seems a radical departure from the assumption of innate knowledge of rules of language structure, there is a common position here: Form is still distinguished from function, and the mastery of formal structures is seen as preceding the use of the structures.

This position runs counter to Halliday's; for him, form and function are not dichotomized in this way. Rather, he draws attention to the close relation between the nature of the system and its use. According to Halliday, linguistic form is best viewed as functional in nature. This can be taken in two senses: First, grammatical structures are functional; they serve to make meanings, and a child will develop them to do just this. Rather than form preceding function, the two are seen as mutually dependent. Second, language is a functional resource in that the language system as a whole can be viewed as having the form it does because of what it is called upon to do—the needs of language users have shaped the linguistic system itself.

I will first clarify these remarks by discussing briefly both the fundamental needs of speakers and Halliday's view of language as organized to respond to those needs. Having looked at the evolved language in these terms, I will turn to a consideration of language development. Here, two central questions would be: What is the child making his symbolic system do for him? and How does the child's symbolic system change in response to his changing needs and goals? Following Halliday, my central thesis will be that the system of language develops in response to the child's needs; and using the system at his disposal creates additional needs and goals which will, in turn, lead to further changes in the system. Language development is seen, then, as an ongoing process in which what is being done now becomes an impetus to the exploration of how the system may be changed to meet new needs.

1.2 Halliday's Approach: A Descriptive Outline

Turning then first to the role language plays in all our lives, it has been suggested that language is by its nature our principal means for creating "intersubjectivity" (Berger & Luckmann, 1966); it is the means by which we allow our fellows to share our experiences of ourselves, of each other, and of the environment. We make sense of ourselves and of our world by interpreting our experiences into language and having others "validate" that experience by understanding us. We can see then why most scholars concerned with functions of language agree that it involves at least two things: both interpretation of experience (which allows it to be talked about) and interaction with others (in which that experience is made available for validation).

These two basic functions of language are termed the **experiential** and the **interpersonal metafunctions.** Halliday sees adult language as organized into two relatively distinct sets of grammatical resources serving these two functions. In addition, in order to fulfil these two basic functions, language needs a further set of resources by means of which any part of an ongoing text is linked to the rest of the text as well as to the context—this is the **textual metafunction.**

Let us consider a short extract of conversation between a mother and her child of 2 years, 9 months, in these terms:

(1)   (Child Stephen gets into bed with parents in early morning)
    S: Are you waking up, Mummy?
    M: Yes, darling
    S: Talk!
    M: (laughs)
    S: Talk!
    M: Oh, all right
            I'm talking
    S: What you got in your ears?
    M: These? (touching earring)
    S: Mm
    M: That's an earring
    S: Oh, earring
            I haven't got earrings
    M: No, you haven't got earrings
    S: And Hal hasn't got earrings (Hal = brother)
    M: No, Hal hasn't got earrings
    S: (turns to F and reaches hand to face)
            And Daddy hasn't got earrings
            Daddy's got bristles
    M: Mm, he has, hasn't he?
    S: I haven't got bristles . . .

We can see here that the partners in this dialogue accept and adopt various speech roles, and that these are expressed by particular grammatical choices. For example, to open the communication, the child begins with a question (coded as a polar interrogative). The affirmative response he gets is a minimal one, so he tries a more direct approach to get the conversation going, by directly demanding a service of M (expressing this with the imperative *talk*). His attention is attracted by M's earrings and this leads to an exchange in which the child first seeks specific information (using a *wh-* interrogative) and then goes on to provide related information himself (using declaratives; e.g., *I haven't got earrings*).

The speakers are thus taking up interactional roles via the grammatical system of mood (see Halliday, 1985b, for explanation of all technical terms used here). In addition, the topic of conversation moves from M's behavioral state to various characteristics of significant persons (the former coded as "behavioral" processes *(wake up; talk)*, and the latter as attributive "relational" ones *(is, has got)*. These choices of process are independent of the choices of mood discussed above, though they are expressed simultaneously in the utterances spoken. Thus, each speaker in this fragment of conversation can be seen as making simultaneous selections from the interpersonal system of mood, and the experiential

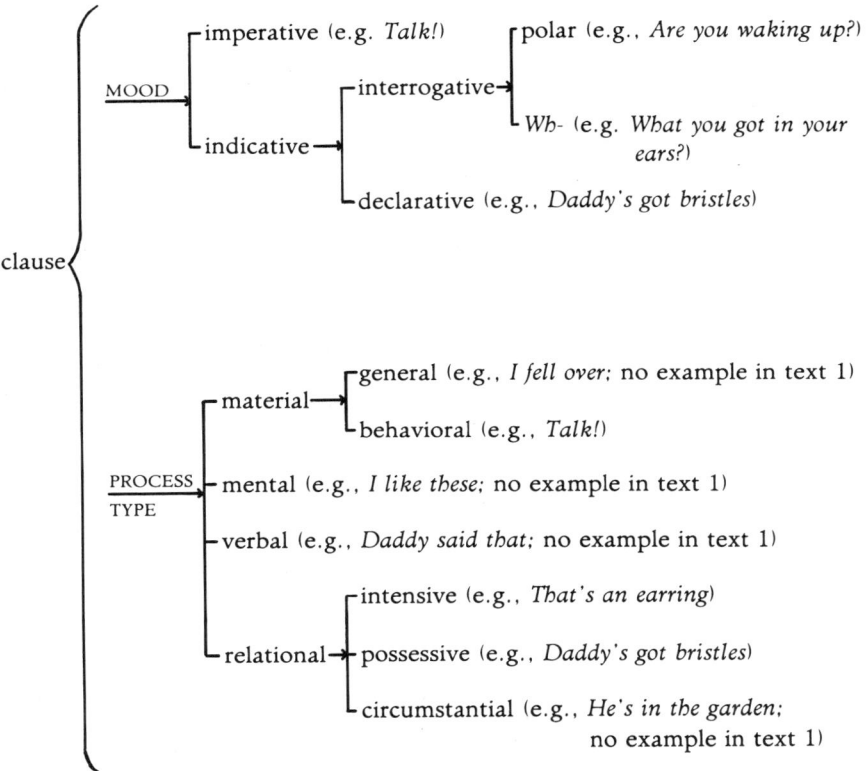

The [denotes an either-or choice (e.g., either imperative or indicative, either material or mental or verbal or relational). The { denotes 'simultaneous choice'—in this case that every clause must embody a choice of options from both the mood system and the process-type system.

Figure 1. Outline of mood and process-type options at clause rank

one of process type, as shown in Figure 1. (Note that other systems are involved too, e.g., interpersonal ones of vocation, polarity, and ellipsis).

Furthermore, because the dialogue is a text, realized as sequential utterances spoken over time, and is not just a random series of sentences, there are also textual systems deployed at the same time as the interpersonal and experiential ones outlined in Figure 1. Textual systems used here include those of Theme and Information. The child's Themes (realized by first position in the clause) map onto key mood-defining elements throughout as shown in Table 1.

For the first half of the conversation, then, his "point of departure" is the gaining of a response, and Themes are interrogative or imperative elements indicating this. Once the information exchange is under way,

Table 1. Themes from Text 1

Thematic choices Expression in clause			"Point of Departure"
Text.[a]	Int.	Exper.	
S:	Are	you	request yes/no information on addressee
M: Yes		(I)	affirmative answer about speaker
S:		talk!	request speech from addressee
M: Alright			accede to request
		I	about speaker
S:	What———		request information about something
M:		that	about that (earring)
S:		I	about speaker
M: No		you	response about addressee
S: And		Hal	continuing, about Hal
M: No		Hal	response about Hal
S: And		Daddy	continuing, about Daddy
		Daddy	about Daddy
M: Mm,		he	response about Daddy
S:		I	about speaker

[a]Text. = textual Theme; Int. = interpersonal Theme; Exper. = experiential Theme

Themes from both parties are the names of members of the family, preceded often by other cohesive elements (No and Mm from M, linking the discourse by acknowledging the previous speaker, and and from the child, marking his statements as further information). Many of the person Themes are also marked by intonation as "new information," allowing one person to be contrasted with another in a series of parallel structures.

So far, I have been suggesting that the linguistic system is organized into three (relatively independent) sets of resources. One (which includes the mood, ellipsis, and polarity systems of the clause) is concerned with the interpersonal function—involved in talking to another; a second (which includes the process-type system) is concerned with the experiential function—involved in talking about something; and a third (which includes the clause systems of theme and information and the discourse systems of reference and conjunction) is concerned with the textual function—involved in the creation of coherent text over time. I will now look very briefly beyond the linguistic system to consider what influences the choices made within it on any particular occasion such as this, and here we will need some notion of context.

It is generally agreed that language varies according to the context in which it occurs. Some studies have used a scale of degrees of formality as a contextual means of explaining variation (e.g., Labov, 1970). And there have been various other attempts to determine which kinds of factors influence grammatical or phonological choices made, or likely to be made, in a particular situation (see, e.g., Firth, 1950; Hymes, 1967). Halliday's contribution has been to hypothesize that if language is organized meta-functionally as three sets of coexisting resources, then the context for any text should be viewed as a corresponding tripartite construct, each aspect of the context influencing choices made in one metafunctional area of the grammar (Halliday, 1974; Halliday & Hasan, 1985).

One aspect of the context—the **tenor** (Gregory 1967)—involves the re-lations between speaker and hearer, or reader and writer, in terms of power, contact, and affect relations (see Poynton, 1984). These factors influence choices made within the interpersonal systems of the grammar (including the degree to which the choices made are reciprocal between speakers).

In text 1, we have a parent and child conversing, and even though the child is leading the interaction for the most part, he has to establish his right to do so initially because the parent is still in bed. (This reflects the inherent inequality of power relations between the two roles since an examination of a larger corpus of material would show that the child does not have comparable rights of privacy requiring such conversa-tional openings.) Moreover, there seems to be a difference in roles taken up with regard to the knowledge exchanged. The parent would appear to be the chief source of information, not only in being the one to supply the initial piece of information, but in preferring nonellipitical acknowl-edgments of the child's statements on the whole. This pattern suggests that the parent's moves are something other than typical acknowledg-ments and serve in a tutorial way to confirm the child's propositions.

Another component of the context is the **field**, and this influences experiential choices from the linguistic system. Field concerns not just the topic of the text but the social process being achieved by it. The child's purpose is to establish interaction with a family member and to explore a particular domain of reality. For the parent, the goal is chiefly one of "phatic communion" (oiling personal relations), but this involves helping the child achieve his purposes. The move from focusing on M's state of readiness for talk to the salient characteristics possessed by fam-ily members reflects the attainment of these ends and determines the move in the text from behavioral processes to attributive possessive ones. The lexical choices of family names and facial adornment reflect the domain being explored.

The third component of the context is the **mode**, which concerns the role that language plays in the process, and which has an effect on the deployment of textual systems. Language is doing much more here than simply accompanying a social process, as when speakers are engaged in a joint nonlinguistic task (e.g., doing a jigsaw puzzle together). Conse-quently the text needs few "stage directions" to be understood by us out of context. But because of shared knowledge between the interactants and the face-to-face nature of the interaction, it is unnecessary for all the entities under discussion to be introduced and contextualized through "presenting" reference (Rochester & Martin, 1979). *Hal* and *Daddy* are part of the shared world while the identities of *I, you, that,* and *these* are in fact simply "retrieved" from the situation (see Halliday, 1985b; Halliday & Hasan, 1976, 1985).

Each aspect of the context will therefore have its influence on the speaker's "choice" of meanings within a particular metafunction. In this way language is organized to respond to context and the interpretation of context by the speakers affects the way the language is deployed in any specific instance.

2.1 How Does Language Begin?

The child in text 1 has already developed a metafunctionally organized linguistic system that allows him to talk about things to other people, thus manifesting intersubjectivity. But we still need to explore how and why he developed such a system. To do this, we shall consider the journey a child takes from birth onward, examining what needs of the child motivate him to develop language and how his experiences as a communicator using the system at his disposal encourage him to move in the direction he does.

Such a perspective makes it unnecessary to assume the existence at birth of innate grammatical or other linguistic knowledge, but it does lead us to inquire whether the neonate might come into the world with some inbuilt needs or predispositions to provide the foundation of communication. Such a hypothesis is supported by recent findings in developmental psychology that suggest that babies have a general innate motivation to explore the environment of persons and of objects (Trevarthen, 1980). The neonate's exploration of the human element in the environment takes the form of closely attending to persons communicating with it, and this attention is manifested in facial, vocal, and bodily movements directed toward the other person. The communicating partner reciprocates this attention by continuously "mirroring" back to the infant his communicative moves. The effect is that after a few months the two have achieved a pattern of conversationlike interaction, in which the vocalizations and gestures produced by each interactant are synchronized with the partner's response (Bateson, 1975; Brazelton & Tronick, 1980; Sylvester-Bradley & Trevarthen, 1978; Trevarthen & Hubley, 1978). An innate predisposition to intersubjectivity—to attend to the human element in the environment—thus develops through social contact into a communicative game with an adult partner.

This is admittedly a rudimentary form of communication. The sounds and movements made by the baby are sensitive to the partner's behavior but have not been organized into any nonrandom system, and there are no identifiable meanings being exchanged at this stage—the "communication" is a matter of a synchronized cooperative exchange of attention. But once this form of communication has been achieved, a new possibility arises for the baby. He is no longer obliged to continue his investigation of the world of persons separately from his parallel investigation of nonhuman objects; he now has the possibility of using communication with another person to help him explore the world of objects (Trevarthen & Hubley, 1978). For example, an infant may try addressing another person in order to act on an object in some way—perhaps to have it manipulated, removed, or put within reach—as an alternative to acting on the object directly and physically. If the infant's communicative behavior of this kind, whether gestural or vocal, receives an interpretation by the partner that is satisfactory to the child, then it can be regarded as an act of meaning, a symbolic act. If the child is to repeat a successful act of meaning he has to interpret a new instance of experience as a communicative occasion comparable to the original one, and from all his possible expressive behaviors, he may be most successful if he "reproduces" the vocal or bodily gesture that was successful before. Thus, at about 9 or 10 months, children begin to use the same vocal or bodily gesture in what can be interpreted by the partner as the same circumstances. An example from the case study of my son, Hal, can illustrate this. At 10½ months Hal would address the sound [amama-mama] to us on occasion; we were always able to interpret it as meaning "I want that food there."

So the perfecting of synchronized exchanges of attention makes possible a more complex kind of interaction in which attention is jointly focused on an object. But the successful management of a more complex interaction in turn requires—or at least is facilitated by—the creation of a symbol. Moreover, if the infant has a range of needs that can be met by acting on the world symbolically, then we can expect him to create a range of symbols to serve those purposes. And this is exactly what appears to happen. There is a growing body of evidence that infants create a "protolanguage" of symbols to fulfill certain functions that arise from the universal conditions of infancy, such as physical dependence on others as well as predispositions to interact with others and to explore the environment (see Bates, Camaioni, & Volterra, 1979; Bruner, 1978; Carter, 1978; Dore, 1973, 1978; Ferrier, 1978; Halliday, 1975, Oldenberg, 1986; Painter, 1984; Qiu, 1985).

The functions Halliday has proposed as arising initially are as follows:

Function name	Use of protolanguage symbols
Instrumental	to obtain objects (and services)
Regulatory	to control others
Interactional	to share and cement relationships with others
Personal	to express a sense of self—by reacting to the environment or by expressing curiosity toward it

The nature of the protolanguage and the functions it serves can perhaps be made clearer if we look at some examples of typical conversations in which Hal at 10½ months is using his own protolanguage—his system of vocal symbols—and the parent is responding in English.

(2)   H: [amamamama] (reaching gesture toward biscuit tin)
        M: Okay, you can have one. (opens lid)

Hal's vocalization here clearly serves the Instrumental 'I want' function.

(3)   H: (looks up and smiles) [x : : :]
        M: Hello, sweetheart. How are you today?

Here the vocalization is a kind of greeting, an expression of 'togetherness' serving the Interactional function.

(4)   H: (loudly) [ga] (holding up a toy to M)
        M: Ooh, what you got there?
        H: (loudly) [ga]
        M: Ooh, yes.

The function here is Interactional again, but this time an object is used as a focus of joint attention.

(5)   H: [gai gai gai] (after finishing his bottle of milk)
        M: (approaching) Feel good now, do you, darling?

Here Hal is reacting to a pleasurable experience, using language in the Personal function.

(6)   H: [ga] (pulling at object)
              [ga, ka] (tapping it on ground)

This final example again uses protolanguage in the Personal function; Hal is expressing his engagement with the environment of objects here and is not particularly concerned about gaining an addressee response.

There is not time here to illustrate Hal's complete range of symbols at this point, but if we accept that texts given are typical examples we could infer a simple protolinguistic system of the kind given in Figure 2 below. Thus the utterances given in examples 2–6 are to be seen as instantiations of such a system.

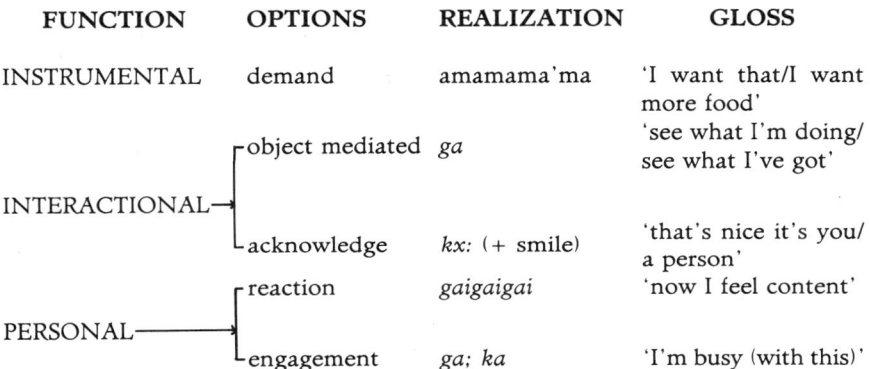

FUNCTION	OPTIONS	REALIZATION	GLOSS
INSTRUMENTAL	demand	amamama'ma	'I want that/I want more food'
INTERACTIONAL	object mediated	*ga*	'see what I'm doing/ see what I've got'
	acknowledge	*kx:* (+ smile)	'that's nice it's you/ a person'
PERSONAL	reaction	*gaigaigai*	'now I feel content'
	engagement	*ga; ka*	'I'm busy (with this)'

Figure 2. Protolanguage system inferrable from text examples 2–6

Thus the protolanguage system illustrated here serves only three functions, but within two of these there is the potential for two different meanings to be made.

At this stage it may be useful very briefly to point out again what the child has gained by creating this system, and then to consider what the limitations are that may provoke further changes.

Looking at the gains first, we see that the use of protolanguage in conversations with significant others allows a child to interact with a partner in ways not open to a prelinguistic child. For example, in addition to maintaining interpersonal contact as before, Hal could now also use objects as a means of regulating joint attention in various ways. In the Instrumental function he could begin to control the environment through the persons he communicated with, and in the Personal function a sense of personal identity could also begin to develop once his reactions to aspects of reality were interpreted back to him by adult responses.

We can see, then, that the social experiences of the first year of life will take a child like Hal a considerable way toward language. But when we compare the kind of conversation Hal was engaging in at this stage with that of the child in our original dialogue (text 1), certain differences are immediately apparent. For one thing, Stephen was able to refer to specific objects (bristles, earrings) and persons (Mummy, Hal, Daddy) and actions (wake up, talk). Hal, as a protolanguage speaker, could indicate that his communication involved particular objects or actions only by such behavior as reaching to the biscuit tin or holding up a toy. This means that he could 'talk about' something only in the here-and-now context, since objects and actions would have to be present and visible to both parties for this strategy to be successful.

One way a protolanguage speaker could overcome this would be to create many more symbols—for example, a distinct Instrumental sign for every different desired object. But this would still not allow the speaker to do what Stephen can do, for the following reason. If an object such as a peg were desired on one occasion, used in an interactional give-and-take game on another, and investigated privately on another, three different symbols would be needed, as three different functions would be being served. There would be no symbolic way of identifying the peg as a specific object common to all three contexts. There would in fact be no way of coding the experiential meaning of *peg* separately from interpersonal meanings of 'I want,' 'here you are' or 'I'm interested.' Stephen and his mother, on the other hand, can encode a meaning such as 'talk' or 'earring' as a particular activity or object, whether desiring it, inquiring about it, describing it, or anything else.

A further major difference between Hal's protolanguage conversations and the conversation between Stephen and his mother concerns their dialogic nature. We saw how Stephen could ask a question ("What you got in your ears?") and use the information of the answer ("they're earrings") as the basis for a fresh move ("I haven't got earrings"). For Hal, as a protolanguage speaker, dialogue is limited to an initiation of some kind (repeated if necessary) to be followed by a response—for example, child demand + adult compliance, as in example 2, or child attention-claimer + adult acknowledgement, as in example 4. The same exchange can be endlessly repeated, but conversation cannot be extended by making the partner's response the linguistic context for a new departure.

2.2   Use of the Protolanguage Leads to Change

We have considered some of the limitations of the child's protolanguage as compared with the adult system; the question we now raise is why and how the child's system develops further. My thesis is that the child's experience with the communication system he has developed sets up the conditions for placing new requirements on the system, and these in turn change the nature of the system. This means at this point that while using his protolanguage does serve his needs, using it also pressures him to require more of his symbolic resources.

Why then should the child wish to do something his protolanguage cannot manage? To address this question, to explore why a child would feel the limitations of his protolanguage, we have to remember that he is developing language in interaction with others. His experiences of having his symbolic purposes recognized by others (who unconsciously respond to his protolinguistic vocalizations) will surely encourage the child to view those others as themselves meaning-makers. This in turn prepares him to attend to the meanings offered by those he addresses, who of course can talk back to him only using their own language system; and so the child's system changes in a certain direction under pressure from the adult system. A direction that entails, in the first instance, the development of names.

Let us look a little more closely, then, at the linguistic responses that Hal received in a small sample of conversations that served a Personal function for him between the ages of 11 and 15 months, to get an idea of how this process of change happens through interaction with others.

(7) H: [ga] (pointing at dog)   (gloss: 'that's interesting')
     M: Yes, that's a dog
     H: [ga]
     M: Mm, a dog; a big dog

Here we can see that the adult responds to Hal's act of meaning as an expression of curiosity and interest but responds also as though the child were attempting to identify things by name. While one could not make too much of a single occasion of this kind, conversations of this type were repeated dozens, even hundreds, of times. Other typical conversations are given below:

(8) M: Where's the birdie, Hal?
     H: [ga] (pointing)
     M: Yes, good boy
         That's the bird
     H: [ga]
     M: Yes, birdie

(9) H: [ga] (getting a book out of toy box)
     M: What have you got there?
     H: [ga] (turning it around)
     M: A book
     H: [ga] (opening it)
     M: A big book
     H: [ba]

In these two examples, the parent is using requests for the location of a named object or for the identification of an unnamed object under attention, as a means of eliciting expressions of interest from the child. And again names are offered by the adult as the means of acknowledging Hal's responses.

When we look at such conversations, we can see how the adult is continually highlighting for the child the value of language as a means of typifying different instances of things as "the same" by naming them. In doing this of course language symbols will be imposing—or creating—a different kind of order to existence from that imposed by the protolanguage. And it is not only in interactions where language is used in the Personal function that the adult directs the child's attention to naming. If we turn our attention now to the Interactional function, we can find many examples of the same kind of process going on. In the following example, the child is already anxious to share attention with the conversational partner by focusing on an object, and so will probably be very receptive to the name being offered:

(10)   H: [adʒa] (holding up toy)   (gloss: 'look what I've got')
        M: Got a peg there, have you?

Evidence of Hal's growing interest in the adult language forms can be seen in the following text where he is requesting a specific vocalization:

(11)   (M & H reading picture book)
        M: Here's a pussy
             Pussy goes mioau (turns page)
        H: [da]   (gloss: 'you make the noise')
        M: woof-woof
        H: [da]
        M: cock-a-doodle-do! (etc.)

Interactions of this kind then developed into conversational games of the kind shown in example 12.

(12)   H: woof woof   (gloss: 'I say, now you say')
        M: woof woof
        H: miaou
        M: cat goes 'miaou' (etc.)

Transparent symbols such as conventionalized animal noises are easy for any child to recognize, and in these last two examples we can see

Hal trying out the role of requesting a specific vocalization and then of systematically exchanging a shared range of expressions as an interactive game.

We have had time to look at examples of Hal's protolanguage used in only two functions, but even this partial picture helps us to see how changes to the system occur. In all these conversations Hal was using his protolanguage and satisfying his needs with it. But at the same time this experience was making him aware of other possibilities—of the possibility of a symbolic system as a repertoire of names and of the value of exchanging shared symbols which relate to something in experience. So he then tried out these possibilities, beginning to adopt expressions from the adult system into his protolanguage. And we will see that once this happens, the way is open for really fundamental changes in the purposes and nature of his symbolic resources.

Before we look at how this occurs, we can perhaps make one or two general points relevant to pedagogical interests here. We have begun to see the way that language is learned interactively, and there are two related aspects to this which can perhaps be brought out now. First, making meanings with the parent creates a dialogue that achieves something more than the child's utterances considered alone. And it is by having his meanings responded to that the child is guided, or pushed, to attempt new things. Second, we can see that the notion of 'practice' may be a highly relevant one in language learning as long as we do not limit it to practicing skills of sound discrimination and articulation. What I would prefer to stress is the need for practice in semiosis—in making meanings.

2.3   The Effect of Names in the Protolanguage System

I have suggested that the first move beyond the protolanguage is likely to be the child's use of mother-tongue names. We have considered how repeated interactions with mother-tongue speakers will make this a natural next step, but it is a step that would presumably only be taken if the child gained something as a communicator. And so we need to think about what advantages there are for children when they make this move.

At first the gains may be small because each mother-tongue word used by the child may be restricted to one functional meaning. For example *bird* may have only the Instrumental meaning of 'I want my toy bird,' or *Daddy* may have only the Interactional meaning of 'Hello, Daddy.' At this stage, the child's symbolic resources are substantially of the same kind as before—a set of independent "languages," each of which is a set of resources to fulfill a different function; a system of the same kind as shown earlier in Figure 2 in fact, but with some of the vocal expressions "borrowed" from adult language rather than invented by the child.

Even this small difference offers advantages, however. One is of course that communication with a wider audience is possible once shared forms are used. As time goes on, the child does take advantage of this possibility, but it certainly does not seem to be one that motivates change in the first place. There is another advantage, though, that children begin to exploit in a limited way somewhat earlier, and this relates to the first of the limitations of the protolanguage spelled out earlier. We saw that protolinguistic utterances have the disadvantage of being interpretable only with reference to the here-and-now situation. A mother-tongue word, however, is not inherently restricted in this way. For example, an Instrumental expression such as *bird* allows for the possibility of initiating a request for a specific object that is not in view and has not been verbally offered.

And we find again that using the system changes it. In many cases, mother-tongue words will at first be used in only one protolinguistic functional meaning, but once these words are adopted into the system and used in dialogue, the child becomes aware of their potential to act as names, as in adult language. We can see the child developing the notion of a name when he begins to use the same word for **different** protolanguage functions. An example from Hal would be his uttering of the sequence *eyes, nose, mouth* on some occasions as part of a ritual in which the addressee's face is touched, and on other occasions when touching toys or pictures without reference to an addressee. The first case would be Interactional in function and the second Personal. But by using a name Hal was free to express distinctly an experiential meaning common to both situations, thus overcoming the second limitation of the protolanguage, which was discussed earlier.

2.4   The Transition Phase

In overcoming this limitation, the child has changed the nature of his language and enters what Halliday calls the "transition" phase of development. When we see words used differently on different occasions, as with the example of *eyes, nose,* and *mouth,* we may no longer wish to distinguish between them as fulfilling different functions. Even though the one case here was more interactional than the other, both can be seen as fulfilling the same function if we define that more broadly as one of organizing or interpreting the phenomena of experience. This is because in either case the child was engaged in a task of classification, of sorting out phenomena into classes of related things.

So, when "borrowed" mother-tongue words develop into names, a child gains tools for learning, for sorting out and categorizing experience. And he has come to require this of his symbolic resources not just because of his need to know the world, but because his interactions with others have highlighted for him the possibility of language serving this need in this way.

However, not all utterances of mother-tongue words were directed primarily to this learning function. Hal followed a typical developmental pattern in maintaining a certain functional restriction on the use of vocabulary items at first (see also Bloom 1970; Carter, 1979; Menn, 1978; Nelson, 1973). I am not talking about restrictions in terms of the initial protolanguage functions now, but in terms of only two broad functions for language. One of these is that already mentioned, using language as a means of organizing experience, which Halliday has termed the **mathetic** function. The other function is that of language used as a form of action—to control others, gain goods and services, and intrude upon the world, which Halliday terms the **pragmatic** function.

This pragmatic function is a generalization of the protolinguistic Instrumental and Regulatory functions. The freeing of these demanding functions from the immediate situational context, which is made possible by using vocabulary, probably encourages the child to generalize these functions and to begin to make broader pragmatic meanings. For example, Hal might now utter a world like *porridge* with a pragmatic meaning of 'Porridge—something needs to be done!' This might be glossed as 'I want porridge' or 'Let me see the porridge' or 'Lift me to stir the porridge' or 'I've dropped the porridge—help!' depending on the occasion.

Let us step back now and look at the language system lying behind the kinds of utterances we have been discussing. I have suggested that it is typical for new vocabulary to be restricted to either mathetic or pragmatic uses at first. When this is the case, the child will have a set of mathetic words and a different set of pragmatic words. So if we wish to characterize the nature of the child's symbolic resources at this point, we can suggest that the system has been reorganized into two independent sets of resources, as shown in Figure 3. And the child will make use of whichever set of resources is appropriate, depending on the values he has assigned to the context for discourse. If it is one for learning about and reflecting on reality, he will make use of his mathetic resources; if it is one for acting on reality, he will call on his pragmatic resources. We can see the similarities here with the earlier protolanguage system which was organized as a set of meaning options for each protolinguistic functional context.

Many studies have reported that children separate their words into

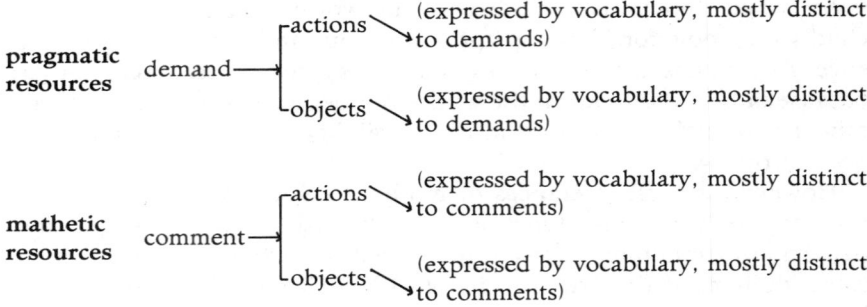

(The sloping arrow indicates "is realized by" or "is expressed by.")

Figure 3.   Simplified outline of early transition linguistic system

two functional classes. There is also growing evidence that children develop different versions of their vocabulary items according to which function is being fulfilled (see Dore, 1973; Greenfield & Smith, 1976; McShane, 1980; Menn, 1978; Oldenberg, 1986). Both Hal and Halliday's subject, Nigel, distinguished the function of early words through tone. Both used a falling tone with mathetic utterances, while pragmatic ones had a nonfalling tone. The tone served to signal the function and thus to mark the interpersonal status of the utterance, as a (mathetic) comment or a (pragmatic) demand that someone had to meet. This can be taken as further evidence for the reorganization suggested in Figure 3. But it also means that now, for the first time, the child's linguistic resources can be compared with the metafunctionally organized adult resources outlined earlier in Figure 1. In considering the adult language we saw how interpersonal mood choices coexist with experiential choices of process type and how each kind of meaning has its own realizational thread in the uttered structure. For the transition-stage child, experiential choices of meaning expressed by lexis would coexist with interpersonal choices expressed by intonation, as illustrated in Figure 4.

It is possible then, to stress the likeness of the transition system to the adult metafunctional one. Yet if Hal's case is typical, only a small proportion of the mother-tongue expressions will be used on both tones at first. This means that the system is probably more fairly represented as reorganized into two independent sets of resources, as in the earlier Figure 3.

The child's reorganization of his linguistic system in such a way can be interpreted as a move that provides him with more effective resources for achieving his current purposes. His protolanguage had certain limitations as a symbolic system. I cited some evidence that the experiences

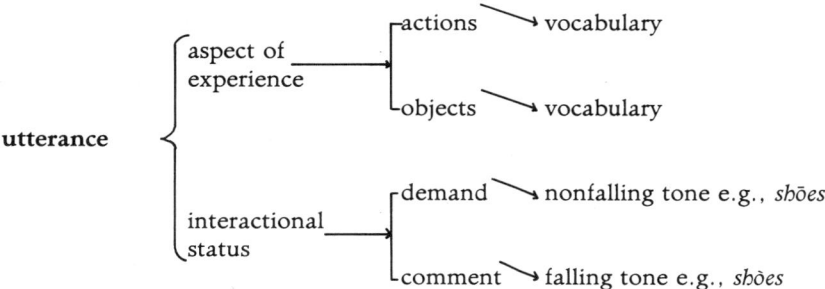

Figure 4. Simplified outline of early transition linguistic system

of making protolinguistic meanings in conversations with adults led the child to focus on naming; this led to other achievements and to engaging in dialogue games involving shared symbols. At the same time, other conversations, in the Instrumental and Regulatory functions, were confirming the effectiveness of symbols as a means of acting on the world of persons and objects to achieve more concrete goals. By reorganizing his linguistic resources, the child is able to attend separately to the two functions that his experiences have made most salient to him—that of construing the world and that of interacting with others as a way of acting on the world—the mathetic and pragmatic functions, respectively.

2.5.1 Developments in the Transition Period: Pragmatic Function

Let us take up the story now by looking at the development of language for each of these functions in turn. We can begin with the pragmatic function as it developed for Hal. Pragmatic function is the use of language to make an effect on the world—to intrude, to change the situation in some way, which usually involves interacting with others. So development within the pragmatic function is largely concerned with the nature of interactional roles. Months of protolanguage experience had led Hal to assign a range of possible roles to the addressee. These were:

provider of valued objects and food (Instrumental)
provider of assistance in routines of dressing, eating, etc. (Instrumental)
provider of entertainment (sing, etc.) (Regulatory)
provider of company (be with me) (Interactional)

I have already described one effect of adopting names into this area of the language. It led to the generalization of some protolanguage functions (Instrumental, Regulatory, and some Interactional meanings) to a broader function of acting on the world with the aid of language. This in turn allowed for the emergence of more general social roles. In Hal's case a new meaning of 'I want to do' emerged as he took on a more general "intruder" role, and at the same time he assigned the addressee a more general role of provider of goods and services.

Although the addressee was required to provide goods and services rather than to interact linguistically, the adult naturally spoke to the child at the same time as giving the required goods and services. Alternatively, of course, pragmatic demands may not have been met and verbalization may have been all that the child received. On these occasions the adult's speech may be specially relevant, so it may be useful to look at a few such instances here. The following conversation took place soon after Hal began using words:

(13)   (H gets out stacking-baskets toy at bedtime)
        H: bāskēt
        M: No, we're not going to do baskets
            Get another book
        H: bāskēt; bāskēt; tōwer
            (to F) tōwer
            (F builds it; H knocks it down)
            tōwer

M's countersuggestion was ignored by Hal here, but as in many other conversations, Hal was being offered speech rather than the goods or services demanded.

The following case shows how compliance with a demand was also accompanied by speech, and how an inability to comply was likely to be explained verbally.

(14)   (H playing with doors on toy cars)
        H: ōpen
        M: There, it's open;
            shut (shutting it).
        H: ōpen (struggling with another)
        M: That one's broken, love

Finally, two examples in which the adult offers verbal explanations for refusals to meet demands.

(15)   H: sīde sīde; sīde; sīde
       M: You go outside,
            I'm a bit tired

(16)   H: gēt; gēt; mōre; mōre
       M: What do you want, darling?
       H: mōre; mōre; mōre; mōre; mōre
       M: Oh Hal, you're not having any more.
            That's Michael's drink;
            Michael's gone,
            and you don't have his drink

Verbal replies from the adult, whether refusing or promising to meet a demand, were usually ignored at first, but repeated experiences of this kind led Hal to accept a verbal rejoinder as an appropriate response to a pragmatic utterance. We can see this happening where he appears to be working at interpreting the verbal response given, by adding a mathetic utterance of his own, as in the following examples:

(17)   (H goes to back door)
       H: Outsīde; outsīde
       F: It's cold outside, Hal
       H: Outsīde; còld
            Outsīde
            Còld

(18)   (M and H are out on walk)
       H: Drīnk; orānge
       M: Okay, we'll go to those tables (pointing to café) and have a nice drink of orange
       H: Drīnk. tàble. nīce

What Hal was learning in all these interactions was that speech may be an appropriate response to a request to do something. It is not surprising, then, that he began actually to solicit speech rather than action next—to move from desiring a pragmatic response of 'do!' to one of 'say!' And this development was then instrumental in further moving pragmatic speech beyond the protolinguistic anchorage in the here and now. We will look briefly at three attested ways this soliciting of a verbal response can take place.

The first is for a child to formulate an intention and test its acceptability on the addressee, as Hal does in example 19:

(19)   (H has pencil and paper)
       H: (looks up at M with pencil poised)
            Páper?

M: Yes, you can write on the paper
H: Pàper (doing so)

A second related way that Hal used pragmatic speech to demand a verbal response was to call upon the adult to engage in role play to test his interpretation of a situation, as in the following example:

(20)   (H pouring salt on table)
       H: Nāughtȳ (looking round at M)
       M: Mm? (laughs) Oh yes, you are naughty naughty . . . (etc.)

Again he can be seen as bringing to bear on the current situation experiences from the past which allow him to interpret and predict.

A third way that experience with pragmatic language interactions may move the child to require a response of 'say' is illustrated from the data on Nigel. Halliday (1975) has detailed how Nigel's demands for services began to include demands for linguistic services. These included requiring the adult to verify a hypothesis about the nature of things, as in the next examples:

(21)   N: That blue train might brèak;
             réd train might break?   (Halliday, 1975; p. 96)

(22)   N: Turn róund? (trying to fit shape into puzzle)
                                                        (Halliday, 1975; p. 95)

Alternatively, the linguistic service required might be the supply of information—initially names—as in the following example:

(23)   N: What's thát?
       F: Butter
       N: Bùtter   (Halliday, 1975; p. 49)

Although Hal did not demand information at this stage, his growing orientation to the social roles adopted in pragmatic contexts as being primarily linguistic ones could be observed. Evidence is provided by his gradual shift from high-level tone (pragmatic tone) to falling tone for those demands that were uttered in response to adult verbal offers:

(24)   (H has just finished food on plate)
       H: Mōre; mōre; chēese
       F: All right, Daddy will cut you a little piece
       H: Pièce; eàt; pièce

(25)   (H is reaching up to table)
   M: Do you want to get that cup?
   H: Cùp (assenting)

The "demand" status of the utterances in such cases did not need to be encoded tonally when it was made clear by the interactional structure of the conversation.

In this discussion of the pragmatic function I have tried to show how the pragmatic linguistic resources were used initially as a form of action, to get (nonlinguistic) things done. But the conversations that the child engaged in toward this end let him to see the interactions themselves, and the responses required from an interacting partner, as primarily linguistic ones. Thus it would appear that the child's use of language in the pragmatic function is largely concerned with defining and redefining the possible social roles of interactants.

If we now look at the linguistic resources built up by Hal and Nigel for use in pragmatic contexts, we can see that they are largely those relevant to the achievement of pragmatic ends. On the whole, the resources developed were those of the interpersonal component of the mother tongue: an imperative mood system, which included a "polite" option for Hal; a person system distinguishing 'I do' from 'you do' (from 'let's do' in Nigel's case), and a polarity system (*no* was for Hal a purely pragmatic item for a considerable time). Some experiential structures however were also developed and used by both children because of their relevance for pragmatic contexts. For example, two particular nominal group structures were used by Hal only in the pragmatic function at first. These involved two kinds of modifiers: *more* for supplementary requests and the deictics *this* and *that* which served to specify the desired object from an array of possibilities (cups of different colors, different items of clothing, etc.). All these particular linguistic forms, then, developed at this stage because they were functional in Hal's life. A child does not learn structures and then look for meanings to attach to them. He is engaged in the business of making meanings and therefore develops functional structures that will do this.

It is important to understand this in the educational context. If we conceive of forms and structures as though their mastery were a distinct and prior enterprise from successful use, then we will be making the learner's task unnecessarily difficult. On the other hand, if we recognize that form is functional, we can aim to focus on the meanings the context requires. This does not mean that linguistic form is unimportant. On the contrary, a focus on meaning will **entail** developing functional structures—generic text structures as well as clause structures—since these forms realize meanings.

2.5.2   Development in the Transition Period: Mathetic Function

Let us now turn to the mathetic function to see what developments take place there. In the mathetic function the focus is not on interacting and doing, but on observing and understanding. From the Personal function of reacting to the environment and the Interactional function of engaging another person's attention through the objects of the environment, the child begins to interpret the world in terms of the entities, actions, locations, qualities, and relations embodied in the mother tongue. I am suggesting then that reality is not "given" to the child in the form of innate linguistic structure, nor is it "given" in the material environment, waiting to be mirrored in language (see Butt, chapter 2 of this volume). Experience has to be interpreted, it must be construed by the child with the help of the conversational partner; and language in the mathetic function is the tool for doing this.

We can begin to exemplify this by looking at vocabulary development and what is involved in this. As a starting point we can look at a typical brief conversational exchange from Hal's transition phase:

(26)   (H appears uninterested in the apple being cut up for him after lunch)
       M: Don't you want your fruit? (i.e., finished your meal?)
       H: Not frùit; (= that's not fruit)
          That's àpple

Here Hal is using his mother tongue, but there is a minor communication problem. What is involved in each of these things? First, for Hal to have the name *apple* as part of his resources, he will have been engaged in the process of typifying experience. That is to say, necessarily distinct individual sensory perceptions will have had to be interpreted in language as "the same" in order for him to have developed a name such as *apple*.

But this is not all that is involved in building up lexical resources. The child's task is not just a matter of matching a set of labels to a set of objects. A name serves to differentiate a typified object (or quality or action) from some other, and the choice of name in any instance depends on what has to be differentiated in that particular case. This is the source of the communicative problem that arose in the exchange between Hal and his mother. When he rejected the label *fruit*, on the grounds that the object in question was an apple, he had not yet understood that *fruit* was a superordinate term which includes apple, and that it was a preferred choice since what was being discussed was a dessert course rather than the main part of the meal. In Hal's system, *fruit* (a term he also used) and *apple* were at the same level of generality.

The source of the difficulty was a mismatch between the lexical tax-onomies of the participants to the conversation—a mismatch ultimately in the way each party was construing reality. A trivial example in this case, perhaps, but it can illustrate the general point that when parents and teachers correct 'errors of fact' made by children (see Clark & Clark, 1977), what is involved is a linguistic matter—a mismatch between the realities constructed by each party as embodied in their linguistic sys-tems. And the importance of appreciating this is that it leads to the recognition that most learning—certainly most school learning—is ulti-mately a matter of language development.

To return to the transition-phase child, the point I have been making is that lexical items, as they are incorporated into the child's system, are built up into taxonomic sets. Items may be related in terms of hy-ponymy (class-member), as in the example we have been considering, or in terms of meronymy (part-whole) and synonymy relations. Initially, names are organized into sets centering on the different areas of the child's life—dressing/clothing, washing/grooming, eating/food, places/outings, play/playthings, and so on, with additional fields introduced through books (such as wild animals, forms of transport, etc.).

Before leaving the topic of lexical development, I propose to look at a number of typical early occasions where Hal's language was used in the mathetic function. This is in order to get a better idea of how they represent possible learning occasions enabling him to develop his lexical resources.

First an example where Hal "practices" a name:

(27)   (M and H have been outside looking at the moon.
       H runs back in)
       H: Moòn, moòn
       M: You gonna tell Daddy what you saw?
       F: What did you see?
       H: Moòn
            (Goes off and rummages among books. Finds two with pictures
            of moon; points to each in turn) Moòn; moòn

Here the child is engaged in the task of generalising experience—of treating different instances of moons (actual and symbolic in this case) as equivalent.

(28)   (H and M are walking)
       H: (pulling his T-shirt) Shìrt; shìrt; shìrt
            (Looks at M, pulls her dress)
       M: Dress
            Mummy's dress and Hal's shirt

> H: (beaming) Shìrt (pointing to it)
>   Drèss (touching it)

In this example we see the parent helping the child to build up a lexical set. But a conversational partner was not necessarily involved in every occasion of language used in the mathetic function. In the following case no adult participated.

(29)   (In park, dog wanders up)
         H: Dòg!
               tail, èyes, eàr, nòse (touching each in turn)

Hal appeared to be trying out a meronymic lexical set here and was satisfied with his own success.

Finally we can observe further cases involving a mismatch between the child's and the adult's classifications, as in the next example:

(30)   (The radio comes on in adjacent room)
         H: Noìse
         M: Well, its music,
               it's a nice noise

On the many occasions of this sort the adult helps the child to become aware of a mismatch between their systems and simultaneously helps the child to gain access to the adult taxonomy. In the following example, Hal rejects a superordinate term, demonstrating that his taxonomic hierarchy is not the same as M's.

(31)   M: Here's some fish (preparing lunch)
         H: (bossily) Not fish, sardines!

Equally often, of course, a more specific term will be rejected, as in the next case:

(32)   (M and H reading animal dictionary picture book)
         M: And do you know this one?
               That's a goanna
         H: Not goanna; that's a lizard

It is possible that these texts are unconvincing as occasions of learning, but that is because we are looking at single instances of conversations. It is not to be expected that every utterance or exchange will "teach" the child a new word or result in a readjustment to his lexical system. We are looking here at tiny fragments of a continuous process in which the child is making meanings for himself. He may be satisfied with his own efforts on a specific occasion without receiving any overt validation of his interpretation by others, or even in the face of a noncomfirmatory response. But repeated semiotic practice in the presence of others means a constant subtle encouragement to interpret reality in the same way that they do. And this means, among other things, developing the same lexical taxonomies.

Building up taxonomies of object names is one important aspect of interpreting reality and involves the linguistic organization of the things of the world. But the "goings-on" of experience also need to be made sense of, and one way many children learn to organize this aspect of experience involves them in a "running-commentary" kind of discourse. What the child does here is to typify experience by interpreting into language what he is doing or observing as it takes place. As with the labeling texts, Hal did not seek a linguistic response on these occasions, but nonetheless he made use of those provided, often repeating to himself the adult version. In the following examples of running-commentary texts, Hal is interpreting experience by using one word at a time:

(33)   H: bròken, flòwer, nàughty (as he rips up a flower)

(34)   H: brèad, eàt, bìrdies (watching seagulls eating)
        M: Mm, the birdies are eating all the bread up

(35)   H: Rùn (watching jogger go by)
        M: Yes, the man's running, isn't he?
        H: Màn; rùnning
              (after a few minutes) gòne
        M: Yes, he's gone now

So far we have been looking at texts produced in the mathetic function at a fairly early stage. Texts are instances of the language system, and we can now move from the texts to consider the system the speaker calls upon when producing them. When we do this, we can infer Hal's system of resources for the mathetic function as being something like that given in Figure 5.

Figure 5 indicates that Hal was building up different lexical sets and subsets associated with each of some five major aspects of experience. This constituted his linguistic organization of reality at this period.

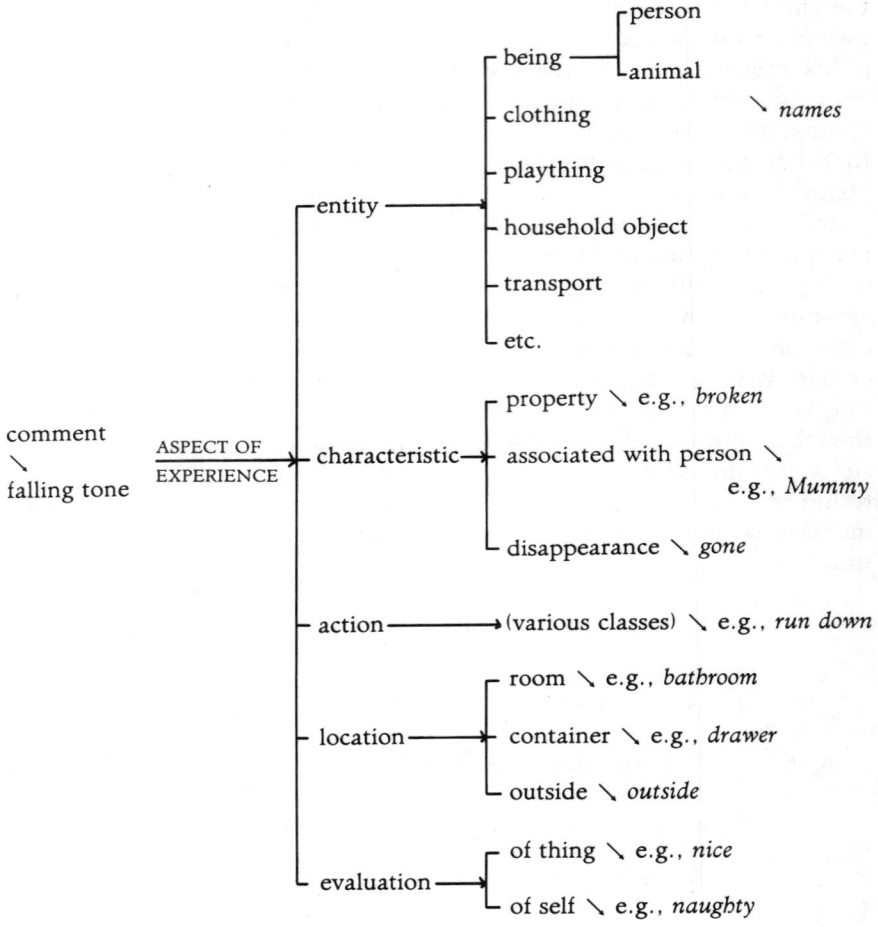

Figure 5. Simplified outline of Hal's mathetic resources at the 'one-word stage'.

2.5.3 Development of Linguistic Structure Within Mathetic Function

At this stage, then, a child like Hal has a set of resources for construing reality which allows him to express meanings in single-word utterances. And we know that the next step will be for him to use two- or three-word linguistic structures. Again, if we are to understand how this process of language development takes place, we need to ask why the child should take this step. There is, of course, a definite advantage to be gained by using linguistic structures: By combining word units into wholes, and recombining the same units into different wholes, the speaker clearly increases his meaning potential. But it is not the case that the "one-word child" has run out of new lexemes to learn and therefore **has** to take this step if he is to increase his meaning potential. Nor is he cognitively unable to keep adding and adding to his lexical resources (think of multilingual children). The child makes the move into linguistic structure because this is one possible way of increasing his meaning potential **and** it is the way that has been modeled for him by those he interacts with. And the same pattern of development can be expected in later language development. It is not that the child is preprogrammed on to a certain course and need only be left to it. The learner (perhaps as a writer in school) will take a developmental step only if there is something to be gained by it, **and** if in some way that particular route has been made obvious to him.

Let us look at the kinds of structures Hal produced at first so that we can examine more carefully what the move "into structure" entails. First, we can observe that Hal classified the things around him with structures of the following kind:

big apple
big pillow
soft pillow
soft pussy

When he produced utterances on this pattern, we can claim that he was using a Modifier + Head structure. In other words the child was treating the different qualities of (here) bigness and softness as comparable in some way, as being two ways of qualifying some entity.

At the same time, Hal was encoding "happenings" with comments like these:

bite big apple
bite book
buy book
buy apple
eat apple

Here distinct goings-on such as biting and buying are treated as comparable in that they are processes standing in the same kind of relation to a participant entity. In each case there is a process and something affected by it, or involved in it—a Process + Medium structure.

Thus the move from lexis only to combinable and recombinable structural elements greatly increases the child's meaning potential. And it does so by a further generalisation of experience. In order to develop names, the child must class different instances of reality as equivalent. In order to develop structures, different classes of properties or things or happenings (encoded by different lexical items) must be interpreted in context as being equivalent in their function as Modifier or Medium or Process. Thus the representation of reality in grammatical structure requires an interpretation more general than that encoded directly by lexical items. So as well as having an efficient way to make new messages, the child gains a more coherent, or tightly organized, view of experiential reality.

I have stressed that the child makes the move into structure under the influence of the adult system used with him. But it is equally important to note that, in Hal's case, the structures developed differently within the two functions. Not only were structures used earlier and more frequently in the mathetic function, but the structures used in the mathetic function were different from those used in the pragmatic function. This constitutes further evidence that it is the function of the system for the child that determines the way the resources develop, that forms evolve to realize meanings.

2.5.4 Mathetic and Pragmatic Structures Compared

To develop this point, we will now compare the structures produced by Hal in each function and the linguistic systems underlying them.

2.5.4.1 Nominal group. We can begin by looking at examples of typical nominal group structures:

pragmatic function	mathetic function
more drink	big truck
(later) this cup	blue shirt
that book	Daddy's coffee

The nominal group is the structure that represents the things or entities of experience. At a time when the only group used pragmatically was *more* + noun, there was no such quantifying Modifier in nominal structures used in the mathetic function. The majority of structures in mathetic contexts used quality or possessive Modifiers: *big truck, blue shirt, Daddy's coffee,* and so on. We can explain this difference in terms of the different kinds of meanings relevant for the child in the two functions. *More* expressed a meaning much more relevant to Hal when making a demand than when in the mathetic, observer role. In mathetic contexts, he found quantifying and demonstrative identification of less relevance

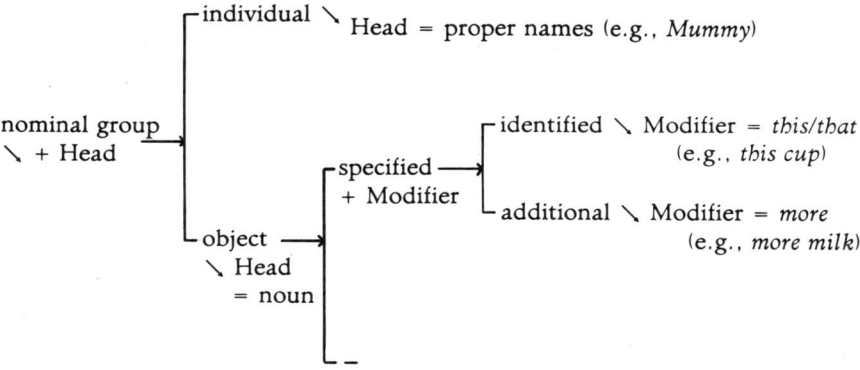

Figure 6.   Simplified outline of Hal's pragmatic nominal group options, midtransition

at first than characterizing objects in terms of salient properties or association with familiar people. (On the other hand, of course, children with siblings would be likely to develop possessive Modifiers in pragmatic, rather than mathetic contexts.) Hal's two nominal group systems underlying the example utterances given above are characterized in Figures 6 and 7.

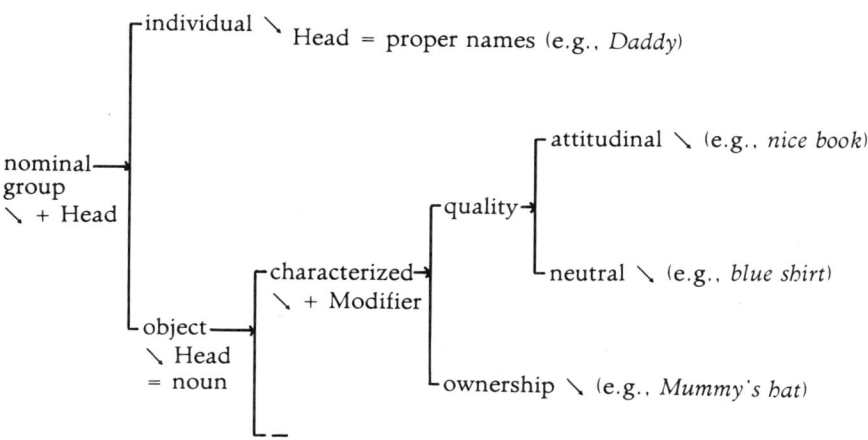

Figure 7.   Simplified outline of Hal's mathetic nominal group options, midtransition

2.5.4.2 Mathetic clause structures. At clause rank the "happenings" in the world are interpreted into language, and there are again differences between the structural patterns produced by Hal in the two functional contexts. The two element structures produced by Hal in mathetic contexts of observation and recall were almost all of the following kind:

Daddy coming	break car
girl run	bite apple
teddy jump	buy book

There were thus intransitive clause structures, such as *Daddy coming*, and transitive structures that "lacked" an Actor role, such as *break car*. In all cases, therefore, there was a Process element encoding the activity and a second element that Halliday (1985b) refers to as the Medium. *Daddy* in *Daddy coming* and *car* in *break car* encode the entity most closely affected by the process, the entity through which the process comes about (hence the term "Medium"). So mathetic material-process clauses all had a Process+Medium structure, though word order varied. And in addition to these material process clauses, there were also "relational" clauses such as *Mummy's busy* and *birdies in trees* used in the mathetic function.

2.5.4.3 Pragmatic clause structures. The two-element structures that Hal produced with a pragmatic function differ from the above. There were no relational clauses at all here, and the material processes had the following pattern:

Mummy sing	Mummy cut
Hal sit (= I want to)	Hal break

Here, too, all structures had a Process element encoding the activity; however, the entities associated with the processes had the role of Doer or Actor. They were, therefore, different from structures produced in the mathetic context. In the pragmatic function, the structure of material process clauses was Actor + Process. So where the adult language would have a three-element transitive clause such as *Mummy cut paper*, Hal would have two possible two-element structures: *Mummy cut* or *cut paper*. If he were demanding an action, the former would be used; if he were observing an action, the latter would be used. Figures 8 and 9 depict Hal's meaning choices at clause rank for the two functions, shown in general terms at the midtransition period.

Once again we can explain the development of different structural patterns for each context if we treat linguistic structures as function/form complexes rather than arbitrary patterns. I would suggest that it

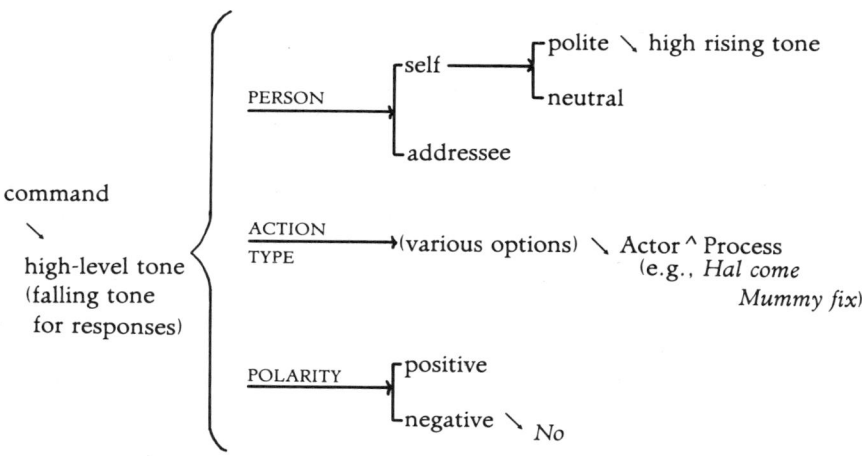

Figure 8. Outline of pragmatic options at clause rank, midtransition

is because pragmatic speech attempts to have an effect on the world, that the model of reality built up here by Hal was one of Actors doing things. Mathetic speech, on the other hand, attempts to interpret the goings-on of experience from an observer's standpoint, and Hal's understanding appeared to be that a happening involves a process and an entity through which the process comes about.

Here, then, we have a further exemplification of the statements made initially that forms evolve to actualize meanings. Because Hal was mean-

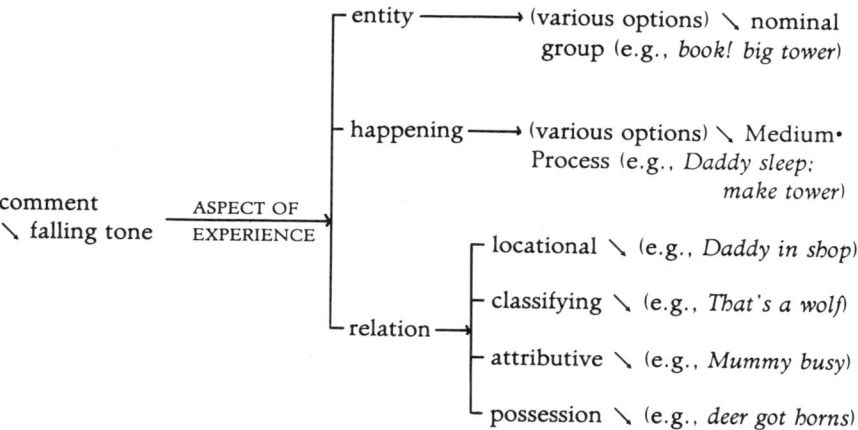

Figure 9. Outline of mathetic options at clause rank, midtransition

ing different kinds of things depending on the functional context, he evolved different kinds of structures. The development of linguistic structures, then, is not to be explained simply as a matter of perfecting the sensorimotor or "cognitive" skills which will allow words to be joined together in longer and more complicated patterns. The child extends his symbolic resources to serve his developing needs. Because he does this by making meanings in cooperation with other speakers, we can expect that—as in Hal's case—the clause structures developed will be compatible with those of the mother tongue.

2.6   Further Developments

In the last section I described how Hal built up a set of resources for acting on reality (pragmatic function) and a set of resources for reflecting on reality (mathetic function). I will now look at the way using this system for these purposes resulted in further development in the direction of the mother-tongue system; in particular in the ability to exchange information with others and to construct longer texts.

In using language within the mathetic function the child builds up a linguistic system in order to reflect on, indeed to organize, reality. Mathetic speech, for both Nigel and Hal, was not primarily directed at another person in order to gain a response from that person; often in fact it was self-addressed. But as a response to certain pressures, the child begins to adopt the role of information giver and to focus on linguistic interaction when using language in the mathetic function.

If Hal is typical, one possible kind of pressure arises from the child's need for sympathy when hurt or scolded. This is suggested by the nature of Hal's earliest informative utterances which were in situations of the following kinds:

(36)   (M hears Hal cry and enters room)
  M: Ooh, darling
  H: Bùmp

(37)   (M scolds Hal, who goes over to Granny)
  H: (to Granny) Mùmmy

(38)   (H is scolded by M for pulling cat's tail)
  H: (to F) tàil; tàil; pùssy; tàil; pùssy; tàil; pùssy; badbòy

These occasions suggest that the child's emotional needs may be one motivation for interacting through information giving. An even stronger pressure comes from the way other speakers behave. The mathetic utterances made by Nigel and Hal, even when self-addressed, were always being treated by the adult partner as though they were informative ones requiring acknowledgment, even though they did not tell the adult anything new. Many of the examples already given show the adult taking on the role of information receiver in this way (see examples 34, 35).

In addition, children like Hal may frequently be placed in an information-giving role by being asked questions by an adult who is actually in control of the information being ''sought.'' In the following examples we see Hal using language for his own mathetic purposes, but he is being assigned an information-giving role by the addressee:

(39)   (M and H are reading)
        M: And what's the antelope got?
        H: It's got horns

(40)   H: Aeroplane (picking up toy)
        M: Who went in the aeroplane, Hal?
        H: Daddy

(41)   (H enters holding hat)
        M: What have you got there?
        H: Hat

So interaction with others highlights for the child the possibility of using for information-giving purposes the resources that were originally developed in order to reflect on the world. The key role of such conversational interactions is also made evident when we look at how Hal and Nigel first produced informative utterances when there was no eliciting or questioning prompt from the addressee.

As the following examples show, Hal sometimes adopted the strategy of marking his information-giving utterances as such by prefacing them with an interrogative utterance of his own:

(42)   (H approaches M with a bag)
        H: What's in there?
            What's in there?
            What's in there?
            Tĕddy

(43)   (H enters holding two of his T-shirts)
        H: Which one d'you want?
            Thís one? (holding up one)
            Thís one? (holding up another)
            Thìs one (choosing)

(44)   (H shows M a book)
       H: What's thàt?
              Mònkey

Nigel too showed the influence of pressure from interactions with others in the way he marked his information-giving utterances. He did this more systematically than Hal but in a related way: He coded information givers as interrogatives. Thus *did Nila drop it* would mean 'Nila dropped it, and this is something you don't know.' Both children therefore seem to display clear evidence of taking up a role they were conscious of having had assigned to them by others. And without doubt when a child tries out the possibility of information giving, he will find he has a new and very rich way of interacting with others through reference to the outside world. In this way, the mathetic function, which primarily builds up experiential language systems and involves uttering self-contained comments, gradually comes to require the adoption of interactive speech roles.

Information exchange involves demanding information as well as giving it, of course, but Hal did not begin to do this until he had gained some experience in taking on both dialogue roles himself, as we saw him doing in examples 42–44. Presumably he was able in this way to focus first on the new social role of information giving and on the conversational exchange structure in which it could typically occur. Only when he had become more confident and experienced in taking on the information-giving role was he able to assign that role to others by asking genuine questions. Seeking information may therefore arise as a natural development from experience in the mathetic function. The child comes to terms with the complex notion of information, as we have described, and is then able to use questions as a productive way of learning about the world.

Information seeking may also arise from the pragmatic function, however, where interacting with others has always been to the fore, and utterances have always been demands of some kind. We have already seen how their conversational experiences pushed both Nigel and Hal to demand linguistic, rather than physical, responses from the addressee. While this was happening they were engaged in repeated interactions where they were treated as information givers. Once having appreciated the possibility of information as a commodity for exchange, it is a natural next step for the child to demand responses in the form of information when using language in the pragmatic function. And this was Nigel's preferred route into questioning.

So experience in using language for both mathetic and pragmatic purposes is likely to contribute to the child's use of language in order to exchange information, and hence to take on (and assign to others) roles such as Questioner, Answerer, Acknowledger, and so on.

Finally, I wish to consider the development of informative texts that involve the child in more than a straightforward clause-length response to a question. The most prominent of these are linguistic recounts of personal experience. Two threads need to be traced here—the variation in the mode element of the context involved when talking about something beyond the here and now, and the creation of a text that may concern a number of related incidents rather than a single event.

The first—distancing speech from the here and now—is a possibility as soon as the child embarks on the mother tongue, and has been mentioned as one of its advantages over the protolanguage (allowing for the demand of nonpresent objects, for example). One way the possibility is taken up in mathetic speech is in the form of predicting from previous experience (e.g., advancing toward a radiator cautiously, saying *hot*) or verbalizing an intention (e.g., saying *bring water* before setting off to do so). And just as these mathetic predicting and planning utterances help the child to organize experience, so can occasions of recalling past experience by means of language. In example 38, gaining sympathy was only one motive for the creation of that text; another motive was to reconstruct an immediately past event into language in order to reflect on it and understand it better.

But the experiences the child wishes to reflect on may not be individual happenings; they might be a series of events sequenced in time. Managing to represent this linguistically constitutes a task distinct from the matter of giving information, and one that the child attends to separately. We find that most early recounts of personal experience are not informative in function but take the form of "shared recall" with a conversational partner. Either party may initiate a dialogue in which experience is jointly reconstructed as a way of feeling close, as in the following texts from Nigel and Hal:

(45) (N and M have been shopping together)
      N: Our light said walk
          and we went in a shop
      M: And you were very good
          and crossed the road quickly
          and held Mummy's hand
      N: And you went on a wall (you = I)
          and you went on a bus
      M: And we went to the shop
          and we bought you two pairs of trousers and—
      N: And a red jumper . . .   (Halliday, 1984b)

(46) H: (cuddling a toy giraffe)
          I saw a big giraffe

> M: Yes, what was the giraffe doing?
> H: Eating the leaves
> M: What about the little giraffe?
>   Remember what he did?
> H: Go peepbo (i.e., stretched its neck out of the shed)
> M: Yes, he was looking out of the door, wasn't he?

Such occasions allow the child to make sense of the events of his life through a shared creation and understanding of a linguistic interpretation of shared experience. The experience is too complex to be encoded as a single clause or utterance, so a more complex text is required. But, unlike running commentaries, reconstruction texts involve the selection of events from memory and their representation as a sequence in time. Jointly produced texts concerning shared experience, such as those above, obviously help the child to do this and offer models for him to build on when he comes to produce monologue texts. In addition, before an **informative** recount of unshared experience can be confidently constructed, the child will need to be able to manage the further tasks of introducing participants into a story and providing an appropriate shape to it, including some kind of climax or high point. Again, the conversations he enters into provide him with guided experience, sometimes putting him into the information-giving role vis-à-vis an adult who shared the information. We can see this happening in the following example:

(47)   M: Where did you go yesterday?
       N: Clinic
       M: You went to the clinic
           And what did the doctor give you?
       N: Chocolate
       M: And what did the doctor say?
       N: No more
           (to F) Nila went to the clinic   (Halliday, 1984b)

There are many formal language-learning situations in which students are required to produce narratives of personal experience: perhaps in a new language or a new medium (writing), or for a new kind of audience (teacher or "generalized" audience). From the examples we have looked at we can get some idea of the number of different things the language user must learn to manage, and how the immature speaker is guided in parent-child interaction toward the successful creation of such texts.

In particular, it seems that the kind of dialogic creation of recounts that we have seen has two advantages. It provides a way of making the requirements of the task transparent to the child and it minimizes the need for the child to handle all aspects of the task simultaneously. Language learners of all kinds will extend their language abilities only by being challenged or by feeling the need to do new things, but they should not necessarily be expected to manage unaided a new task if it involves a whole complex of new challenges. We have seen at several points now that the child avoids focusing his attention on everything at once in the process of language learning. For example, the creation of the mathetic/pragmatic dichotomy avoided the need to focus on interpersonal and experiential matters simultaneously. And the information-giving self-created dialogues, such as examples 42–44, allowed Hal to concentrate on just one speech role at a time. In the same way, the joint creation of personal recounts treats selected recall of incidents, introduction and keeping track of participants, and the creation of an appropriate generic shape, as matters which the child may take more or less responsibility for on particular occasions.

When teachers encourage their students to produce spoken and written texts of various kinds, they will need (from linguists) adequate descriptions of the kinds of texts they intend their students to create or participate in. (Are spoken recounts of the early years the same kind of text as written personal narratives, for example? How does a short story differ from either of these?) With such descriptive tools, we will be better able to determine the kinds of new challenges a specific new task represents. In addition, interactional "scaffolding" techniques analogous to those we have seen used by parents may prove fruitful in the classroom (see Painter, 1986, for development of this idea).

2.7   Disappearance of the Pragmatic/Mathetic Dichotomy

In the last section I examined the development of information exchange and of more complex meanings that need to be structured into longer discourse. It is time now to consider how doing these new things—making these new kinds of meanings—has affected the underlying linguistic system.

It may already be apparent that in developing the resources for exchanging information, the distinction between the pragmatic and mathetic functions will have disappeared. Let me briefly retrace the steps by which this has come about.

The child's experiences in using protolanguage highlighted for him two principal functions for language, so instead of having symbolic resources for a number of narrower functions, he develops two sets of resources—one for interpreting the world as an observer, and one for acting on the world as an intruder. Acting on the world by means of symbols involves above all interacting with others, while reflecting upon it by means of symbols need not.

But, of course, acting on the world using mother-tongue linguistic forms also involves categorizing experience, even though this is not the primary goal. Thus, *apple* from Hal was a demand, but one involving some specific class of entity, even though the child was not focusing his attention on the categorization itself. Similarly, observing the world is not carried out in solitude, and using language for his own mathetic purposes with other speakers encourages the child to take account of the addresser-addressee relationship in this context too. Thus using the language for the two functions he initially found relevant to his purposes led Hal in all contexts to represent experiential reality and to take on speech roles to interact with others. Once both "pragmatic" and "mathetic" utterances are doing both these things, it is impossible to distinguish the one kind of utterance from the other. Any utterance is not just one or the other, but both.

This has two consequences: the context for speech has to be construed differently, and the linguistic resources called upon in speech have to be reorganized. Instead of construing contexts as involving either speaker-hearer relations (tenor) or involving the representation of experience (field), the child has been pushed to the adult way of construing all contexts for speech as involving both. Moreover, the functional separation of resources into two relatively separate systems no longer serves his needs and has to be abandoned along with the two-way tonal distinction. Soon after Hal reached two years of age (doubtless there is a great age variation in this as in other things) one can infer that he had a single transitivity system of process types used, whether giving information or demanding it, whether offering goods and services or demanding them, and he had a complementary mood system to distinguish all those different speech functions (all except offers, at least, which get coded by interrogatives as do questions).

In the following figures, a schematic outline of the options available at the end of the transition period is presented. First, in Figures 10 and 11, we can see the "end point" of development of the mathetic and pragmatic resources. But once they have reached this point of development they can be represented as a single integrated metafunctional meaning potential, as shown in Figure 12. Figure 12 represents the same kind of system as that initially outlined for adult language in Figure 1.

I have not detailed the development of textual resources since these develop not from a basic function for language, but as a means of allowing the other metafunctions to produce text. In order to use language to talk to others and to talk about things in sustained discourse, the speaker will need systems for making links within and beyond the text,

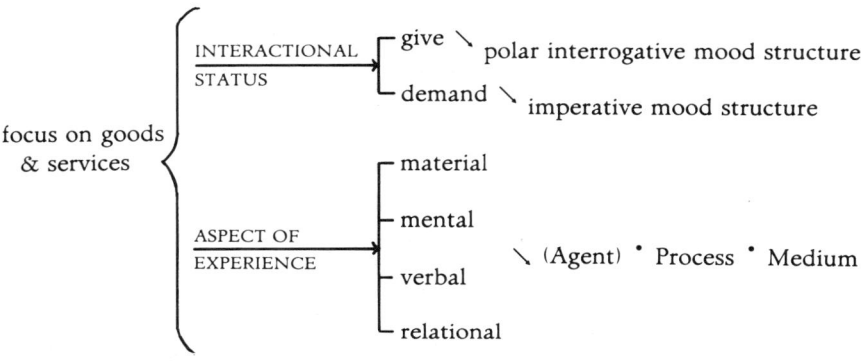

Figure 10. Simplified outline of Hal's "pragmatic" options at clause rank—End of transition phase

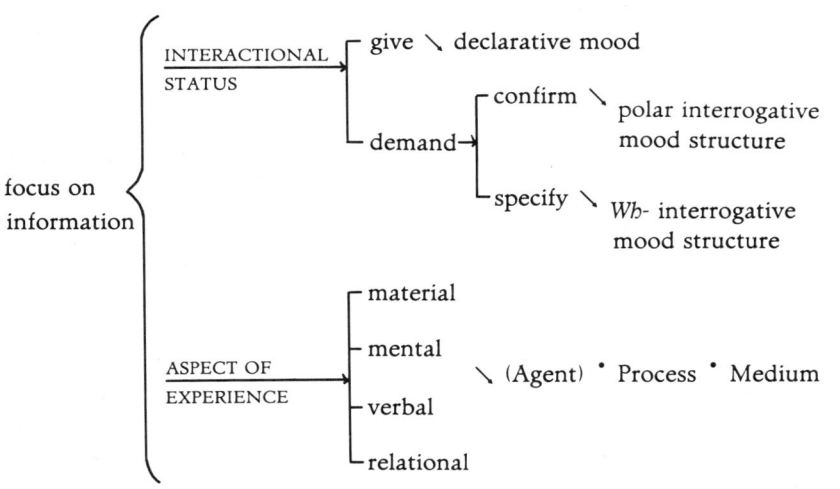

Figure 11. Simplified outline of Hal's "mathetic" options at clause rank—End of transition phase

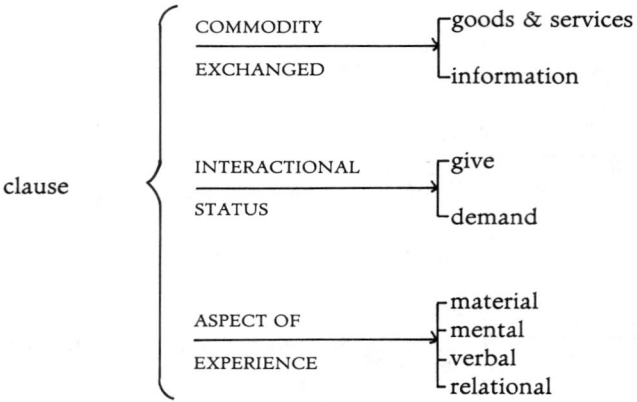

Figure 12. Alternative outline of Hal's end transition linguistic potential represented as a single integrated "metafunctional" system

for foregrounding and backgrounding information, for keeping track of the entities being talked about, and so on. Thus it is only with the development of the systems of mood and transitivity (which make possible dialogue and narrative modes of discourse) that the speaker will need to develop textual systems of marked and unmarked Theme, conjunction, anaphoric reference, and so on. One of the earliest systems to develop here is that of Information, in which intonational prominence is assigned by the speaker to the part of the utterance to be taken as "New Information." This is a crucial system for coherent text in the spoken mode, and thus naturally one the child will feel the need for very early on (see Halliday, 1979a, for a discussion of Nigel's development of textual resources).

The Commodity exchanged and Interactional status systems are realized through the grammatical system of Mood, so this system represents the grammatical potential described in Figure 1.

2.8   Milestones in the Development of the Mother Tongue

This account of language development has been a fairly lengthy one since it has attempted to look simultaneously at how an individual's symbolic resources develop in the first years of life and why the child takes the developmental steps he does. At the same time, I have attempted to illustrate all general claims with details from the individual case histories of Hal or Nigel. At this point, then, it may be helpful to summarize the most significant moves the child finds it necessary to make.

1. Innate motivation. The child is born with built-in motivations to interact with others. This results in adult-child communication of a sort in the earliest months.

2. Development of symbols. The establishment of interpersonal communication patterns allows for the possibility of bringing the world of objects into the communication. This motivates the development of communication through symbols—the beginning of the protolanguage phase.

3. Development of "naming." Adult language used to the child suggests to him not only that symbolic expressions can be shared, but that language can interpret experience by classing separate instances of experience as the same.

4. Development of mathetic and pragmatic functions. Experience with protolanguage demonstrates to the child his ability to have an effect on the world through symbols. The development of names not only extends this potential but also involves the child in seeing the interpretation of experience as a key function for language. Out of this, the child finds language serving him in two principal ways—as an instrument for reflection and as a tool for action.

5. Development of linguistic structure. The child's potential for acting on the world symbolically is extended by developing certain kinds of linguistic structures; his potential for interpreting the world symbolically is extended by developing other kinds of linguistic structures.

6. Development of information exchange. Using language for pragmatic and mathetic purposes with others makes the child aware of, and eventually able to participate in, the exchange of information.

7. Development of a metafunctionally organized system. When exchanging information the speaker is both "doing" with language (asking, answering, querying, etc. . . .) and representing states of affairs with language. The interpretation of any context for speech as one for both doing and representing allows for the possibility of meaning two kinds of things at once—as the adult clause does, but as the protolinguistic utterance cannot. Thus this point of development is the consequence of the movement from 1 to 6.

3. A Functional View of Language Development

In this final section I would like to draw together a number of points relating to this view which seem relevant for educators, although there will be other chapters in this volume that address much more directly the question of how Halliday's insights might relate to classroom practice.

Perhaps the first points to be made here should focus on the implications of the term **functional**. One clear implication is that children learn language in order to achieve something—to understand the environment, to feel close to family members, to obtain desired goods, and so on. Another aspect of this is that language learning involves making meanings in a context from the earliest use of symbols. Language forms are not developed for their own sake and then put to use. On the contrary, forms (words, structures, and discourse structures) develop in order to actualize meanings, and so the linguistic system is functional in a real sense.

If we think about these points in an educational context, we can see that language learning here too needs to be functional. We cannot realistically expect children to develop their linguistic resources further unless they are engaged in tasks in which they achieve something by means of language. Our approach should not be based on attempts to ''teach'' language items that have not arisen in any functional context for the learner, in the expectation that they will then be available to the child to use when an appropriate opportunity arises. If we reject the dichotomy between form and use which is embodied in the pragmatics school of thought, this becomes obvious.

Another point to consider is that since the grammatical system is functional, errors of ''form'' made by students (a different matter from mother-tongue dialect differences) can be seen as arising from problems in creating particular kinds of meaning in context. Since form is functional, the attention of teacher and pupil should be directed to what the language user is or should be trying to do, and how this can be effectively achieved linguistically, rather than on mere ''correction'' of forms. Of course to do this effectively we may need to have better descriptions of the kinds of discourses any student group is likely to be engaged in, so that we have a systematic basis for considering how ''what the user is trying to do'' can be effectively realized linguistically.

A second theme of this chapter relevant for applied programs concerns the question of what motivates development in language. I hope to have shown that at each phase of development the child's linguistic system changes in response to pressures arising from the individual's needs, and that both the needs and the responses to them may be shaped by interactions with other speakers.

Let me briefly point to two examples given earlier in the chapter. One concerns the move out of the protolanguage. The protolanguage is a limited resource for learning, but it is only the child's experiences in using it to engage in various types of interactions which highlight for him the possibility of the mother tongue as an effective instrument for learning. We could say that the conversational partner in a sense pushes the child to realize the mathetic potential of the mother tongue. But at the same time the child is able to respond to that pressure only by perfecting exchanges that fulfill his original purposes in the Personal and Interactional functions.

As another example, consider the development of questions by the child. The transition system has limitations as a tool for learning as long as the child cannot make the best use of other people as a source of knowledge by demanding information from them. How does a child come to appreciate this possibility? I have shown that for Hal it was partly through using his own system for mathetic purposes: In the resulting interactions information was offered to him even though he did not ask for it. At the same time, when he did ask for other things, he was given information as well as (or instead of) the desired commodities. These (i.e., the move into the mother tongue and the move into information giving) are two examples of how the child uses language to satisfy his needs while at the same time his social experience of languaging shapes those needs.

In what way can we draw on these understandings in an educational context? First, we can recognize that an individual's linguistic system will be extended only if that person finds it necessary to do more things with language. Such a need may arise outside the language classroom from the student's other social experiences (for immigrants learning a second language, for example, or for schoolchildren coping with curriculum subjects). But this will not always be the case, and in both mother-tongue and second language learning contexts it may be up to the teacher to find ways to challenge students to extend their linguistic resources in particular directions.

But being pressured to achieve something new is barely half the story. There is also the vital matter of getting the student to achieve the desired goal. We may make explicit the expectations we have of the learner but this does not mean that he is innately endowed with the linguistic resources and experience to fulfill them. Here it is important to consider how much the young child is guided by those around him to achieve success in language development. One factor I have emphasised several times is experience—in the sense of experience in meaning-making. Learners need opportunities, and perhaps repeated opportunities, for making meanings relevant for the achievement of any language development goal we may set. And practice in making meanings probably has to occur in interactions with others, even for older children, and even when they are developing essentially monologic genres such as most of those important for success in school, university, or public life.

I have shown how in the early years a process of interactive modeling takes place continually. This serves not only to covertly nudge the child into attempting new meanings, but also demonstrates ways to actualize them. While I would certainly not suggest that classroom methodology has to mimic slavishly the conditions of a parent-infant dyad, I would suggest that making meaning requires interaction and success in making meanings requires models. There is nothing new, of course, in the idea of providing models of language for students to learn from, at least in methodologies of second language learning. The difference with a functional approach is that models of language will not be conceived of and presented as models of arbitrary patterns of forms (text structures, clause structures, vocabulary, or whatever else), but rather as models of text actualizing meanings in a context (see Gray, 1984; Rothery, 1986a, for illustrations of how this can take place in mother-tongue classrooms).

It is probably in mother-tongue classrooms that teachers will be most wary of the idea of interactive modeling, feeling that this may be an interference with the child's unique creative talents. Yet it is never suggested that parent-child interaction in the first two or three years does this. On the contrary, these years are held up as a model of natural language development unsullied by interference from others (Cambourne, 1984). I hope that a closer understanding of how development actually takes place in the early years will show that this attitude is naive, and that although the child is indeed engaged in developing linguistic resources to serve his own purposes, both the purposes and the resources are constructed through social interaction.

A third aspect of the functional view of development concerns the nature of the linguistic system and its relation to the contexts of use. An important strand to our discussion of early language learning has been that language develops in the life of the individual as distinct sets of resources for "doing" and for "representing," which eventually come to be used simultaneously. This developmental trail has two consequences for the mature system. First, it results in a linguistic system organized as complementary sets of options which are relatively independent of one another. For example, a particular Actor + Process construction can be represented in a number of different mood forms, because process-type choices are independent of mood ones. Second, it means that any text, any occasion of language spoken or written at any particular time, will embody options from each metafunction. Choices made will depend on how the context is construed; what the social goals of the discourse are, what the field is understood to be, what tenor relations are relevant, and what the mode factors are (e.g., spoken or written channel, language constituting or incidental to the social activity engaged in).

An understanding of the relationship between the system and contexts of use is highly relevant in teaching. It makes it possible both to interpret language problems and to plan for further language development in a principled way. For example, a student who fails to use vocabulary of an appropriate degree of technicality has probably not understood the field requirements of the context; a failure to construct a text with the appropriate generic shape is likely to be the result of a failure to understand how to fulfill the goals of the discourse; on the other hand, if the learner does not use the appropriate degree of "formality" or tentativeness/certainty, or appropriate expressions of personal attitudes, this suggests a failure to appreciate the tenor requirements of the context; or the problem may be a failure to "self-contextualize" a written text, suggesting that mode requirements have not been considered; and so on. (Of course, once the nature of any context of situation is familiar and understood, it is always possible to choose to act unpredictably or "inappropriately" in order to achieve some particular effect.)

Moreover, understanding of the relation between the linguistic system and contexts of use provides a way of planning to develop language further. It allows us to be systematic in attempts to extend students by challenging them in respect of one particular contextual variable at a time, or with respect to whichever contextual variable relates to the grammatical systems in which current problems have been observed. At the very least it allows us to have a means of assessing the difficulty of new tasks and of clarifying for the learner all the contextual values he will need to be clear about in order to perform any required task using language.

A final and very important point about a functional view of language development is that it raises our consciousness that all school learning will be a linguistic challenge of some kind. Even if the systems of grammatical and lexical options of the mother tongue do not develop so dramatically as we get older, we are always being called upon to fulfill tasks for which our previous experience has not prepared us. These tasks will require the creation of new kinds of texts (spoken and written), and to succeed in constructing them we usually need help and we usually need models. Success in using the linguistic system at our disposal in any instance depends on understanding the requirements of the context of situation and gaining experience in fulfilling them. Both the understanding and the experience may need to be achieved with the help of others—particularly teachers, whether or not those teachers are generally viewed as having responsibility for language development.

CHAPTER 2

THE OBJECT OF LANGUAGE

David G. Butt

National University of Singapore

> "*A child is learning a semiotic system, the culture, and simultaneously he is learning the means of learning it—a second semiotic system, the language, which is the intermediary in which the first one is encoded. This is a very complex situation.*" (Halliday, 1975, p. 122)

It is a paradox that much contemporary literature on child language development—or language acquisition, as it has often been called in the last two decades—constitutes the first obstruction to understanding the "complex situation" described by Halliday. The metaphor of acquisition in itself highlights the particular orientation of the period, especially up to 1975: as if language were not progressively learned, but rather something the child obtained with maturation, like teeth or hair. Research in education and psychology, as well as in linguistics, was dominated by the Chomskyan notion that language was a kind of mental organ (Chomsky, 1975, p. 59), and that, by elucidating principles of linguistic structure which could not be motivated by function, linguistics would achieve a description of the deep properties of the human mind (Chomsky, 1972, p. 41).

For the lay person who missed the Chomskyan revolution, however, it would be a shock to realize how much of what one takes for granted has only more recently returned as the subject matter of respectable academic discourse. A case in point is the idea that mothers teach and children learn. It was not that the nativist hypothesis denied teaching and learning between mother and child: It merely claimed that mothers did not teach 'language.' While it was conceded that caregivers expand, extend, and occasionally correct the form of their children's language, such behavior was regarded as incidental to the direction, quality, and possibly even the rate of the process of 'acquisition.' (e.g., Brown & Cazden, 1975, and Cazden, 1972, pp. 90–122). One particularly influential conclusion presented by Brown, Cazden, and Bellugi (see Cazden, 1972, p. 115) did much to downgrade the role of mothers in linguistic development. Essentially the researchers claimed that the grounds upon which parents approved or disapproved a child's utterance "were not strictly linguistic at all": The mother's response was to "the truth of the proposition the child intended to express."

> In general, the parents fitted propositions to the child's utterances, however incomplete or distorted the utterances, and then approved or not according to the correspondence between the proposition and reality. Thus, *Her curl my hair* was approved because the mother was, in fact, curling Eve's hair. However, Sarah's grammatically impeccable *There's the animal farmhouse* was disapproved because the building was a light-house, and Adam's *Walt Disney comes on on Tuesday* was disapproved because Walt Disney came on on some other day. It seems, then, to be truth value rather than syntactic well-formedness that chiefly governs explicit verbal reinforcement by parents—which renders mildly paradoxical the fact that the usual product of such a training schedule is an adult whose speech is highly grammatical but not notably truthful. (Brown, Cazden, & Bellugi, quoted in Cazden, 1972, p. 115)

Unwinding the implications of this passage is very instructive for anyone reflecting on theoretical assumptions in developmental studies. And I will return to details of the passage in section 3 below. Even the final ironic observation reveals something of the climate of theory—as though training were clearly irrelevant or counterproductive to the achievement of complex behavior. The aspect of the passage that requires most careful appreciation, however, is the emphasis on syntax and grammaticality. The implication here appears to be that a strong boundary exists between syntax and semantics, between grammatical knowledge and other forms of knowledge—even knowledge of the meanings of individual words. And this emphasis on "syntactic well-formedness" implies that language is essentially a set of forms independent of the contexts of its use in the house, neighborhood, and school. In short, it is a view of language that assumes a maximal distance between culture and language, as if the vast networks of social interaction could be stripped down into an unambiguous contrast between content and form, with the former being culture or 'knowledge of the world' and the latter, language.

It is the relationship between culture and language that I examine, in the light of Halliday's statement quoted at the outset. To interpret that relationship, I analyze three kinds of social context: mother-child exchanges, at home (with the child 3 years, 9 months old); teacher-pupil and peer interaction in the first weeks of attending school (with the child 5 years old); and infant-mother interaction during the first year of life. Each of these contexts is discussed in a separate section. The non-chronological order of the discussion—namely, (a) the child at home; (b) the school novice; (c) the infant—is a concession to the difficulty of interpreting infant behavior. The orientation of sections 1 and 2 prepares for the paradoxical notions which need to be considered in section 3. From the interpretation of these three contexts, I review the general significance of the analyses: namely, how they throw light on the situation of the child who is simultaneously learning the culture and the language. In particular, I focus on the role of language as both instrument and object, the tool of the learner and the "thing" to be learned.

The direction of the argument can be stated briefly. The opposition of the terms "culture" and "language" may be useful in certain forms of discourse. Such an opposition may even appear necessary to the achievement of particular academic and educational needs, for example, the writing of grammars and the formulation of curricula. But culture and language are two terms on a continuum of saying—a gradient of processes of meaning. When linguistic theories and educational practice stress an opposition between culture and language, or between context and linguistic code, the relationship of the child to the environments of home and school is totally misconstrued.

Below section 1, there is presented a series of exchanges between a small girl (aged 3 years, 9 months). and her mother. Each exchange is a virtual snippet from representative home contexts: helping with the cooking; dressing; getting ready for preschool; and cutting and pasting while the mother sews and watches television. After each exchange I analyze and comment on the text in relation to the preceding discussion. The examples are also given a characterizing title to facilitate subsequent reference.

These exchanges, like the school transcripts discussed in section 2, are taken from recordings made on a research project conducted by Ruqaiya Hasan at Macquarie University, and funded by the Australian Research Grants Scheme. (For a fuller outline of the project, refer to Cloran chapter 3 of this volume. For other discussions relating to the materials and orientation of the project, see Hasan, 1984a, 1986.)

SECTION 1. BEFORE SCHOOL

Meaning as Doing.

Text 1.1
1 M: . . . . Now I'll cut up the onions and capsicums.
2 And I'll get you to grease the dish.
3 C: What's grease?

4 M: I'll put a little bit of oil in that dish.
5 C: Mm
6 M: And then I want you to rub it around with your fingers . . . .

The child's question is answered here, but in a way that may appear indirect: The mother does not adopt the explicit definitional form of equative clause *(Grease is . . .* or *To grease means . . .);* she offers the child a "meaning-as-use" approach to the word. But there is an additional factor for which an explication might prepare the child: namely, that there is a term *grease* (the thing, as a noun: gris) as well as *grease* (the process, as a verb: gri:z). It is important to note that the mother's response encompasses both the thing and the process (messages 4 and 6, respectively). By introducing paraphrase (i.e., *a little bit of oil* and *rub it around)* and putting it to work in a set of instructions which continue for another six messages, the mother virtually delimits a chunk of activity and leaves the child to a certain amount of inference.

Your Meaning, My Wording

Text 1.2
1 M: But when you do cooking
2   do all the kids cook?
3   or do they choose some of the kids to cook?
4 C: Some of the kids to cook
5 M: I see. . . .

Carefully the mother lays out the contrastiveness of *all* and *some.* The explicitness and the resulting parallelism between 2 and 3 produces a number of results. In the first place the child is not left to construct a meaning so much as select a wording; and select the wording she does in the elliptical 4: (They choose) *some of the kids to cook.* Through the strategy of 'give me the meaning by selecting from *my* wordings,' both difficulty and ambiguity are controlled.

The paradigmatic opposition between "all" and "some" could have been inferred by the child even if the mother had said (the relatively unnatural)

Do all the kids cook?
Or do some of the kids cook?

The mother, however, constructs message 3 in such a way that the syntagmatic relations help to specify the crucial opposition between all/some. If the child understands *choose,* she already understands most of the *all/some* contrast—choice entails a progression from a larger to a smaller set. Without this motivation of clarifying the meanings, it is difficult to explain why the mother would switch Subject from *all the kids* in 2 to *they* in 3. A natural alternative would have been *Or do only some of the kids cook?* This wording (with *only*) does not have the advantages for interpretation that the *do they choose some . . .* message has. In the latter, the mother has enhanced the connection between *choose* and *some* by making *choose* the finite Predicator and main Process—that is, the element around which the clause is organized.

A Part of Speech: A Syllogism

Text 1.3
1 C: Oh, oh (complaining about stirring the onions)
2 M: I know you don't like onions
3   but I always put onions in cornbread
4   and you always like cornbread
5   So I don't think you really mind.

This syllogistic response from the mother serves to remind that there are many levels of structure in language. One of those levels is discourse. And there seems little justification to exclude one level of convention or form because it may be difficult to bring into a closed system description. If there is a pattern in the language which speakers use as a communicative resource then that pattern constitutes part of the language. The importance of admitting meaningful patterns of the discourse level can be seen by trying to explain the mother's response here in terms of the grammatical rank scale—from clause complex down to morpheme. While one might claim simply that messages 2–5 constitute a single clause complex with the organic relations (Hasan, 1984b) explicit: adversative *But*, additive *And*, and the casual *So*, the mother is using a standardized gambit that is itself a unit—a ''move''—at the level of exchange. (See Sinclair & Coulthard, 1975, for proposals concerning such units.)

An important conflict of perspective arises here. One needs to decide whether the mother's syllogistic move is better regarded as one of the community forms of talk—a form with a special, rational status—or alternatively as one of the universal forms of thought, which is merely reflected in language. The difficulties involved in these alternative points of view are considered below in section 2 on school talk, and in section 3: the discussion of structure in the experience of children in their first year. In particular, it is asked to what degree one can regard language as a mirror to thought and states of affairs. For present purposes, however, let us reflect on the ways in which the syllogistic form is actually employed in discourse. It is important to note that it is often used, not for the achievement of some clarity in cognitive meaning, but for the rhetorical force of its apparent rationalism. This is to say that its function is more as a figure of speech than as the test of legitimate argument. An instance of this syllogistic mode, used by a 5-year-old child for rhetorical and heuristic purposes, is discussed in Butt (1985, pp. 91–93).

Text 1.4
The mother and child are sitting together in this exchange. The daughter makes the comment that she hates school, a comment which contradicts her usual statements about school. The mother then decides to ask the child about her teacher, knowing that this is likely to bring out her general enjoyment of school:

M: Do you hate Mrs. McDonald?
C: Do I hate my family?!!
   I'd hate you if I hated her
   Do you hear that?
   'Cause I love her.
   Do you hear that?
   I'd have to hate you!

(Butt, 1985, p. 91)

This is then interpreted in the following way: "In so much as the girl's reaction to her teacher is of the same category as her feelings towards her mother, if her feelings to her teacher were in fact hate (which they are not), then it would follow that the feelings towards the mother would be hate. This is to say A and B are the same with respect to factor C; if the reaction A/C is changed then the relationship B/C is changed in the same way." The reasoning rests on "the fiction of equivalent cases." And in the final clause, *I'd have to hate you*, the child is drawing attention to "a form of logical imperative in the whole fabrication: as if the consequence, hating mum, would be a logical necessity (almost something beyond the influence of the child's own feelings or volition)." The example "reveals the child in the process of constructing "reason." Her argument is already an appeal to an impersonal structure that exists outside her: She has become an agent forced into hating because of the objective nature of the connections between facts. . . . The argument or reasoning is unacceptable. Yet it has considerable interpersonal force" (Butt, 1975, p. 92).

Guidance Versus Correction: The Problem of Disproportionate Feedback

When language is viewed primarily as a potential to mean, rather than (after the manner of formal logic) as a set of well-formed strings, all speaker selections have to be addressed as part of the language and consequently have to figure in one's theory of language development. When the mother and child work together to lay out the meaning system, their strategies do not pertain to one level in the system or to one kind of structure alone. Furthermore, the parent and child, as users of the system, are going to be concerned with a form only in terms of its semantic consequences, including social consequences. In this light, the pattern of corrections found by Brown and colleagues appears consistent—the parent's focus will be on the system as meaning, on the interpretation of the child's behavior. Hence, when the child asks the mother, *Has this got the knot undone up?* the mother does not point out to the child that there is a kind of asymmetry between the antonyms ''done up'' and ''undone'' (do up/undo). To the reader of this transcript—with enough time to reflect—the 'error' suggests that the 4-year-old has developed an understanding of how function determines form: She has discerned that *done up* constrasts with *done* such that the former constitutes an item recognizable even to her as a separate word in the other context; hence she expects the *un-* prefix to apply to the whole from *done up*. The mother 'tells' her about the do up/undo relationship in the only way that makes sense. She replies, *Yes, I undid the knot for you.*

Her response shifts the problematic form *undone up* away from the involved complement structure:

Has	this	got	the	knot	undone

Fin.	Subj.	Pred.			
			Subj.	IS?	Comp.
			Mood		Residue
			Complement		
Mood		Residue			

Instead, the mother chooses a form in which *undid* functions as the Predicator in the clause:

I	undid		it	for you
Subj.	Fin.	Pred.	Comp.	Adjunct
Mood		Residue		

Note that the mother does not just say "yes," which would have confirmed the truth value of the child's proposition (cf. remarks quoted earlier from Brown). Rather, the mother chooses a form that blocks the possibility of the addition of *up* to the clause at any point. This can be seen by changing the Predicator to *did up* or by thinking of comparable cases: processes like "turn off" as in "turn off the lights" and "turn the lights off." From the point of view of the mother as a teacher, we can see that her explicit response, with the Adjunct *for you*, helps to close off any opportunity for tacking on the preposition *up*.

The consequence of the Adjunct *for you* can be seen through the following:

√ I did up the knot
√ I did the knot up
✕ I did the knot for you up

In the adult system, *up* cannot come after the Adjunct, just as one doesn't have the form "undone up." Of course, from the child's point of view—in her system—this limitation may not be salient. Whatever the case, we can see that the mother's response offers two kinds of evidence against the use of her daughter's *undone up*. First of all, the mother simply does not use it herself in the role of Predicator, and second, there is the presence of the Adjunct which diminishes the possibility that the mother has omitted an *up* through a form of ellipsis or carelessness (viz., the alternative answer: "Yes, this has got the knot undone").

The mother's wording is a sound strategy for a nonlinguist (or a linguist, for that matter) in displaying the system *through use*. The mother could have stopped proceedings, of course, in order to draw attention to the 'mistake' in the child's wording. But an explicit correction is not as straightforward a strategy as one might assume. In the first place it gives a negative orientation to the exchanges in that it draws attention to one error rather than affirming the communicative achievements of the developing child. It is interesting to note, for instance, that the child's error is trivial by comparison with the achievements of manipulating the systems of Theme/Rheme and Given/New (in the textual component). Yet it is easy to get the proportions wrong in one's corrections, since errors like *undone up* are overt and easy to be explicit about, while textual systems, which are far more significant to an interaction, pass beneath the threshold of comment—perhaps because they are not realized by simple discrete elements, and because they involve elaborate, shifting patterns of combination. (For a discussion of the relationship between Given/New and Theme/Rheme, see Halliday, 1985b).

Given the likelihood of such disproportionate feedback, the oblique strategy of the mother—that is, displaying the system through use—could well be the optimum method of productively guiding the child. In this regard, it should be emphasized that in any talk, the interaction is a kind of artifact; but it is not the simple combination of two individual, modular contributions. Rather, it is as if the interactions step up and up and up, building a discourse that cannot be adequately described in terms of the psychology of individuals (see Bateson 1980, pp. 146, 153). Therefore, in closing off this subsection on the strategic guidance of the mother, one should draw attention to four implications.

1. Regular interactants, like a mother and a child, develop their own styles as a dyad, their own discourse "fabric," with recurrent motifs and patterns.
2. Guidance is not unilateral: The parent is being led in parenting as the child is being directed in development.
3. The metalinguistic talk sought by researchers during the era of syntactic investigations may be so communicatively dysfunctional (with its emphasis on errors and corrections) that its relative absence can be explained on this ground alone—one may not even need to appeal to the fact that humans are oriented to meanings and activities, rather than to "well-formed formulae."
4. A mother's strategies for drawing attention to language may be far more oblique and subtle than has been usual to concede, (Recall, also, the way the syntagmatic and paradigmatic are interrelated in the "choose/some" example above, in text 1.2.)

Rehearsing Behavior

Text 1.5
1   M: Oh, you're a goose, Ruth. (the baby sister who has caught herself)
2   C: Oh, you're a goose.
3   Do goosies do that?
4   M: No no
5   But you often call people a goose
6   If they're silly.
7   C: Hmm.
8   M: You know, if you eat too much

9		I say you're a little pig.
10		I say you're a little piggy-wig.
11	C:	Yeah. (laughing)
12	M:	Well, if people are silly
13		you say ''silly goose''
14		And sometimes you can say they're a donkey.
15		You silly donkey.
16	C:	(laughs)
17		Silly donkey.
18	M:	And if they are fussy
19		What do you say . . .
20		I think you'd say they're a hen . . . or a mother hen.
21	C:	[?]
22	M:	You haven't got your panties on, have we?
23		Where are they?
24		Goodness me, I put them out.
25		There they are. The blue ones.
26	C:	Hello [? fussy hen]?

The central issue which emerges from this series of exchanges is the way we are to regard the comprehensive listing of expressions that the mother offers the child. The mother explains *you're a goose; you're a little pig; silly goose; you silly donkey;* and *they're a hen . . . a mother hen.* If the child had actually asked about geese, pigs, donkeys, and hens, many linguists might have categorized the talk as essentially about knowledge of the world, about facts, and irrelevant to the learning of language. But since the same lexical items *(goose; donkey;* etc.) are part of what ''you can say,'' the exchanges are unequivocally about language. It is interesting, therefore, to reflect on the similarity between this set of exchanges and other topics discussed by the mother and the daughter.

The exchanges begin with the mother recounting a silly action by the younger daughter, Ruth. This produces the *Oh, you're a goose, Ruth,* which is immediately emulated by the other daughter (note, 10 messages earlier the same had happened with *silly monkey).* The subsequent query *Do goosies do that?* arises out of their engagement with Ruth, much as *What's grease?* arose previously from the cooking. On the surface, then, the questions seem to be a checking of facts; but the answers they receive, as well as some of the circumstances in which each one was expressed, make them somewhat different. The question concerning *grease* is a response to instructions and the only reply it receives is further instructions, albeit broken into component actions. The inquiry about *goosies* comes about in addressing the baby; but the elder child has not been fielding instructions. The mother has just reported to her on the baby. This brief episode—the report—is an activity constituted by language, whereas in the cooking (if not in the teaching of cooking) the talk tends to be ancillary to the activity. Furthermore, the misunderstanding in *Do goosies do that?* brings out an explicit answer *(No, no* etc.), which extends right up to *mother hen* (20). The child is not left simply to infer.

A crucial similarity between the situations, however, is the orientation of the mother's response: In both cases she presents the relevant meanings as forms of doing. It was seen above that the mother did not give a dictionary-like citation for *grease*—nor, for that matter, did she explain that such citations would not be forthcoming! Rather, she showed how to work with the expression *grease the dish*. In a related way, in the series of examples in response to *Do goosies . . . ?* the mother offers no definitional formulations of the idioms she draws upon. Instead we find *you often call* . . . (5); *you know* . . . *I say* . . . (8–9); *I say* . . . (10); *you can say* (14); *what do you say* . . . (19); *I think you'd say* . . . (20). All 'meanings,' so to speak, are rendered as expressions of saying, under different conditions. It is only in the hypotactic clauses of condition that one finds any relational processes, for example, *if they're silly* (6); *if people are silly* (12); *if they are fussy* (18); and these are attributive clauses, quite unlike the identifying/equative structures one can expect with definitions and meanings.

This orientation to doing is also realized in the selections of tenses: for example, *you* . . . *call, I say,* and so on in the main clauses. The value of the present tense here is not exactly iterative, even though something of the meaning over and over is involved. Note that the specifications of *you* . . . *call* or *I say* are in terms of conditional *if* clauses, not temporal adjuncts. These conditions lend an axiomatic force to the mother's statements. In fact, each statement is an axiom of cultural practice—virtually what "people" DO across *all* times, given particular conditions.

It should be appreciated that such statements, from this particular mother, tend to be muted with respect to their force as 'axioms of praxis' or as edicts. This tendency is a domain over which mothers vary. Such variation is usefully regarded, however, in terms of group styles, not just as individual differences. For example, in the *Do goosies do that?* episode, the mother presents the *you often call, I say* . . . , *you can say,* or *you'd say* as a cline of assertion. She begins with the most general and impersonal assertion and moves toward subjective modality and a more personalized focus on the hearer (the child):

(5)   *But you often call people a goose if . . .* : you = impersonal, suggesting all the members of our community; often = usualness, median-value modality

(8-9)   *you know, if . . . I say you're a little pig:* you know = a form of
deferring to hearer; I say you're = this is my practice with respect
to you—hence something that can be checked against our personal
experience

(14)   *And sometimes you can say . . . :* sometimes = low value of usualness; you = again the community you; can = ability/modality

(20)   *I think you'd say . . . :* I think = subjective modality; would =
median-value probability; you = ambivalent between the impersonal you of (5) and the you of the preceding question *what do you
say . . .* (19), which could be again the impersonal/general you

The child is a party to the mother's progression from the relatively
unqualified information following the *No, no . . .* to the projective, self-
questioning style of the final lines. Among other things, the strategy of
graduated or cyclic assertions shows the child that cultural practice is
not monolithic and unambiguous—the episode begins in *No, no . . .* but
closes with the mother trying to arrive at the right wording for when
they are fussy. Even on this very small topic, then, and even with this
very young child, the mother builds the discourse so that it is open for
her daughter to engage in the dialectic. The talk could become a blend
of informing and mutual finding out, with the child picking up on the
crucial speech acts that are directed inward to the mother's own process
of thinking (see, for example, *And, if they are fussy, what do you say?*). In
fact, the mixture of modality and "public soliloquy" beckons the hearer
into the kind of intersubjective engagement that is the foundation of
linguistic and social development. In itself, the example of talk directed
metacognitively must be useful to the child. While it can be claimed that
this discourse style, combining modality and the debate of one's mind,
appears in the talk in every home (between every parent and child), it
is also evident that parents vary with respect to the contexts—the domains of experience—within which such openness and indeterminacy
are options of meaning. We all think out loud; and in that sense we let
others in on our thinking. But this phenomenon does not occur uniformly across topics and activities and families. Consider, for example,
the differences among talk about others, talk about oneself, and talk
about punishment and control.

At least two points deserve reiteration, then, as conclusions in this
section. The first characterizes the responses of the mother, whether
focused on what are taken to be the facts of the world or on saying and
meaning: The responses are activity oriented. In the talk between the
mother and child, any distinction between encyclopedia and dictionary
is irrelevant. The mother is expounding a user's manual on the culture

in general. And from her point of view, as well as the child's, making sense has to be handled by analogy with other forms of making. The second conclusion concerns the mother's expository style. Her cline of assertion suggests one area of iteration in which variability could have important consequences for establishing the child's own orientation to meaning: what is assured, what is debated, what rules are negotiated, and what practices can or cannot become the objects of talk in the home. Consistencies with respect to such styles are part of the unconscious, or covert, structure of interaction.

Turning Mother's Evidence

In this section of textual exemplification, the emphasis will shift toward the child's contribution. The responses, suggestions, and inquiries—even the pattern of the child's tracking—reveal the structure and intensity of reciprocation. In the first place, the activity or 'doing' orientation of the mother's exposition is complemented by the child's tendency to experiment with what she has gleaned from the interaction. Hence, after the list of idiomatic expressions, as the mother turns to the tasks of dressing the older child, Kristy, and her baby sister, Ruth, Kristy tries out the new potential on the baby: *Hello, fussy hen*. And subsequently Kristy can be seen repeating any similar expressions that the mother directs at the younger Ruth:

> Text 1.6
> C: Ruth's got an apple and a banana.
> M: Yes, I know.
>   She's a little possum.
>   Takes bits out of it
>   And leaves it around.
> C: Yeah.
> M: Little possum.
> C: Little possum.
> M: Little cuddly possum.
> C: Little cuddly possum.
>   Can I give her a cuddle?

On occasion, of course, the child's model for an utterance is not immediate; moreover, some segments of her dialogue with the mother might appear puzzling—almost meaningless—when seen in isolation from the reciprocal exchanges of meaning through which the two appear to come together so often in their understandings, whether in conflict or in cooperation. Extract (A) of text 1.7 below furnishes a good example.

> Text 1.7(A)
> 1   C: Um, I just feel crooked today. (complaining)

```
2     M:   You just feel crooked?
3     C:   I can't help the weather—
4          I don't have the weather—
5          It's cold out here in the morning
6          And then it comes hot—
7     M:   I think you are probably feeling crook
8          Just because you have been hanging around the house too long.
9          As soon as we get out
10         You'll feel better.
11    C:   Yeah and I don't know what to do. (half crying)
12         'Cause [?     ]
```

Kristy's use of *crooked* reflects the kind of astute interpretation that children often produce in the face of difficulties in the adult system. The girl is unhappy about going to her day care and she is reaching about for the reasons that might change her mother's mind. The use of *crooked* is the girl's attempt at the adult *I feel crook*. The mother's checking in (2) was probably needed to discount the very common use of *crooked*: 'to be crooked (on),' 'to be angry with.' Having established the drift of the child's statements, the mother carefully lays out the situation, both linguistically and rationally (7–10). But while the mother's focus has been on *crook/crooked*, the reasons given by the child for feeling *crooked* are actually a rearticulation of complex ideas treated in their conversation up to 170 messages before—here presented as messages 13–32 and 33–49 and 50–71 in texts 1.7 (B–D) below, which had preceded 1.7 (A). The actual order of occurrence was B–C–D–A.

It is the activity of dressing which first provoked the discussion of weather; and the mother presented a very full elaboration of the issue in response to what may have been an oblique, opening move in Kristy's attempt to remain at home:

```
Text 1.7(B)
13    C:   Mummy, I think I'm going to get cold today.
14    M:   I have no idea what the weather is going to be like today.
15         I'll send your sweatshirt or your cardigan or your jumper
16         or whatever you'd like over too.
17    C:   I want I want a short-sleeved cardigan—a long-sleeved one.
18         If it goes hot
19         I'll have to wear a short-sleeved one so ⌐—
20    M:                                           └Yep. Well, see yesterday
21         I thought it was going to be cold
22         And you were really hot by the end of the day
23         So I think the best thing is to put a short-sleeved T-shirt on
24         you and a cardigan.
```

25	C:	Yeah . . .
26		I think we don't know what day it's going to be.
27	M:	No, it's a bit [?] in spring and autumn, isn't it?
28		Stand up straight
29		So I can get your duds on.
30		In winter it is cold
31		And in summer it's hot
32		And in the spring and the autumn it's funny.

After the excursus on donkeys and fussy hens, and about a dozen other messages related to dressing, Kristy took up her mother's formulations concerning spring and autumn:

Text 1.7(C)

33	C:	Why is spring and autumn ⌐
34	M:	⌊[Kristy's shoes] (to Ruth)
35	C:	Why is spring and autumn um is is funny?
36	M:	Well, um it is less predictable.
37		You don't really know what it is going to be like.
38	C:	Hmm.
39	M:	In spring the weather is changing from—
40		No, I haven't got your [?leg] in.
41		The weather is changing from cold to hot
42		And in autumn the weather is changing from hot to cold
43		And it's not just in the middle
44		It seems to um ⌐ be colder early in the morning.
45	C:	⌊Hmm.
46	M:	And gets warm later in the day.
47	C:	Yeah. Why does it?
48	M:	I don't understand enough about the weather
49		To be able to explain that

In the light of these episodes, which occurred 100 or more messages before, Kristy's reasons for feeling crooked:

I can't help the weather—
I don't have the weather—
It's cold out here in the morning
And then it comes hot—

become less puzzling both as meanings and as a rhetorical strategy in her attempts to stay with her mother and Ruth. In (3) and (4) Kristy struggles with her mother's formulations of *less predictable* and the mother's disavowal of the knowledge to explain the shifts between hot and cold. In fact, the *I can't* of (3) seems to pick up the *be able to* of (49); and the *I don't* of (4) returns the mood selection of (48). Two forms of disavowing knowledge by the mother—*you don't really know what it is going to be like* (37) and *I don't understand enough about the weather to be able to explain that* (48–49)—are presented back to the mother as grounds for the child's disquiet over leaving home. The forms that the child constructs hardly match the mother's clause complexes (at least, in this case); but even though the elaborate mental projections are not carried over, Kristy does manage to articulate a crucial factor, something like Keats's notion of 'negative capability': namely, that the goings-on of the world around are subject to my observation, but not my intervention. To relate this state of mind specifically to the mother's own sayings, Kristy produces the central, concrete detail in the explanation about the "funny" character of autumn and spring (5–6). The child's exposition actually follows the pattern that she has heard concerning the expression *less predictable*. The mother had unpacked a new and abstract wording through references to shared experience: *You really don't know . . .* (37); *in spring . . . changing from cold to hot* (39–41); *in autumn . . . hot to cold* (42); *colder in the morning* (44); and so on. The wordings construct the shared experiences; thus the mother lets the child in on the more abstract meaning of the wording *less predictable*.

But the rhetorical strategy in exchanges (1–12) is more easily appreciated when seen against a larger cycle of contentions about leaving for preschool. Directly after the mother's *I don't understand enough about the weather to be able to explain that* (48–49), events overtook the topic:

Text 1.7(D)
```
50   C:   [?    ] I'm dressed.
51   M:   You're dressed.
52        We'll have to put your shoes on too, won't we?
53   C:   I'm dressed now [? to go up to Dee's].
54   M:   Good.
55        You'll have a nice day at Dee's.
56   C:   I don't want to.
57   M:   Why not?
58   C:   'Cause um—
59   M:   You tell me why?
60   C:   Because um um ah I don't like playing in sand
61        'Cause you can get your botty hurting.
62   M:   The kids play in the sand at our place.
63   C:   Yeah but—
64   M:   That's good now it's tangled up. (to Ruth)
65   C:   But we have much and much sand.
66   M:   I would say we probably have exactly the same amount of sand
          as Dee.
```

67	C:	Yeah but she's got big school kids.
68	M:	The big school kids were at school
69		When you were there.
70		That goes on Kristy. (to Ruth)
		(Ruth cries)
71	M:	Don't whop her, thank you. (to Kristy)

Here the mother takes the engagement directly to the daughter with *why not?* (57) and *You tell me why?* (59). For a mother who approaches other issues (e.g., deciding group norms) with such graduated indirectness, these explicit demands for a reason seem sharp and confrontationist. The concern and the challenge in the mother's questions can be seen in the shift from an interrogative mood to an imperative which is masked by the presence of the exclusive Subject: *you*. The aim, then, appears to be something quite different from the common parental inquiry to establish the child's state of being. The mother is demanding that an acceptable reason be articulated—it is a demand for a particular rhetorical "piece" and sets a narrow gauge on the discourse that can follow.

Even at the age of 3 years, 9 months, Kristy can meet the discourse criteria implicit in her mother's demands. In (60) and (61), Kristy presents a recursive causal structure, *Because . . . 'Cause . . .* , as if to match each of the mother's uses of *Why*. The daughter's response is very circumspect in that it appeals to, in the first place, her own likes/dislikes. These are in one sense incontestable, though low in status as "reasons." And second, she presents a general point about bodily well-being—which echoes an adult warning sometimes given to children. This has a relatively high value as reason, even though it may be more vulnerable to rejection than assertions of personal preference.

The exchanges develop, then, according to the principle invoked in the mother's demands and the subject matter tendered by the child. In this way, both interactants are determining the syntagmatic axis of their conversation—what counts as a going forward. But the mother maintains the intensity shifting from the demand of a reason to the requirement of consistency (66). Note also that the child is left to infer the significance of the mother's rejoinder about the *sand at our place*. Kristy has no difficulty in this—but her attempt to cap the mother's response does not seem either relevant or productive. In terms of the argument, however, the criterion of relevance *for the child* is merely establishing some contrast between the day-care house and her own: She is moving solely against the mother's claim that the two houses constitute identical cases.

The mother's response (66) appears to make allowance for the rhetorical cul-de-sac that may result if both sides disagree on the simple issue of the amount of sand. In order to have her judgment accepted in this matter the mother produces the combination of overt modality with an absolute measure: *exactly the same amount* (66). It is an indication of the semantic style in this dyad that the conversation does not break down at this point. The involved projected modality

I	would	say	we	probably	have	
Subj.	Fin. Modal	Pred.	Subj.	Modal	Fin.	Pred.
Mood		Res.				
Modal						
MOOD						RES

does not bewilder the child, however. She simply tries to move the contention on to the issue of the big school kids. This too is apparently countered on the grounds of inconsistency—early in the preparations for school Kristy had tried to argue for going to kindergarten school and not going to day care. The child's moves are rejected by the mother as lacking rational validity. In (71) we see one outcome of the mother's success in counterargument: In frustration, Kristy has smacked her sister over some trifle.

Despite the contention between mother and child, what is important is the shared pattern—and the shared assumptions—in their discourse. These are implicit, for example, in the child's recognition that the mother's reasons have been ascendent. Kristy has come to accept that the game will progress in a certain way; and that at some points she will be individually responsible for stating her own case, not merely her likes and dislikes. Should her contributions be rejected, she must find an alternative strategy, or a new articulation of the old strategies the validity of which cannot be faulted. In this event, Kristy does something of both in the section of text 1.7(A) beginning *I can't help the weather–I don't have the weather*. The rhetorical advantages of these lines, and hence their rhetorical sophistication, reside in the fact that they constitute giving back to the mother information she first gave to Kristy (see above, lines (36–46) and (48–49)). Unlike the previous issues raised by the daughter, the mother cannot take an opposing line without being inconsistent herself, since she was the original source of the autumn-spring information. In order to explicate the context and cotext to Kristy's outburst on feeling *crooked* (2), we have had to inquire about the value of a particular meaning in terms of the mother's and child's divergent purposes, as well as in terms of the rhetorical pattern of this particular home.

Culture and Language: The Continuum of Saying

I have emphasized that the mother's responses are oriented to doing rather than defining. Related to this, I have also emphasized the degree to which the child may be left to infer the meaning and structure of linguistic behavior. Such inferences, then, are typically interpretations of action. It should be added, however, that the process of inference itself is often made explicit by parents. And it might be suggested that this tendency to greater explicitness is an indication of two quite different modes of guidance and, therefore, two different ways in which the child is engaged in learning. In short: Do mothers teach thinking in a way that they may not teach talking? Does thinking become the subject matter of their talk in a way that talk itself does not?

The following extracts are a sample of inferences that arise as Kristy is cutting and pasting and her mother is sewing in front of the television.

Text 1.8(A)
1	C:	Mum, what's this?
2		What's this?
3	M:	Ah, I don't know.
4		A windmill maybe, or a ferris wheel.
5	C:	Yeah.
6	M:	It's probably a ferris wheel
7		since that book is about the circus.
8	C:	Pardon?
9	M:	It's probably a ferris wheel
10		since that book is about the circus.
11	C:	Mmm
12		It's not about the circus.
13	M:	Mmm?
14	C:	Not about the circus.
15	M:	It happens at a circus.
16	C:	What happens at the circus?
17	M:	There. Do you think that button is a better color?

Text 1.8(B)
18	C:	I'm taking the balloon out.
19	M:	Okay, well, you better work out what page it sticks onto.
20	C:	What—how you've gotta say—
21		It's from this picture.
22	M:	From that one?

```
23            Ah. It's a balloon, is it?
24    C:      Mmm.
25    M:      Give us a look at it.
26            It's—an well you've got to find one with dots on it . . .
27            There you are.
28    C:      Ah, that's not the right one.
29    M:      I think you'll find it is.
30    C:      It's too small.
31    M:      It's the only one with dots around it.
32            And the stick-on ones have got dots.
33            It does seem a bit small, doesn't it?
34            Ah, I think it seems small
35            because they've left a bit of extra paper around it.
36            You'll find that the pictures are ⌈ the same size

37    C:                                        ⌊ Mmm.
38    M:      But there is extra paper around the picture.
39            Do you want a wettex to stick it on?
```

Text 1.8(C)

```
40    C:      I don't know what that was. (referring to background noise)
41            It's very funny sound.
42    M:      That was an empty truck going along the street.
43    C:      Mmm.
44    M:      They make that sort of rattling noise
45            when they're empty.
46            Can I have a button?
```

In (A) and (B) the mother exteriorizes her problem solving; in (C) she merely indicates the evidence for her statement in (42), thereby suggesting, after the fact, that the claim was arrived at by using knowledge that did not begin in actually seeing this particular truck. In (A) and (B), then, the mother takes a good deal of trouble to assert the hypothetical status of her responses and the interconnected nature of facts. Thus in (3) she begins with a disavowal of certainty, and in (4) offers two possibilities, realized with the modality of *maybe*. This opening, accepted by the child, is then consolidated by (9) and (10)—a statement of probability and a reason. Kristy is still left to make a crucial inference—namely, that *ferris wheel* goes with *circus* in a way that *windmill* does not. She is being presented with one part of a knowledge frame, a connection in a semantic field.

The crucial characteristic of the parent's responses, from the point of view of the child, must be the way the mother appears to have information that has not been given to her in conversation. So the mother says that to paste in the balloon you've got to find the one with the dots on (26). When the child rejects this hypothesis from the mother on the basis of less abstract evidence (i.e., size), the mother brings the full pressure of her reason to bear. Still, the origin of the mother's knowledge constitutes a puzzle for Kristy and she later turns back to the issue of the dots, albeit once more orienting her inquiry to doing rather than knowing (see (57) below).

Text 1.8(D)

47	C:	Where's this balloon going?
48	M:	Well, on the picture that we put the other balloon on.
49	C:	Yeah. Where's the green balloon?
50		There's lots of balloons.
51	M:	Well, look for the one with dots around it.
52	C:	Mmm.
53	M:	There's a little one and a bigger one.
54		Is that the little one or the bigger one?
55		I think that was the bigger one.
56		I'd try putting it there.
57	C:	Why—why did you put it around one that's got dots around?
58	M:	Ah, the pictures have dots.
59		To show you where the stick-on pieces go.
60	C:	Mmm. So do the dots say that's where the stick-on pieces go?
61	M:	The dots don't say it.
62		They're not a special sort of writing or anything.
63	C:	⌈Mmm.
64	M:	⌊But it's just to indicate to you where to put them.
65	C:	Mmm. This book—
66		The balloon won't go in.
67	M:	It won't?**
68		You've licked it too much. . . . Nitwit.

The messages (60–64) are a "crux" in the discourse between this mother and child. I am using the term here as it might be used in the study of literary texts—to refer to points at which a number of interpretive issues meet and cross. Kristy has conjectured that the dots to which the mother keeps referring might be themselves a form of saying. The mother is careful in her rejection of this; but Kristy is closer to the truth than the mother is willing to concede. The mother's reply—*it's just to indicate to you where to put them*—is carefully worded to distinguish writing from a mere pointing function *(just to indicate)*. Still, the child has discerned that the dots have a semiotic, or sign, function, and that the mother has not, therefore, gone beyond the meanings which are physically accessible to them *both*. Kristy recognizes the semiotic continuum of culture and language. The mother, on the other hand, must maintain a boundary that seems natural in a literate culture. The cost of maintaining this boundary is difficult to assess—how important is it to understand that *inference is a form of "reading,"* specifically a "reading" of the culture, a "reading" of semiotic values that do not typically fall within the community notion of language?

At this point in my own discussion, I would suggest that it is important, for linguists and educationalists at least, to envisage a semiotic continuum that includes both culture and language. The reasons for observing a boundary between these two semiotic systems are essentially that (a) the separation has been useful for the scholar in that it has imposed limits and shape in her/his projects of description; (b) the distinction has seemed natural to the layman; and (c) the principles and methods by which one might arrive at the description of a culture as "system" have been elusive. Whatever the role of historical and theoretical factors in establishing a culture/language division, however, one point deserves our attention: We observe a distinction between culture and language because differences of scale, of realization, and of analytical principles have made the semantic continuum across culture and language difficult to perceive. Note, for instance, how analogous differences of scale, realization, and description also pertain across the three levels of language: semantics, lexicogrammar, and phonology. And this also may explain why some linguists have had so much difficulty in including semantics in their conceptions of linguistics (viz., Bloomfield and Chomsky; see, for example, Bloomfield, 1933, p. 140). Nevertheless, linguistics took its most significant step forward when Saussure applied Durkheim's notion of a social fact to his own thinking about meaning in language. Conversely, the analysis of culture has been enriched by tools developed in linguistic structuralism (Eco, 1973). The continuum of culture and language explains this growing academic compatibility. So when Halliday wrote, over 10 years ago, that "the child's construction of a semantic system and his construction of a social system take place side by side, as two aspects of a single unitary process" (1975, p. 121), the use of "side by side" may not have been a reference to any seam in the "unitary" phenomenon, but rather a metaphor for our perspective ("aspect") of analysis—a product of our tendencies to talk about 'languages' and about 'social systems.'

Kristy has recognized the continuity of signs even across the boundaries stated by her mother. But the child has not achieved her insight alone. The patterns of interaction—the strategies by which the mother and child exert on each other a constant semantic pressure—have revealed the breadth of semiosis. In fact, from her point of view as a novice, she is not subject to certain adult obstructions: She is right to see *the dots* as a form of saying. The mother's sophisticated distinction between "saying-writing" and "indicating" fails to deal with the fact that deixis (or pointing and indicating) is one of the fundamental principles around which the meanings of the linguistic system are organized. The linguist must work to clarify such matters since, as one moves toward the study of school discourse (section 2) and as one tries to interpret the stages of prelanguage and protolanguage (section 3), the usefulness of most folk *and* academic categories tends to diminish.

SECTION 2. AT SCHOOL

Whether or not the language of the school constitutes a break with the language of the home is a widely debated issue (McTear, 1985, pp. 208ff). As in many controversies relating to discourse, the controversy is not a case of yes or no, but rather of *both* yes and no: The new context makes new demands on the meaning system of the child, while on the other hand the pattern of neighborhood and family are the foundation upon which newer forms of sense are interpreted. The situation must be seen for both its changes and its continuities. In Kristy's case, for example, it was clear that the mother had already begun to establish a distance between the instrumental, pragmatic, action-oriented approach to meanings and the conception of language passed down by adults and their literate world. As if preparing her daughter for that world and school, the mother was categorical (unusual for her!) about what was or was not writing.

The activities of school make new demands on the child's uses of language—the shifts in tenor suggest this in themselves—but perhaps an equally significant aspect of the process of schooling is the change it demands in the child's conception of language. Whereas, in the discussion above, it was suggested that the child handled the activity of "making sense" in a way analogous to other forms of making, even the first weeks of school involve a reorienting of the child's perspective on communication. The following transcripts help to bring out both the continuities and the shift toward language as something known, rather than done.

Decoding and Tenor

The first transcript illustrates the degree to which language is contextually bound for the 5-year-olds in their first weeks of school. The children cannot decode the wording because essentially they cannot conceive of the social relations implicit in the teacher's question (32): They are unable to envisage themselves in the role of Actor when the teacher or headmaster might be the Beneficiary, since these transitivity roles contradict their notion of authority in the social order of school.

Text 2.1

1	T:	What do you know
2		that the teachers do for you?
3		Susan
4		Alan, come here
5		Alan, quick.
6		Sorry, Susan, what was that?
7	P:	[. . . some things]
8	T:	Yes, you learn things
9		The teachers help you.
10		by teaching you things.
11		How else can teachers help you?
12		Jillian
13		Mmm?
14		Quick, answer the question.
15	P:	[—].
16	T:	It'd help
17		if you were listening, Catherine. . . .
18		Jeffrey
19	P:	Oh!
20		⌈What was the question?
21	T:	⌊Catherine
22		On the other side of Rachel
23	P:	Oh, they help you
24		if you have fallen over
25		or hurt yourself.
26	T:	Good boy.
27		They help you
28		if you've a problem
29		if you've hurt yourself
30		or you haven't got some lunch.
31		Lots and lots of ways.
32		How do you help the teachers?
33		Come on
34		Jeffrey's the only person with his hand up.
35		Susan
36	P:	[By . . . ah . . .]
37	T:	(to class)
38		How can *you* help the teachers?
39		What can you do?
40		Edwin . . .
41	P:	[By helping you
42		to find your line]
43	T:	Good boy

44		That's right.
45		Bit hard at first
46		to find out
47		where your line is,
48		and what you're supposed to do.
49		No sweetie, what can **you**, the children,
50		how can the **children** help the teachers?
51		Terry
52		What can you do?
53	T:	Ah . . . By giving them some work. . . ?
54		By giving them some coloring-in or something.
55	T:	No, you're not listening.
56		How can **you**, all of you, help me?
57		or help Mrs. Michaels
58		or help Mr. Southey?
59		What can you do that helps us?
60		['Cause] we help you,
61		and I'm sure you help us.
62		How do you do that?
63		Rachel.
64	P:	[Pick up rubbish]
65	T:	Good girl.
66		Helping to keep the playground tidy.
67		That's a good answer
68		Louise
69	P:	By doing the right thing on the worksheet.
70	T:	Right.
71		Listening carefully
72		and doing your work properly.
73		David
74	P:	[By taking . . . to] teachers.
75	T:	How can you help me? (correcting the student again)
76		You mean
77		if a teacher needs me
78		you come and give the message?
79		Right, good boy.
80		Hmm . . . Terry

In message (38) the teacher gives special salience to the *you* (i.e., the pupils) as Actor. This prominence is repeated in (49) and (50) with the apposition *you, the children* and by removing the pronoun to make the inference explicit: *how can the **children** help the teachers?* But despite these three modes of making the *you*-as-Actor role emphatic—a phonological, a grammatical and a lexical signal—the teacher is unsuccessful. Terry in (53) and (54) "hears" the question that the culture has prepared the children for: Teachers are givers, doers, helpers, initiators; pupils are receivers, listeners, the helped, and responders only.

The teacher makes an assumption in (55) that is perfectly natural from the adult point of view—*No, you're not listening*. There is clearly no aspect of the wording in her initial or subsequent questions that should present difficulty to the linguistic experience of the pupils *when, at least, that experience is regarded as knowledge of an aggregate of linguistic forms—words, sentences, or "propositions")*. But what the episode demonstrates is that linguistic experience cannot be satisfactorily regarded in this way—as forms known or not known, acquired or yet to be acquired. It is only after the teacher introduces further strategies in (56–62) that Rachel makes rather meek headway toward the teacher's original aim. The teacher concretizes her question with references to the school's teachers and principal; and she emphasizes the reciprocation of helping (60–62). Yet the tension of framing an issue contrary to the context of culture is evident in more than the teacher's assiduous efforts at clarification. The teacher herself "hears" her own question the wrong way round in (43–48). In accepting Edwin's answer she indicates how much the social roles that define an activity or institution are, in fact, part of the system of meaning. Expressed more theoretically, the tenor and the context of situation overall are basic to the patterns or structures that the child "knows" because they define the activities that the child learns. Part of what the adult learns, however, is to put some distance between the coding and the context—at least, to be sensitive to the interdependence of context and code as a language user, but to let the structure of the code dominate in the educated consciousness. Ultimately then, for the children learning the culture and language of school, it becomes important to adopt a rarefied, abstract perspective on their own behavior—on their languaging.

Invisible Shapes and Ideal Forms

The previous transcript suggested one aspect of what is involved in the "complex situation" of learning the culture at the same time as learning the language—one of the systems in which the culture is encoded. It showed that one of the demands of school is to adopt a particular attitude toward language. A more distinct representation of this attitude can be given in the light of the following transcript in which another kingergarten class (again at the beginning of the school year) works with shapes. Certain confusions which arise, between the teacher's point of view and that of a child, are manifestations of two orientations to the message and the code. The distance between the perspectives of the teacher and child is the distance the children will have to traverse in their school experience.

Text 2.2

1	*T:*	Right, will you make a circle, please.
2		Stand up everybody.
3		Now hold hands. . . .
4		Maybe if I pushed the Lego table back.
5		Now put the dolly over on the table, darling.
		(Daren mimics teacher)
6		Oh . . . Daren . . . you're a bit mouthy today
7		Sitting in a circle . . .
8		Let Louise into the circle please, Kenneth.
9		That's the boy, thanks.
10		Now this part of the circle has to move out a bit. (T.'s at-
11		tention is briefly engaged by pupils' questions about the mi-
12		crophones.)
13	*Pupils:*	Oh blocks.
14	*T:*	"Oh blocks."
15		What sort of blocks are they?
16	*Pupils:*	Shapes, shapes . . . (Note: The shapes are in solid rubber.)
17	*T:*	Different shapes!
18		Let's see
19		how clever you are.
20		What's that shape?
21	*P:*	Circle, circle.
22		Square!
23	*T:*	It's a circle, isn't it, Bernadette?
		(T. laughs. . . . Bernadette had called out, "Square!")
24		It's a circle. . . .
25		That's the circle we made.
26		Do you see?
27		Maybe our circle isn't as round
28		as it should be
29		But that one is, isn't it?
30		Yes . . .
31	*T:*	Another. . . ?
32	*Class:*	Circle, circle . . .
33	*T:*	Is this a circle as well?
34	*Class:*	Yes . . .
35	*T:*	It's not the same as that, though . . .
36	*P:*	It's a little circle
37	*P:*	A little circle!
38	*T:*	It's a little circle
39		and this is a . . .
40	*Class:*	Big one. Big circle.
41	*T:*	All right, don't call out this time,
42		I'm gonna see
43		how clever you are.
44		Hands up,
45		if you know

46		what this is called.
47	*Class:*	(calling out)
48	*T:*	Hands up! Hands up!
49		You forgot . . .
50		what's it called, Ellie?
51	*P:*	A triangle.
52	*T:*	A triangle.
53		If I turn it around like that,
54		is it still a triangle?
55	*Class:*	No . . .
56	*T:*	Isn't it?
57	*Class:*	(subdued) No . . .
58	*T:*	Yes, it is . . .
59		It doesn't matter which way I turn it,
60		it's still a triangle.
61		How many sides does a triangle have?
62	*P:*	Four!
63	*T:*	Does it?
64		Count them for me
65	*Class:*	Three, three.
66		one; two-three.
67	*T:*	Yes (grinning), three sides.
68		Count them together.
69	*Class:*	One, two, three.
70	*T:*	How many corners does it have?
71	*Class:*	Three . . . four . . . three . . .
72	*T:*	Let's count them.
73	*Class:*	One, two, three.
74	*T:*	Is there any other shape [that has three sides]?
75	*P:*	No.
76	*T:*	Do you know one, Daren?
77	*P:*	[?No.]
78	*T:*	What is it?
79	*D:*	Another one of them.
80	*T:*	Is there any other shape, *apart from a triangle*, that has three
81		sides?
82	*P:*	A circle.
83	*T:*	Does a circle have three sides?
84	*Class:*	No . . .
85	*P:*	Four . . .
86	*P:*	None
87	*T:*	How many sides does a circle have?
88		Four?
89	*P:*	None . . .
90	*T:*	None?! (with both real and theatrical surprise)
91		This is a side, isn't it?
92		How many sides does a circle have?
93	*Class:*	One

94		Four (more subdued)
95	T:	One!
96		You're right, Daren. (T. has to overlook "four.")
97		One.
98		It's not like these sides—
99		it's curved.
100		See . . .
101	P:	[. . .]
102		[. . . big side]
103	T:	Mmm.
104		It's got a curved side,
105		but it's one big side . . .
106		so a circle has how many sides?
107	Class:	One! [big side]
108	T:	A triangle has how many sides?
109	Class:	Three!!
110	T:	Ooh . . . don't yell, please.
111		What's this called?
112	Class	(minority): Square
113	Class	(majority): Rectangle
114	T:	Sometimes it's called a rectangle
115		but the name we're going to give it is an "oblong."
116		Can you say that?
117	Class:	Oblong!
118	T:	It's a funny word.
119		An oblong—

The discussion progresses toward a working distinction between square and oblong, beginning however with what they have in common: four corners, four sides, and so on. Overall size is rejected as the basis of shape difference, and eventually *two short sides and two long sides* is tendered as the operational description of *oblong*. The teacher then reviews the subject matter of the lesson:

Text 2.2 (continued)

120	T:	. . . Right . . . let's have a look at these shapes.
121		I'm going to hold them up
122		and you have to tell me
123		which is which.
124		This is . . .
125	Class:	Triangle
126		Circle
127		Oblongs!
128	T:	An oblong, right
129	Class:	Square!
130	T:	A square

131	P:	Circle
132	T:	Circle
133	Class:	Square
134	T:	Are you sure?
135	Class:	Yeah
136	T:	How do you know
137		it's a square, Colin?
138	P:	'Cause all the squares are the same.
139	T:	Good boy
140		'Cause all the sides, Daren, are the same.
141	T:	Ellie, did you see that?
142		Colin just said
143		it's a square
144		'cause all the sides are the same
145		So what's this?
146	P:	An oblong.
147	T:	An oblong.
148		And how do you know
149		that this is an oblong?
150	T:	Oh . . . oh . . . don't call out . . .
151		How do you know, Harriet?
152	P:	Because it's got long sides on it
153		and little sides on it.
154	T:	Right!

In this lesson, the child's conception of language becomes an issue between the teacher and the pupils. The subject matter that precipitates the oblique confrontation is the idealization of shapes. The focal point of the issue can be seen in messages (72–104) when the teacher is seeking the number of sides of a triangle in contrast to the side(s) of a circle. Having established the three-sidedness of particular triangles, the teacher finds a way to establish the three-sidedness as a principle: *Is there any other shape [that has three sides]?* (72).

To her surprise—and no doubt most adults in her community would have been similarly surprised—young Daren finds an answer that the teacher had not perceived, but one that reflects the observational methods of the earlier part of the lesson: *Another one of them* (77). The teacher is not fazed by this Wittgensteinian riposte, and she finds a more adequate wording for her original intention *Is there any other shape, apart from a triangle, that has three sides?* (78). This however, produces an even more puzzling answer—sufficiently unexpected to make the teacher assume that it is a total misunderstanding of the lesson activity. Again, her surprise is consistent with an adult point of view. One might even be tempted to say that her surprise is ''natural.'' But the situation is actually more complicated; and even the teacher's careful professional strategy in (80–104) does not bring the source of the confusion to her own attention, let alone into the range of the classroom discourse.

The crucial fact here appears to be the nature of the objects that the teacher uses to exemplify triangleness, circleness, and so on. She does not have drawings on a blackboard or flat cut-outs. Instead, she is holding relatively solid plastic or rubber shapes that are unequivocally three-dimensional; note that the children even refer to them in (11) as *blocks*. Hence, by presenting and holding these objects, it would be difficult to make a child overlook the qualities of mass and depth (the edges), which the adult knows are irrelevant to the flat-surface concepts of the curriculum. The evidence to the child's eye is likely to be that a circle does have three sides—the two flat sides and what could be called the edge. But the lesson requires that $\triangle$ and $\bigcirc$ be expressed as facts of relation, abstract notions divorced from instantiation, or analytic truths. Indeed, all the terms of the discussion—shape, line, corner, side, triangle, and so on—are to be addressed as abstractions. The teacher has in mind idealized forms considered from the point of view of an observer looking down on a flat plane (or of someone seeing only an outline). The adult does not appear to see that the plastic circle shape she holds *does* have three sides: The definitional characteristics of circleness make the instantial reality (i.e., a three-sided, solid figure) culturally invisible.

The other cultural point of view in this case is, of course, that of the nonadult, nonliterate children. For them, the characteristics of a circle are to be established through observation, or through the teacher's edict: Note for example that in (80–92) the class replies lurch from *one* to *four* to *none*, as if the children are trying to guess the teacher's mind, possibly using their memory of a previous lesson on squares. In their world, shapes are basically objects of experience, not axioms of relation. They have only recently begun to construct that elaborate edifice of discourse in which useful intellectual fictions support higher and higher levels of interrelated abstraction. With the developing talk of school, experience will take on an increasingly heuristic, or "as if," quality. This process will not be overt. But one of the elements of cultural experience that most displays a shift in attitude is language itself, as children become aware that their "doing language" is actually being assessed as a form of knowing.

The difficulties that children have to confront in their shift toward axiomatic discourse are intensified by the adult skill at giving a word or meaning a number of orientations. This emerges in the discussion of *circle*. While the teacher's aims have been discussed, it is interesting to note that the lesson began with a far more pragmatic approach to *circle*. The messages (1–10) are concerned essentially with "making a circle";

the children are involved with the meaning as a form of "doing," and the "making" as it applies to meaning—see messages (1), (7), (8), (10). In a similar direction, in messages (133–144), the teacher settles for a relative and context-specific truth concerning squares: 'Cause all the sides are the same. While this description could also apply to the earlier-discussed triangle, it is operationally a useful step toward sorting out the hyponyms square and oblong in relation to the superordinate rectangle. The teacher settles for an exophoric resolution to sorting out the semantic field. Like most of the strategies of this sensitive and outstanding teacher, the mixture of practical and abstract demands on the children has been finely calibrated in order to bring this particular group one manageable step closer to the adult and school ways of seeing. But it should be emphasized that, from the point of view of the child, a conflict exists over the status of empirical evidence: namely, when to rely on what can be seen. The teacher herself is sensitive to the two directions of discourse—the pragmatic and the axiomatic—since she comments on one of the first circles she holds up, in (25–26): Maybe our circle isn't as round as it should be. The modulation should here reflects the idealization involved in axiomatic truths: There is a kind of necessity at work, as if the facts of the world were obliged to meet the specifications of ideal forms.

A last comment must be made about the question of prestige. Despite the teacher's relatively informal and highly supportive personal style, there are various ways in which the prestige of the new way of knowing is communicated to the children. There is, for instance, the half-playful (39–44):

All right, don't call out this time,
I'm gonna see
how clever you are.
Hands up,
if you know
what this is called.

More important may be the simple fact that the students compete for the teacher's acknowledgment. In the following transcript, the prestige of knowing 'what it's called' is more clearly at issue.

"What's the Proper Name. . . ?"

The following short sections of classroom talk arose as parts of a picture talk lesson. The lesson occurred toward the end of the kindergarten year, in contrast with the preceding school transcript, which took place

at another school in the initial weeks. The selections are examples of
the teacher directing the students toward knowing *the* word or *the* formal item. While this teacher does ask the children to fabricate an interpretation of the picture on the basis of their cultural knowledge, the
object or goal of that projection becomes the knowledge of a piece of
the semiotic system—the appropriate word.

The first selection comes as one student has suggested that the girl
in the picture may be putting Dettol antiseptic on the knee of the injured
boy:

Text 2.3

1	T:	It could be Dettol
2		That's right.
3		What do we use Dettol for?
4		What do we usually use Dettol for?
5		Sam?
6	P:	Fix sores up.
7	T:	Yes.
8		What does the Dettol do?
9		Steven?
10	P:	Makes the dirt come all out of the leg.
11	T:	It cleans it, doesn't it?
12		So it doesn't get . . .
13	P:	Gets the germs out of it.
14	T:	Gets the germs . . .
15		If germs get in it,
		what's the word?
17		It becomes,
18		hands up.
19		Who knows the special word?
20	Children:	Oh!!
21	T:	If germs get into the sore,
22		what could happen?
23	P:	Oh . . . it will grow bigger.
24	T:	It could get bigger.
25		What else?
26		There's a special word,
27		if germs get into your knee . . .
28	Children:	Oh! Oh!
29	T:	It becomes . . .
30	P:	Badder. . . ?
31	T:	Nancy?
32	P:	Effective
33	T:	Nearly. (laughs)
34	Children:	Oh! Oh!
35	T:	Alex?
36		"Infected."

37		If you don't clean it,
38		it could become infected.
39		That's when it becomes a lot worse
40		and a lot sorer.
41	P:	If it gets bad infected,
42		you could have to get your leg chopped off. . . .
43	P:	[Yes]
44	T:	Ooh, I hope not.
45		It would have to become very badly infected
46		for that to happen.
47	T:	What is the little girl using
48		to put the Dettol on her knee with?
49		Patrick?
50	P:	[ ] little fluffy thing.
51	T:	Well, what is it?
52		"Little fluffy thing . . ."
53		What's the proper name for it?
54	Pupils:	Oh! Oh!
55	T:	Lisa?
56	L:	Cotton wool.
57	T:	Cotton wool.
58		Look, she's got a little bit of cotton.
59		Where do you think the accident has happened?
60		Whereabout has this accident happened, do you think?
61	P:	I know.
62	T:	Nicola.
63	P:	On the road.
64	T:	It could have happened on the road.
65		Where else?
66		Lisa?
67	P:	On the cement.
68	T:	It could have happened on the cement.
69		If he hurt himself very badly
70		where would they have to take him, do you think?
71	P:	I know.
72	T:	If the little girl could not have fixed him up,
73		whereabouts would they have had to take him?
74		Anna?
75	P:	From the . . . to the hospital.
76	T:	They could have had to take him to the hospital.
77		What part of the hospital do you go to
78		if you've had an accident?
79	P:	To the part where . . . where there's . . .
80		And you ask them for a bed
81		And you—
82	T:	It's got a special name.
83		Does anyone know?
84		The part of the hospital you go to

85		if you have an accident,
86		and you've gotta go there in a hurry?
87	*Pupils*	Oh . . .
88	*T:*	No.
89	*Pupils*	Oh . . .
90	*A:*	Ambulance.
91	*T:*	No.
92		The ambulance takes you there sometimes.
93	*P:*	Theater.
94	*T:*	Not the "theater."
95		That's where you have your operation, in the theater.
96		It starts with /k/ . . .
	P:	[. . .]
		(laughing)
97	*T:*	"Casualty."
98		The casualty department—that's where you have to go
99		if you have an accident.
100		Is that where they had to take your dad?

The same pattern continues with other sophisticated items: "anesthetic," for example. It is not that the teacher directs the pupils away from their own experiences; she rather demands that they renovate their experience according to adult categories. And the first step in this change is the restructuring of cultural knowledge around the dominant taxonomy.

Argument over Evidence

The axiomatic mode discussed in section 2 above has been presented here in particular association with school discourse. Yet it was also claimed in section 2 that the language of school involved both contrast and continuities with respect to the language of home. The following extract suggests the degree to which the children (from very much working-class homes) are already developing their peer-group discourse in a direction paralleling the teacher's emphasis on rationalization. As in the earlier transcript, the discussion of shapes, the following exchanges show that the demands for consistent abstraction can overrule the evidence of the senses.

The children are wearing small radio transmitters on belts. These relay their speech without an adult being visibly present. One transmitter is not showing its "on" light, despite the fact that the child's voice is being transmitted in the normal way. This failure of the "on" light becomes the topic of conversation since the children are naturally worried about a malfunction. The complicating factor is that the light is not visible anyway in direct sunlight, but appears pink indoors or when shaded by the hand.

Text 2.4

1	*Child:*	Aah! (into microphone)
2		Doesn't work.
3	*Gail:*	Yes, it does.
4		⌈They just put another battery in.
5	*Karen:*	⌊That's for . . .
6	*Child:*	Oh . . . the light's on
7	*Karen:*	No . . . it
8		when you cover it up
9		it goes pink;
10		but when you go like that. . . . [?]
11	*Leonie:*	Yeah, because of the sun.
12	*Gail:*	Cas, cas . . . I'll show you something.
13	*Karen:*	No, it was like that inside Leonie. (child 4)
14	*Child:*	Is yours the same?
15	*Karen:*	⌈Yeah
16	*Beth*	⌊But when it's dark,
17		when it's dark
18		it's red.
19		. . . Pink, I mean . . .
20		Look.
21	*Gail:*	Show ye something?
22	*Child:*	What?
23	*Karen:*	But it was like that inside.
24	*Leonie:*	Yeah, because . . . because . . . inside
25		It's not dark inside.

The crucial issue here is how one interprets the fact that the light is not on at that moment in the playground. Karen, in (13), points out that it cannot be attributed to the bright sunlight in the way that Leonie has implied in (11). Karen's argument is that the light was also off when they were in class. How can the quandary be resolved, given that the light shows pink when it is dark? Leonie is equal to the problem. She simply asserts that *It's not dark inside*, and thereby removes the inconsistency. Her assertion has something like the value: The light in the classroom is not dark enough to make the "on" light pink; and this can be arrived at through the knowledge that

1. the light is supposed to work;
2. the transmitter has a new battery;
3. the light usually does not show in bright light;
4. the light was seen to be off in the classroom.

Leonie's conclusion/explanation achieves the assent of the group—they do not contest the issue further, at least. This shows, then, that these children will put what they have seen to one side in order to maintain a consistency in the discourse. The "inside" of their building, though not uniformly dark, was more than sufficient to perceive the light; but this perception is jettisoned for the sake of making the *because . . . because* of (24–25) confirm the reason in (11). What makes sense becomes what is real.

At this point one can see that the experience of these children—their culture—and their language are mutually defining. In this way the situation is analogous to Saussure's view of the unity of the signified and signifier within a sign. It is as important to say that the experience, even the perception, of the world is discourse directed as it is to make the more conventional claim, namely, that experience directs discourse. Neither assertion can have priority.

SECTION 3: PRELANGUAGE AND PROTOLANGUAGE

When developmental studies "marched to 'syntax-semantics' music," as Bruner has called it (1983, p. 165), the tendency was to focus on the ages between 1 year, 6 months, four years, in which, it was claimed, the child progresses from holophrase to a "mastery" of the mother tongue. In fact the dramatic speed imputed to the development of a child's language depended on first confining language to what went on in these two years. Subsequent reorientations of research—first toward meaning and then to pragmatics (Bruner, 1983, chapter 9)—have widened the focus of study in both directions: from two years to newborn, as well as from 4 years to high school age. The shifts in developmental linguistics were reinforced by interdisciplinary research on the earliest patterns of mother-child dyads. In particular, the motivation here related to the interpretation of communication failure, in autism for example (Bullowa, 1979). The result of the wider focus on development has been to remove the idea that language appears de novo, as if out of nothing. Rather, the image now would be of a process with a certain logic—a series of stages in which higher levels of development can be related to what precedes them. Hence, emphasis has been given to isomorphism between the structure of action and the child's system of signs, as well as to the basis of intersubjectivity between the mother and child (Bruner, 1975).

Halliday has consistently focused on the logic in the development of the individual's potential to mean. The basis of this logic, he shows, is function—the demands of interaction with another, and within the context of culture more generally.

By reflecting on Halliday's notion of "social semiotic" (Halliday, 1978a,c), one can bring out the "logic" of development, as well as clarify the "complex situation" of learning the culture and learning the language. In achieving these two clarifications, however, much that is taken as common sense about the world undergoes reorientation. In fact, in my further discussion of these issues—the meaning of "semiotic"; the logic of development; and the relationship between culture and language—the emphasis will seem paradoxical, at least initially. This is because a semiotic approach to cultural experience involves more than linguistic and philosophical arguments; it involves a new way of looking at things.

One strategy for appreciating this way of looking is to consider the experience of a child from birth to around 9 months, and to review the patterns of order which lend form to the child's sense of the world. One can begin here by reflecting on the notion of an object. For the adult, the status of objects is unequivocal. An adult definition, or dictionary meaning, of *object* is as follows: that which is "given . . . thrown down"; that "of which one thinks, has cognition," about which "a report or image can be produced," and to which "action, thought, or feeling" can be directed. (OED). It is useful to reflect, then, on the confidence adults express about their object world when the notion of object itself can include so much. The dictionary gloss begins with the concrete and moves into the indeterminate, the all-encompassing. The difficulties bring one back to ask, "What exactly about our experience is "given" or "thrown down" before us?"

A first, general response to this question might be: "Certain kinds of patterns—essentially, the reports of the senses." But what appears as an incontestable substratum in the experience of the adult is, in fact, something that the child arrives at only with time and, typically, after the mediation of other people. Such a counterintuitive state of affairs has begun to emerge with the fine-grained analysis of the first 6 months of a child's development. Although it is not necessary to reiterate the details of relevant studies here, their overall conclusions should be summarized in order for their significance to be assessed.

Concerning Objectness

For a newborn child the concept of an object is neither a 'given' of perception nor an idea arrived at totally through the aggregation of experience. The concept is neither a priori nor totally synthetic. The work of Bower (1971), for example, suggested that even a child just 2 weeks old recognizes the "tactile consequences" of an approaching object that is merely seen. Similarly, children of the same age confronted by illusory ('virtual') objects were considerably upset by their inability to grasp the apparent object in front of them. Bower concludes that "there is a primitive unity of the senses, with visual variables specifying tactile consequences, and that this primitive unity is built into the structure of the human nervous system" (1971, p. 32). This would seem to suggest that there is very little interpretation and experience involved in an important dimension of objectness.

Yet other findings by Bower himself turn this suggestion around. Extensions of his experiments have led Bower to claim that infants less than 16 weeks do not respond to "moving objects but to movements" (1971, p. 37). In addition, such young infants respond not "to stationary objects but to places." Bower goes on to explain the situation after 16 weeks, stressing that this is after the child's "discovery of the object concept" (p.38 :

> In contrast, older infants (i.e., > 16 weeks) have learned to define an object as something that can go from place to place along pathways of movement. They identify an object by its features rather than by its place or movement. For them different features imply different objects that can move independently so that the stopping of one does not imply the stopping of the other. (Bower, 1971, p. 37)

So the children *less* than 16–20 weeks old live in "a grossly overpopulated world. . . . The infant must cope with a large number of objects when only one is really there" (p. 38) Bower poses the question, then, why must the object concept be discovered rather than wired into the neural system. And given that something of the child's "error" persists in adult perception, Bower conjectures that the concept may be "outside the limits of intrinsic neural specification" (p. 38).

A conclusion we can draw from this is that the relationship between 'things' and the structure of human perceptual systems is far more equivocal than most laymen or researchers are ready to concede. Certainly, Popper is making an important point when he stresses that even human anatomy needs to be regarded as hypotheses concerning the nature of the world (1972, p. 145): Structure in a living organism cannot exist without consequences for that organism. But the challenge in developmental studies—and perhaps across many intellectual disciplines—is to *reconcile the notion of structure with the fact of process*. One has to relate "morphology" to changes in potential; relate an initial state to its emergent system; and allow for changing values in the relationship between an element and the ensemble within which the element is being interpreted. These are three injunctions that can be derived from the perception of objectness. And, as can be seen in Popper's reference to human form, physiological and neural structure can be viewed negatively or positively—either as setting limits on the possible forms of experience or as a basis for (possibly novel) transactions with the world.

Now, while the tendency of both philosophy and linguistics has been to emphasize the former view, the limiting case—see for example Kant's notion of the forms of possible knowledge and Chomsky's pursuit of possible human grammars (1972, pp. 20ff)—more recent work in neurosciences has concentrated on the problem of plasticity and nonlocalized functions in the brain (Wilber, 1982). One arrives then at a kind of ambivalence about the perceptual system and the givenness of the object world which adults take to be primary. First of all, it should be stressed that nothing can happen or be done in the total absence of structure; in that sense, the idea of the brain as a tabula rasa is incoherent. On the other hand, the idea of structure has to encompass metamorphosis—the fact that form has to be responsive to changing functional demands. In all transactions with the world, the functional demands on the infant are mediated by a caregiver. And the patterns in this mediation have come to dominate as the focus of infant developmental studies.

The Meaning of a Dyad

The use of the term *dyad* in referring to the infant-caregiver relationship has the advantage of drawing attention to the unity the two persons constitute. They are ethnographically and ethologically a "unit." The significance of this unit for enculturation, as well as the development of intelligence and language, has been examined by, among many others, Trevarthen, Brazelton, Newson, and Condon. Although none of these researchers is a linguist, the work of each has been part of the widening focus on and reinterpretation of the roots of communication. Their work helps in the present discussion in at least two ways: it describes just the sorts of patterns and consistencies in which the infant is immersed; and it prepares the ground for discussing "social semiotics," or the life of signs in the community.

Trevarthen's work on infants began with a search for a latent innate structure of intelligence. This investigation brought him to the view that communicative, interpersonal exchanges between mothers and children from birth to 6 months of age are the basis of intelligence.

We conclude that human intelligence develops from the start as an interpersonal process and that the maturation of consciousness and the ability to act with voluntary control in the physical world is a product rather than an ingredient of this process. (Trevarthen, 1974, p. 230).

Careful study of split-screen recordings (showing the mother and infant simultaneously), along with the knowledge that children of 2 months differentiate strongly between attention to persons and attention to objects, ultimately led Trevarthen to propose two stages of intersubjectivity and an "innate human mode of psychological function that requires transactions with other persons." He adds

> This function includes rudiments of the quite unique human activity of speech, which becomes the chief medium of individual human mental growth and the essential ingredient of civilised society. (1974, p. 235)

Those in contact with contemporary research in psychology and education may well see in Trevarthen's emphasis some affinity with the growing interest in the Russian theorists Vygotsky and Luria. The point of particular relevance is the idea that social interaction is the central source of structure in the mind of the individual (see, e.g., Luria, 1975).

Brazelton et al. (1974) suggest, like Trevarthen, that the child is not predominantly a receiver/imitator in the reciprocity between mother and infant. In terms of the metaphor of a dance, the infant takes the lead and the mother builds on the child's behavior and transfers the elaborated structure back to the infant.

> Most mothers . . . are unwilling or unable to deal with neonatal behaviours as though they are meaningless or unintentional. Instead they endow the smallest movements with highly personal meaning and react to them effectively. They insist on joining in and enlarging on even the least possible interactive behaviors, through imitation. (Brazelton et al., 1974, p. 68)

In the work of Brazelton and his colleagues, the idea of patterning is itself elaborated and enhanced. The "successful" interaction seems to depend on the mother's sensitivity to cycles in the attention of the child so that the child's attention can be sustained and intensified. In this regard "rhythm" becomes a many-valued term, depending on the level of description under focus: for example, cycle of attention, bodily-kinesic patterns, speech rhythms, and so on. The situation can be gleaned by the following concluding remarks:

> This interdependency of rhythms seemed to be at the root of their "attachment" as well as communication. When the balance was sympathetic to the needs of each member of the dyad, there was a sense of rhythmic

interaction which an observer sensed as "positive." When the balance was not equalized, and one member was out of phase with the other, there seemed to be a "negative" quality in the entire interaction. At the periods of new acquisitions (e.g., at 8 and 12 weeks) when the infant was out of phase, the mother reflected the stress she felt in not being able to communicate. (Brazelton et al., 1974, p. 74)

The work of Condon echoes the metaphors of Brazelton. Condon has developed an ethological scheme for delicate description involving hierarchical units that are an attempt to have discreteness subordinate to the way "behaviour flows" (1979, p. 135). As early as 1963, Condon presented the notion of "interactional synchrony" to refer to the listener's pattern of movements in response to another's speech. Such patterns are indicative, Condon says, of a kind of entrainment. And thus "responsive entrainment" is crucial in establishing the functional patterns of behavior and culture. Dysfunctional categories (e.g., autism, aphasia, hyperactivity, and reading disability) have been found by Condon to involve delayed and "multiple entrainments," creating perturbations and loss of phase in the "interactional synchrony" (1979, pp. 142ff). Condon's approach to the structure of behavior—the tension between 'unit' and continuity; the emphasis on relations of relations—has an affinity with Saussure's conception of semiology and sign. Condon describes the "forms" of behavior as "relationships of patterns of change in relation to one another" (1979, p. 135). This is a highly sophisticated notion of interaction; one is not addressing a single pattern as the vehicle of communication in itself. Rather, it is the relation of patterns to each other, in a kind of orchestration, that is significant. This emphasis is consistent with certain of the strictures that Saussure placed on what could and could not carry the value of a sign. Putting the situation most abstractly, it allows for both intersystemic and intrasystemic shifts in the value of units—the thread of meaningfulness is, in fact, the product of such variation!

Given the range of material treated in this chapter, it is useful to note that Dore has studied the orienting movements of teacher and pupil with respect to reading failure. His microanalysis of video recordings also suggests the salience of the "dance" metaphor—with some children engaging and others not (Dore, talk given at Sydney University, 1984). To become a successful reader, one first has to "read" the semiotic value of the intricate patterns of teacher-pupil cooperation.

In the work of Newson we find some of the clearest generalizations from the studies of infant-mother reciprocation (1979, pp. 207–216). Newson clarifies the role of the "contingent reactivity" of the mother; the "massive and continuous" social programming which is a concomitant of the care of infants; and the way the world of objects receives its order from the social programming (1979, pp. 214–215). In particular, his remarks on the latter point bring the discussion in this chapter back to the general significance of the culture-language continuum and the 'logic' of language development:

> The ability of an infant to reach, with co-ordinated grasp movements in a manner appropriate to size and distance of objects, tells us virtually nothing about the way in which he comes to conceptualise, at a mental level, an out-there world of differentiated objects. (Newson, 1979, p. 215)

Mothers exert an almost constant semantic pressure on the wakeful infant. Such pressure takes the form of continuous interpretation, passed to the child through the "reactivity" of the mother. For the child, however, it would seem that development is not merely a receiving, but rather a process of achieving "phases" amid layers of behavioral regularity. The achievement is, of course, not the achievement of the individual child. Each child has to negotiate a place with respect to the patterns of behavior; yet the negotiation is handled by "units" within which the child (or any individual) constitutes but one role. The mother-child dyad, the family, the extended family, the neighborhood, the school—these are all units of mediation. Since they are institutions of gradually diminishing reciprocation, they increasingly challenge the child to reinterpret her or his orientation to doing and meaning:

> The child is born into a society already keyed for his coming. A system exists into which he must be assimilated if the society is to sustain itself. If his behaviour cannot, after a period of time, become predictable to a degree expected in that society, he must be specially treated. In some societies the nonassimilator will be allowed to die; in others he may be given special institutional treatment. This special treatment can range from deification to incarceration. But ultimately the goal is the same: to make that child's behaviour sufficiently predictable that the society can go about the rest of its business. (Birdwhistell, 1970, p. 6).

Being "in phase" might be viewed as the first and most pervasive meaning of human behavior. Such a use of meaning must be, of course, distinguished from the symbolic process by which Halliday identifies a protolanguage at around 9 months (Halliday, 1975; see also Painter, 1984, 1985). But the interactional synchrony of the dyad can be interpreted as realizing a meaning: namely, what from the adult point of view is "receptivity to other." When this most generalized signaling is regarded as the ground for the development of communication, conventional wisdom on the relationship between the natural order and social order has to be turned on its head.

The world of objects—of things "given" or "thrown down" before our objective apprehension—is a fiction. This is not to say that objects do not exist. Rather, it is a claim about the mediated character of human contact with the world. It is to say that the world of objects is never a world of things "thrown down," an order prior to all else. The roots of communication suggest that before the world has taken on the regularities of adult perception, the child is already participating in patterns of exchange derived from the social order. In this sense, then, our external world has to be negotiated, like all our experience, through the semiotic filter of cultural salience. From parenting onward, the culture provides mechanisms for experiential foregrounding. Hence, the system of things that exist in one's experience is built up like one's potential to mean: as Halliday expressed it, through "context-specific micro-paradigms" (1975, p. 125). This buildup is like that of the semantic system because, ultimately, it *is* the semantic system. Things do not first exist as objects and then as meanings, as with members of a taxonomic set. Objects/things are bequeathed their status by the social "games" within which they function. Therefore, one might need to say that objects begin as meanings.

By reflecting on three institutions of socialization—mother-child exchanges; school discourse; and mother-infant reactivity—we can begin to understand why it is misleading to separate learning language and learning culture. Of course, there is no purely linguistic domain of experience; but more crucial, there is no activity outside the semiotic organization of the culture, since even the delimitation of events and objects must be deferred to the social order. That we cannot envisage this situation as adults is a result of the illusion of self-evidence. We are now too far away from the building up of those "context-specific micro-paradigms." So much so that it is difficult to "see" the process in the small children we can observe. It has been all too congenial to reify language, to turn it into a form of knowledge—the kind of material that can be projected through curricula and evaluated. Then, when language has been formalized and made a thing apart from human activities, one is forced to address such questions as "What impels development?" (Brown & Cadzen, 1975, p. 304).

Like most intellectual fictions, the priority of the object world has probably been as useful an idea as it has been a misleading one. It led Newton to the belief, for example, that "there were no assumptions in his physics which were not necessitated by the experimental data" (Northrop in Heisenberg, 1958, p. 3). The data were truly, as the Latin indicates, the "given." In contrast to this situation, there is little relating to the fiction of language as knowledge which makes me confident that this idea has been useful. While on the one hand there has developed a highly sophisticated discourse on formal languages (e.g., philosophical grammars and AI proposals) as well as on the formal properties of metalanguages (e.g., syntactic descriptions), these have to be weighed against the ways in which language is used as a vehicle of discrimination throughout institutions of learning—especially, the way a particular orientation to meaning, based on a student's different pattern of cultural experience, can be interpreted as a limitation of knowledge, or as evidence that the child "does not have what it takes." But such claims require their own separate treatment—a study of how it has come to pass that academia has demanded evidence of explicit teaching by mothers amid the implicit meanings of home, but at the same time discouraged teachers from anything like the systematic discussion of language in their explicitly educational environments.

Halliday's perspective, however, has been one of the few points of reference which have worked as correctives in the language development imbroglio. Through his work it is possible to appreciate both the semiotic structure of culture and the cultural transmission involved in language.

CHAPTER 3

LEARNING THROUGH LANGUAGE: THE SOCIAL CONSTRUCTION OF GENDER*

Carmel Cloran

*Macquarie University
New South Wales, Australia*

INTRODUCTION

Learning through language, according to Halliday (1980), "is just another facet of the same basic phenomenon of language development" described in the previous chapter. In this chapter we shall consider how the child learns through language—how it is that, through language, the child builds up a picture of the world in which he lives, including his own place in it. In the following pages it will be shown that learning through language and learning language are "two aspects of a unitary process" (Halliday, 1975, p. 121) for, in constructing a semantic system, the child is at the same time constructing the culture since the one realizes the other. Clearly, modalities other than language participate in the construction of culture for an individual. Language, however, is the major modality in this process.

   In order to illustrate this phenomenon of the simultaneous construction of the culture and the semiotic system which expresses it, we shall focus on a single but pervasive aspect of the child's world—indeed, an aspect that shapes the child's own personality, namely, gender. Gender, defined as "the socially imposed division of the sexes" (Rubin, 1975, p. 179) is thus a social construct. The way children use this social construct as a principle through which to organize and interpret their experience of the world will be shown in a brief ethnographic account of the talk of preschool children in interaction with their mothers. Here it will be seen, also, that children's construction of their world—specifically gen-

I am grateful to Professor Ruqaiya Hasan, not only for her encouragement during the preparation of this chapter but also for reading and commenting on earlier drafts.

der—occurs through and in interaction with significant others (see Painter, Chapter 1, and Butt, Chapter 2 in this volume). The interactions in which learning occurs are by no means specifically designed for this purpose. Rather, "the most ordinary uses of language in the most everyday situations" (Halliday, 1973, p. 45) serve as the environments for the construction and transmission of the systems of values and knowledge of the culture.

In section 3 of this chapter, an empirical account of the social construction of gender will be presented, and here it will be shown that this social construct—gender—actually shapes the child's own personality. Finally, and in relation to this last issue, the way the social structure is involved in the child's construction of reality will be explicated. Halliday (1975, p. 128) observes that the social structure is involved in the child's construction of reality in two ways: "In the first place it is a part of the environment; hence it is a part of what is being transmitted to the child through language. In the second place it is a determinant of the transmission process, since it determines the types of role relationships in the 'primary socialising agencies.' " Gender is certainly an aspect of the organization of society but this is by no means the complete picture. The relationship between gender and another crucial aspect of social organization—social class—should also be considered. The consideration of this relationship will then bring us back to question the basis—indeed, often the justification—of gender as a social construct, that is, the natural environment or biological determinism.

1.1 Language and Gender

Like social class, gender is a basic facet of the organization of society. Physical configuration provides the basis for some differentiation in all societies. Goffman (1977, p. 302) remarks that "for these very slight biological differences . . . to be identified as the grounds for the kind of social consequences felt to follow from them requires a vast, integrated body of social beliefs and practices." Gender differences are held to be so important and basic that all languages offer some resource for distinguishing the sexes. For example, many languages grammatically encode gender; that is, they either overtly (e.g., French) or covertly (e.g., English—see Whorf, 1956, pp. 90–92) assign nominals to a gender class, while many other languages do not have 'formal' gender systems, for instance, Farsi, Finnish (Ibrahim, 1973, p. 70). Among the languages having grammatical gender, there is considerable variation in the following:

1. The number of terms in the system: two—masculine/feminine, as in Semitic languages; three—masculine/feminine/neuter, as in

many Indo-European languages; more than three, as in Bantu languages.

2. The extent and constancy of gender concord, that is, whether concord is invariably applied and whether such application is restricted to nominal group elements or extends throughout the clause to both nominal and verbal groups. Urdu, for example, has invariably applied clause extensive concord while in French concord is restricted to nominal group elements. Ukrainian, while having clause extensive concord, limits agreement in the verbal group to verbs in the singular past tense (Ibrahim, 1973, p. 99).

This brief survey of variation in the grammatical encoding of gender across languages raises two questions:

1. What, if anything, does the presence or absence of grammatical gender in a language tell us about the cultural significance of the sexes to speakers of languages varying along this dimension? (See for example Cameron, 1985.)
2. What, if any, are the consequences for the establishment in the individual of gender identity?

The second question has been investigated by social psychologists and we will return to it presently (section 2.2). The first question can be answered simply: nothing. Sapir (1949, p. 26) observes that the presence or absence of grammatical gender in a language does not "seem to have any relevance for our understanding of the social organisation . . . of the associated peoples." Indeed, to assume that it is through the grammatical encoding of gender that the male and female personalities are constructed is to assume that languages having no grammatical gender do not socially distinguish and differentially evaluate the sexes. Such an assumption, notes Poynton (1985, p. 44), has no basis in reality.

The cultural significance of the sexes is not to be found, then, through an examination of any isolated lexicogrammatical patterns but only through a study of the patterns of language which, in Whorf's (1956, p. 83) terms, are in configurative rapport. The position to be demonstrated in this chapter is that gender roles are constructed through what Hasan (1948a) terms "habitual forms of communication." These habitual forms of communication are distinct constellations of meanings that can be shown to occur in the environment of one sex as opposed to the other. They express, therefore, the different ways of being, behaving, and saying that are seen as gender-appropriate. It is in the assignment of these constellations of meanings to one or the other sex, rather than in the assignment of nominals to a gender class, that the cultural values concerning the sexes is revealed.

The area of sex differences in communication has been the focus of much research, particularly in the last 10 years. The literature pertaining to this research is highly relevant to the discussion of habitual forms of communication. In the third section of this chapter we examine the habitual forms of communication in an empirical account of the talk of mothers and their preschool children; the literature relating to sex differences in language use will be reviewed then. At this point let us consider the ontogenesis of general behavioral differences manifested through the form of early interaction involving the child. From there we will turn to an ethnographic account of the talk of mothers and their preschool children, where the child's active participation in the social construction of gender will be highlighted.

2. CONSTRUCTING GENDER:
AN ETHNOGRAPHIC ACCOUNT

2.1 Introduction: Parent-Infant Interaction

A number of studies have shown that from the time of their birth male and female children are perceived, evaluated, and treated differently by interacting adults. Rubin, Provenzano, and Luria (1974), in a study of adult perceptions and evaluations of newborns, found that the newborn girls were described as softer, smaller, and cuter than the male neonates despite the fact that there were no objective differences in height or weight. Indeed Seavey, Katz, and Zalk (1975) found that adults respond differently to the *same* child according to whether it is perceived to be male or female. Boys are apparently handled more roughly (Lewis & West, 1972) than are girls. Moss (cited in Birns, 1976) affirms that male infants get more attention than females who learn to be content when they are ignored. Studies such as these confirm the view that adults, possessing internalized cultural constructs of masculinity and femininity "transmit these very directly, if at times unconsciously, by their behaviour towards their infants" (Birns, 1976, p. 242).

Birns notes that studies of children's behavior have reached a level of sophistication not yet achieved in studies of parental socialization practices. One of the reasons is that while children may be directly observed without jeopardizing the naturalness of such a study, the same cannot be said of adults. Thus studies of socialization practices have tended to use questionnaires and interviews rather than make detailed observations of parent-child interaction. Data thus collected is severely restricted, relying as it must on the often unreliable reports of displaced behavior or alternatively on predicted behaviors in hypothetical situations. In other words, it is suggested that discrepancies often exist between what people say they do in particular situations and what they actually *do* do. Particularly in the area of sex-differential socialization people tend to be "blinkered" concerning their practices. How often does one hear, "I don't treat Mary and Jim any differently"—often with the rider "Of course I don't have to be as hard on Mary as I am on Jim because she's such a compliant child and he's so headstrong." In other words, the cultural constructs concerning male and female are so internalized that they have become invisible. Quite often they do become fleetingly visible when questioned by those being initiated, namely, young children, and this will be evident in the following ethnographic account. Parents, on the whole, tend to account for any differential treatment of their children in terms of temperamentally related individual differences. Such an appeal is undoubtedly justified up to a point. Beyond this, however, are the background cultural prescriptions and prohibitions governing expectations concerning the behaviors seen as gender-appropriate.

If we accept that the child brings certain temperamental predispositions—of whatever origin—to interactions, the extent to which these are influenced by cultural constructs concerning gender-appropriate behaviors would seem to affect gender socialization. For example, such temperamental characteristics as high levels of intensity of reactions and persistence in actions, if viewed as precursors to the development of independence, are likely to generate different parental responses, depending on whether the child is male or female. In other words, in terms of gender socialization, parents' attitudes and behaviors with the child are influenced by the degree of congruence between parental expectations and the behavior of the child. Thus gender socialization runs the risk of forcing the suppression of those temperamental characteristics that are considered gender-inappropriate.

While males and females are perceived, evaluated, and treated differently from birth, gender socialization through language begins in earnest in the second year of life (Buss & Piomin, 1984, p. 58) as the child's language develops. In order to investigate the gender-socialization practices of parents, what is needed—either to augment or to replace existing interview/questionnaire data—is a record of the naturally occurring interaction between parents and children in their customary environments.

2.2 Interaction in the Preschool Years

The data on which the present account is based were collected in a project directed by Ruqaiya Hasan and funded by the Australian Government Research Grant Scheme. Twenty-four mothers, contacted through preschools in and around Sydney, were asked to audiotape up to 6 hours of their verbal interaction with their preschool child during the course of the family's daily routine activities, with no outsider present. Mothers did the recording, taking on average about 4 weeks, and using cassettes and equipment with which they had been supplied. While the mothers themselves may have initially been self-conscious when they switched on the tape recorder, the quality of the data suggests that they soon lost this because of the demands of the interaction with the child. The 24 mother-child dyads represent two socioeconomic groups defined by reference to the degree of autonomy that the occupation of the family breadwinner permitted. In 12 families the breadwinner held a job that permitted little or no autonomy in making decisions related to work and little or no control on the work life of others in the workplace. These low-autonomy-profession families will hereafter be referred to as LAPs. In the 12 high-autonomy-profession families (HAPs) the degree of autonomy in decision making and control on others in the workplace was relatively much higher. HAP parents had higher levels of education than did LAP parents, none of whom had been educated at the tertiary level. Male and female children were equally distributed in the two social groups, as indicated in Table 1.

Table 1.   Distribution of
24 Dyads by Sex and Social
Group.

	Girls	Boys
LAP	6	6
HAP	6	6

The natural mother-child interaction recorded in Hasan's project goes a long way toward providing the kind of unself-conscious information that is usually missing from questionnaire and interview data. While limited in that fathers were all but excluded, these recordings of parent-child interaction during daily routine activities nevertheless provide some interesting insights into the ways in which children are brought to a knowledge of the norms and social expectations of themselves as males and females. Of the 24 children, 8 were followed up, 18 months later, into their first year at school. In this second phase of Hasan's project, each of the 8 children was recorded in a variety of contexts, including that of an interview with a relatively unfamiliar adult (Dr. David Butt). While the following ethnographic account draws mainly on the data from the first phase of the project (parent-child interaction), some data from the project's second phase is also included.

The children in Hasan's project have had, on average, 3 years, 8 months of interaction with parents and significant others in their social world. They have learned during this time that they belong to one of two categories of people. They have heard on many occasions in the course of routine interactions that they are good, naughty, clever, grubby, cute, strong, brave, and so on boys or girls; that they are Mummy's, Daddy's, Grandma's, little or big boy or girl; and in many cases that Mummy, Daddy, brother, or sister is ''she'' or ''he'' as are similarly referenced friends, cousins, and, often, pets and toys. So by 3½ years of age these children, who are probably fairly representative of the 3½-year-old population of Sydney, have internalized their own gender identity and have learned that maleness and femaleness is an attribute of both humans and animals. The exchange in (1), for example, occurs while Peter and his mother are engaging in fantasy play together:[1]

(1)   *Mother:*   I'm Tarzan
      Peter: Oh yeah—no! You're a girl.

In (2) Colin and his mother are admiring a kitten:

(2)   *Mother:*   Oh look at that black kitten! Isn't she beautiful!
      Colin: No, it's a boy.

It is not clear whether in (2) above Colin is denying the beauty of the kitten as well as the gender assignment encoded by the mother's use of the feminine 3rd-person pronominal. Kress and Hodge (1979) note that certain adjectives such as *beautiful* have feminine valency since they are more frequently used with reference to females than to males. The valency of adjectives is thus an aspect of the covertness of gender classification in English.

In addition to classifying the human and animal world along gender lines, children learn that surrogates may be so classified. Jane's mother inquires, ''Is Teddy a boy or a girl?''

---

[1]Transcription conventions used in examples:
  (   ) enclose contextual comment or interpretative source of pronominal referent;
  [= simultaneous or overlapping talk;
  [? item] = item not clearly intelligible but interpreted by reference to contextual, cotextual, or phonological clues;
  [?   ] = unintelligible and uninterpretable.

A child's own gender identity is usually established by 2–3 years (Kohlberg, 1956) although in languages with a high gender-loading (i.e., clause extensive concord), such as Hebrew, gender identity may be achieved earlier. Guiora, Beit-Hallahmi, Fried, and Yoder (1982) have found that the achievement of gender identity closely parallels the gender loading of the language spoken. Thus "a Hebrew-speaking child is made aware of gender distinctions sooner and more frequently than his or her Finnish- or English-speaking counterparts" (Guiora et al, 1982, p. 982), since Hebrew speakers must encode the sex of the addressee as well as their own sex as speaker. English does not require this and, even at 3½ years, English-speaking children such as Alan, in (3) below, may still be unsure of the gender identity of others.

(3) Alan: I'm a big boy
     Mother: Yeah
     Alan: Same as Daddy and me
     Mother: Yeah
     Alan: Not you
     Mother: No not Mummy
     Alan: You're a little boy
     Mother: Mummy's a little boy?
     Alan: Yeah
     Mother: No, Mummy's a girl
     Alan: Mummy's a girl.

In (3) above, Alan's method of establishing gender identity—by a principle of comparison and contrast with intimates—is apparent. This same child is also unsure of the gender identity of one of his preschool peers—perhaps because of this child's behavior and role in Alan's world.

(4) Mother   You don't fight with Sally anymore, don't you? . . . Or Sally doesn't fight with you.
     Alan: Nup
     Mother   She looks after you, doesn't she?
     Alan: Yeah, she won't let anybody bash me
     Mother   She won't let anybody bash you?
     Alan: No, she smacks 'em back
     Mother   She smacks 'em back, does she?
     Alan: Because Sally's a big boy
     Mother   Eh?
     Alan: Because Sally's a big—
     Mother: Sally's a big *girl*
     Alan: Big girl, Sally's a girl and I'm a boy
     Mother: That's right.

Again Alan is rehearsing gender identification by means of comparison/contrast. Since in the previous example (3) he had nominated his mother as "boy", size relative to himself does not seem to be his criterion for gender identification. Perhaps "benefactor" is his criterion for assigning maleness, since the protective Sally would fall into this category, as would his mother and father. (The notion of "benefactor" as an attribute of maleness will be considered in a later section.) Alternatively, "aggression" might figure in Alan's classification of Sally as a boy. Maccoby and Jacklin (1974) cite aggression as one of the few behavioral differences between males and females that have been consistently identified in studies of sex differences, and Birns (1976) found, in a survey of the literature, that even in the preschool years boys are more aggressive than girls. However, Ruble and Ruble (1982) note that children under 7 have not yet internalized the more abstract traits (such as aggression) held to characterize males and females in our culture.

That abstract sex-appropriate attributes are not internalized by age 3½ is not to say that children are not exposed, at this age, to the cultural norms and expectations concerning such attributes. Such instruction occurs, as is to be expected, in opportunities arising from daily routine activities. One such opportunity arises for Cameron's mother when, during lunch, she and Cameron are recalling Cameron's tumble while he was riding his bike:

(5) *Mother:*   Mm . . . You were certainly very brave
     Cameron: [I wasn't] *very* brave
     Mother: Yeah, you were brave; you mightn't think you were brave but I think you were
     Cameron: What for?
     Mother: ⌈Because you acted in a very brave way
     Cameron: ⌊No
     Mother: You hurt yourself and you cried and that's good to cry when you hurt yourself but you only cried for a little while and then you climbed back on your bike
     Cameron: ⌈And didn't—
     Mother: ⌊And when you were a little boy, you know what you would have done?
     Cameron: What?
     Mother: You would have run back to Mummy, crying really loudly, shouting, and you didn't do that, you acted like a big boy.

Sam's mother recalls a visit to the doctor:

(6) *Mother:*   You had a needle, didn't you? . . . It didn't hurt you, did it? You were a good boy, the doctor said . . . Big

Sam: What?
Mother: And strong.

A conversation between Nathan and his mother shows how Nathan is trying to make sense of his social world in terms of gender classification. The following exchange occurs while Nathan's mother is cutting his hair:

(7)   Mother: When Santa comes creeping in at dead of night, he'll see a handsome boy
      Nathan: Santa?
      Mother: Yeah
      Nathan: Handsome boy?
      Mother: Mm
      Nathan: What's handsome boy?
      Mother: Well, it means that you look smart . . . all clean ⌈and—
      Nathan: ⌊Crisp?
      Mother: Crisp
      Nathan: Fresh
      Mother: And fresh (laughter)
      Nathan: Do girls be fresh?
      Mother: Yes
      Nathan: Do boys?
      Mother: Yes

There are no examples in the data of mothers imparting information to their daughters concerning desirable feminine attributes—which of course does not mean that they do not do so. Helen tells her mother: "I'm Nana and yours [little girl] first [before Daddy and Grandpa] because the girls have to be first and the men have to be last." This expression of traditional gender-associated courtesy must have been imparted to Helen at some stage.

While learning that as members of a gender category certain attributes are expected of them, children also learn that certain attributes and behaviors judged undesirable for those who are members of one category may be held desirable for members of the other. Thus males learn to inhibit behavior that is considered appropriate for members of the category "female," and vice versa. Early lessons in gender-appropriate behavior occur with toys. David is playing with his sister's doll; Mother warns him to be careful because his sister will be upset if the doll is broken:

(8)   David: No, she won't
      Mother: She sure will, it's her doll
      David: My doll
      Mother: Don't be silly! Boys don't play with dolls.

Children quickly generalize the gender circumscription of toys and activities. Michael, while playing with a toy racing-car set, speaks to his mother:

(9)   *Michael:*   How about buying one of these (sets) for Elsa? Are they only for boys?

Daniel and his mother discuss an earlier visit to see an orchestra:

(10)   *Mother:*   I liked the ladies doing the violins
        Daniel: I like—you can't—but do men do it too?

Michael's mother assured him that racing car sets are for girls too and Daniel's mother saw no reason why both men and women can't play any of the instruments. The fact that these children sought to bring order into their world by appealing to sex classification shows how well this principle of organization is internalized by 3½ years of age.

In addition to learning gender-appropriate activities, children learn that the way they interact with others is determined by the gender identity of others. Colin's mother specifies that aggressive behavior toward girls is unacceptable:

(11)   *Colin:*   We punched her, don't we?
        Mother: You don't punch girls, do you?

She is rather noncommittal, however, when Colin describes his plans for Kevin:

(12)   *Colin:*   And Kevin smacks me on the head
        Mother: Does he?
        Colin: And I—I will—I kick him up the wall . . . and he went [crashing down] and he will go (CRASH) in the water.
        Mother: Oh will he?
        Colin: Yeah, but I will kick him up to the sky and then he will fall in the water . . .
        Mother: Have you finished your drink?

Just as aggressive behavior has to be controlled by reference to the sex of the interactional partner, so too does affection. Julian and his mother play the game "How much do you love Mummy/Daddy/baby sister?" and then continue:

(13) *Julian:*   Who else d'you want me to love?
      Mother: You can love whoever you want
      Julian: Can I love Peter? . . . Can I?
      Mother: No, I think that's more like friendship.
      Julian: Pardon?
      Mother: Thought you'd say that. It's like friendship isn't it? . . . You're friends with Peter, aren't you?
      Julian: Yep . . . Mum
      Mother: Yes
      Julian: When I get old as you and Maree likes me, could we marry each other?

We may infer from Julian's last question that he has understood something of what was behind his mother's prohibition on loving Peter.

While boys learn patterns of appropriate behavior through explicit sayings or through what is implied—for instance, that they can fight males but cannot love them and that they cannot fight females but can love them—what is the situation with regard to girls? It would seem that girls are more oriented toward nurturance, much of which is learned by following the behavior of their mothers. Thus, we find girls at 3½ interpreting representations of such behavior, and also rehearsing such behavior themselves in play. In (14) Carol and her mother are looking at pictures in a magazine:

(14) *Mother:*   What is the lady doing?
      Carol: Um pouring out um coffee or tea for father.

And in (15) Mother is making scones and gives Carol some scone mixture:

(15) *Mother:*   You're going to make a nice little scone. Who's it for?
      Carol: For Teddy.

Interestingly, Carol does not regard the nurturant role as an exclusively female one:

(16) *Carol:*   I'm going to pretend that the mother is going to work and the father is going to stay home minding the bear—
      Mother: That's a good idea
      Carol: Minding the child.

However, Christine appears to expect nurturant behavior only from her mother:

(17) *Father:*   Look at you! You look like you've been making mud pies or something and eating them.

Christine: Mum, you better wash my face.

It is not suggested that fathers do not display nurturant behavior but rather that children have learned, within these years of maximum dependence on their parents, that it is Mum who usually sees to their physical needs. That girls are oriented to this role is made very explicit by Helen's mother in (18), when she urges Helen to tidy her room.

(18) *Mother:*   If you don't do your own work now, when you grow up and have your own little babies you won't know how to look after them, will you? So you'll have to learn how to do those things when you're little, won't you?

Girls thus learn to expect that, as females, they will grow up to be mothers themselves and their role will then be the same as that of their mothers, namely, cooking, cleaning, and looking after the children.

The fact that children are oriented at an early age to the sex roles they will be expected to fulfill as adults is implied by Hasan (1986). Using the same mother-child talk as that on which the present study is based, Hasan discusses the early origins of the ideology of women's work and identifies four aspects of this work as it relates to children: the mother is (a) an instructor, (b) a laborer, (c) an emotional support, and (d) her child's companion. Discussing mothers' laboring role, Hasan notes that "mothers are lavish in the expression of appreciation whenever the child helps in the house—*this happens more often with girls than with boys*" (Hasan, 1986, p. 136; my emphasis). Thus Cameron's mother, in an affort to get him to go off with his father for a while, tells him, 'It'd be much more interesting going to the tip than helping Mummy do the vacuuming.'' In her discussion of mothers' role as emotional support, Hasan quotes two extracts from the data in which mothers themselves seek such support from their children. In the first extract Karen's mother seeks this support:

(19) *Mother:*   Oh I've got a bad cold
      Karen: Oh
      Mother: Are you going to look after me . . . eh?
      Karen: Oh
      Mother: Oh ah, sorry (COUGHING AGAIN)
      Karen: I can't when I have to go to school
      Mother: But you don't have to go to school for a few days
      Karen: I know
      Mother: You going to look after me?
      Karen: Yeah
      Mother: Okay.

In the second extract Nathan's mother asks him to look after her:

(20)   *Mother:*   I have to lie down and put my leg in the air. Will you look
                     after me?
        Nathan: No
        Mother: You won't! (SURPRISED)
        Nathan: Why?
        Mother: You won't look after me?
        Nathan: Where are you—where are you gonna do it?
        Mother: In the loungeroom [I think]
        Nathan: No, do it here.

It is interesting that Karen finally undertakes to look after her mother
(since she doesn't have to go to preschool), while Nathan is quite be-
wildered by the request and at no point appears to grant it.

Given that the ways of being and behaving transmitted to boys are
somewhat different from those imparted to girls, one might ask: Are
such socialization practices related to the fact that by 3½ years of age
children prefer their own sex as playmates? Peter's mother, for example,
inquires about his friends at preschool:

(21)   *Mother:*   Have you got any girls down at kindergarten?
        Peter: Like my friends?
        Mother: Yeah
        Peter: Nup

Talk continues about preschool and then Mother comes back to the
subject of playmates:

        Mother: Is there any girls you play with at kindergarten?
        Peter: Nup

Again the talk takes another direction before the mother pursues the
subject of playmates:

        Mother: Who's your mate down at kindy?
        Peter: Ivan.

Mother continues to elicit the names of Peter's playmates, all of whom
are boys. David's mother tries to persuade a reluctant David to go to
school:

(22) *Mother:* You've got other boys and girls to play with at school
      David: No I haven't got—I didn't play with girls

Finally, note Michael's response:

(23) *Mother:*   Did you play with all the girls and boys (at kindy)?
      Michael: Oh no . . . I only played with the boys

The social psychological literature suggests that same-sex preference is associated with gender constancy, that is, with the knowledge that the gender identity of self and others does not change despite changes in hairstyle, clothes, and so on. Research findings on the age at which such stability is achieved vary but the earliest seems to be around 4½ to 5 years (Ruble & Ruble, 1982). The positive evaluation of one's own sex and the negative evaluation of the other is also said to be linked with gender constancy. If these two phenomena—same-sex preference and positive evaluations—are indeed associated with gender constancy, then it would seem that at 3½ years Peter, David, and Michael have achieved this constancy, as has Jenny who remarks, with reference to her nagging cough, "Naughty boy," Jenny is one of the children who participated also in the second phase of Hasan's project. In an interview 18 months after the above remark, Jenny clearly articulates her perceptions of the differences between the sexes with regard to preferred activities, and her evaluation of such preferences. Jenny and the interviewer, David, are discussing Care Bears:

(24) *Jenny:* But I don't like one Care Bear and that's Grumpy Bear
      David: Oh no, who wants to put up with a Grump, eh?
      Jenny: Not me but I think the boys would.
      David: The b—why would the boys like it?
      Jenny: Because they like bad things
      David: Do they?
      Jenny: Yeah, like we have Rainbow Bright things
      David: Yeah
      Jenny: And they have murkyish things like murkyish castle or Skeletor or all those things.

Such positive evaluation of one's own sex and negative evaluation of the other is also clear in 5-year-old Alison's talk with the same interviewer about goings-on at school:

(25) *Alison:* We've got snakes and things on that big grass around the back
      David: Yes, yeah

Alison:	And people—you have to get the teachers—tell 'em to get the ball
David:	Mm
Alison:	'Cause um people kick it over the fence
David:	At school they kick it right over the fence!
Alison:	Yes and the girls don't, they play out in the good part
David:	Who does, sorry?
Alison:	The girls
David:	The girls, yeah
Alison:	The girls are better than boys.

There is little doubt that children socialize one another. Male and female siblings do this within the family, and experiences in the wider world of preschool provide reinforcement. The extracts of mother-child talk presented in this brief ethnography exemplify many such instances of the transmission of sociocultural values, beliefs, and customs concerning gender-appropriate behavior. What the child must do as a boy or girl is learned at the mother's knee, as it were, not only from the mother's direct prescriptions or prohibitions but also from her lack of expression of these. The child's efforts to make sense of his world are evident as well, and it seems clear that by 3½ years children have internalized the fact that the sex distinction is one way of doing this. Thus, in Goffman's (1977, p. 314–315), terms, "what will serve to structure wider social life is given its shape and its impetus in a very small and very cosy circle."

3. AN EMPIRICAL ACCOUNT

3.1 Introduction

In the preceding section we saw how mothers, in the course of daily routine activities, transmit to their children the behavior held to be gender appropriate, either explicitly through their prescriptions, prohibitions, or simply comments, or implicitly by not commenting. In this section I will use the same mother-child data that served as the source of the ethnographic material presented in section 2.2, in order to empirically investigate the constellations of meanings exchanged by mothers and their sons/daughters. Here I will show also how it is that gender interacts with the social group membership of the family in the construction of these meanings. First, however, let us consider some of the research evidence that has already accumulated concerning sex differences in communications.

3.2 Sex Differences in Language Use

While there is no single feature of spoken English that is used exclusively by one sex or the other, studies show that certain kinds of linguistic behavior are more frequently associated with one sex than with the other. However, single features in isolation do not characterize speakers on the basis of sex, and this factor has led to inconsistencies in the results of studies seeking evidence of sex differences in language behavior. For example, in a review of the literature Haas (1979) reports that there are mixed results in studies of such features as verbosity or quantity of talk and the use of low-value modals as expressions of uncertainty. However, the major focus of research in recent years has been on co-occurring features in the speech to and of males and females. The stimulus for this research was provided by the work of Lakoff (1975), who categorized the speech style of women under three headings— phonological, lexical, and syntactic-pragmatic traits.

Women's style, according to Lakoff, is characterized by imprecise intensifiers, frequent expressions of emotion, infrequent expressions of anger and hostility, politeness, correct pronunciation, tag questions, and low-value modals as expressions of uncertainty (Lakoff, 1975, pp. 53–55). Lakoff's work gave impetus to further research not only into stylistic patterns in the speech of women and men but also into stereotypes (as revealed by speaker judgments) concerning ''sex-appropriate'' speech styles, and into the consequences for interaction of this variation in habitual communicative behavior.

Haas (1979, p. 623) found from a survey of the research into male/ female speech styles that apparently men ''use language to lecture, argue, debate, assert and command''—all processes associated with power. The existence in the community of stereotypes of men's and women's speech was revealed by the work of Siegler and Siegler (1976), Edelsky (1976), and Kramer (1974), who asked subjects to attribute speaker/ writer sex to statements containing typical male or female speech features. In a later study, Kramer (1978, p. 158), found that male speech is described as attention-seeking, dominating, aggressive, and frank by comparison with female speech, which is held to be ''friendly, gentle, enthusiastic, grammatically correct, but containing gibberish on trivial topics.''

What are the consequences of these distinct speech patterns for interaction between males and females? Haas (1981) found that from an early age boys, in interaction with girls, are more assertive, giving more information and making more direct requests (imperatives), while girls are higher on verbal compliance. This result is consistent with Strodbeck and Mann's (1956) finding that women agreed, concurred, complied, accepted, and supported other speakers almost twice as much as men who were more assertive, antagonistic, and offensive. This brings us to Fishman's (1978) analysis of recordings of 52 hours of the routine conversational interactions of three married couples. Fishman found that the work of maintaining the interaction fell to the women who, to achieve this end, more often asked questions and used attention-getters, and actively maintained and supported their male partners in conversation. As far as the introduction of topics to talk about is concerned, Fishman (1978, p. 404), found that "Both men and women regarded topics introduced by women as tentative. . . . In contrast, topics introduced by the men were treated as topics to be pursued; they were seldom rejected." Fishman concludes that it is the male who chooses "what part of the world the interactants orient to, construct and maintain the reality of . . . yet the women labour hardest in making the interactions go" (p. 404).

Poynton (1985) provides a comprehensive account of what she calls 'gender-based codes," which, she demonstrates, are expressed through different selections at all levels of the linguistic system—from phonology to genre. The literature thus presents some convincing evidence supporting the existence of distinctive male and female communicative styles. What we want to consider now is the origin of these styles in the lives of individuals—a matter that has received little attention because of the difficulties pointed out in section 2.1. In the account that follows we will focus on the choices available to speakers at the semantic level in order to discern the constellations of meanings defining the habitual forms of communication used by mothers in interaction with their preschool sons and daughters. This will enable us to see that communicative styles are not simply aggregations of different features but rather are patternings of features such that each pattern forms a coherent whole whose meaning can then be interpreted at a more abstract semiotic level.

3.3 Habitual Forms of Communication

3.3.1 Method and procedure. The talk of the 24 mothers and children who participated in Hasan's project was segmented into messages and analyzed with a message semantics framework devised by Hasan (1983). In all, about 20,000 messages were coded and stored on computer. The semantic features of each of these 20,000 messages referred to the following:

1. textual features—the status of the message as a component of the ongoing discourse (e.g., topic maintaining, response requirement, etc.);

2. interpersonal features—the semantic features of each message as exchange (Halliday, 1985b) including attitudinal features;
3. ideational features—features of the role of participants in the processes encoded, as well as the features of each message as an elaboration of other messages.

Each message was thus described in terms of 50 features, on average.

In order that the linguistic behavior be the single variable distinguishing the population, the frequency of occurrence of a number of the features of the 20,000 messages was tabulated and subjected to analyses by the principal components method of factor analysis. A factor-analytic method was used as a means of discerning the regularity and order in the linguistic phenomena. Factor analysis would seem to be particularly appropriate in the analysis of linguistic data since, as Rummel (1967, p. 445) observes, it "takes thousands and potentially millions of measurements and qualitative observations and resolves them into distinct patterns of occurrence. It makes explicit and more precise the building up of fact-linkages going on continuously in the human mind."

Horvath (1985) pioneered the application of the principal components technique to linguistic data in her study of phonological and textual variation in Australian English. She points out that the principal components technique is particularly appealing to linguists since it "allows groupings of speakers according to their linguistic behaviour rather than according to their place in a social grid. . . . As linguists it is the linguistic categories that we are most concerned about and most knowledgeable about" (Horvath, 1985, p. 66). Once speakers have been grouped on the basis of their linguistic behavior, the groups can then be examined in order to identify their social characteristics, if there exist any consistent ones.

The principal components procedure, like other methods of factor analysis, reduces the large number of variables to their common factor patterns. It selects, from among a set of variables, a subset of variables that together form a coherent pattern identifying the behavior of the group upon which the measurements of the variables were taken. This pattern is then interpreted on the basis of the subset of variables strongly associated with it, namely, those variables in which 25 percent or more of their variation are involved in the pattern (Rummel, 1967). Part of the appeal of this procedure is that it appears to build on the interpretation of behavior which people constantly apply in their everyday lives in order to make sense of an individual's behavior and perhaps to characterize that individual. For example, if we meet a person who in conversation among strangers contributes little, we may also notice that this person appears interested in the conversation, smiles, establishes eye contact, responds appropriately when addressed, and so on. On the basis of our observations of these behaviors we may conclude that this person is shy. In other words, these behaviors we know from our everyday experiences are, when combined, indexical of a person commonly interpreted to be a "shy person."

To continue our commonsense example, let us hypothesize that a group of people have been measured on the following list of behaviors and the measurements have been subjected to a principal components analysis. The results might be as follows:

Variable	PC1	PC2	PC3
contribution	−high	−high	+high
eye contact	+high	−high	+high
smile	+yes	−yes	+yes
tracks (e.g., nods)	+yes	+yes	+yes
responds appropriately	+yes	−yes	+yes
winks	—	—	+yes
laughs	—	—	+yes
raises eyebrows	—	—	+yes
frowns	—	—	−yes

The entries "+high" and "+yes" indicate that these are the behaviors that are relevant to the interpretation of this component. Their value would be .25 or more (rather than "+high" and "+yes"). Where there is no entry against a variable (−), the associated behaviors are not relevant in the interpretation of the component, that is, their value would be less than .25, or statistically speaking, less than 25 percent of the variation of these variables is involved in the component. Where a variable is negatively associated with a component (e.g., "contribution" on PC1), this variable is relevant to the interpretation of the component. What is relevant about it is that it does *not* occur in the behavior of people who score high on the component.

Let us now try to interpret PC1. People who score high on PC1 contribute little in conversation (−high); however, they do allow eye contact to be established, they smile and nonverbally indicate interest in the conversation, responding appropriately when addressed. The rest of the behaviors—winking, laughing, raising eyebrows, and frowning—are not relevant to the interpretation of this component. On the basis of (a) the behaviors that are relevant and (b) the fact of their positive or negative loading, one would say that this component delineates a pattern of behavior that is typical of shy people. Let us therefore name PC1 "shy people."

PC2 describes a pattern of these same behaviors. However, they load (are associated) differently with the component. People scoring high on this component do not contribute much when in conversation, nor do they allow eye contact to be established; they do not smile and they tend not to respond appropriately when addressed, but they do non-verbally indicate interest in the conversation. This combination of behaviors may be interpreted as describing "uninvolved people."

PC3 delineates a pattern made up of nearly all the behaviors. Note too that, with the exception of the last variable, all of the relevant behaviors are positively loaded. Thus people who score high on PC3 tend to be major contributors to conversation where they allow eye contact, smile, indicate interest, and respond appropriately; they are also given to winking at others and laughing, but they tend not to frown. This combination of behaviors suggests a pattern typical of a "friendly, gregarious person."

The foregoing is a highly simplified account of the interpretation of principal components, and some important details have been omitted. It is hoped, however, that some idea of the principal components procedure has been conveyed so that the analysis presented in the following pages will not be too obscure. An important point to note is that the principal components technique allows subjects to be compared and discussed in terms of the dimensions identified by the components rather than in terms of the original large number of variables on the combination of which each dimension or pattern is constituted.

For the statistically minded, the principal components procedure used here focused on the regularity in the data from the point of view of the variation of the variables. In other words, an R-mode analysis based on the matrix of correlation coefficients among the variables was employed. A major drawback of the principal components method is that it demands a ratio of 3 to 1 subjects to variables. The number of subjects when considered in terms of speakers was 48 (24 mothers and 24 children) so that the linguistic features had to be broken down into groups of 15–20 variables and separate principal components analyses computed. The results of two of the principal components analyses computed so far are alone relevant in the present discussion of gender construction and these will be presented below. First, however, it might be helpful to outline the variables subjected to the principal components procedure in each of the analyses.

The first principal components analysis involved the linguistic variables associated broadly with what may be termed initiating types of messages. Included were question types: *how/why* questions or questions seeking specification (e.g., *When did you . . . ?*) or confirmation (e.g., *Did you . . . ?*); types of demands for good and services: assertive (e.g., *Do . . . !*), consultative (e.g., *Would you . . . ?*), or suggestive (e.g., *Shall we . . . ?*); ways of giving goods and services, that is, consultative versus assertive offers; and ways of giving information—giving reasons in various ways, making announcements concerning activities, reiterating one's own or the other's messages, recounting, supporting, evaluating, and so forth. These variables are listed in Table 2 together with their associated component loadings.

The second principal components analysis involved the linguistic features associated with (a) discourse features of messages—topic maintenance or change, overt expression of the logical relationships between messages; and (b) speakers' expressions of attitude and point of view as indicated by the use of modals, projection, and orientation to time. These variables are listed with their associated component loadings in Table 3.

For each of the two principal component analyses, a separate analysis was carried out for mothers and children. Further statistical tests were performed (on completion of each principal components analysis) using the scores of each subject on the identified components. Analyses of variance revealed the presence or absence of significant differences in subjects' scores in association with the independent variables: social class membership and sex of child. Finally, the correlation between the principal components of the two separate analyses was checked as a way of reducing, to some extent at least, the handicap of having to separate the linguistic variables into groups. The results of the analyses of variance as well as the correlations among components will be drawn upon in the following discussion of the interpretation of the principal components identified.

3.3.2 Results. Principal Components Analysis 1 as in factor analysis generally, the first factor pattern or principal component delineates the largest pattern of relationships in the data, the second delineates the next largest pattern that is uncorrelated with the first, the third delineates the next largest pattern that is uncorrelated with both the first and second, and so on. The amount of variation in the data described by each component thus decreases successively with each component. The amount of variation accounted for by a component is indicated by its eigenvalue, and from this is derived the percent of total variation among the variables that is contributed by each component.

The principal components shown in Table 2 will be discussed first in terms of those delineating the behavior of mothers. The interpretation and discussion of those referring to the behavior of children will follow.

Patterns in Mothers' Talk: The variables associated with the first principal component (PC1) refer to a pattern of behavior in which mothers habitually tend.

1. to demand goods and services by using exhortative commands (realized typically by the imperative forms, e.g., *Don't do that*, or by

Table 2. Variable Features of Principal Components Analysis 1

Initiating-type Utterance Variables	Mothers Component 1	Mothers Component 2	Children Component 1	Children Component 2
Confirmation/Specification questions[a]	−.34	.00	−.05	.04
How/Why questions	−.34	−.00	.05	−.04
Direct commands	.41	.14	−.27	−.01
Indirect commands	−.25	−.06	.23	.01
Suggestions	−.37	−.15	.20	−.07
Assertive offers	.09	−.04	−.05	.07
Consultative offers[a]	−.09	.04	.05	−.07
Reasons appealing to tradition	.24	−.38	−.10	−.25
Reasons appealing to internal consequences	−.36	.34	.29	.55
Reasons appealing to bribe/threat	.32	−.19	−.27	−.48
Empathetic reiterations	−.03	.06	−.46	−.13
Reinforcing reiterations[a]	.03	−.06	.46	.13
Announcing completion/inception of activity	−.26	−.39	.41	−.36
Recounting past event/happening	.05	−.37	−.29	.11
Adding information	.22	.55	−.21	.35
Reassuring/sympathizing	.18	−.16	.36	−.29
Guiding interpretation of own utterances[a]	−.18	.16	−.36	.29
Praise	−.19	.09	−.03	.07
Criticism[a]	.19	−.09	.03	−.07
Eigenvalue	4.1	2.07	3.2	2.1
Percent total contribution per eigenvalue	29.5	14.8	23	15

[a]Variable whose association with a component was deduced since it represented the other member of a binary category.

using high-value modals such as *must, have to, gotta,* etc.) rather than the more discretion-giving consultative or suggestive type (realized by interrogatives, e.g., *Would you do it?* or *How about doing it?*;

2. to give rationalizations by appeal to bribes or threats rather than to consequences inherent in an act (e.g., *if you touch the hot stove, you'll burn yourself*);

3. to demand information using *how/why* questions rather than speci-
fication-seeking questions (e.g., *What happened?)* or confirmation-
seeking ones (e.g., *Did you cut yourself?);*

4. not to announce the commencement of some activity (e.g., *I'll just
go and hang out the washing)* or its completion (e.g., *I've finished my
lunch now).* The significance of this negative loading appears to be
that such a speaker is not overtly concerned with the involvement
of the addressee in the ongoing activity.

The combination of these variables suggests that they delineate a pattern of mothers' control style. Thus mothers scoring high on PC1 allow
their children no discretion when demanding goods and services and
such demands are supported by bribes or threats. The use of *how/why*
questions by these mothers suggested that these were part of the control
strategies of such mothers and further investigation revealed that indeed
such questions were used rhetorically or to counter the children's utterances. Peter's mother in the following extract exemplifies the behavior
identified by this component. Peter is drinking milk and pretending that
it is orange juice; Mother goes along with his game until it becomes too
boisterous:

(26) *Mother:* Don't do that . . . Now look, you'll get it all over me
     Peter: (LAUGHS)
     Mother: It's not funny. What's funny about that?
     You do it again and I'll whack you.

Peter's mother uses a direct command *don't do that* and rhetorically
demands an explanation for his behavior: *what's funny about that?* Finally she threatens him: *You do it again and I'll whack you.* This threat
is a last resort, for she had previously reasoned by appealing to the
inherent consequences of his behavior: *Now look, you'll get it all over me.*
This episode illustrates two important points:

1. It is not the case that mothers having a particular pattern of behavior never use features other than those constituting that pattern;
thus, while Peter's mother does appeal to inherent consequences by way
of rationalizations, the fact that she scores high on PC1 indicates that
she selects this way of reasoning with less frequency.

2. It is impossible to illustrate the fact that a person does not select
a particular feature; that Peter's mother, for example, is not given to
involving Peter in the ongoing activity by announcing the commencement or completion of some activity is apparent only when the interaction of this dyad is contrasted with that of another.

Analysis of variance of the mothers' scores on component 1 indicates that significantly it is mothers of boys rather than mothers of girls (p = .02) who habitually use this control style.

The variables combining to produce PC1 account for 29.5 percent of the total variance in the data. PC2 accounts for a further 14.8 percent of the total variance. The variables combining to constitute PC2 both refer to the giving of information. PC2 thus identifies mothers who

1. give additional information rather than simply announce the completion or inception of some activity or recall past events;
2. give explanations appealing to inherent consequences rather than to tradition.

Such mothers are significantly mothers of boys (p = .04).

In the following, Stephen's mother exemplifies such behavior. Stephen has just finished eating his lunch and begins to chew on a nearby blind cord:

(27)   *Mother:*   I don't think Nana wants her blind cord chewed. Yuk, it's filthy, darling, very dirty. All that dirt's going into your mouth and down into your tummy. It's really best not to fill your tummy with dirt. . . . Would you like some mandarin to put in your tummy instead?
       Stephen: Yes.

The core of this message to Stephen is that he is not to put the blind cord in his mouth. However, Stephen is bombarded with additional information: (a) the blind cord is filthy; (b) the filth is going into his system; (c) filth in the system is undesirable; (d) his grandmother possibly wouldn't like it. While (a), (b), and (c) are appeals to consequences inherent to the child's act, the status of (d) is somewhat ambiguous. Why would Nana not want "her blind cord chewed"? It is possible that she will be concerned for a possibly damaged blind cord or for the well-being of her grandson. Whatever the case, the rationale presented by Stephen's mother is a typical form of what Bernstein (1971, pp. 182–183) calls personal control. Where control is personal "Causal relations at the interpersonal level are made. . . . There is the appearance of the child having a choice (discretion). If the child raises a question more explanation is given. The mother, so to speak, lays out the situation for the child and the rule is learned in an individualised inter-personal context."

Bernstein distinguishes two modes of control: an imperative mode and a mode based on appeals. The latter mode is further distinguished on the basis of whether appeals are positional or personal. Where the

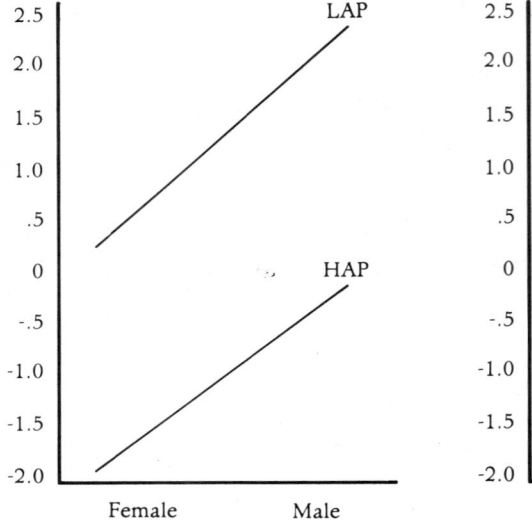

Figure 1(a). Mean scores on PC1

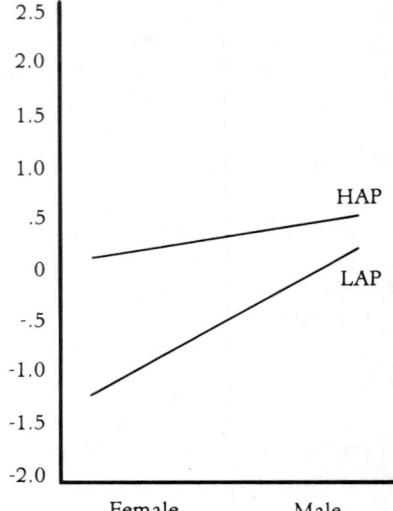

Figure 1(b). Mean scores on PC2

mode of control is imperative, the degree of role discretion accorded to the child is reduced, allowing the child "only the external possibilities of rebellion, withdrawal or acceptance" (Bernstein, 1971, p. 180). Where the mode of control is based on positional appeals, "the child is explicitly linked to others who hold a similar universal or particular status" (p. 181). Positional appeals refer the child's behavior to the behavior traditionally expected of members of his age, sex, family, or social group. Personal appeals, on the other hand, "focus on the child as an individual rather than upon his formal status" (p. 182). The basis of control by personal appeals "lies in linguistically elaborated individualised meanings" (p. 184).

Principal components 1 and 2 would appear to delineate two of the modes of control identified by Bernstein: PC1 indicates an "imperative" control style and PC2 a "personal" mode of control. Bernstein predicts that these contrasting modes of control are associated with the location of the family within the social structure. Analyses of variance of the scores of mothers on PC1 and PC2 show that the imperative mode of control is significantly associated with LAP mothers ($p = .003$), while the personal style of PC2 is associated, though not significantly, with HAP mothers. Figure 1 shows the association between mothers' control style and social group. Figure 1(a) is a graph of the mean scores of all mothers on PC1: imperative control style. LAP mothers of both boys and girls have a higher mean score than do HAP mothers. Figure 1(b) shows the mean scores of mothers on PC2: personal control style. Here, HAP mothers of boys and girls have a higher mean score.

In case one should be tempted to assign relative social value to these two control styles, it is worth noting that each style has both positive and negative consequences for the child. On the one hand, "where control is positional, and even more, where it is imperative, the child has a strong sense of social identity but the rules which he learns will be tied to specific contexts and his sense of autonomy may well be reduced" (Bernstein, 1971, p. 184). On the other hand, where control is personal the child attains autonomy though at the expense of a weakened social identity. "Such ambiguity in the sense of social identity . . . may move such children towards a radically closed value system and its attendant social structure" (p. 184).

Patterns in Children's Talk: The variables associated with PC1 for *children* delineate an attention-seeking pattern or behavior. Children who score high on this component

1. reiterate their own utterances;
2. announce that they have completed or are about to begin some activity;
3. provide support for their mothers in the form of sympathy and reassurance;
4. tend not to recall past events or happenings (for which, after all, assurance of the interactional partner's attention is necessary);
5. provide rationalizations by appeal to consequences that are inherent to an act. (This would seem to be characteristic of all children's rationalizations since such young children are in no position to appeal elsewhere when giving reasons, i.e., they are not yet sufficiently familiar with traditions to make these the basis of their appeals, nor do they have the power base necessary for serious appeal to such external consequences as bribes or threats.)

In order to exemplify some of the variables associated with PC1, let us consider the following extract. Rosie is playing ball in the house; her mother has cautioned her to throw the ball softly:

(28)   *Rosie:*   Mum, was that softly? . . . Was it? . . . Mummy, sorry
                  (AS MUM IS HIT)
       Mother: That wasn't very nice, Rosie
       Rosie: I'm sorry. . . . Mummy, I said sorry ⎡didn't I?
       Mother: ⎣Right, good girl

> *Rosie:*   I won't throw it at you. . . . Mummy, it won't hit the tape
> that's on
>
> *Mother:*   Don't throw it near the video

Here Rosie reiterates her question. Clearly her mother's attention is engaged elsewhere until she is hit by the ball. Rosie reiterates the apology, which was tendered even before her mother's reproach. The apology is again repeated until her mother indicates that it is accepted. Rosie then assures her mother not only that she won't be hit again but also that the ball won't hit the tape recorder either.

It is not always possible to exemplify all the variables associated with a component in one short extract of talk. The following extract from the same dyad illustrates variable 2 as well as variable 1. In this extract Rosie is again playing ball in the house:

(29)   *Rosie:*   I'm gonna play cricket. . . . Oh I [?   ]
       Mother: Where did you do that? . . . .
       Rosie: Mummy, I won; Mummy, I won
       Mother: Did you?

Analysis of variance of scores on this component indicates that this attention-seeking behavior tends to characterize girls more often than boys. However, this difference is just short of significance ($p = .08$).

PC2 has been excluded here since it is not associated, either directly or indirectly, with sex differences. The variables associated with PC3 delineate informative behavior in children. Children scoring high on PC3

1. provide explanations appealing to inherent consequences;
2. provide additional unsolicited information;
3. endeavor to make their meanings explicit by guiding their mothers' interpretation of their messages.

Andrew's remarks in the following extract exemplify the behavior identified by this component. Andrew's mother is preparing him for bed because he is too tired to undress himself:

(30)   *Andrew:*   I been in the sandpit
       Mother: Oh the sandpit at school, have you?
       Andrew: Yeah
       Mother: Oh I think you'd better have a bath after all, eh, if you've
       been in the sandpit
       Andrew: That's why I said
       Mother: Mm?

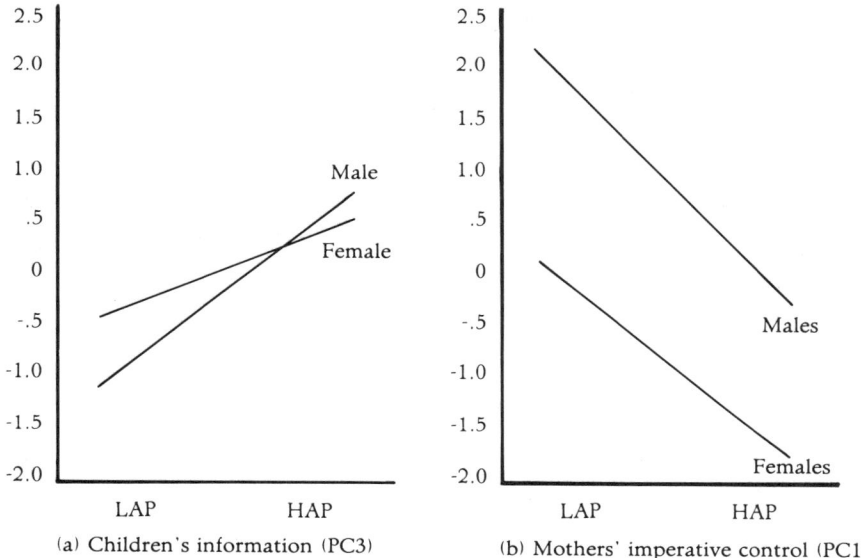

Figure 2. Mean scores by gender and social group

> *Andrew:* That's what I mean. That's why I said I have to have a bath.
> Got sand on my feet.

Andrew volunteers the information that he has been playing in the sandpit. His mother then realizes that he must therefore be more in need of a bath than she had anticipated. Andrew agrees: *That's why I said.* This is still apparently somewhat obscure and in response to his mother's *Mm?* he makes his meaning clear. Condensed in Andrew's message and perhaps left implicit because of his weary state is the explanation which may be glossed in the following terms: I played in the sandpit; consequently I've got sand on my feet; consequently I need to have a bath in order to be clean.

While sex differences in scores of these more or less "informative" children are not significant, there is a significant social group effect ($p = .01$). Furthermore, this component is negatively associated with that delineating mothers' imperative control style ($r = -.56$). Thus it seems that when mothers are highly direct in their control style, children are not given to volunteering information. This situation is represented graphically in Figure 2.

Figure 2 shows that the least "informative" children—LAP boys—are also the most highly imperatively controlled by their mothers. The least imperatively controlled children are HAP children and these are the most "informative".

Table 3. Variable Features of Principal Components Analysis II

	Mothers			Children	
Variable	PC1	PC2	PC3	PC1	PC2
1. Topic maintaining	.03	−.26	−.38	.26	−.24
2. Topic changing[a]	−.03	.26	.38	−.26	.24
3. Logical relationships	.11	−.33	−.34	.18	−.04
4. Actual time: past-present	−.44	−.15	.23	.34	.28
5. Actual time:habitual	−.10	−.22	−.41	.31	−.05
6. Possibility	.09	−.20	.40	−.36	.07
7. Prediction	.43	−.10	.15	−.27	−.36
8. Obligation	.25	.42	−.25	−.31	−.21
9. Total projection	.00	−.47	.00	−.16	.32
10. Projection: interpersonal	−.02	−.37	.07	−.15	.43
11. Projection: cognition	−.18	.18	.21	−.04	−.05
12. Projection: perception	.07	−.07	−.30	−.14	.29
13. Projection: verbal	.37	.21	−.07	.43	−.11
14. Projection: reaction	−.31	.10	−.17	.07	−.42
15. Projection: ability/permission	.32	−.05	.06	−.12	−.11
16. Nonassumptive	−.35	.21	−.25	.28	.28
17. Assumptive[a]	.35	−.21	.25	−.28	−.28
Eigenvalue	3.1	2.9	1.9	3.2	2.7
Percent total contribution per eigenvalue	21	19	13	21.7	18.5

Principal Components Analysis 2. Before considering this analysis separately for mothers and children, it is worth noting that some of the variables serve to distinguish mothers from children. Mothers are more likely than children to express assumptiveness, grant permission, change topic, and express modality. Mothers use different liguistic resources from those used by children to express point of view—either their own or that of others. Mothers express point of view mainly through modals, while children, being concerned with actuality, employ projecting clauses to make explicit the fact that a message is expressing their own ideas, perceptions, saying, and opinions, or those of others. This is not to say that modality is not a feature of children's talk or that mothers do not encode point of view via projections but simply that these features, when they occur on the components with which we are concerned, are negatively loaded.

Patterns in Mothers' Talk: The following interpretation and discussion will be concerned only with the second and third components as these alone are associated, directly or indirectly, with gender.

The variables involved most strongly in the delineation of PC2 indicate that mothers scoring high on this dimension

1. do not express point of view via projections (see Hasan, 1985b);
2. are concerned to make explicit obligations or absolute standards of behavior;
3. are not concerned to make explicit the connections between states of affairs.

This component is associated with that delineating mothers' imperative control style ($r = .48$). Two points should be made about this correlation. First, the fact that there is a positive association between the component identifying highly directly controlling mothers is to be expected since modals of obligation are used to encode direct commands. They are not used exclusively for this purpose, however; the encoding of direct commands is but one aspect of their use. The second point concerns the fact that the expression of obligation combines with the lack of encoding of point of view. These two features are not necessarily exclusive, that is, the use of one does not preclude the use of the other, a fact shown on the first component. It does appear, however, that mothers given to frequent or habitual use of direct commands tend to be the mothers who encode obligation in contexts other than that of control and such mothers tend not to express point of view. These mothers thus appear to be more concerned to sensitize their children to fixed patterns rather than to the possibilities of variation in perspective. Since highly directly controlling mothers tend to be mothers of boys, the fact of the association between this dimension of mothers' control style and that identifying obligation-expressing-non-point-of-view mothers suggests that it is mothers of boys who socialize their sons into these fixed patterns of being and behaving. David's mother exemplifies such behavior in extract (31); here she is bathing David:

(31) *David:*   I want to still play in here, Mum. It's nice and warm
      Mother: Bend over David . . . so I can do your ears. . . . Turn around. . . . Don't put the bath water in your mouth . . . Come on, time to get out. . . . Daddy'll be home soon. Quickly . . . come on, David. I've got to get the dinner on the stove. Just leave everything as it is, please, and get out . . . quick.

David's mother expresses not only his obligations but also her own: *I've got to get the dinner on the stove.* While she implicitly links what David has to do with the imminent arrival of his father, this circumstance is probably also the source of her own obligations—a fact David may or may not infer.

Girls, on the other hand, are sensitized to variation in possible ways of viewing the world, as indicated by the distribution of mothers on PC3. The variables involved most strongly in the delineation of PC3 indicate that mothers scoring high on this component tend

1. not to express habitual time;
2. not to encode obligation;
3. to express possibility;
4. to express assumptiveness;
5. not to make explicit the logical relations among messages.

These mothers are thus not concerned with absolute standards of behavior—neither the personal nor the traditional/communal type, but rather with the various possibilities that are open. Since they assume a certain rapport with the interactional partner, namely the child, the overt indication of the relations between states of affairs is not needed. These mothers of girls rather than mothers of boys ($p = .02$) tend not to be highly controlling on either of the two dimensions of control ($r = -.48$; $r = -.42$, respectively). Jenny's mother, in the following extract, is typical of the mothers who score high on this component. Jenny is helping her mother make little cupcakes and is having difficulty spooning the rather sloppy mixture into the trays:

(32)   *Mother:*   Mightn't be too easy, might it? Perhaps it's just a weeny bit difficult. Tell you what: you can have the spoon to lick and you can count for me
    Jenny: Yes
    Mother: Mm . . . It's not quite as easy as Mummy thought it might be for you

Jenny's mother expresses possibility using the median-value modals *might* and *can* and the modal adjunct *perhaps.* Assumptiveness in information seeking is indicated in her use of the negative in *Mightn't be too easy, might it?*

Support for the interpretation of these two dimensions of mothers' behavior—that they socialize their sons into fixed patterns of being and behaving while their daughters are sensitized to variation in possible ways of viewing the world—is to be found in the distribution of mothers and children on the second component of an analysis in which mothers and children were combined. The variables loading most strongly on this component are

1. probability/possibility, realized by median-value modals (Halliday, 1985b);

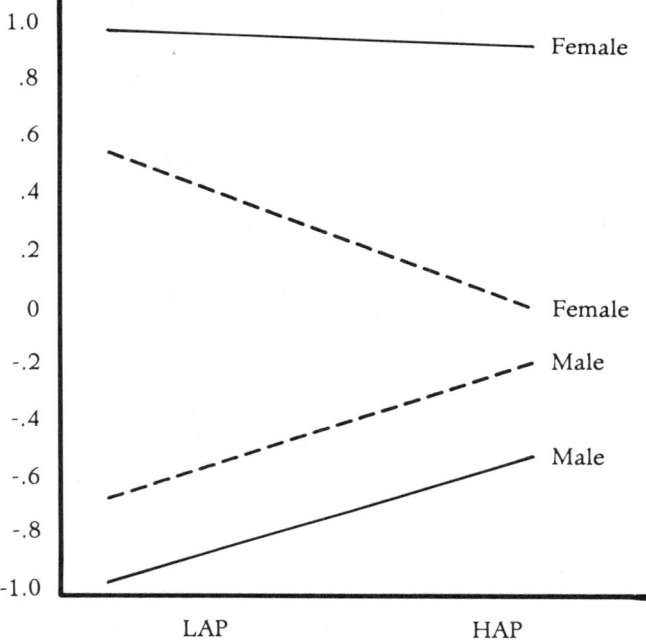

Figure 3. Mean scores of mothers (dotted lines) and children (solid lines) on point-of-view component

2. predictive time reference;
3. assumptiveness in information seeking;
4. actual (realized by past and present tense) and habitual time reference;
5. verbal projection

The first three variables are positively associated while the latter two are negatively loaded. Thus this component identifies mothers and children who are concerned with possibilities and probabilities/predictions rather than with actuality/usuality. These mothers and children take much for granted in their exchanges and tend not to be concerned with reporting or quoting their own or another's sayings. 'What could be' thus seems to dominate this component on which mothers of girls and girls themselves score significantly higher than mothers of boys and boys ($p =$ .007). The mean scores of both mothers and children on this component are shown in Figure 3.

A striking aspect of this component is the similarity in the scores of mothers and their sons ($r = .72$) in comparison with those of mothers and their daughters ($r = .29$). While Figure 3 represents the mean scores on this component, the similarity between mothers and sons is nevertheless evident. Figure 3 also shows that boys' scores tend toward the bottom end of the scale while girls' scores tend toward the upper end in comparison with those of their mothers. That girls tend even more than their mothers to be given to expressing point of view while boys do so even less frequently than their mothers suggests that there is more socialization pressure on boys to conform to "what is" as opposed to 'what could be.''

Also worthy of note in Figure 3 is the comparatively higher scores of LAP girls and their mothers; this suggests that, as a group, these girls are being more sensitized to the possibility of variation in perspective. This would appear to be a rather unexpected phenomenon. One possible explanation of this anomaly would be to consider LAP girls as the group most likely to be upwardly socially mobile. Logically an appreciation of the perspective of others would seem to be a prerequisite for the assimilation and, possibly, the transmission of the others' point of view (as when, for example, upward social mobility occurs via marriage). Given the potential social mobility of LAP girls, then, their sensitization to the possibility of variation in perspective is not surprising. Figure 3 thus provides a picture of an aspect of socialization to change as well as to maintenance.

Patterns in Children's Talk: The variables associated with PC1 indicate that the underlying dimension here is a concern with the "actual", including usuality. Boys score significantly higher than girls ($p = .04$) and, in addition to their concern with actuality, they tend to make their own and others' sayings the object of talk. In extract (33) below, Julian's talk illustrates the variables which identify this component. Julian is giving orders to the dog:

(33) *Julian:* Now stay there (TO DOG)
      Mother: All right, bossy boots
      Julian: Why do you say "bossy boots"?
      Mother: 'Cause you are
      Julian: Is that how you say it . . . Is it?
      Mother: Yep
      Julian: [?   ] . . . Mummy
      Mother: Mm
      Julian: Daddy said I—I could play down the park today

In Julian's exchanges with his mother, there are six clauses, five of which refer to actual/usual time. His concern with sayings is also evident: He queries the saying of his mother, reports that of his father, and seeks confirmation about the generalization he draws from his mother's saying (i.e., *Is that how you say it?* may be glossed as "Is that the communally recognized way of saying that a person is bossy?").

PC2 indicates that girls more than boys tend to express point of view—both their own and that of others—although this difference does not reach significance ($p = .1$). Children scoring high on PC2 tend to make explicit the fact that a message is their own or another's perception or opinion. Preferences, however, are not so encoded. Christine, in the following extract, exemplifies this behavior while playing with her doll:

(34)   *Christine:*   I think I better put it [?   ] I . . . I think it's very sunny now in the house. I better put this up . . . I better put this up 'cause it's very sunny. I better put this up
        Mother: Yes, you better
        Christine: 'Cause it's very sunny in the house
        Mother: You might hurt her eyes
        Christine: You see if she's crawling. You see if she's crawling

Christine, in her first two messages, makes it clear that what she should do is a matter of her own opinion, as is her reason for doing it. Her concern with her mother's perceptions *(You see if she's crawling!)* is possibly an attempt to engage her mother in active participation in the game.

From the previous discussion of Figure 3, the tendency for girls to score higher than boys on this point-of-view component is predictable.

The dimensions identified in this second principal components analysis of children's behavior confirm the previously stated view that girls are oriented to "what could be" while boys are oriented to "what is." Let us now speculate on the origin and function of these differing orientations, taking into account at the same time the associated social class differences.

The possibility of social change is an essential aspect of any theory about society and the transmission of culture. According to common wisdom as well as to anthropological scholarship (Friedl, 1975, p. 137), in modern industrial societies females in their primary role as caregivers are charged with the task of the transmission of (sub)cultural norms and expectations. In order that any change in these norms and expectations be assimilated and so transmitted, it would seem to be imperative that those responsible for their transmission be flexible enough in their attitudes to consider adapting their own ways of being and behaving to accommodate any changes and so to transmit them. Males, on the other hand, are by tradition charged with the task of providing food and shelter for their families. The ability to consider and adapt to the perspective of others would seem to be of greater or lesser importance, depending on location in the social division of labor. Occupations demanding a high degree of decision-making affecting the lives of others, for example, would seem to require such ability, but not so occupations involving the implementation of others' decisions. Thus, in terms of the future occupational expectations of the mothers for their children, the children's sensitization to point of view, as shown in Figure 3, is explicated. Girls are most sensitized to the possibility of variation in perspective since, as potential mothers themselves, they will need to adapt to and transmit changes in social values and expectations. LAP girls may have to adapt to and transmit the norms and expectations of the HAP group if they marry into it. HAP girls, as mothers, will need to socialize their sons as well as their daughters to point of view. HAP boys, as potential executives, must be aware of the point of view of others, but there is no such necessity for LAP boys.

The components in the second principal components analysis, while referring to mothers' and children's concern with actuality and point of view, have been interpreted at a higher order of meaning as identifying a dimension which is crucial to the process of subcultural transmission, maintenance, and change. It is only when the components are considered in relation to each other—children in relation to mothers, and mothers and children together—that this picture is built up. It may seem extraordinary to view 3½-year-olds as habitually encoding ways of being and behaving that are related to their future adult roles, yet at 3½ years children are rehearsing adult roles in many ways during the course of their daily activities and interactions (as was shown in the ethnographic section). These behaviors are not found to be remarkable, rather, they are expected, indeed demanded, as evidence of the development of gender-appropriate behaviors.

Coda. Analysis of the features of mother-child interaction by principal components procedure is still incomplete. One aspect of interaction yet to be included is the assignment by mothers to children and of children to themselves of such transitivity roles as actor/acted upon and benefactor/beneficiary (Hasan, 1985b). Preliminary tabulation of the frequency of occurrence of these categories indicates that there is, predictably, a gender influence particularly in the assignment by mothers of these roles and, to a lesser extent, the adoption of these roles by the children. Thus, when encoding benefaction, mothers almost exclusively assign to their sons the role of benefactor and to their daughters the role of beneficiary; and when children are assigned the role of ''actor'' they tend to be boys, while the ''acted upon'' tend to be girls. Given

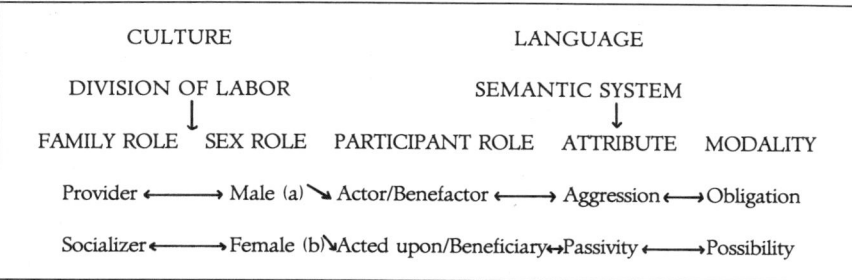

Figure 4. Language as the expression and the symbol of culture

the evidence from previous research in this area (e.g., Thwaite, 1983), and in the light of the preceding discussion, these findings are hardly surprising.

Summary

The principal components analyses presented in this section identified components describing underlying patterns in the behavior of mothers and their children and distinguished the boys and mothers of boys from girls and mothers of girls purely on the grounds of their linguistic behavior. It has been shown through statistical tests of significance on subjects' components scores that mothers of boys are more highly controlling, encoding obligation in other contexts as well as that of control and not encoding point of view. At the same time they tend to give more unsolicited information. Girls, on the other hand, are oriented by their mothers to "what could be" and are concerned with this themselves, unlike boys who, not surprisingly, are more concerned with actuality. The fact that girls more than boys bid for their mothers' attention reflects the fact that, on the whole, girls are given less attention than are boys.

CONCLUSION

Halliday (1977, p. 25) notes that language serves "both as a vehicle and as a metaphor, both maintaining and symbolising the social system." The study of the social construction of gender presented in this chapter can be shown to illustrate this point. Let us consider the following diagram.

In Figure 4 the slanting arrows indicate a realization relationship between categories, the vertical arrows indicate that the relationship between categories is one of subordination and the horizontal arrows indicate an associative relationship. Thus we say that any aspect of the culture, such as the division of labor, is realized by or expressed in the semantic system of that culture's language. Family roles are aspects of the division of labor and are associated with sex roles. These roles are realized by (expressed through) categories of the semantic system, specifically participant roles, attributes, and modality which are therefore associated. The family roles are those of Provider and Socializer. These are realized linguistically by the selections made in the semantic categories: Participant Roles, Attribute, and Modality.

Let us focus, for the moment, on the subcategories of the semantic system, putting to one side the fact that the values of these semantic subcategories are realizing aspects of the division of labor in the culture. There are no linguistic reasons for the above correlations of specific participant role-attribute-modality configurations with male or female. To put it another way, if (a) and (b)—the specific values of the semantic subcategories—are considered to be structures, there is nothing in the linguistic system to prevent a member of a particular subcategory—for example, participant role in (a) being freely interchangeable with a member of the same subcategory in (b). Thus, from the point of view of the linguistic system, the following combination is permitted:

PARTICIPANT ROLE	ATTRIBUTE	MODALITY
Actor/Benefactor	Passivity	Possibility

Such a combination is, however, ruled out if one is seeking to describe the structure that realizes the Male (or for that matter the Female) Family role. The structures (a) and (b), then, are seen as the linguistic realizations of a higher-order semiotic, namely, the sex roles operating in the culture.

Now there is nothing in the structures (a) and (b) to indicate any inherent value. Value is revealed only by considering (a) in relation to (b). It is then that we see that the terms in the semantic subcategories are in opposition in each structure. The paradigmatic relations between the two structures are thus antonymous. But which is the more valued habitual form of talk, and how is this value transmitted? The answers to these questions are to be found in the empirical account of mother-child interaction. Recall that mothers attended to boys more than to girls in that boys were controlled more and given more information by their mothers, who also tended to maintain the topic of talk with boys. The fact that boys tend to receive more attention from their interactional partners—in this case the mothers—is recognized by girls who, more than boys, tend to bid for their mothers' attention. Thus it is through the style of mothers' interaction with their sons and daughters that the cultural value of each of the sexes is established. In the same way the cultural significance of each is transmitted for, as Goffman (1977, p. 314) points out, "family life ensures that most of what each sex does is done in the full sight of the other sex and with full mutual appreciation of the differential treatment that obtains."

The examination in this chapter of the social construction of gender has attempted to illustrate the importance of what Whorf (1956, pp. 258–261) called "patternment" in language. In the social construction of gender, sex role identities and behaviors are built up through the patterns of language, rather than through referential items such as those indicated by the grammatical encoding of gender in a language. Sapir (1949, p. 26) points out that "the cultural significance of linguistic form . . . lies on a much more submerged level than on the overt one of definite cultural pattern." On this submerged level, then, lie the sets of linguistic patterns or, in Hasan's (1986, p. 143) terms "a constellation of patterns in rapport with each other." In Figure 4, the constellation of Actor/Benefactor + Aggression + Obligation is one such constellation; this constellation in the data discussed is associated with male gender.

The principal components analyses have shown that these configurations of linguistic patterns may be considered correlations within language itself, not because the linguistic system determines such configurations but because these patterns are correlated also with the social system, as the analysis of variance of component scores has shown. In this way the system of language is said to provide the resources for the social construction of meaning. This study of the social construction of gender thus accords with Halliday's (1977, p. 17) recommendation: "The questions of sociolinguistics . . . involve correlations of some kind between language and society. . . . These may need to be approached through a consideration of correlations that are found within language itself."

The preservation of the division of labor based on sex/family roles is often justified by appeal to the natural environment, that is, to the biological facts of pregnancy, childbirth, and the dependence of the young on the mother for succor. In other words, the person who bears the children is seen as the natural choice for the task of socializing them. Stated in these terms, the argument is less contentious than appeals to the social environment, that is, to the greater suitability of women for the task because of personality attributes. Since suitability in terms of personality is, as we have seen, a socially constructed phenomenon, there is no reason why males could not learn the task-appropriate behaviors, given the opportunity. Men and women have much more in common than the culture, through its linguistic patterns, would have us believe. The mutually exclusive categories indicated in the linguistic patterns are social, not natural, constructs. To learn the gender-appropriate ways of being and behaving (Hasan, 1984c) involves, in some degree, the suppression of behaviors considered gender-inappropriate. As Rubin (1975, p. 180) observes, such insistence upon the division of personality oppresses everyone.

To paraphrase Lakoff (1975), men and women produce the speech they do, not just because it is how men and women are naturally inclined to speak but because it fits with the personalities they develop as a consequence of sex role requirements. It has been argued in this chapter that children construct through language the social reality of gender and its requirements. The ethnographic account showed how children learn to classify ways of being and behaving, using gender as a basic principle of classification and how, in daily routine interactions with mothers and significant others, they learn the details of the culturally specified gender-appropriate behaviors. The empirical account tried to show how habitual forms of communication are associated with the higher-order semiotic, which, based in the social and gender-specific division of labor, views the female as responsible for the transmission of the culture to the next generation and the male as responsible for the economic maintenance of the family and of the social structural status quo.

It is not remarkable that the gender division of labor is resistant to change, since the ranking member of the two sexes—the male—is oriented to the maintenance of the status quo, namely, to "what is." Females, being oriented to "what could be" and to variation in perspective, are in a better position to create and adapt to change, but being of lesser rank and therefore lesser power they rarely find themselves in a position to implement changes. Rather, women expect, and are expected, to adapt to the existing states of affairs, and this applies to the position of women in other institutions as well as the family. Thus the status quo remains, since its adherents hold the power. In the foregoing discussion I have argued that this situation is due not to a conspiracy, as has been suggested by some writers, but rather to different orientations originating in socialization practices which once were (but can no longer be held to be) functional. Thus it seems that change can occur only when the status quo is questioned, as it has been more and more during the last 25 years, thanks to the consciousness-raising efforts of feminist critique. The examination of habitual forms of communication presented in this chapter shows, however, that the division of labour based on gender is very much alive and well and firmly entrenched in households in Sydney and surrounding suburbs.

CHAPTER 4

LANGUAGE DEVELOPMENT IN EDUCATION

Frances Christie

Deakin University
Victoria, Australia

1. INTRODUCTION

The difficulty with language is that it is invisible: so much taken for granted that its true significance in the structuring of school experience, and hence in the processes of school learning, is consistently over-looked. Indeed, in the late 20th century, for reasons to do with the steady growth of public education over the last 200 years, teachers now operate in schools with a number of traditional attitudes about educa-tion that effectively diminish and sometimes even deny the role of lan-guage in schooling. Such an observation may seem somewhat surprising, for since the 1960s in particular we have witnessed a considerable growth in interest in language and learning throughout the English-speaking world, and it is sometimes suggested therefore that in contemporary educational practice language is now accorded its due significance.

It is true that since the '60s, and partly because of the contributions of scholars such as Halliday (e.g., the Nuffield/Schools Council Pro-gramme in Linguistics and English Teaching; see Chapter 7 in this vol-ume) and others, there has been considerable interest in research into language and its role in schools. However, useful though many of the new directions and initiatives have been, they have nonetheless been hampered by older and stronger traditions of thinking about learning and knowledge, whose effect has been to give language a peripheral rather than central status in discussions of schooling.

Specifically, as part of our broader cultural tradition, and not uniquely as a feature of schooling, a strong belief prevails by which both knowl-edge and intellectual skills of various kinds are understood to have sta-tus in some way independent of the language patterns in which they come into being. At best, in most contemporary discussion of curriculum practice, "skills" in using language are normally acknowledged as important in promoting growth in "thinking," and in developing control of "content" or knowledge. But "language skills" are generally understood to develop alongside a range of other skills—"cognitive," "emotional," and "social," such that these are viewed as having parallel yet independent existence. Similarly, "knowledge" or "content" to be learned is understood to have a status independent both of language in particular, and, in general, of the various kinds of desired intellectual skills that schools are intended to confer. It is certainly true that schools *are* in the business of teaching knowledge and of developing various desirable mental skills. However, the central role language has in the development of these things remains obscured because language is perceived to have no more than an "instrumental" function. In the prevailing views, language is an essentially neutral if useful commodity which merely serves to "give expression" to the thoughts, ideas, and information that individuals acquire. Rarely in practice is it acknowledged that the development of the desired mental skills is entirely dependent on mastery of the linguistic patterns in which these skills are realized. Equally rarely is it acknowledged that "knowledge" itself is constructed in varying patterns of discourse.

To understand why this is the case, it will be useful briefly to review some of the major trends in the development of educational theory which have been responsible, for in doing this we can establish a context within which to consider what actually happens in the name of language education in many contemporary schools. In the light of this discussion, we will examine in detail one teaching episode involving a class of young children learning to write. We will argue that the activity offers very limited learning experience, in that no useful knowledge is learned, and that this is because the language the children learn is itself so limited. Further, we will argue that this limitation comes about because the teacher assumes she can separate content and language skills. Like many teachers of young children, she seeks to develop literacy skills in a manner that suggests these can be usefully developed apart from considerations of content. The result, we will suggest, is that neither literacy nor grasp of knowledge is significantly enhanced.

2. THE EDUCATIONAL TRADITION

The study of education, as it began to emerge in the 19th century, blossoming into a major area of enquiry in the 20th, has always focused on two related preoccupations, evidence for which can be found both in the early manuals about teaching practice developed for the first teacher-training institutions in the 19th century, and in contemporary studies of education as taught in universities and colleges of education.

The first preoccupation has always been pedagogical, dealing with what are deemed to be desirable principles of teaching, and hence of directing and guiding children's learning. In the 19th century, this involved a concern with "classroom management," and in the 20th century, it has been variously referred to by such terms as "teaching methods," "teaching methodology," "classroom practices," and, more recently, "classroom processes." The shift from the term "management" to "process" no doubt reflects a general interest in processes in the late-20th-century social sciences. As a term, it does imply a greater awareness of the dynamic nature of human behavior than does the term "management," and the distinction is to that extent an important one. However, while this represents an important shift in emphasis, it remains true that the preoccupation with understanding what steps teachers should take in order to guide their students' learning has remained a constant theme in educational research and thinking, so that it continues to constitute a significant element in the professional studies offered to teachers.

The other preoccupation has been with theories of learning, and with notions about the processes of children's mental growth. Childhood is perceived as a significantly different period of life from either infancy or adulthood, and, together with adolescence, which has been in particular a 20th-century area of interest, it has been the focus of a great deal of educational research. Generally speaking, such research has sought to identify the characteristics and the needs of children and of adolescents, with a view to understanding how they learn. Courses in "learning processes" and the like currently constitute significant areas of study in the professional preparation of teachers.

Associated with both the broad preoccupations we have identified are a number of important if frequently unacknowledged ideologies about the nature of persons, about the nature of human development, and also about the nature of knowledge.

A fundamental belief about the educational process has always been that it will enhance the development of persons, able, as one 19th-century authority put it, "to *live* a fuller, a richer, a more interesting and a more useful life" (Fitch, 1880, p. 34). This theme has been in particular associated with a view of persons as *individuals*: a major function of schooling is the development of individuals, capable of exercising independence of judgment and point of view. One recent Australian curriculum document intended to guide teachers in planning their work with children in primary social science adopts as a basic background assumption "the belief that a major goal of education is to aid the individual in his growth as an active, thinking participant of society'' (Education Department of Victoria, 1981, p. 3). "Individual growth" and "individual difference" have both, in the 20th century, become important notions which are dealt with in teacher training and which, theoretically at least, teachers are asked to take into account when planning and implementing educational programs.

If we are quickly to characterize the individual so conceived, it is as a person possessed of certain inborn features and attributes of a distinctive kind. It is these that give the person "individuality." The successful individual also learns to function appropriately in a social sense, responding to society and its demands, while retaining his or her individuality. In this tradition of thinking, the individual exists independently of society and must learn to become part of society, learning how to reconcile the claims of individual needs and those of social responsibilities. One function of schooling will be to enable the individual to learn to act responsibly in relation to society. In other words, persons achieve identity as a consequence of inner and inborn characteristics, and these characteristics essentially shape the identity recognized by others. Society itself has little significance in shaping the individual, though it is certainly recognized that the person must function responsibly as a member of society.

It is just such a view of individuality, long established in our Western tradition of education, that Halliday actually challenges when he suggests that humans are primarily social beings, who shape and structure their identity in the complex processes of interaction with others which commence at birth, and which remain critically important in defining the nature of the person throughout all of life.

The prevailing view of individuality, it should be noted, presents a number of significant theoretical problems, not all of which it will be necessary to comment on here. However, it is noteworthy that a reified view of the individual and of that individual's processes of development throughout childhood and adolescence does cause difficulties precisely because it neglects the social. That is to say, it neglects to have any clear perspective on the ways children develop as they interact with and are guided by significant adults. Good educational programs must involve direct intervention by teachers in the selection of learning activities, in identification of strengths and weaknesses in children's school performance, and in the provision of appropriate models for children to learn. A theory of persons as shaped primarily in response to innate or inborn capacity rather than to the needs and challenges of interacting satisfactorily with others, necessarily has little of use to say about any of these matters. Educational discussion for many years has been bedeviled by constant argument over the need to 'make theory relevant to practice.'

A theory of individuality that is not informed by any rigorous understanding of how individuality is shaped in social processes simply has nothing of use to say about practice.

Prevailing theories of children's development have always had important consequences for a great deal of school practice. For example, children come to school, so tradition would suggest, to develop various skills and abilities, and to acquire significant and useful knowledge. They will do these things in deliberately planned and structured phases or steps through which they will pass: hence the practices of grading children, which commence soon after their entry to school. Hence too the processes of curriculum planning, by which programs of work in different school subjects or 'content areas' are devised for the successive years of schooling, with an intended increase in difficulty over time.

Nowadays, so most programs for the training of teachers and most guidance to teachers in schools indicate, it is argued that since knowledge is constantly changing, the skills to be developed in children are more important than the knowledge to be learned. The Australian social science curriculum document cited earlier, for example, refers to the "knowledge explosion," associated among others things with "the requirement of the individual to handle vast amounts of information" and "the continual revision of theories and the consequent rejection of notions once believed to be true, which means that it is no longer possible for an individual to learn, when he is young, all of the facts that he might need to know during his life. . . . Later, the document notes that "traditionally, the teacher's role has been the dissemination of information. Effective teaching methods were considered to be those which resulted in pupils retaining large amounts of specific information, that is, learning a large number of specific facts." But in the contemporary world, and because of the knowledge explosion, the teacher must help children learn "to organise knowledge" and to think (Education Department of Victoria, 1981, pp. 4–7). Mental skills and abilities properly developed, so the argument goes, equip children to move into subsequent new life experiences, and into capacity to process and deal with new knowledge and information; but mere acquisition of 'content' or knowledge will not equip children to encounter and deal with new knowledge and life experiences.

Skills and content, it should be noted, are thus understood as clearly separable. It is a separation, as we hope to demonstrate, that has had very serious consequences for much educational practice.

Historically, the tradition of making such a separation goes back a long way, back indeed to the Greeks. For the present discussion, however, it will be sufficient to go back to the 19th century, and to the educational theory that was a feature of the first teacher-training institutions which opened their doors in that period. This educational theory not only became the subject of a large number of textbooks for teachers, but it also formed the basis of various official circulars prepared for the guidance of teachers in schools. This discussion draws to some extent on official advice to Australian colonial schools (reviewed in Christie, 1976), but it is based primarily on an examination of several of the textbooks produced in England and, in one case, in Australia (Currie, who produced two influential volumes, n.d., but used extensively throughout much of the century; Dawes, also not dated; Dunn, 1837; Fitch, 1880; Gill, 1883; Gladman, n.d.; Laurie, 1867; Robinson, 1867; Wilkins, 1886).

Fundamental to the prevailing educational theories throughout the 19th century as a belief in the presence of mental faculties. The term 'faculty'' (itself taken originally from the Scholastics) referred both to a mental power or ability and to the process or mental operation implicit in that ability. Certain laws, it was held, governed the existence and growth of faculties, and these were essentially the same in all individuals. They were all intimately related, and they developed in a deliberate ascending order, each dependent on both the successful development and the continuing exercise of the earlier ones. A paramount function of schooling was "the training of the faculties" (Fitch, 1880, p. 199). The emergence of a faculty in any child would be apparent in the ability to do certain things, and it was the teacher's business to understand what these things were, in order to recognize the stage of development reached by the child, as well as to understand what activities should be introduced to foster or "exercise" the different faculties.

In infancy, strictly speaking, there were no faculties present as such, though the potential for their emergence was present at this point, principally in the existence of the five sense. Stimulation of the senses was a necessary part of preparation for faculty development. The first faculties to emerge in early childhood were the imitative, perceptive, and language faculties (some authorities differed in the terms they used, but those used here are the most representative). The imitative faculty involved such matters as ability to distinguish size, weight, and shape, or to reproduce simple objects in drawing. The perceptive faculty involved ability to distinguish simple relations between objects. Significantly, the language ability was understood as ability to "attach labels" to objects.

Later childhood involved the representative faculty (also known as "conceptive" or "cognitive"), which was expressed in a number of abilities, including the ability to use language with ease, especially in reading. There was also some development of the imaginative faculty, involving such matters as ability to concentrate, to memorize, to form ideas, to compare and classify, and finally, to imagine, though since this faculty was a "higher-order faculty," belonging in particular to the creative impulse, it was held to be fully developed only after the years of schooling had finished. A faculty belonging to the period of youth was that of reasoning or judgment, involving abilities to generalize, to reason, and to abstract.

All of the abilities thus referred to (with the possible exception of some aspects of the imaginative faculty) belonged loosely to what in the 20th century would become known as the "cognitive domain" of development. There was in addition another faculty whose development, it was held, followed after the emergence of that of reasoning: it was the development of "sentiment" or of feeling, involving the growth of finer feelings and sensibilities of a kind stimulated in particular, for example, by the reading of poetry. Loosely, the faculty referred to here (as well as aspects of the imaginative faculty) would in the 20th century come to be identified as belonging to the domain of "affective development."

Where in the 19th century educational theorists wrote of the faculties and their development, in the 20th they were to think in terms of developmental stages and associated learning tasks (Connell, 1980, p. 67), and they were to ponder how the nature and sequence of the stages and tasks might be determined. "The really important question for the teacher," wrote one theorist early in the century, "is this: What are the conditions that must be fulfilled before the mind is prepared for a new step in development? . . . If we know the conditions and can control them, we can then produce the phenomenon at such a time as we may deem appropriate" (Judd, 1903, quoted in Connell, 1980, p. 97). Educational interest in developmental stages and tasks was to remain an important theme in courses for the preparation of teachers throughout the 20th century. The present writer can recall, for example, course work in her own professional preparation in the late 1950s that examined the concept of children's "developmental tasks" as treated by Havighurst (1953).

Turning from theories of development to theories of knowledge, in the 19th century a distinction was drawn between that which was "instrumentary" and that which was "general" knowledge (Currie, n.d.-b, pp. 74–85). While authorities differed over what they included in the second category, all agreed that the "instrumentary" group included literacy and numeracy, for acquisition of these was instrumental to the learning of other forms of knowledge.

This view of knowledge was in many ways consistent with the view of human growth and cognition implicit in faculty psychology. Certainly, it is clear that in both cases the view of language was the same in relation to knowledge. Language was essentially just a useful instrument. Even the language faculty which developed in early childhood was understood primarily as the ability to label objects. Thoughts, skills, ideas, information, all existed at some "higher-order" plane than language: language merely "clothed" or "gave expression" to these.

With the expansion of 20th-century psychology, attention turned away from the notion of "faculties," and though few psychologists today would use the term, most remain interested in such notions as mental development, cognitive development, and social and emotional development. In addition, school practices, supported by much educational psychology, have tended to propose the presence of "stages" of growth—mental, emotional, social, as well as physical—through which children pass in the process of achieving maturity. It is true that some contemporary psychologists now actually question the evidence for the existence of stages of mental growth. Nonetheless, schools continue to operate with a tacit understanding that such stages do exist. Thus, children are normally graded in schools, always on the basis of age, and frequently, in addition, on the basis of "levels of ability," as measured by IQ tests, or on "levels of attainment" of various kinds, as measured by scholastic testing of some sort or other. Frequently, grading is done on the basis of a combination of IQ and scholastic scores. The traditional separation of mental skills and knowledge remains, and language is still largely invisible in prevailing conceptions of the nature of both mental development and knowledge.

The Taxonomy of Educational Objectives (Bloom, Englehart, Furst, Hill, & Krathwohl, 1956; Krathwohl, Bloom, & Masia, 1964) probably provided the 20th century with its most thoroughly systematic model of a view of teaching and learning in terms of sets of mental skills. These mental skills were thought of as apart from language on the one hand, and from knowledge, on the other. Though a large number of people worked on the Taxonomy, it has frequently been referred to simply as Bloom's Taxonomy. Planned initially at a meeting of the American Psychological Association Convention in Boston in 1948, the Taxonomy aimed to adapt the notion of a biological taxonomy to the needs of education, more specifically of examination of educational objectives. It was "intended to provide for classification of the goals of our educational system" (Bloom et al., 1956, p. 1). While it was thus principally a tool for evaluation and assessment, its developers argued that it could also be a source of help in planning curriculum activities generally. Significantly, the Taxonomy was planned and its categories created by reference both to prevailing teaching practice and to the kinds of categories and procedures teachers commonly used and therefore felt comfortable with, and also to contemporary accepted psychological principles and theories. It was therefore no innovatory document: in the principles the

Taxonomy adopted, it sought to systematize existing practices rather than introduce new ones, and its categories thus offered a very complete reflection of prevailing attitudes toward mental development and knowledge.

Three broad domains of educational effort were identified: cognitive, affective, and psychomotor. In practice, nothing was done about the last domain since on the evidence schools did little about promoting development in this area. Within the cognitive domain two broad areas were identified: that of "knowledge," and that of "intellectual abilities and skills." The areas of knowledge involved at one end knowledge of "specific and isolable bits of information." The material identified here was "at a very low level of abstraction," and might be thought of as "the elements from which more complex and abstract forms of knowledge are built" (Bloom et al., 1956, p. 201). At the upper level of abstraction there was "knowledge of theories and structures," involving "knowledge of the *body* of principles and generalizations together with their interrelations which present a clear, rounded, and systematic view of a complex phenomenon, problem, or field" (p. 204). Of the intellectual abilities and skills, that at the "lowest level of understanding" was "comprehension" of material (p. 204), which subsequent categories built up over areas to do with "analysis," "synthesis," and, thence to the highest level of "evaluation," involving at first judgments in terms of "internal evidence," and later judgments in terms of "external criteria," for instance, "the ability to compare a work with the highest known standards in its field—especially with other works of recognized excellence" (p. 204).

The volume devoted to the "affective domain" noted that this was an area in which it was difficult to set up principles of classification because less was done systematically about promoting development in this area in schools, than in the cognitive domain. Nonetheless, some principal categories were created which were arranged again in an ascending order of levels. They were: "receiving" or "attending," "responding," "valuing," "organization," and "characterization by a value or value complex." While the first three are probably self-evident, a word or two may be needed to explain the latter two. It was held that at the fourth level of organization, the learner has been internalizing values, which now achieve some organization into a value system. At the final level, the values, now arranged into some kind of hierarchy and in some "internally consistent system," are generalizable, and they assume the character of the individual's "philosophy of life" (Krathwohl et al.; 1964, pp. 184–185).

The entire two volumes of the Taxonomy were remarkable for a number of reasons, not all of which need be discussed here. Principally we should note as relevant to the present discussion the complete absence of any serious discussion of or interest in language. As had been the case a century before, to the extent to which language rated a mention at all, it was in an essentially neutral and expressive role that it was understood. Thus, for example, in the cognitive domain, mention was made of the need for ''knowledge of conventions,'' where this involved ''familiarity with the forms and conventions of the major types of works, e.g., verse, plays, scientific papers, etc.'' Pupils, it was also noted, should be made ''conscious of correct form and usage in speech and writing'' (1956, p. 202). Discussed in these terms, knowledge of language ''conventions'' was perceived as no more than knowledge of linguistic good manners. A kind of etiquette applied, was the implication, and it was necessary that children learn it in order to give appropriate expression to the new knowledge they acquired.

In fact, with a more sophisticated appreciation of the significance of language, of the kind Halliday's work in particular has made possible, it would have been recognized that those who wrote the literary pieces referred to—verse or plays—and those who wrote the scientific papers also identified in passing needed to exercise choices in the linguistic system to realize the kinds of meanings, or to construct the kinds of knowledge, that were their concern. Capacity to exercise these choices is very much a matter of opportunity, so that a primary responsibility of schooling will be to teach children to be able to make such choices. Following Halliday, we would argue that each generic pattern or linguistic form represents a culturally significant and valued way of ''making money,'' as Kress (1982) set out to demonstrate in his study of writing development, and as Martin and Rothery (1980, 1981) have also demonstrated in their study of children's writing development. Understood from this point of view, the so-called language conventions and the various linguistic patterns they help to shape are essential to successful production of any ''content.'' Thus, for example, the content of science—be it a natural science such as physics or chemistry, or a social science such as history or sociology—comes into being in characteristic discourse patterns. To learn the content of a science is therefore necessarily to learn the linguistic patterns in which that content is encoded or comes into being. Similarly, to learn to make the meanings particular to literature, or mathematics, geography, economics, or any other other ''content area,'' is to learn to deal with experience in certain characteristic ways, all of which are recognizable only because they are created in distinctive patterns of language.

Much contemporary discussion about children's writing development continues to be confused by debate over the apparently rival claims of ''conventions'' and ''content,'' or of ''form'' and ''content.'' This is principally because researchers persist in seeing a distinction where none really exists. Reviewing several models of English teaching as they were originally described by Dixon (1967), Wilkinson, Barnsley, Hanna, and Swan (1980, p. 5) comment on the "skills model," which they argue had some value, though in others ways it was limited. "By working on spelling, punctuation, paragraphing, direct and reported speech, forms of address in letters, arrangement in composition, one can certainly make improvements in performance." But, they go on, such a model is inadequate because it "concentrates on mechanics and techniques of expression rather than on the nature and quality of what is expressed." The tendency to concentrate on such matters as spelling, grammar, and punctuation particularly at public examinations, they note, causes these to be overemphasized at the expense of "more ambiguous features such as style or imagination."

One can agree that a preoccupation with such things as spelling and punctuation is an insufficient basis for the teaching of writing, particularly where these are pursued as ends in themselves, and out of any context of real use. However, the difficulty with the way Wilkinson puts his argument is that he begs the question of what constitutes a written text of "quality," showing good "style" and "imagination." A language model that recognizes that the act of writing always involves the selection and creation of a particular linguistic pattern, genre, or form will also recognize that the successful production of a genre demonstrating the qualities of good style alluded to must involve appropriate selection of all the relevant linguistic features. That is to say, all aspects of the English writing system are essential features of the actual text produced; they are necessary elements of the way it means. It is for this reason that the distinction between convention and content is seriously misleading and unhelpful.

Among many educationists, the call to resist a preoccupation with conventions takes on the character of a defense of the individual against undesirable conformity. In a discussion of the strengths and limitations of the approach to curriculum involved in Bloom's Taxonomy, Stenhouse (1975, p. 59) quoted one statement of objective devised by Popham and Baker in 1970:

> The student will write a 500-word essay with a topic sentence, development by example, and a concluding statement. The topic of this essay will be Negro contributions to the culture of the United States.

Stenhouse dismissed this on the grounds that it seemed to him to "stereotype undesirably the pattern of the essay" (1975, p. 60) Elsewhere, he wrote of the essay (a term by which he meant "not merely a written piece, but also an oral performance or a painting or the playing of a piece of music or designing and making a standard lamp'') that it ''should be individual and creative and not attempt to meet a prespecification'' (1975, p. 82).

Like Moffett (1981), a contemporary American authority on writing, Stenhouse appears to see ''conventions'' and their control in writing as leading to clichés, and to the loss of individual creativity. This is a particularly unfortunate position to adopt, principally because it is confused about the nature of individual creativity and how it is developed. The confusion is brought about by the well-established tendency in our intellectual tradition referred to earlier, to focus on the individual rather than the social. As Halliday has noted more than once (e.g., 1974, p. 48), when we shift our attention from man the individual to man as ''social man,'' we are forced to focus on the complex of human relationships and activities in which persons interact, shaping and defining their identities. A principal behavioral resource with which persons do these things is their language. We regularly operate in socially defined contexts of situation, in which, in order to operate successfully at all, we must select the appropriate behavioral resources, including the linguistic ones. Thus, in writing as much as in speaking, we must select the ''conventional'' linguistic patterns appropriate to the meanings we need to make. A primary function of schooling is that children be taught to recognize and use conventions in language, precisely because that is a necessary part of learning how to mean successfully in their culture. Once children have mastered the conventions, as is the case for skilled adult writers, they can manipulate and experiment with them. It is in this process of manipulation and experimentation that the capacity for individual self-expression so valued by Stenhouse, Moffett, and others is actually achieved.

Like Bernstein (1973), with whom Halliday worked closely for some years, Halliday has argued that in an important sense much school failure is language failure: failure to understand and use the linguistic patterns appropriate to the range of information, attitudes, and ideas valued in schools. The reason Stenhouse's position in particular is so unhelpful is that it fails to acknowledge that essays of the type he dismisses as stereotypical are among the number of linguistic patterns children need to master in order to be successful in their school learning. Where teachers neglect to teach appropriate essay forms they disadvantage many of the children in their care. In general, we would argue, the children who cope despite such a failure on their teachers' part are those who share and understand many of the ways of working valued in schools, and to which Bernstein referred when he wrote of ''elaborated codes.'' Those who fail to cope, not managing to master essay forms, among other aspects of their schooling, are those operating with "restricted codes," which, relevant though they are in many contexts, too often provide little entry to the language of school learning.

As we earlier noted, the Taxonomy was remarkable for the thoroughness with which it constructed its categories of human development from prevailing teaching practices, as these were sampled in the United States, at any rate, and it pursued the implications of these categories for curriculum planning very fully. When it first appeared, the Taxonomy was cited as authoritative, though it is difficult to estimate how widely it was actually employed throughout the English-speaking world. Certainly, it was extensively used in the US and received a great deal of attention in other English-speaking countries, and attempts were made to devise whole approaches to curriculum design based on it. The Taxonomy did subsequently fall into disuse, and it is rarely cited today.

However, its general tendency to view human development in terms of a set of independent categories remains, as does the tendency to see language development as merely instrumental to development in the other "higher-order" areas of cognitive or mental growth. The study by Wilkinson and his colleagues (1980), for example, cited earlier, proposes four models of development of the human mind, which underlie the approach adopted to the study of children's development in writing. The four are a cognitive model, an affective one, a moral one, and a stylistic one. The study seeks to elicit principles by which development in children's writing in each of these areas may be analyzed. Though Wilkinson claims a degree of originality (Wilkinson et al., 1980, pp. 44–45) for the model of human development he proposes, as the above discussion should have served to demonstrate, he operates with what are in fact certain time-honored and very familiar assumptions about the nature of the human mind, about knowledge, and about the role of language. Like many educationists and scholars before him, and like many others in contemporary educational discussion, he maintains the tradition by which knowledge and skills, including language skills, are separated, and language is assigned the relatively lowly and largely invisible status of being merely expressive of knowledge and skills.

3. LANGUAGE AND KNOWLEDGE IN THE CONTEMPORARY SITUATION

Today, most curriculum practices, like most discussions about learning in schools, are posited on an assumed separation of knowledge and skills and equally on an assumed "instrumental" or "expressive" function of language in the acquisition of knowledge and in the development of desired mental, emotional and social skills.

The deleterious effects of the continuing tendency to separate language and "content" or knowledge may be seen at all levels of education, including tertiary. However, they are particularly marked in the earliest years of schooling. It is there that literacy is first established, and it is there too that in many subtle ways children are initiated into the processes of formal education. We will shortly examine one teaching/learning episode involving 25 children in year 2, their third year of schooling, with a view to considering how the traditional assumptions about language and knowledge fundamentally determine the course the activity takes, and hence the language the children use. We will argue that where the teacher works with a view that considerations of language skills may be divorced from considerations of content or knowledge, then neither the skills developed nor the content dealt with may be said to be of a useful or rewarding kind. Significant language skills, we will suggest, can be developed only in contexts where the need is to grapple with significant meanings, and hence to construct significant knowledge.

In the discussion above it was argued at one point that when students learn the different subjects or "disciplines" of schooling, be they mathematics, one of the natural or social sciences, or English literary studies, they actually learn a "content area" which is recognizable because it is structured in particular language patterns. It is in this sense that to learn a subject at any time is always to learn language. To put the point another way, we may say that each of the different subjects taught in schools, particularly in the upper primary and secondary years, represents a way of exploring some aspects of experience and of asking questions about it. Each takes shape in characteristic linguistic patterns. As we also suggested earlier, it is because of the presence of such characteristic language patterns that we recognize the particular subject in question, whether it be social science, mathematics, English language arts, or school science. To learn a school subject is to learn how to deal with experience in a particular way. It is to learn to operate as a social scientist, a mathematician, a natural scientist, or as a writer of literature, for example, where each of these involves learning to adopt the appropriate behavior, including in particular language behavior. An area of knowledge or a subject is thus a way of knowing about some aspect of experience. The natural scientist, for example, explores phenomena of the natural world, be they the life cycle of the butterfly, how electricity is made, or how the principles of gravity operate. The social scientist tends to explore aspects of human society and behavior which, may include the historian's interest in exploring details of the past, or the sociologist's concern to study features of contemporary society. The mathematician uses formal numbering systems for exploring problems and for dealing with notions of space, distance, or weight. The writer of literature tends to explore the nature of human experience, both real-life and imagined, creating works of art in language. Learning a subject, then, involves learning how to go about dealing with experience in the manner appropriate to that subject, understanding how to ask questions and to answer these, or how to identify phenomena and to deal with them.

Typically, much school practice, especially that of the kind we will examine in our selected teaching episode, does not view knowledge in these terms at all. On the contrary, an attitude seems to prevail that "knowledge" or "content" is some kind of "product" waiting to be passed on to the children at appropriate times in their school careers. The problem is one serious manifestation of the difficulties caused by the separation of skills and content, and the associated instrumental or expressive role accorded to language, both of which we have discussed above at some length. Where knowledge or content is viewed as a product, and language as having a merely instrumental function in relation to content, it leads, for example, to the view that the primary purpose of the first years of schooling is that young children should acquire "skills," such as literacy, so that in subsequent years they will be able to deal with "content." In the early years, this view would have it, children will learn to talk, particularly in such activities as morning-news or show-and-tell sessions, where the interest from the teacher's point of view is less in what the children might choose to talk about, and more in having the children talk at all. Similarly, it is expected that young children will learn to read and write, with the interest less in what they write and read about, and more in establishing what are termed "basic literacy skills," conceived of as apart from the information dealt with in language. Thus, for example, Singer (1979, p. 10), an authority on reading, has suggested that the first years of school involve "reading acquisition," and that the later years, after about year 3, involve "learning from text." Thus, he suggests that "instruction shifts from teaching (the children) how to read to teaching them how to learn subject matter." Children learn to talk, to read and to write in the first 3 to 4 years of schooling, is the implication. Subsequently, in the upper primary, secondary, and even tertiary years, they will learn content.

Such a position does significant harm in educational practices, both in the first years of schooling and in the subsequent years as well. That is because it denies the primary function of language in the construction of meaning. It is quite contrary to children's most fundamental understandings about their language and how and why they use it, to suggest that they learn "to use it first," and then go on to employ it in dealing with content or meanings later. Earlier chapters in this book (particularly chapters 1 and 2) have examined carefully the processes by which young children in the preschool years learn their mother tongue. That they learn to talk at all is born of the constant need to achieve some control over experience, and hence to make meaning. They thus are already able to talk when they arrive at school, though one of the tasks of schooling will be to assist children to develop control of an expanding range of new registers. It is impossible to use language without dealing with experience and hence constructing meanings of some kind. However, the worst programs for the teaching of initial literacy frequently deny this, making the task of learning for young children needlessly hard. Early reading and writing programs that concentrate on teaching sound-letter correspondence and mastery of spelling and handwriting, at the expense of interest in meaning in constructing texts, sacrifice children's capacity to deal with significant experience, to the detriment of their writing and reading development.

Turning to the later years of upper primary, secondary, and even tertiary studies, we would argue that the preoccupation with content at the expense of interest in how content is structured and comes into being has consequences quite as serious for students' learning as those associated with the early years. Where teachers remain insensitive to the ways in which differing linguistic patterns or genres realize the different meanings associated with the subjects they teach, they fail to offer useful guidance to their students in how to structure and hence learn the appropriate content. Success in mastering a content area is actually a matter of mastering the necessary linguistic resources with which to deal with that content—this implies knowing how one's discourse is to be structured.

Since it is impossible to use language without dealing with experience and hence constructing meanings of some kind, it will be instructive to consider the kinds of meanings or knowledge our teacher does in fact involve her children in creating. As we shall seek to demonstrate, there is a very intimate relationship between the nature of the knowledge dealt with and the actual language used. Specifically, we will argue that the curriculum activity constitutes no significant learning challenge for the children: that the poverty of the language used by the children, both in talk and in the written texts they produce, is itself a manifestation of the poverty of the "knowledge" with which they are asked to work. Both language capacity and knowledge are trivialized, and the result is a curriculum activity of a kind in which little of value takes place.

In undertaking the investigation of our chosen curriculum activity, we will employ principles of systemic linguistic analysis, primarily as proposed by Halliday (1985b), though also developed by Hasan (1984b, 1985c) and by Rochester and Martin (1979). This framework for analysis offers a powerful means for understanding what goes on in such a curriculum activity, for it provides a functional interpretation, enabling us to appreciate precisely how the learning experience and the "knowledge" involved are actually constructed.

First, the curriculum activity we will discuss is an example of a curriculum genre. The term "genre" as it is used here bears a relationship to its traditional usage, particularly in literary discussions. A text may be said to have "generic structure" because it has an overall characteristic pattern or shape, making it identifiably different from some other genre, whose functions will of course be of a different kind. What marks the present use of "genre" as different, however, from its traditional usages, is the fact that it refers as much to spoken as to written texts. It is suggested that it is in the nature of the social construction of experience that human beings generate texts which have distinctive overall patterns or shapes, through which meanings pertaining to the given context or situation are created. The definition adopted here owes much to the somewhat differing but related usages of Kress (1982), Martin (1984), and Hasan (1985c). It will be argued, following Martin in particular, that where teachers and children work together in the classroom, they engage in "staged, purposeful, goal-oriented activities," which lead to the construction of "curriculum genres" (Christie, 1985a, 1985b, 1985c). Our teaching/learning activity we will thus term a curriculum genre, and we will also examine one of the written texts that the children involved produced.

4. A WRITING CURRICULUM GENRE

Text 1 is in fact is an extract from a longer interaction. The first part of the morning's proceedings had involved both roll call and morning news, and these have been omitted, since it would be impossible to do them justice. Lines 1–14 of the text actually constitute a phase preliminary to the commencement of the writing activity, and for the purposes of the analysis to be undertaken we will exclude these from our discussion. We will in fact argue that the writing curriculum genre commences at line 15. The genre was developed as one of a number in a major thematic unit of work on foods which lasted about 10 weeks. As is customary in such approaches to the curriculum, the theme of food was explored in almost all areas of the school day. On the day before text 1 was recorded, the children watched their teacher cook spaghetti bolognaise, had eaten it, and had been asked to copy the recipe from the board into their books. In this particular lesson, the teacher intended that the children learn to write by taking selected aspects of the activities associated with the spaghetti bolognaise.

Text 1

1	*T:*	All right, hands up, any people who haven't finished
2		writing out the spaghetti bolognaise recipe from yes-
3		terday.
4	*Stacey:*	Not me, I've finished it.
5	*T:*	Where are you up to, Jodie? (Jodie has put up her
6		hand.)
7	*Jodie:*	I'm up to (lost).
8	*T:*	Right, where are you up to, Simon?
9	*Simon:*	I'm up to the one where it says, um, packets of spa-
10		ghetti.
11	*T:*	Right, you people, some time today, try and get that
12		finished so we can clean our blackboard again. Hands
13		up, the people who haven't finished writing out our
14		five food groups (Several raise their hands). Well, we
15		might have to have a finishing-off hour after play.
16	*Jodie:*	I'm not, I'm only up to the second
17	*Another child:*	I've finished.
18	*Lucy:*	I love spaghetti bolognaise (muttered into the micro-
19		phone).

Task Orientation

20	*T:*	All right, well, what we're going to do today, we're
21		going to have a look at our recipe from yesterday.
22		Simon (addressed to attract his attention), and we're
23		going to make from our recipe a shopping list. Now,
24		the things that we have to buy for our spaghetti bol-
25		ognaise are the things we put on our shopping list.
26		We don't have to think of anything new, because
27		they're all written there. The only thing we have to
28		think about is where we would buy them. We didn't
29		find them all in one shop. When Mrs. S and I went
30		shopping to buy all those things, we didn't just go to
31		one shop and buy them all. We went to different
32		shops. The different things we put into the spaghetti
33		and the spaghetti bolognaise sauce, you get in differ-
34		ent places. Put up your hand if you can tell me one
35		of the shops we might have gone to, to get something
36		there. (Here she gestures up to the recipe written on
37		the board). Have a look. We had to buy meat, we
38		had to buy soup, tomato paste, carrots, onions, spa-
39		ghetti, and all these herbs and spices. Now, one of

40		the shops would have been what, Joseph?
41	Joseph:	Uh . . . Coles?
42	T:	What's Coles?
43	Joseph:	Coles New World.
44	T:	And what's that? What do we call that type of shop?
45	Susy:	C . . . Village (a reference to the shopping complex
46		in which there is a branch of Coles New World su-
47		permarkets).
48	T:	Stacey (who is whispering to another child), if you
49		don't want to help us p'raps you'd like to ask some-
50		one else to mind you. What do you call Coles New
51		World, Frankie? What sort of a shop is it?
52	Frankie:	C . . . Village
53	Kelly:	Shopping centre.
54	T:	It's in the C . . . Village. What sort of shop is it,
55		Simon?
56	Simon:	Shopping centre.
57	T:	No. C . . . Village is a big shopping centre. What sort
58		of shop is it, Elvira? (no reply) David? (no reply)
59		Daniela? (no reply) Jodie? Come on, I want some
60		thinkers. You've been there with your mum. What
61		sort of shop is Coles New World? (There are a few
62		quiet murmurs at this point, too soft to be recorded.)
63	Mark:	Supermarket? (Apparently T doesn't hear him.)
64	Helen:	Spaghetti shop.
65	T:	Spaghetti shop? (A general laugh greets this.) Who
66		said that?
67	Jeffrey:	You buy spaghetti there.
68	T:	You buy spaghetti there, I know, but what sort of a
69		shop is it? What do you call a shop that has all those
70		things? Helen?
71	Helen:	Food shop.
72	T:	No. In the shopping centre, but it's a certain kind of
73		shop. Christopher, do you know?
74	Christopher:	Supermarket?
75	T:	Good boy. It's a supermarket.
76	Mark:	I said supermarket.
77	T:	(writes ''supermarket'' on the board) So we had to
78		go to the supermarket. That was one shop we had to
79		go to. What other shop did we have to go to? Have
80		a look here, and see if, what else we might have had
81		to go to, to buy something for our spaghetti bolog-
82		naise. Come on, all these people who didn't have
83		their hand up last time. Jodie?
84	Jodie:	A vegetable shop.
85	T:	What do we call a vegetable shop? (a long pause)
86		Does it have a special name, or do you just call it the
87		fruit shop?

88	*Lucy:*	The fruit and vegetable shop.
89	*T:*	The fruit and vegetable shop. (She writes this on the
90		board.) Now there's somewhere else. It's the most
91		important thing that we needed for our spaghetti
92		sauce. Another important shop, where we had to
93		buy? . . . Simon, you're not listening. . . . A very im-
94		portant shop, where we went to buy the meat.
95	*Several children:*	I know. I know. The butcher. The butcher.
96	*T:*	Everyone should know this. Um . . . Frankie, where
97		does your mum buy the meat? Do you know the
98		name of the shop. (Frankie looks a little puzzled, and
99		shakes his head.) Do you know it in Italian?
100	*Frankie:*	No.
101	*T:*	What she calls where she goes to buy the meat? Have
102		you been with her when she goes shopping?
103	*Frankie:*	Sometimes.
104	*T:*	Does she go into a special shop that only has meat?
105		(Again he appears uncertain.) David?
106	*David:*	Butcher.
107	*T:*	Butcher. Right. Those are the three different shops
108		we went to. (She writes ''butcher shop'' on the
109		board.) Right, on our shopping list, Mrs. S and I had
110		written down ''mince.'' Elizabeth, you shouldn't be
111		talking.
112	*Kelly:*	She's been talking a lot to the microphone.
113	*T:*	Well, face the front. We had a shopping list, and we
114		had all these things written down. We had how many
115		kilograms we needed, how many tins of tomato soup
116		we needed, how many jars of tomato paste, how
117		many carrots, onions, packets of spaghetti, and then
118		the herbs and spice, and then off we went shopping.
119		We went to the butcher, and of course what did we
120		buy there?
121	*Class:*	The meat.
122	*T:*	That's all we bought. We bought two kilograms of
123		minced topside. Mrs. S bought two kilograms of
124		minced topside. That was all we had to buy in the
125		butcher shop, because there's nothing else there the
126		butcher sells. (She writes ''number 3'' next to ''2 kg
127		minced topside'' on the board.) Then we went to the
128		fruit and vegetable shop. Put up your hand and tell
129		me what we would have bought there. Luelle, can
130		you see something?
131	*Luelle:*	Steak?
132	*T:*	Well, this we bought at shop number three. All right?
133		(She points to it on the board.) We're at the fruit and
134		vegetable shop, and we're looking at our list. What
135		are the things we're getting at the fruit and vegetable

136		shop, Mark?
137	*Mark:*	Um, Carrots and onions.
138	*T:*	Good boy, so that's at shop number two. (She writes
139		"number 2" next to "carrots" and "onions.") We
140		bought the carrots there, we bought the onions there,
141		at shop number two. We write "spaghetti" here.
142		(What she says here about "spaghetti" is not clear.)
143		Now let's have a look over here. (She points to the
144		recipe.) Is there anything else we could have bought
145		there?
146	*Several children:*	Parsley.
147	*T:*	We could have bought fresh parsley leaves, at shop
148		number two. (She writes "number 2" next to "pars-
149		ley leaves.") Well, if we only bought those things at
150		those two shops, where did we buy all the other
151		things?
152	*Lucy:*	At the supermarket.
153	*T:*	At the supermarket. So all these other things, the
154		soup, we went to shop number one, the tomato paste,
155		shop number one, spaghetti, shop number one, all
156		these herbs and spices . . .
157	*Class:*	Shop number one (T "shop number 1" next to each
158		item).
159	*David:*	The water's not in there. (He laughs, for this is a
160		comment on the fact that the recipe on the board
161		lists water as one ingredient needed in the spaghetti
162		bolognaise. T smiles.)
163		(A series of laughing responses from other children
164		about the water is too quiet to record here.)

Task Specification

165	*T:*	All right, now what I want you people now to do, in
166		your blue books, or pink books, whatever you're in,
167		I want you to make me a shopping list.
168		David mutters quietly into the microphone: My
169		shopping list.
170	*T:*	Now I don't want it written out like that (points to
171		the recipe), like a recipe, I want it written out as if
172		you had to go shopping. Now the first shop you're
173		going to shop at is the supermarket, so I want you to
174		write on your shopping list "Supermarket," and I
175		want you to pick out all the things from our spaghetti
176		bolognaise recipe that you would have to buy at the
177		supermarket, and that's very easy, because all the
178		things with a number one beside them are the things
179		that we bought at the supermarket.
180	*Joel:*	Do you copy number one?
181	*T:*	Yes. Then on your shopping list, you first of all write,

182		I need to buy two tins of tomato soup, a jar of tomato
183		paste, three packets of spaghetti. That will leave
184		crushed garlic, oregano leaves, beef cubes, Worces-
185		tershire sauce, salt, and pepper. Then at the next
186		shop, which is the fruit and vegetable shop, I had to
187		buy three carrots, four onions, and some parsley.
188		Then at the next shop which was the butcher shop,
189		I had to buy. . . ?
190	*Several children:*	Meat.
191	*Several children:*	Minced meat.
192	*Several children:*	Topside.
193	*T:*	Topside. All right, hands up if you don't think you
194		know what to do. (No one raises a hand.) Now, when
195		your mum goes shopping, she probably doesn't have
196		to write down all the shops that she buys things in.
197		She probably knows where she's headed, she needs
198		to go to the butcher, she needs to go to the deli, and
199		she needs to go to the fruit shop, and she needs to
200		go to the supermarket or the dry cleaners, or wher-
201		ever else she needs to go.
202	*David:*	The milk bar?
203	*T:*	What was that, David?
204	*David:*	The milk bar.
205	*T:*	The milk bar, if she needs to go there.
206	*Child:*	You could get the meat at the supermarket at C . . .
207		Village.
208	*T:*	You could, but we bought it at the butcher shop.
209	*Susy:*	You could go to the donut shop.
210	*Jodie:*	We go to the butcher shop near the donut shop.
211	*T:*	The butcher on the corner? We went to the other
212		butcher around near V . . . around near the deli. All
213		right, these people can start . . .
214	*Child:*	Can you write the number one?
215	*T:*	Can you write down what?
216	*Child:*	The number one.
217	*T:*	You can write "number 1, supermarket," and then
218		all the things that you need . . . Hullo. (She breaks
219		off as Mrs. L, who takes three children for lessons in
220		Croatian, comes into the room to fetch them. The T
221		had forgotten that she would be coming.) Do you
222		want these? (She nods toward the two children who
223		have stood up in readiness to depart as Mrs. L en-
224		tered the room.)
225	*Mrs. L:*	Yes.
226	*T:*	(indecipherable) It's half past nine, is it?
227	*Mrs. L*	(smiling) Yes.
228	*T:*	Never mind, by the end of the year I'll have learned
229		what time. (This is a reference to her tendency to

230		forget that the children should regularly withdraw at
231		this time. The children leave with Mrs. L.) Right, so
232		number one is the supermarket, and all the things that
233		we got there.
234	*Stacey:*	Number two, the fruit and vegetable shop.
235	*T:*	Number two, the fruit and vegetable shop and the
236		things we bought there, and number three is the
237		butcher. So that if you went to your mum and said,
238		"I need to do the shopping, I have to go to the su-
239		permarket, I have to go to the fruit shop, and I have
240		to go to the butcher," she'd know exactly what to
241		buy in each one.
242	*David:*	What if the shop's a long way away?
243	*T:*	I beg your pardon?
244	*David:*	What if the shop's a long way away? (He smiles, as
245		he plainly intends this as a joke.)
246	*T:*	You'd have to ride a long way.
247	*Child:*	Go by car. (A little laughter greets this.)

Task

249	*T:*	All right, stand up, the girls, mind the cords on the
250		floor, just look where your feet are going.
251	*Recorder:*	Step over it, and I'll get it out of the way now.
252	*T:*	Now the boys. Get your books from your lockers,
253		and you can all start to write your shopping lists.

The text is very representative of the kinds of writing curriculum genres familiarly found in the first few years of schooling. The object is to develop some literacy skills, and the teacher seeks to do this by drawing on the actual experiences of eating the spaghetti bolognaise and of writing out the recipe, as well as drawing on the children's knowledge of their own family's shopping habits.

In terms of schematic structure, the text has three elements, which have been indicated in the text. They are Task Orientation (TO), Task Specification (TS) and Task (T). They may be represented thus:

$$TO \wedge TS \wedge T,$$

where the symbol $\wedge$ indicates sequence. Sometimes texts of this kind will have an additional element, which we have elsewhere referred to (Christie, 1985c) as Task Reorientation (TR). Such an element, following upon TO, and involving some recasting of at least some of its features, is thus an optional element, whose presence would be accepted by participants as unremarkable, indicating that it was reasonably routine and commonplace. However, the three elements identified in text 1 appear to be obligatory, in that unless they are found to be present, we are not justified in identifying the text as an example of a writing curriculum genre. (The distinction between obligatory and optional elements is one taken from Hasan; 1978; 1979; 1985c).

We will begin our analysis by focusing on theme in the discourse, and we will subsequently examine transitivity processes as well as lexical cohesion and reference. We will argue that a focus on all these linguistic features clarifies our understanding of how the text is put together and therefore of how its meanings are realized. Such an analysis, we will suggest, reveals why the language used by the children is so limited, and hence why the learning experience and the content dealt with are of such a disappointing kind.

It is one immediate measure of the value of Halliday's functional grammar, that a focus on Theme as it is realized in the text will take us a significant part of the way into understanding how the text is constructed, and hence how the meanings in it are made. Indeed, Theme as it is realized in this text is one of the most significant measures of its status as a curriculum genre, delineating much that is most characteristic of the relative roles of teacher and pupils. When we concentrate on Theme, we focus on one aspect of the way the message of any clause is organized: Theme is the starting point of the message, and in English at least, it is realized by first position in clause structure (see Fries, 1983; Halliday, 1985b). Table 1 considers Theme as it is identified in the teacher's opening discourse, in the element of the text we have identified as Task Orientation (where an embedded clause is Theme, no analysis of theme within that clause will be provided). All clauses (apart from minor ones) will have a topical Theme, and they are all identified in the Table. Clauses may or may not have Themes that are interpersonal and textual. There are no interpersonal themes in the passage of discourse involved here, and for that reason the tables offers no analysis of interpersonal Theme. However, the pattern of textual Theme is important, for reasons we will discuss below. Note that there are several subclasses of textual themes, some of which are found in this text, and they are labeled accordingly in Table 1. Note also that the first element identified in the teacher's discourse is not shown with conventional Theme-Rheme notation, because we identify this structure as functioning at another level from subsequent elements of the discourse. That is to say, the opening structure, *all right well what we're going to do today*, has status as marking the first element of the schematic structure of the curriculum genre. It is significant that this represents an incomplete clause complex. A similarly incomplete clause complex also marks the commencement of the element of the text we will call the Task Specification.

Two kinds of textual Theme are apparent in this segment of the teacher's discourse: they are continuatives, *now*, and structural Themes

Table 1: Theme in Task Orientation (lines 20–40)

Theme		Rheme
Textual	**Topical**	
	we	're going to have a look at our recipe from yesterday
and (Structural)	we	're going to make from our recipe a shopping list
now (Continuative)	the things that we have to buy for our spaghetti bolognaise	are the things we put on our shopping list
	We	don't have to think of anything new
because Struct.	they	're all written there
	the only thing we have to think about	is where we would buy them
	we	didn't find them all in one shop
when (Struct)	Mrs S and I	went shopping to buy all those things
	we	didn't just go to one shop
and (Struct)		buy them
	we	went to different shops
	the different things we put into the spaghetti and the spaghetti bolognaise sauce	you get in different shops
	put up	your hand
if (Struct)	you	can tell me one of the shops we might have gone to, to get something there
	have	a look
	we	had to buy meat
	we	had to buy soup, tomato paste, carrots, onions, spaghetti, and all these herbs and species
now (Conti)	one of the shops	would have been what, Joseph

such as *because, when,* and *and.* Textual Themes function primarily to tie the text together, and to foster the direction in which the discourse will proceed.

The teacher makes more frequent use of textual Theme as even the short extract examined reveals than do her pupils, and this is consistent with her role as teacher and authority figure, particularly in this, the opening of the Task Orientation: she is pointing the direction of the Task, while her choices of topical Theme indicate the content or the experiences on which the children's attention is to be focused. An examination of the rest of Task Orientation will reveal that textual Themes remain a relatively frequent feature of the teacher's discourse, though the choices of textual Theme shift interestingly. Continuatives diminish in frequency, and structural Themes predominate for the rest of the Task Orientation. A selection of Themes in the teacher's discourse for the rest of the Task Orientation is presented below:

> *and what's that*
> *what do we call that type of shop*
> *what sort of shop is it Simon*
> *no C . . . Village is a a big shopping centre*
> *but it's a certain kind of shop*
> *so we had to go to the supermarket*
> *right those are the three different shops*
> *well this we bought at shop number three*
> *so all these other things the soup*

In all the teacher uses only three continuatives after the opening portion: *no* (used twice), *right*, and *well* (used twice, once for the purposes of disciplining a child). The structural Themes are conjunctions (e.g., *but*, *so*).

Now consider Theme in the children's discourse, for it is in noting the contrast with that of the teacher that we can see very clearly the ways the different roles are both identified and created in the discourse. Significantly, the children's contributions are normally not substantial enough to involve the creation of messages having Theme at all: for example, *Coles, shopping centre, supermarket*, and so on. Where the children are permitted by the terms of the discourse patterns to create complete clauses, Theme is always topical as in:

> *you buy spaghetti there*
> *I know*

Overall, whoever controls textual Theme holds the power, and it is the teacher who overwhelmingly controls what is going on here. At no point do the children participate in the construction of the discourse on what might be considered equal terms with the teacher. If they did, one manifestation of an enhanced capacity to participate and hence contribute to the direction the discourse might take would be apparent in capacity to create textual Themes. Given the teacher's role, it must be expected that she take a significant hand in the shaping of the discourse. However, it need not follow that those who are learning are so totally denied effective capacity to influence the direction of the discourse. Indeed, were the children to be permitted genuine intellectual effort and inquiry, they certainly would take a more substantial role in directing the course of the discussion. Now let us turn to the Task Specification, and consider Theme here.

The commencement of Task Specification is apparent in another element marking a step in the schematic structure of the text, and for that reason, as with the element introducing Task Orientation, we will show no Theme/Rheme notation. As we have earlier noted, the element involved is an incomplete clause complex. This would appear to be a frequent though not universal feature of those elements of classroom texts which mark the presence of a new step in the schematic structure.

One of the measures of the fact that a new phase in the text has been reached, justifying our terming it a Task Specification, will be found in the manner in which the teacher reverts to using a more significant number of continuatives as textual Theme than was true in the latter part of Task Orientation. After the initial orientating phase, she is moving to define the task preparatory to the children's writing. Continuatives are reasonably frequent in the teacher's discourse in the Task Specification, and they are also distributed throughout this element of the text. In Table 2, we will first of all consider the opening two passages of teacher discourse, from lines 167 to 179, where continuatives and structural Themes are frequent.

Note the following parts of the teacher's subsequent discourse, in which continuatives are used:

yes then on your shopping lists
all right hands up if you don't know what to do
now when your mum goes shopping
right so number one is the supermarket

Significant in the overall pattern by which the Task Specification is put together is the use of conjunctions. The interrogatives have largely disappeared, because the relevant information has been elicited, and the teacher's intention now is to build connections between appropriate aspects of that information, as part of specifying the task. Some of the conjunctions have been noted in the short passage examined above, but there are more:

then on your shopping list

Table 2.   Theme in Task Specification (lines 167–179)

Theme		Rheme
Textual	**Topical**	**Rheme**
	I	want you to make me a shopping list
now *continuative*	I	don't want
	it	written out like that like a recipe
	I	want
	it	written out
as if *structural*	you	had to go shopping
now *cont.*	the first shop you're going to shop at	is the supermarket
so *struct.*	I	want
	you	to pick out all the things from our spaghetti bolognaise recipe that you would have to buy at the supermarket
and *struct.*	that	's very easy
because *struct.*	all the things with a number one beside them	are the things that we bought at the supermarket

then at the next shop
then at the next shop which was the butcher
now when your mum goes shopping
and she needs to go to the butcher
so that if you went to your mum

The final element in the schematic structure of the genre, which we have labeled Task, starts at *all right stand up the girls mind the cords on the floor just look where your feet are going*. This does in fact begin with a continuative, but since the element has status as part of the schematic structure we will not examine its significance in thematic terms. One continuative is used in the Task: *now the boys*.

One other textual Theme appears in the Task, *and you can all start to write your shopping lists*, but at this stage, since the Task Specification is completed, there is no further use for them.

When we come to consider Theme in the children's discourse, not surprisingly we find an inequality in the varying roles of participants similar to that found in the Task Orientation. Sometimes the children's contributions are again too limited to carry Thematic significance (e.g., *meat*). Elsewhere, Theme is a finite, hence having a function in an interpersonal sense, and being used to clarify the teacher's expectations of the children:

> do you copy number one?
> can you write the number one?

Or more commonly, Theme is once again topical, and has to do with self or family:

> you could get the meat at the supermarket
> you could go to the donut shop
> we go to the butcher near the donut shop

Significantly, only once does a child use an interrogative, which, since it is intended as a joke, is quickly (though quite kindly) disposed of by the teacher, because of its marginal relevance to the task at hand: *what if the shop's a long way away?*

In summary, the above brief review of Theme in text 1 has served to demonstrate two matters, to both of which we have already referred. First, an analysis of Theme and who "owns" what kind of Theme reveals a good deal of the ways the roles of teacher and pupils are both defined and created in a curriculum discourse. Second, in that it has indicated how differing kinds of textual Themes are distributed across the three elements of the text, the analysis has provided support for the claim that a particular schematic structure does in fact apply here. Both observations are of considerable importance to us in the present discussion, for they tell us a great deal of the ways meanings are created in the early years of primary school.

Those meanings, it should be noted, are of two broad kinds. First, there are meanings that deal with the nature of the teacher's authority and the relationship of the children to her; second, there are meanings that deal with the kind of knowledge the children are required to construct and how they are to construct it. With respect to the former of these two meanings, we would argue that acknowledgment of the teacher's authority is so determining a factor here that the children are left with very little capacity for independence of action: An important but largely unconscious ideology pertains, that children will do what the teacher tells them. Independence of action on their part is not encouraged, even though the teacher is herself a kindly woman. As we noted earlier, it must always remain the case that the teacher acts with authority in any curriculum genre, but the exercise of this authority need not involve such unquestioning acquiescence from the children. On the contrary, given the avowed commitment of English-speaking countries to the development of habits of intellectual independence, we would suggest that such a pattern of unquestioning following of teacher authority should in fact be broken, even in the earliest years of schooling.

That the pattern is not even acknowledge, let alone broken, is related to the ideology of knowledge operating in such curriculum genres. About that it will now be appropriate to say a little more.

5. KNOWLEDGE CONSTRUCTION IN THE WRITING CURRICULUM GENRE

The discussion of Theme has already thrown some light on the ways knowledge is constructed in text 1. In both the Task Orientation and the Task Specification, the teacher focused through topical Themes, on the experiences to be written about: spaghetti bolognaise, the ingredients, shopping. Her use of interrogatives, particularly in the Task Orientation, was designed to elicit certain information about these experiences, and throughout the text the use of continuatives and other textual Themes was an important part of building up and connecting information relevant to the writing task. The nature of the connections built is an important aspect of the kind of knowledge constructed. The collective function of the continuatives, of the conjunctions chosen (notably coordinating ones such as *and, then,* and *so*), is that the process of information construction is one of building connectedness between the events involved in the activity of going shopping. The knowledge is thus of a sequential kind, consistent with reconstruction of personal experience. By contrast, the pattern of textual Theme would be very different in a text in which the teacher sought to build connectedness through processes of explanation, or of examination of casual relationships between events or phenomena. Such a text, we may speculate, would make much greater use of topical Themes, realized for example in *wh*-elements such as *why* or *how,* or by structural Themes dealing with causal relationship, such as *because, although, unless,* or in modal adjuncts such as *perhaps.* The point will be worth bearing in mind as we begin to examine transitivity, for this necessarily throws a very different light on the nature of the knowledge construction in the text. As Halliday (1985) points out, transitivity processes tell us what is "going on" in a text, and they therefore have a significant role in building the experiential component of any text.

Broadly, two kinds of transitivity processes predominate in the teacher's discourse; they are material and relational. The former have to do with re-creation of the experience of shopping and buying ingredients for the spaghetti bolognaise; the latter deal with creation of assertions about what is factually true of these matters, mostly concerned with identification. Such a finding complements the findings of our examination of Theme, confirming the feeling that the primary purpose of the text is to involve the children in re-creation of familiar experience. Some examples will serve as illustration. Consider again the opening passage of the teacher's discourse from the point of view of transitivity.

Most of the processes used here are material, part of the re-creation of the activity of shopping. The final process is identifying in *now one of the shops would have been what Joseph?* and it signals that the teacher is moving into elicitation of information from the children. For a time in the Task Orientation, there is considerable use of attributive processes, part of the continuing business of eliciting factual information from the children:

> C . . . *Village is a big shopping centre*
> *what sort of shop is it??*
> *it's a supermarket*
> *does it have a special name?*
> *those are the three different shops*

The pattern continues throughout the rest of the Task Orientation, interweaving relational (either identifying or attributive) and material processes, as the fabric of the text is constructed, and a "knowledge" about the activities of shopping is built up. While material and relational processes are characteristic of the Task Orientation, the paucity of mental processes is another noteworthy feature. In the above analysis the teacher uses two in her opening discourse (*think* used twice) and at one point several children say *I know*. In general, however, the Task Orientation is remarkably free of mental processes.

Significantly, for it is further evidence for the presence of a new element in the overall schematic structure, the teacher makes considerable use of the same mental process (*want*) at the start of the Task Specification, because it is at this point that she begins to direct the children's writing:

> *now what I want you people now to do*
> *I want you to make me a shopping list*

Table 3: Transitivity in Task Orientation (lines 20–40)

all right well	what	we	're going	to do	today
	Goal	Actor	Material or Process		Circumstance: Time

We	're going to have	a look	at our recipe from yesterday
Behaver	Behavioral Pro	Range	Goal

and we	're going to make	from our recipe	a shopping list
Actor	Mat Pro	Circ: Means	Goal

Now	the things [that	we	have to buy	for our spaghetti bolognaise]	are	the things [we	put	on our shopping list]
	Token				Identifying Process	Value		
		[Actor	Mat Pro	Goal]		[Ac	Mat Pro	Circ: Purpose]

we	don't have to think of	anything new
Senser	Mental Pro	Phenomenon

because	they	're all written	there
	Range	Behavioral Pro	Circ: Place

the only thing [we	have to think about]	is	[where	we	would buy	them]
Value		Identifying Pro	Token			
[Senser	Mental Pro: Cognition]		[Place	Ac	Mat Pro	Goal]

we	didn't find	them all	in one shop
Actor	Mat Pro	Range	Circ: Place

when	Mrs. S and I	went shopping
	Actor	Mat Pro

to buy	all those things
Mat Pro	Goal

we	didn't just go	to one shop
Actor	Mat Pro	Circ: Place

we	went	to different shops
Actor	Mat Pro	Circ: Place

the different things [we put into the spaghetti and the spaghetti Bolognaise sauce]		you	get	in different places
Goal		Actor	Mat Pro	Circ: Place
	[Ac	Mat Pro	Circ: Place]	

Table 3: Transitivity in Task Orientation (continued)

put up	your hand
Mat Pro	Goal

if you	can tell	me	one of the shop [we	might have gone to]
Sayer	Verbal Pro	Receiver	Range	
			[Actor	Mat Pro]

to get	something	there
Mat Pro	Goal	Circ: Place

have	a look
Behavioral Pro	Range

we	had to buy	meat
Actor	Mat Pro	Goal

we	had to buy	soup, tomato paste, carrots, onions, spaghetti and all those herbs and spices
Actor	Mat Pro	Goal

now	one of the shops	would have been	what	Joseph
	Value	Identifying Pro		Token

> *now I don't want it written out like that*
> *I want it written out*
> *so I want you to write*
> *and I want you to pick*

At one other point, the teacher uses two mental processes: *hands up if you don't think you know what to do.*

At no point in the Task Specification do the children use any mental processes, for the contributions the children are constrained to produce by the demands of this context of situation are of a different kind. In fact, for reasons already indicated in the above discussion of Theme, the children overall produce few clauses anyway, and in those they do produce, for the most part they use material processes, or occasionally verbal and behavioral process:

> *I said supermarket*
> *she's been talking a lot*
> *do you copy number one*
> *can you write the number*

In a text not remarkable for the number of variety of transitivity processes in the children's discourse, it is significant that of the few produced, two (the verbal) involve some commentary on pupil behavior and two others *(do copy* and *can write)*, both behavioral, involve clarification of the nature of the task to be done. The others are material, relevant to the reconstruction of personal experience of shopping. None of these processes has any role in construction of experiential meanings that have to do with speculation or inquiry, though theoretically speculation and inquiry are intended to be features of the experience of learning.

How then does this brief discussion of transitivity shed light on our interest in the kind of knowledge being constructed in the curriculum genre in text 1 and the processes of its construction? Overall material and relational processes predominate; their primary functions are to reconstruct personal experiences (shopping for spaghetti bolognaise ingredients) and to make assertions about that activity, with a view to clarifying it. The experience of teaching and learning as realized in this curriculum genre, then, requires no more than the reconstruction of personal experience: it is this which is the ''knowledge'' involved.

Such a form of knowledge involves no intellectual challenge for the children—no pursuit of new ideas and information—and therefore no development of associated mental skills of a worthwhile kind. While there is a sense in which mental skills and knowledge may be thought of separately, it does not follow that the two have any real independence of each other, such that mental skills may be developed regardless of content. This is why the contemporary view in much curriculum discussion is so misleading, when it suggests that teaching practice should see the development of mental skills as more important than the control of knowledge, because the latter dates so quickly. The mental skills children develop are very much determined by the kind of knowledge they are asked to deal with, and, as our discussion has served to demonstrate, knowledge and control of it, like the associated mental abilities in handling it, come into being in the patterns of language that children and teachers create.

Two other areas of the text will now be worth exploring briefly, for what they reveal of the way the knowledge in the writing curriculum genre is constructed. They are lexical cohesion and reference. While the transitivity processes clearly create a great deal of the experimental component of the text, the lexis has a major role as well.

Tables 4 and 5 set out lexical cohesion and reference in the Task Orientation of Text, commencing at line 20. The general method of examining both lexical cohesion and reference follows Halliday and Hasan (1976) and Martin (1979). In the Task Orientation two strings predominate, one to do with the *things* on the *shopping list*, and the other to do with the *sort of shop* in which these things are purchased. These two

Table 4. Lexical Cohesion in Task Orientation

"hands up"	"shopping list"	"sort of shop"
TASK ORIENTATION		
	shopping list	
	things	
	spaghetti bolognaise	
	things	
	shopping list	
	anything	
	thing	
	buy	
		shop
	buy those things	
		shop
	buy	different shops
	different things	
	spaghetti, spaghetti bolognaise sauce	
		different places
put up your hand		
can tell		one of the shops
	something	
have a look		
	buy meat	
	buy soup, tomato paste, carrots, onions, spaghetti, all these herbs spices	
		one of the shops
		Coles
		Coles
		Coles New World
		type of shop C . . . Village
don't want to help		
ask someone else to mind you		

Table 4. Lexical Cohesion in Task Orientation (continued)

"hands up"	"shopping list"	"sort of shop"
		Coles New World
		sort of shop
		C . . . Village
		shopping centre
		C . . . Village
		sort of shop
		shopping centre
		C . . . Village, big shopping centre
		sort of shop
come on		
want some thinkers		
		sort of shop, Coles New World
		supermarket
		spaghetti shop
		spaghetti shop
		spaghetti
		spaghetti
		sort of a shop
		call a shop
		food shop
		shopping centre
		certain kind of shop
		supermarket
good boy		supermarket
		supermarket
		supermarket
		one shop
		other shop
have a look	buy something, spaghetti bolognaise	
see		
come on		
hand up		
		vegetable shop
		vegetable shop
		fruit shop
		fruit and vegetable shop
		fruit and vegetable shop
	spaghetti sauce	

Table 4. Lexical Cohesion in Task Orientation (continued)

"hands up"	"shopping list"	"sort of shop"
		another important shop
not listening		
		very important shop
	meat	
		butcher
	meat	
		name of the shop
	buy meat	
	shopping	
		special shop
	meat	
		butcher
		butcher
		three different shops
	shopping list	
	mince	
talking		
talking		
face the front		
	shopping list	
	these things	
	kilograms	
	tins of tomato soup	
	jars of tomato paste	
	carrots, onions	
	packets of spaghetti	
	herbs and spice	
	shopping	
		butcher
	buy	
	meat	
	bought	
	two kilograms of minced	
	topside	
	two kilograms of minced	butcher shop
	topside	butcher
	buy	fruit and vegetable shop
put up your hand		
	bought	
see		
	steak	
		shop number 3
		fruit and vegetable shop
	list	
	things	
		fruit and vegetable shop
	carrots and onions	

Table 4. Lexical Cohesion in Task Orientation (continued)

"hands up"	"shopping list"	"sort of shop"
good boy		
		shop number 2
	carrots	shop number 2
	spaghetti	
let's have a look		
	anything else	
	bought	
	parsley	
	fresh parsley leaves	shop number 2
	bought these things	those two shops
	buy all the other things	
		supermarket
		supermarket
	all these other things	
	the soup	
		shop number 1
	tomato paste	shop number 1
	spaghetti	shop number 1
	all these herbs and spices	
		shop number 1

strings are an essential part of the process of building the experience or the "content" that the children are learning and about which they will be asked to write. An additional smaller string, labeled *hands up*, involves lexical items that have to do with teacher directions to the children about their general behavior.

In the Task Specification (although the analysis of this section could not be included here), the lexical items in the latter string become more numerous, at least initially, as the teacher seeks to specify the nature of the writing task. The strings to do with the *shopping list* and with the *sort of shop* remain important, for the process of task specification requires reiteration of most of the items initially identified in these two strings in the Task Orientation. The need to *write* is referred to several times toward the end of the Task Specification. In the Task, the string to do with direction of the children's behavior predominates, and reference is made once only to the *shopping list*.

Table 5 confirms the same general trend as Table 1, though there is a sense in which it adds to our overall understanding of the kind of knowledge constructed in the text. The principal items referenced apart from *shops* and *things* to buy, are class members and that significant family member *your mum*. This confirms the overall sense we have already established of the kind of knowledge dealt with here: it is the knowledge of personal and family experience.

Table 5. Reference in the Task Orientation

"we"	"the things"	"a shopping list"	"the spaghetti"	"the shop"
TASK ORIENTATION				
we				
we,				
our recipe				
Simon				
we,				
our recipe		a shopping list		
we,	the things			
our spaghetti bolognaise				
we,	the things			
our shopping list	they			
we	the only thing			
we				
we				the one shop
we				
we	them			
Mrs. S, I				
we	them			
we	them			
we	the different things	the spaghetti bolognaise, the spaghetti bolognaise sauce		
your hand				
you, me				
we				the shops
we				
we				
Joseph				the shops
we				
Stacey				
you,				
us				
you				
you				
you, Frankie				

Table 5.   Reference in the Task Orientation (continued)

"we"	"the things"	"a shopping list"	"the spaghetti"	"the shop"
Simon				
Elvira				
David				
Daniela				
Jodie				
you, your mum				
you				
you				
I				it
you, Helen				
				it
Christopher, you				
I				it
we				the supermarket
we				
we				
our spaghetti bolognaise				
who,				
their hand				
Jodie				
we				
we				the fruit and vegetable shop
				the fruit and vegetable shop

Table 5. Reference in the Task Orientation (continued)

"we"	"the things"	"a shopping list"	"the spaghetti"	"the shop"
	it, the most important thing			
we, our spaghetti sauce we Simon, you				
we	the meat			
				the butcher the butcher
Frankie, your mum	the meat			
				the shop
you				
she she you her she she	the meat			
David				the three dif- ferent shops
we our shopping list Mrs. S				
Elizabeth you she				
we we we we we				
	the herbs and spice			
we we				the butcher
we				
we	the meat			
we				

Table 5.   Reference in the Task Orientation (continued)

"we"	"the things"	"a shopping list"	"the spaghetti"	"the shop"
Mrs. S				
we				
				the butcher shop
				the butcher
we				the fruit and vegetable shop
your hand				
me				
we				
Luelle				
you				
we				
we				the fruit and vegetable shop
we, our list				
we	the things			
we, Mark				the fruit and vegetable shop
we	the carrots			
we	the onions			
we				
we				the supermarket
we				
we				
we	all the other things			
				the supermarket
we				
	the soup			

6. KNOWLEDGE AS SPECULATION AND INQUIRY

There is nothing wrong in principle with drawing upon children's personal experience when they learn. In fact, a great deal of learning would not be possible at all without recourse to what the learners already know, as a basis upon which to proceed. However, what makes the curriculum genre in Text 1 remarkable is its complete failure to take children beyond reconstruction of personal experience. It is in this characteristic, that the text is very representative of the curriculum genres of much early school education. Much earlier in this chapter I argued that areas of knowledge, particularly as they are defined in educational institutions, represent varying ways of asking questions about experience, and of answering these. If we are to understand the matter in these terms, we should recognize that the pursuit of knowledge is also necessarily speculative: it involves developing various mental skills and habits of inquiry. The text we have been examining not only fails to involve children in speculative activity: it causes them to engage in other kinds of activities, constructing the kinds of "content" or "knowledge" which effectively denies children opportunity to develop both more powerful knowledge and more powerful mental skills.

Consider, for a moment, one example of the shopping lists produced by a child called Joel. It is entirely representative of the class texts generally (the original spelling is preserved).

Shopping List

1 Supermarket
2 tins of tomato soup
1 jar of tomato paste
3 packets of Spaghetti
basil leaves
crushed garlic
oregano leaves
worchestershire sauce
salt and pepper
2 Fruit and Vegetable
3 carrots
4 onions
parsley leaves
3 Butcher
2kg mince topside

The above text emerged from the curriculum genre we have examined. Indeed, given the terms of the writing activity as the teacher defined it, Joel has understood the task well. It is, however, difficult to see the actual educational value of asking children to write such a text, for it poses little challenge to the children to construct knowledge in new ways. The writing of the recipe for making the spaghetti bolognaise, after the children had engaged in the activity of assisting the teacher to make it, would, for example, have been much more valuable. It would have had the merit that it would have involved more than mere recall and reconstruction of a list of the items needed to do the cooking. It would certainly have required capacity to recall and reconstruct such a list—the basic experiential component of the lesson. But it would also have involved creation of a text representative of a socially useful genre (the recipe), requiring attention both to construction of the steps to be taken in doing the cooking, and to the desirable sequence of those steps. For such young children, to deal with the need to handle these two matters properly would be to construct new and socially useful knowledge, making new demands on their linguistic capacities. It will be recalled that the teacher had actually written up the recipe on the board for the children to copy it out in every way a less significant learning experience, because it offered no challenge to them as learners.

The curriculum genre under discussion here is very representative of the curriculum genres of much early schooling. As such it reveals the paucity of the models of knowledge and of learning which are a feature of much school practice. Too many children are not challenged to speculation and inquiry by the terms of the curriculum activities in which they engage. On the contrary, they are often so constrained that they are denied opportunity to develop both powerful mental skills and mastery of significant and rewarding knowledge. If children were permitted to enter into genuine inquiry and to develop skills of questioning and speculation, the linguistic capacities they developed would necessarily be very different from those revealed either in the spoken discourse of text 1 or in the written texts the children produced.

The nature of their relationship with the teacher would also be fundamentally different. While her authority would remain, the exercise of that authority would be of a different kind, for she would seek to develop more genuinely collaborationist teaching/learning activities, in which the children took a significant share in directing the course of those activities. They would, for example, control textual as well as topical Themes, and, whatever the "content," experience, or knowledge with which they were dealing, the actual linguistic choices they exercised would realize much greater speculation. They would, for example, use a much greater range of transitivity processes, including no doubt a number of mental processes, and they would make greater use of modalities of various kinds.

It is possible that unless we knew the curriculum context in which Joel's text was generated, we might well dismiss it as a reasonably poor piece of writing. However, as we have already noted, given the terms of the curriculum genre, we can see that his written text is a reasonably good one. It should be stressed that where children do produce what we might think are poor or limited pieces of writing, they are frequently responding as best they can to poor directions from their teachers. A badly focused and uncertain sense of knowledge and of inquiry will necessarily beget disappointing written texts. Knowledge and language are indeed indivisible. Hence it makes no sense at all to argue, as it is sometimes, that the knowledge dealt with at any time is of less importance than the mental skills developed in children. The only way to develop significant skills will be in the pursuit of worthwhile and challenging knowledge and information. Furthermore, as this whole discussion should by now have made clear, both the grasp of worthwhile knowledge and the associated development of significant mental skills will be realized in the relevant linguistic behavior. Language does not merely "give expression to" or "label" information, knowledge, and mental processes of reasoning. On the contrary, it is in language that we actually create or construct these things.

7. LANGUAGE AND THE CONSTRUCTION OF KNOWLEDGE

We began this chapter with a discussion of some very old educational traditions which provide so much of the background framework of beliefs and assumptions against which contemporary school practices need to be understood. The most damaging and enduring of these, we argued, were the related assumptions, first, that a useful distinction may be made between knowledge and skills and, second, that both knowledge and mental skills have a status independent in some way of language. For the most part, as would appear to have been the case in Western thinking for some centuries, language is still understood to have only an "expressive" or an "instrumental" role in the communication of meaning. Because of this teachers continue to operate like the teacher in text 1. Our analysis of the writing curriculum genre involved in text 1 has sought to demonstrate how critical are the implications for children's learning of the supposed separation of knowledge and skills, including especially language skills.

It is the particular achievement of Halliday's approach to grammar that it focuses our attention on function and meaning—on the ways linguistic resources are deployed for the creation of experience, including of course the experience of schooling. Our investigation of the ways in which the curriculum genre in text 1 is constructed, and hence of the kinds of meanings encoded in it, has helped illuminate a great deal of familiar curriculum practice, enabling us to understand the causes in linguistic terms of a great deal of the poverty of much curriculum practice. It exposes the folly of a model of knowledge or content as something existing apart from the language in which it is encoded.

A very general view prevails that the lower years of primary school will be devoted to the teaching of "basic literacy." At least one recent authority on the teaching of reading (Singer, 1979) has suggested that the initial years of schooling are for teaching basic skills of reading, while the subsequent years will take children into learning to read in the various "content areas." It is because of a very general commitment on the part of teachers to this view that they continue to use the numerous series of basal reading books for teaching introductory reading, despite the fact that the pedagogical value of these series has often been questioned, in one case at least some 80 years ago (Huey, 1908)! We refer here to those early readers most remarkable for the ruthless manner in which they sacrifice sense and meaning in the pursuit of teaching sound-letter correspondence. Only in situations in which teachers actually believe that considerations of meaning or "content" in using language may be relegated to a position of secondary significance is it possible to use such reading materials.

The teacher engaged in teaching writing in text 1 actually subscribes, albeit unconsciously, to a similar set of beliefs about early writing development. It does not matter what the children write about, she reasons, as long as they write. Hence, in the lesson examined, the teacher selects as her theme certain aspects of the children's experience and she asks them to reconstruct these as a basis upon which to write. Like many teachers of young children, she believes that such recourse to personal experience is a suitable basis for the provision of a "content" about which the children may write. Later on, in the subsequent years of schooling, they will learn to write "content," by which she means the content or knowledge of the different school subjects.

Such a view has equally serious consequences both for the development of children's skills and for the learning of knowledge. Knowledge and learning are trivialized, and as we have seen, children such as those involved in text 1 are not offered the opportunity to explore new experiences or acquire new information. Where curriculum activities are designed so that children do explore new experiences and acquire new information, they are encouraged to employ their linguistic resources in new ways. In meeting the challenge of dealing with new contexts of situation in the classroom, they extend their linguistic resources, thus mastering an expanding range of new registers. It is a fundamental responsibility of schooling that it teach children an ever-growing number of new registers, preparing them to interpret and use the varying generic patterns in which knowledge and information are encoded in our culture. In order satisfactorily to provide educational programs in which children can be taught such things, it is essential that teachers themselves understand the relationship between language and experience, and hence between language and school knowledge. Armed with such an understanding, they can go on to create curriculum contexts in which the need is for children to model and use various linguistic resources such that they learn to create new genres. Thus, when any new area of school knowledge is to be taught to children, teachers should always consider what it is that the children must be able to do in language in order to be successful in mastering that knowledge. To approach the matter in these terms is to give language the ''visible'' status it deserves, so that it becomes, quite properly, an object of overt study in the classroom. Where this happens, language becomes no longer the ''hidden curriculum'' of schooling, but rather the flexible and vital resource with which children learn to deal with experience and information in new ways.

Our discussion has been developed around examination of a curriculum activity involving young children, and we have seen the ill effects of the traditional failure to take language seriously, and to accord it a ''visible'' rather than an invisible and merely expressive role in the processes of learning. But the effects of this failure have serious consequences at later stages of schooling as well. As children grow older, moving into upper primary and thence to secondary and even tertiary education, they encounter the view of knowledge as ''product'' referred to earlier in this chapter. For the most part, commonplace practice for the teaching of knowledge in this sense pays scant attention to the role of language at all. Once again, language is invisible, and such is the strength of our prevailing educational traditions that teachers focus upon ''mastery of content'' at the expense of interest in how knowledge is created.

Yet knowledge is created in patterns of discourse, and successful mastery of a ''body of knowledge,'' like the associated development of various mental skills of reasoning, speculation, and inquiry, is entirely dependent upon mastery of the linguistic resources necessary for these to come into being. It is for this reason, contrary to prevailing custom, that good teaching practices should always have an overt and explicit interest in the nature of the language students must learn to use. The most important proposition Halliday has ever offered education is that learning language is learning ''how to mean:'' how to master the appropriate linguistic resources in which significant and valued meanings, and the associated mental processes, are created. All teachers are teachers of language, for language is the behavioral resource of central significance in the forms of learning for which schools are particularly responsible.

CHAPTER 5

LEARNING ABOUT LANGUAGE*

Joan Rothery

University of Sydney
New South Wales, Australia

In a very important sense it is impossible to separate learning language, learning through language, and learning about language. All three aspects of learning are likely to be going on as young children use language in interaction with adult caretakers. Various chapters in this volume illustrate the phenomenon clearly. Claire Painter, in the description of her son's language development, shows that as children learn language they learn through language. David Butt, in his analysis of some segments of linguistic interaction between mother and child, shows that as children learn language they learn about it, in the sense that they learn about the potential of the language system for meaning in different contexts. Carmel Cloran reveals how very young children learn through language about their social environment and the role they are accorded in it according to gender. It is a sad reflection on educational contexts for language development, as Frances Christie's chapter reveals, that there is an impoverished environment for all aspects of language learning in the classroom. Her analysis of classroom discourse for teaching writing shows how the children she writes about were given minimal opportunities to further their language development.

This chapter too will encompass more than one aspect of language development. The focus once again will be on educational contexts in which the aim is to promote children's language development through their use of language. What will be in the foreground, however, is learning about language in quite an explicit manner, both as a tool for planning and implementing the language curriculum and for children to use

I am most grateful to Guenter Plum of the Linguistics Department, Sydney University, for his permission to use the oral narrative about Cleo which is part of his research data, and to Barbara Ryan of North Sydney Demonstration School, who learned about language and taught grade two about language with much skill and enthusiasm.

in developing their language abilities, particularly in regard to writing. Learning about language is seen, then, as a conscious resource for meaning. Of course this is another instance of children learning through language as they learn about it.

Learning about language is commonly regarded as learning about the structure of the language system. The perspective taken in this chapter is different in that learning about language is seen to encompass learning both about the structure of the system and about how language is related to its sociocultural context. Such a perspective follows naturally from Halliday's description of language as a resource for meaning whose structural shape, so to speak, reflects its sociocultural functions, the research of Halliday and Painter (Halliday, 1975; Painter, 1984) shows early language development as an interactional process comprising activities that are socially and culturally based. Both focuses are seen to be essential in educational contexts that aim to develop children's abilities to use language effectively.

The first part of this chapter will survey some important developments in mother-tongue teaching over the last two decades. It will also introduce some theoretical issues concerning language and text and context within a systemic linguistic framework and examine their relevance for language development programs in school. The second part will examine some aspects of teaching writing in the primary school in a program that is language-based and takes account of the relationship between text and context.

THE PLACE OF LEARNING ABOUT LANGUAGE IN THE SCHOOL CURRICULUM

Learning about language is a rare occurrence in Australian schools. Two decades ago it was considered valuable for children to have explicit knowledge about language, both for its own sake and for the benefit of their language use. The climate of English teaching has changed greatly in the intervening period. The current view is that children's language development is best promoted through frequent and varied opportunities for language use. It is believed this development will proceed without any need for conscious knowledge about the system that enables us to mean.

Little credence is given to learning about language for its own sake. The observations of Jean Piaget, long influential in educational theory, are invoked to support this stand in the primary school (Ginsburg & Opper, 1969). Piaget's view that children are unlikely to undertake certain abstract intellectual activities, described by him as formal operations, until around the ages of 11 to 12, is given as an important reason for omitting learning about language in the primary years. In the secondary school, developing language abilities has been given priority over systematic language study. For these reasons English teaching syllabuses now omit any systematic study of language for students in primary as well as secondary schools.

The changes in teaching practice that have taken place in regard to learning about language are the consequence of changed views about the nature of language and how it is learned. Learning about language was seen to be important in previous years largely because it provided children with a "correct" model for their own language use. The rules that were learned about grammatical relations within the clause and between clauses were seen as means for regulating the child's language use in speech and writing. Exercises on the basis of these rules were set to eradicate incorrect usage or "bad" grammar (Department of Education, New South Wales, 1968, p. 35). This model of language and language learning had prevailed in New South Wales schools since the mid-nineteenth century when compulsory schooling was introduced. The grammar course described by Christie in her study of the school curriculum during that period was almost identical with that set down by the New South Wales Department of Education in the English curriculum for primary schools of 1968 (Christie, 1976). A prescriptive view of language learning prevailed within school contexts because educators had little or no understanding of dialect or register variation or of the child's expertise in language, particularly in regard to spoken language. Although Australian English syllabuses endorsed learning about language for its own sake, as well as for assisting language development, in practice the former was a secondary consideration: Learning about language was learning rules for regulating language use.

The inadequacies of this model for language development programs became apparent as knowledge about the extent of children's preschool language development became widespread in the 1960s and throughout the 1970s. The first wave of research in the United States during the 1960s, focused on the child learning syntax (Brown & Bellugi, 1964; Ervin, 1964; Menyuk, 1969, Smith and Miller, 1966). It drew educators' attention to the considerable progress made by very young children in learning the grammar of their language. By the 1970s a more functional perspective on child language development had developed amongst linguists. The American linguists Courtney Cazden and Lois Bloom were influential as far as educators were concerned because they, like the British linguist Michael Halliday, attempted to take account of how the context of situation influenced the child's meanings (Bloom, 1970; Cazden, 1972; Halliday, 1971a). Halliday, in particular, was concerned with viewing the child's development within the framework of a functional model of language in which language development was described in terms of the young child learning a set of functions for language (see Painter, chapter 1 of this volume). There was also a strong input into educational thinking about language development from the work of ethnographers such as Dell Hymes who also sought to take into account how the context of situation influenced language use (Gumperz & Hymes, 1972; Hymes, 1968).

At about the same time educators became aware of linguistic approaches to language variation on a broader basis than that of child language development. These approaches eschewed any global notions of "correct" or "incorrect" language but focused rather on language variation according to purpose and geographical location (Halliday, McIntosh, & Strevens, 1964; Labov, 1972). The relationship between language and cognition received careful attention in the work of Luria and Vygotsky and this too made a considerable impact on educators (Luria & Yudovich, 1971; Vygotsky, 1962). There was, in fact, a veritable explosion of knowledge about child language development during this period, together with some new perspectives on the nature of language variation in the course of daily life.

In the United Kingdom a group of educators, most notably James Britton, Douglas Barnes, John Dixon, and Harold Rosen, were particularly influential in taking these linguistic insights into the classroom in respect of their implications for teaching. They were eclectic in their approach in that they took from different theories and studies what they saw as insightful or relevant to education and welded these to develop a markedly different practice for language development than that of previous years. What emerged very clearly for them from the linguistic research was that language was learned through use and that oral language was crucial for the child exploring and learning about his environment. One of their most important aims was to change the status of oral language in the classroom. Silent classrooms had hitherto been considered ideal for learning. The teacher spoke; the child listened and answered questions with one or two words. Barnes pointed out, most effectively, the inadequacies of classroom contexts that did not take account of children's strengths in language use and did not assist the learner to move into new ways of using language (Barnes, Britton, & Rosen, 1971).

The insights of child language studies had also thrown into doubt the value of learning about language as a means for aiding language development. They made it clear that children's proficiency in language was not the result of formal grammar teaching. It was the consequence of innumerable opportunities for using language for many different purposes in the course of daily life. Educators such as Britton (1970) and Rosen and Rosen (1973) drew teachers' attention to the child's proficiency in oral language, which was already well advanced by the time she or he started school. As a result, learning about language was increasingly seen as an irrelevant part of the English curriculum

The educational philosophy that brought these linguistic insights together is most clearly expounded in John Dixon's *Growth Through English* (1967). The book was written after a major English teaching conference at Dartmouth College in the United States at which the British view of teaching for language development was strongly expounded by Dixon, Britton, Rosen, and Barnes, among others. From their educational stance the insights of linguistic research pointed to language development as a means for personal growth and development. Although many of the insights embraced came from a sociocultural perspective of language, that language was learned through use and in interaction with adult caretakers, the overriding educational perspective was one of the role of language in the life of the individual and, in particular, the inner life of the person. Such a focus was more in keeping with the romantic literary tradition regarding the nature of childhood and the development of personality. In a sense this focus was not surprising as the teaching of literature was preeminent in the English curriculum. As a consequence the school focus on language development that emerged from the Dartmouth conference was strongly psychologically and individually oriented.

The practice that was advocated at this stage to achieve language development can best be described as child-centered and facilitative. The child's language and experience were seen to provide the starting point for language development programs. The teacher's role was a facilitating one. It was thought that if the child's preschool oral language developed so well without formal teaching, but in contexts where there were plenty of opportunities for language use, a similar policy should be adopted in schools. To accommodate this view teachers were encouraged to develop thematic approaches that took account of the children's interests and gave a common focus for talking, reading, listening, and writing. The teacher developed activities that were seen to "draw out" the child's language abilities in a way that promoted language development. Such approaches were seen to be relevant from the first years at school until at least the middle years of the secondary school.

Two language programs emerged from this period that were somewhat different in conception and practice from those described above. They were *Breakthrough to Literacy* (Mackay, Thompson, & Schaub, 1970) and *Language in Use* (Doughty, Pearce, & Thornton, 1971). (See chapter 7 in this volume). Both were based on specific linguistic insights regarding the nature of language and language development although these were not made explicit in the teaching materials. The idea was to be able to give them to teachers who had no specialist language knowledge but who could still use them successfully in the classroom. *Breakthrough to Literacy* marked a new departure in teaching early literacy: the method of teaching was experience-based but carefully planned to take into account what children had to learn to do with language in order to read and write successfully. One of its most important features was that it freed children from having to write by hand while they were coming to grips with composing in the written mode. *Language in Use* also aimed to develop competence in language through use. But in addition it aimed to develop students' awareness of their language use in different contexts. The development of awareness was seen to be a crucial factor in students' coming to grips with the language demands of different contexts (Halliday, 1971a). In several respects *Language in Use* was different from other language experience programs: It focused on the nature of language as a system for meaning and saw a greater awareness of language as a crucial factor in language development.

In Australia the "new English," as the orientation to language development through language use came to be called, was endorsed in curriculum documents from 1970 onward. These documents, like their predecessors, stated that the goal of school language programs was for children to learn to use language successfully. But whereas this had previously been defined in terms of quite specific tasks such as writing a story or report or giving a short lecture, it was now much more general: to use language successfully in a range of contexts (Christie & Rothery, 1979 Rothery, 1986b, 1986c). It is significant to note the social focus of this goal, although a great deal of classroom practice and teaching materials were based on a view of language as a means for personal growth and development. It was quite deliberate that no more specific goals were given as programs were to be developed according to the particular needs of children in different schools. Such a goal showed the influence of linguistic investigations of variation, particularly those which showed how language varied according to purpose in a particular context of situation (Halliday et al, 1964; Gumperz & Hymes, 1972; Hymes, 1967). The ideal then was for students to learn to use language that was appropriate to their purpose in different contexts.

These insights into language and language development were clearly incompatible with a model of language that viewed language use and development primarily in terms of learning language rules suitable for all occasions. The belief that language development was aided by learning grammar seemed discredited by child language studies (Rosen & Rosen, 1973, p. 253). Nor was there any point in students learning rules and correcting ''errors'' in sentences when language variation was now seen to be the norm rather than the exception.

The move to eliminate language study from the school curriculum gained further support from numerous research studies that sought to establish what relation there was between learning about language and the development of writing abilities. From the early years of this century, starting with a study by Hoyt in 1906, there has been a steady stream of research that has claimed to demonstrate there is no beneficial relationship between systematic knowledge about language and the development of writing abilities. Recently some of the studies frequently cited in this area have been reviewed by Kolln (1981), who has revealed serious defects both in the methodology of the studies and in the interpretation of their findings. As Kolln rightly points out, a great deal depends on what is meant by ''teaching grammar.'' Many studies do illustrate that teaching about language as a separate subject in the curriculum without making links with students' writing is of no benefit to the development of writing abilities. However, there is also evidence from the same sources that when grammatical knowledge is taught in the context of students' own written texts their writing benefits from the instruction. For some reason, never made explicit where these studies are referred to, making conscious application of grammatical knowledge in one's language use is not counted as demonstrating that systematic knowledge about how language means is of relevance to improving writing abilities.

In developing new approaches for mother-tongue teaching educators abandoned the traditional school grammar which had been the staple of such teaching throughout this century, but at the same time they endorsed insights drawn from various schools of linguistics. Studies using transformational grammar had been used to illustrate the extent and nature of the child's mastery of grammar in the preschool years; studies from systemic linguistics were cited to illustrate the functional nature of the child's language use, perhaps best encapsulated by Halliday's description of language development as learning how to mean, and linguistics generally was the source for insights into language variation. It was clear that traditional school grammar was inappropriate for a model of language in use, but educators in Australia and the United Kingdom were reluctant to endorse another description of language for schools. The model that had gained supremacy in the late '60s and early '70s, in terms of widespread use, was transformational grammar, which sought to articulate native speakers' grammatical knowledge of their language. Like traditional school grammar it dealt with an idealized corpus of language; it was not directly concerned with language in use. Educators were aware that development needed to be assessed and kept track of over a period of time, but there was a strongly expressed view that teachers should develop what the English educator Barnes described as "their own maps" to trace development in language (Barnes, 1977). However, neither Barnes nor any other educator has given any suggestions about what such maps might look like.

The "new English" has now been seen to carry its own problems. While children have undoubtedly benefited from approaches that took account of their language expertise and sought to provide stimulating and interesting situations for language use, the evidence from the classroom is that more is needed to help children to develop their language abilities, particularly their writing skills. Let us try to articulate some of the major problems that are now apparent in current approaches to language development. First, there are no clear goals. It is all very well to aim to develop language use appropriate for different purposes but teachers cannot hope to include every aspect of language use in the curriculum. What are the goals in writing, for example? Are there certain varieties or genres that all students should learn to handle? Which ones? Why are they chosen in preference to others? Second, teachers currently have no objective, systematic means for characterizing successful language use. What does language appropriate to context mean? How is it recognized? Without being able to characterize "good or successful writing," for example, there is no way of mapping development or describing in a positive way a student's achievement or approximation to the goal. Third, some students still experience considerable difficulty in language development, particularly as far as writing is concerned. An absence of goals and their linguistic characterization makes it very difficult for teachers to develop strategies to teach children to use language successfully.

By and large, teachers have not made progress in developing their own means for tracking language development as suggested by Douglas Barnes, nor have other disciplines, such as educational psychology, provided them with the means for doing so. They have been presented with approaches to language development that are linguistically based but have no language knowledge to interpret their significance for classroom practice adequately. As a consequence they and their students suffer. As far as writing is concerned teachers have fallen back on the same vague and negative comments that have been the hallmark of English teaching from time immemorial: "vague ideas," "awkward" or "clumsy expression," "neat work," "tidy work," "good," "very good," and so on, none of which informs the writers in any precise way about their strengths or weaknesses or offers strategies for improvement. As far as students are concerned the nature of their learning has become increasingly invisible (Bernstein, 1979, 1986). This is not such a problem for that small group of successful writers who need minimal assistance from the teacher, but it is a serious concern for the majority of children who at some stage or another need help with their writing. Nowhere is this more evident than in the senior years of the secondary school when students are required to undertake a range of factual writing across the curriculum. Many students grapple in the dark and are seriously disadvantaged by what has become the hidden curriculum of writing development.

AN ASSESSMENT OF THE NEW ENGLISH

There is no doubt that the British educators who were largely responsible for the shape of the new English in Australian as well as British schools were deeply concerned with providing better opportunities for all students to develop their language abilities. In the United Kingdom educators had worked in an educational climate that more often than not rejected the child's home dialect, if it was other than the standard, and took little account of such children's language abilities because they did not fit easily into the school framework for language development. They were aware that the consequence of this for many children was failure in school; a vicious cycle was set up whereby their language was seen to be deficient for educational purposes and the possibility was raised that they were potentially less able intellectually than children from backgrounds where a different variety of language was used. Quite rightly these educators saw that the linguistic research of the '60s and '70s refuted this interpretation and provided a means for redressing this situation so that a more equitable schooling and ultimately a more equitable society should come into being.

A fundamental problem in the way the British educators interpreted the linguistic research for application in education was that, although they were deeply concerned about social outcomes, they gave a strong psychological focus to language work that often led to a disproportionate emphasis on talking and writing about personal and vicarious experience, particularly in the primary and junior secondary schools, at the cost of a wider range of language experiences. Underlying this was an individualistic view of human development that believed changes could be wrought by people developing their linguistic strengths and abilities to the utmost so that they could create more effective contexts for learning. Consider, for example, the following statements about the nature of the relationship between language, the language user, and the context of situation:

> A much more dangerous conclusion would be that language is predetermined, that words use us rather than that we use words, that we move from one context of situation to another submitting to its constraints. For not only can the individual change the context of situation unilaterally, since he is a component of that situation, but every context of situation is susceptible to change by all those who participate in it. (Rosen & Rosen, 1973, p. 258)

The Rosen's view of the relationship of language, language user, and context is individually oriented. The relationship is a much more complex one than the above statement suggests, as the remainder of this chapter will attempt to illustrate (Halliday, 1974, 1975, 1978a; Halliday & Hasan, 1985; Hasan, 1978, 1984a, 1984c; Martin, 1984a, 1985a). Nevertheless, it is probably true to say the Rosens' view was typical of those of many educators involved in disseminating ideas about the new English.

The dominance of an individual and psychological perspective of language use meant that the child's language and the child's meanings were seen as the hub of the language development program. What was lost sight of, ignored, or insufficiently taken into account was the nature of language itself as a system for making meaning and the crucial role of interaction and negotiation in making meanings and hence in effecting change. In other words, as can be seen from the Rosens' statement quoted earlier, there was no serious consideration of language as a social instrument for making meaning. These omissions were largely responsible for the failure of the new English to come to grips with social goals for language development and with classroom strategies of negotiation rather than those of telling or simply giving children the opportunity to use language. Taking into account the nature of language as a system for making meaning and its relationship with situational and cultural contexts makes it possible for educators and students to decide what students need to learn to do with language in order to be effective participants in a range of contexts.

Developing classroom strategies for teaching the new English was critical to its success. Encouraging children to use language in an environment that was supportive was a starting point, but classroom experience over the last decade has shown that language use does not equate with language development. Outside school the young child's oral language development is a complex matter that takes place through innumerable negotiations with adult caretakers where each party has a crucial role to play. The school too needed to develop practices in which language development occurred through negotiated exchanges. In this case, however, there was also the need to identify these practices in as precise and systematic fashion as possible so that they could be introduced to teachers and student teachers as ways of doing—in this case teaching— that could be learned. This meant that teachers and students needed an understanding of the nature of language as a system for making meaning so that they could see how the resources of the system were deployed in the negotiation of meanings in the classroom. At least part of the reason that this need was not addressed was that just as the language curriculum had become hidden in the new English because of the lack of explicit developmental goals, so language, as a consequence of omitting learning about language, had become increasingly invisible.

Perhaps the last words, or almost the last, can be left to Basil Bernstein, who saw clearly that the new pedagogy, if successful, was not simply a matter of "drawing out" the child's language but was rather a negotiated interaction between teacher and children. He could see, too, the dangers involved in leaving so much invisible about ways of teaching if the new methods were to survive.

> In the old pedagogical practice, repetition is ingrained in the structure; it is not a property of an individual or a set of individuals. The old structure carried within it, its own reproduction. But with the new pedagogical practice—based on interactions between individuals in groups in a *participated, negotiated relationship*—we have yet to discover how this practice can be reproduced. It is very fragile—very fragile—not only because of the weakness in its material base, but also because when one or two leave a school it tends to collapse. (Bernstein, 1979, pp. 297–298, emphasis added)

An essential aspect of reproducing new classroom strategies is identifying in a systematic way their characteristics as linguistic behavior. The most effective means for doing this is through analyzing classroom discourse so that teachers can see how they and their students use language to mean. The success of this procedure, of course, depends on learning about language.

THE SOCIOCULTURAL IMPORTANCE OF LANGUAGE DEVELOPMENT

In this chapter it will be argued that learning about language is essential for teachers and students if the principal aim of English-teaching syllabuses, to develop students' language abilities, is to be achieved. The first step in this argument is to consider why it is important for students to develop language, in particular literacy, to the maximum extent possible. Literacy is the principal means for effective participation in the community. It is the key to choice of occupation and to effective participation in a range of community matters and organizations. It not only gives access to the mainstream meanings of the society but also provides the means for influencing these so that the society itself may be changed. In short, literacy is empowering within the sociocultural context.

The school has the responsibility for teaching literacy and for developing it to the utmost for all students. This expectation is held by all members of the community regardless of racial or cultural background. If students are to be given the best possible opportunity to develop their language abilities, clear goals and carefully developed strategies are needed to achieve them. It is far too important a matter to pin one's hopes on indirect methods and intuitive hunches. The students who suffer most in the existing hidden curriculum of language development are those whose families have not developed high levels of literacy or those who are speakers of English as a second language. (The latter group is likely to include Australian Aborigines as well as children from immigrant families.) These are the children who need to get most from the school system in order to become effective participants in their own society. At present they are the ones who very often get the least. To put it briefly, implicit programs of language development discriminate against students from certain socioeconomic and language backgrounds.

It is sometimes argued that educational programs that aim to make the mainstream meanings of the culture accessible do so at a cost. Children from the different groups mentioned above may experience some loss of their own culture in respect to their own dialects, values, and so on. It must be recognized, however, that because literacy in our society, as in most others, is a function of schooling there are no traditions from a range of social groups to build on. The situation is different, of course, in respect to oracy, and the proponents of the new English made some attempt to address this in stressing the importance of the school respecting and working with the child's language as much as possible. The other factor that should be kept in mind is that there is a considerable difference between a program that leaves goals and strategies implicit and one that makes them explicit. Explicitness in the language curriculum gives students a conscious awareness of learning and the use they can make of it. How they adapt this to their purposes is their decision, but without access to the mainstream meanings of the culture, which is the likely result from an implicit program, they have far fewer choices available.

Learning about language, given an appropriate language model, becomes an enabling or facilitating factor in language development. It enables teachers and students to do the following:

1. To articulate language goals in terms of what students have to learn to do with language so that teachers and students alike know what they are aiming for.
2. To assess students' language use so they receive a positive picture of their efforts in respect of approximating a successful model.
3. To develop writing abilities by applying explicit language knowledge relevant to the task at hand.
4. To develop and replicate strategies of classroom negotiation for teaching language development.

The main section of this chapter will deal with two terms' work in a Sydney primary school where learning about language was used to achieve the above goals. First, however, we need to deal with the matter of choosing a language model appropriate to the stated aims of language development in the school curriculum.

THE SYSTEMIC FUNCTIONAL MODEL AND THE LANGUAGE CURRICULUM

Primary and secondary syllabuses for English teaching define language development in terms of learning to use language appropriately for different purposes. This definition gives language development a dual focus: the first is using language which entails a focus on meaning. We write and speak in order to mean. The second focus is appropriateness according to purpose. The latter focus takes us outside the language system and places us firmly in the sociocultural context for language use. Appropriateness involves understanding the purposes for language use in the society and how language is used to achieve them. Let us consider briefly a common purpose for language use in most societies, that of buying and selling goods. In most Western societies, for example, buying and selling transactions in shops and stores provide for little if any negotiation regarding the price of goods. This is not the case in many Asian societies, where bartering about the price is an essential aspect of the transaction. Here we have an example of a purpose common to many societies but involving quite different social judgments about what is appropriate language behavior for achieving the purpose.

There are other matters that play a part in appropriateness: how subject matter is handled, how the audience is addressed, how language is used according to whether the mode is spoken or written. In secondary

schools, subject matter is one area that is well recognized for its significance. Unless speakers and writers have some knowledge about the topic
at hand, their language use will suffer. Consequently, there is a fairly
widespread acknowledgment that students must be given the time and
opportunity to become familiar with a topic before they can be expected
to talk or write about it successfully. It is also recognized that different
audiences influence the way speakers and writers use language. There
are differences here between speech and writing. As students move into
factual writing, which is so important in the secondary school, they have
to learn to take up a neutral stance toward their reader. It is not appropriate in this kind of writing to express personal opinions such as ''I
like.'' There is a vague recognition too that speech is different from
writing although the two modes draw on the same system (Halliday,
1985a). But how they are different remains unclear. The impression is
given in syllabus documents that subject matter, audience, and language
mode are part of appropriateness, as is purpose. What remains completely obscure is how these factors are related to purpose of language
use and how all of them are to be dealt with in the classroom.

Language as a Resource for Meaning: A Systemic Description of the Language System

A systemic functional model of language is well suited to an educational
program that aims to develop language through use, for a number of
reasons. First, it has a semantic orientation that is appropriate for a
language development program with focus on meaning. One aspect of
this is its description of the resources of language as system networks,
or bundles of choices, enabling us to identify the particular choices for
meaning that speakers and writers make in a given context (Halliday,
1973). In the following section, the transitivity system, the system for
experiential meanings in the clause, is described. The significance of a
description that is oriented to choice will be explored in the discussion
of the relationship between text and context. A second aspect of the
semantic orientation of a systemic description is its functional description of lexicogrammatical structures (Halliday, 1985a). The sections that
follow will also deal with the experiential structure of the clause and, at
a later point, with the nominal group structure. Finally, the systemic
functional model incorporates a description of the text-forming resources of language that enables us to account for texts, the stretches
of language exhibiting semantic unity which speakers and writers typically produce (Halliday & Hasan, 1976; Martin, 1983). The importance
of this aspect of the description cannot be underestimated, as it is text
that Halliday identifies as the semantic unit of language in use. Whether
they are using language in the school or in the community, children are

largely engaged in producing texts. One of the serious drawbacks of many language descriptions for educational purposes is that they are clause-based descriptions of language that, when applied, reveal only a partial picture of how we use language to mean.

Experiential Choices for Meaning in the Clause: The Clause as Process

> What does it mean to say that a clause represents a process? Our most powerful conception of reality is that it consists of ''goings-on'': of doing, happening, feeling, being. These goings-on are sorted out in the semantic system of language, and expressed through the grammar of the clause. Parallel with its evolution in the function of mood, expressing the active, interpersonal aspect of meaning, the clause evolved simultaneously in another grammatical function expressing the reflective experiential aspect of meaning. This latter is the system of *transitivity*. Transitivity specifies the different types of process that are recognized in the language, and the structures by which they are expressed. (Halliday 1985b, p. 101)

The transitivity system specifies choices for experiential meanings in the clause. The system is a paradigmatic description. That is to say, it presents the *choices* available to a speaker of English for meanings about process. The choices are given semantic labels, thus highlighting how language is structured to mean. The system network represented below shows the choices for meaning in respect of process in English. The entry condition in the grammar for making this choice is the unit clause.

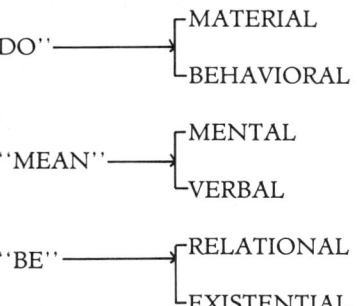

Figure 1.   Simplified system of English process

The system network depicted in Fig. 1 gives English speakers three main options for experiential meanings in the clause: those of doing, meaning, and being. Each of these options opens up further choices. The choice of [DO] leads to a choice between [MATERIAL] and [BEHAV-

IORAL]; the choice of [MEAN] leads to a choice between [MENTAL] and [VERBAL] and the choice of [BE] leads to a choice of [RELATIONAL] or [EXISTENTIAL]. Let us consider the meanings of each of the choices in more detail.

Doing processes are processes of *action*. *Behavioral* processes differ from *material* ones in that they are to do with physiological and psychological behavior. The following illustrates how each of these choices can be realized:

Doing Processes
material: run, move, fight, hit, etc.
  I *broke* the glass vase.
behavioral: sleep, laugh, eat, sneeze, etc.
  She *sleeps* soundly.

Meaning processes can be *mental* or *verbal*. Mental processes are about *perception*, *reaction*, and *cognition*. Verbal processes are processes of "saying." Below are some examples of realizations of choices for meaning processes:

Meaning Processes
mental: think, believe, like, see, fear, etc.
  I *like* apples.
verbal: say, tell, etc.
  She *told* him to come down from the tree.

Verbal processes carry a wider meaning than that of saying through language: "saying" can cover any kind of symbolic meaning in the clause, as in The sign *says* to slow down.

Being processes can be *relational* or *existential*. Relational processes identify participants or assign attributes while existential ones state their existence. Both types of processes are often realized by the verb *be*.

Being Processes
relational: seem, become, turn, appear, etc.
  She *seems* pale today.
existential: be
  There *are* many different types of cats.

The system network provides a good illustration of what Halliday means by language as a resource for meaning. It presents the potential for meaning at a given point in the grammar, in this instance the potential for process meanings, which speakers and writers draw on according to the demands of the different contexts of situation they encounter.

The Experiential Structure of the Clause: Process, Participants, and Circumstances

A process may comprise three components:

1. the process;
2. participants in the process;
3. circumstances associated with the process.

The choice of Process in the transitivity system is realized by a transitivity structure in the clause. The transitivity structure is a configuration of functions which encodes the semantic options of process, participants, and circumstance. The following examples of clauses show the configuration of functions that realize choices in this system.

Example 1

The giant	grabbed	the boy	outside the window.
Actor	Material Process	Goal	Circumstance of Location

Example 2

James	likes	cats.
Senser	Mental Process	Phenomenon

As the examples above clearly illustrate, the configuration of functions that constitutes a transitivity structure has a semantic orientation so that the grammatical description enables us to develop our understanding of how language is structured to mean.

Participants in the Clause: The Structure of the Nominal Group

Transitivity structure has to do with the grammar of processes, what Halliday describes as the "goings-on" of our experience. The nominal group structure has to do with the grammar of the participants who play a part in the process. In this chapter there is a particular concern with how language means in the nominal group, as this was the part of the grammar taught to a grade-two class as part of a language-based writing program. The children were taught the configuration of functions that constitute the structure of the nominal group, with labels appropriate for their age group, as part of their work in developing mastery of Report writing. The structure will be introduced using Halliday's description (Halliday, 1985b). Consider the following nominal group: *these two beautiful old lace cloths with fine embroidery*. The group exhibits the full range of functions: Deictic (D), Numerative (N), Epithet (E), Classifier (C), Thing (T), and Qualifier (Q), as the analysis below shows:

Example 3

these	two	beautiful	old	lace	cloths	with fine embroidery
D	N	E1	E2	C	T	Q

The structure above is experiential. It specifies a class of *things*, in this case *cloths*. The functional label *Thing* is given to the element expressing the class. Typically class membership is expressed by one or more of the above functions *Deictic, Numerative, Epithet, Classifier, and Qualifier*. Example 3 indicates all these functions. Let us examine them briefly one by one.

Deictic. Deictic picks out participants. Deictic elements can be subclassified as specific or nonspecific. Specific deictic can be further subclassified as demonstrative or possessive. Both types of deixis locate the Thing by reference to the speaker: demonstratives in terms of proximity and possessives by possession. In the clause *This book is mine*, the deictic, *this*, locates the book in terms of close proximity to the speaker. On the other hand, in the clause *My book is here*, the deictic, *my*, locates the book in terms of the speaker's possession. In Example 3 *these* has a deictic function locating the cloths in terms of close proximity to the speaker.

There is one other specific deictic, *the*, which has a different meaning. As Halliday says, the occurrence of *the* in the nominal group means the following: "The subset in question is identifiable; but this will not tell you how to identify it" (Halliday, 1985b, p. 161). In fact, where *the* occurs, the identity of Thing in the nominal group may be retrieved either from the surrounding text, in which case the reference is endophoric, or from the context of situation, in which the case the reference is said to be exophoric. In the fairy tale "Little Red Riding Hood," for example, the character may be referred to as *the little girl* after she has been introduced in the text. In this case the reference is endophoric, as the identity of *the little girl* can be retrieved from the text. On the other hand, a mother talking to her small child might refer to *the book* the child is looking at. In this instance, the identity of book is retrievable from outside language, in the context of situation. The reference is therefore exophoric.

There are also nonspecific Deictics, such as *a* and *some*, which convey the sense of some unspecified subset. The deictic *a* is commonly used to introduce new participants into a text. In the clause *I saw a strange cat in the garden yesterday*, the deictic, *a*, signals a new participant in the discourse.

Numerative. Numeratives measure participants. The function, as the name suggests, indicates some numerical feature of the subset. *Two, three; second, third; few, more;* and so on are Numeratives. In Example 3, *two* has the function Numerative.

Epithet. Epithets give qualities and attitudes. The function indicates some quality of the subset which may be an objective property of the thing or may be an expression of the speaker's attitude toward it. The former group of Epithets, identified as experiential ones, includes such items as *red, blue, fast, slow, large, small.* The latter group, identified as attitudinal, includes items such as *silly, cute, friendly.* Attitudinal Epithets usually precede experiential ones. We tend to say, for example, *the silly little dog*, not *the little silly dog*. Note too that a verb may have the function of Epithet in the structure of the nominal group. In the group *the barking dog*, *barking* has the function Epithet. In Example 3, there are two Epithets, *beautiful* and *old*. *Beautiful* is an attitudinal Epithet while *old* is an experiential one.

Classifier. The Classifier indicates a particular subclass of things. For example, we identify *brick* fences, *stone* fences, or *wooden* fences, among others. *Brick, stone,* and *wooden* are Classifiers in their respective nominal groups. *Lace* is Classifier in Example 3 above. Sometimes the same word may function as Epithet or Classifier. For example, when we talk about *red kangaroos* we are identifying a subclassification of the species. Thus, *red* is a Classifier. However, when we refer to a *red dress* the function of *red* in the nominal group is Epithet.

Thing. Halliday describes the function Thing as "the semantic core of the nominal group" (Halliday, 1985b; p. 159). It may be a common noun, a proper noun, or a personal pronoun. In Example 3, *cloths* is Thing in the nominal group structure.

Qualifier. The function Qualifier follows Thing in the nominal group. It differs from the preceding functions in that it is either a phrase or clause. In Example 3, the phrase *with fine embroidery* is the Qualifier.

However, the Qualifier could have been realized by a clause, as in the following structure: *these two beautiful old lace cloths which my grandmother embroidered*. In this instance the Qualifier is the clause *which my grandmother embroidered*.

Halliday draws attention to the ordering of functions in the nominal group and points out that there is a progression from left to right as far as the functions preceding Thing are concerned, from the element that has the least potential for categorization, the Deictic, to the one that has the most, the Classifier. So, for example, in the nominal group *these two beautiful old lace cloths*, the Deictic, *these*, has the least potential for specifying *cloths* while the Classifier, *lace*, has the greatest. Another way of viewing this progression in specification is that the most permanent quality of the thing in question is that which comes immediately before Thing in the group and the most transient is that which occurs farthest away.

Text-Forming Resources: Theme and Cohesion

Another aspect of the semantic orientation of a systemic description is its ability to deal with text. As noted previously, text can be described as a stretch of language of indeterminate length exhibiting semantic unity. A text may be only a few clauses or it may be many thousands; the issue is not so much one of length but of semantic unity. The semantic unity of a text is derived in part from a grammatical choice for ordering the message of the clause in terms of Theme and Rheme and from cohesion.

Choice in Ordering the Message of the Clause: Theme and Rheme

One important aspect of creating text is the ordering of the message in the clause (Fries, 1983). In English, speakers have a choice of what occupies first position in the clause: this is known as *Theme*. Theme is the point of departure for the message of the clause. (For a discussion of the significance of Theme in spoken discourse, see Christie, chapter 4 in this volume.) The remainder of the message is identified as *Rheme*. For example, it is possible to write either of the following:

1. *Red Riding Hood* stopped to pick flowers on her way to her grandmother's.
2. *On her way to her grandmother's* Red Riding Hood stopped to pick flowers.

In the first example the participant, *Red Riding Hood*, is Theme; in the second a circumstantial role, *on her way to her grandmother's*, is Theme.

The choice the writer makes depends very much on how he or she is using Theme to develop a text. In a Narrative such as the fairy tale "Little Red Riding Hood," there is a tendency for the main character to occupy first position in the clause so that the participant role becomes the method of development for the text. However, this may change at certain points. Often the writer chooses a circumstantial role to mark the beginning of a new stage of the text. In other words, the choice of Theme plays an important part in making the text "hang together" as a semantic unit.

In addition to the lexicogrammar there are other resources for creating text, which Martin identifies as belonging to the discourse stratum of language (Martin, 1985a). Halliday and Hasan identify such resources as being responsible for cohesion in a text, where cohesion means that "the interpretation of some element in the discourse is dependent on that of another" (Halliday & Hasan, 1976, p. 4). The resources for cohesion are substitution, ellipsis, reference, conjunction, and lexical relations.

Let us consider some aspects of one of these, reference, in the tale "Little Red Riding Hood," in order to see what is meant by the interpretation of some element depending on that of another. The pronoun *she* occurs many times throughout the story. In many instances the interpretation of the identity of *she* is dependent on *Little Red Riding Hood*. The text can be properly understood only by interpreting the dependency relationship between *she* and *Little Red Riding Hood*. This type of dependency relation is identified as *reference*. What happens too, as this pattern continues throughout a text, is that chains of reference are set up for this and other characters whereby the identity of each participant is retrieved by reference to another item. The following reference chain is only part of the one pertaining to Red Riding Hood.

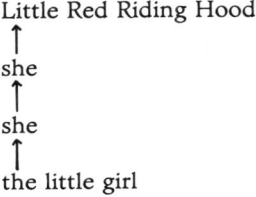

Little Red Riding Hood
↑
she
↑
she
↑
the little girl

Each item in this chain, after the introduction of the main character, is interpreted by reference back through the chain to Little Red Riding Hood.

A program of language development that aims to develop language through use is concerned primarily with texts. In the past, educators have been critical of language descriptions that are clause-based and that do not take account of meaning, as these have, quite rightly, been seen to be limited in their scope. The criticism has not been directed at the quality of the description but rather at its appropriateness for educational contexts. A systemic linguistic grammar is a functional one that illuminates how language is structured to mean in both the clause and the text. It is also a grammar developed around the notion of choice: the system networks present choices for meaning at a given point in the grammar so that language can be seen as a resource for meaning that is drawn on according to situational demands. The relationship between text and context will be taken up in the following section of this chapter, as that, too, is a matter of concern for educators.

LANGUAGE IN USE: THE RELATIONSHIP BETWEEN TEXT AND CONTEXT

The sociocultural orientation of a systemic functional model of language enables systematic links to be established between a text and its contents so that teachers and students can perceive how factors outside of language influence its use. It is this relationship that constitutes appropriateness, which is aimed for in language development programs. The model assumed in this chapter regarding the relationship between a text and its sociocultural environment is that developed by J. R. Martin. Martin, following Hjelmslev (1961), distinguishes between "denotative semiotics, which have their own expression form, and connotative semiotics, which do not" (Martin, 1986, p. 266). Thus, language, which has a phonology for making meaning, is a denotative semiotic. Martin distinguishes two semiotic levels which are connotative and find their expression through language (Martin, 1984a). These are register and genre. It is these two semiotic levels that are responsible for the distinctive patterns of meanings found in texts. The relationship between the three is represented in the diagram below.

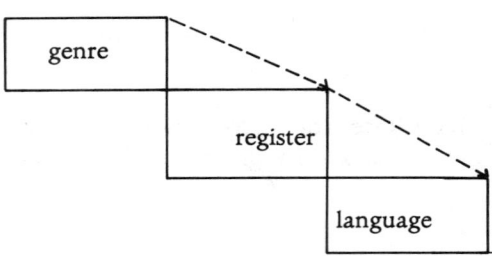

In this chapter only one of the connotative semiotics, genre, will be dealt with. Register, the other connotative semiotic, is just as crucial to successful language use: its scope corresponds roughly to subject matter, audience role, and speech/writing differences. These aspects of language use have already been referred to as playing a part in successful writing. Any comprehensive account of learning about language would need to include an account of register and how it is realized in language. That, however, will not be attempted in this chapter.

Genre, as a connotative semiotic, lies outside language in the context of culture: it is best described as a language-based theory of culture. It interprets culture as a system of social processes which can be recognized and analyzed in terms of their distinctive stages. These stages are the processes by which the culture manifests itself. The stages are the means for realizing purposes or goals through language. The cultural nature of genre has already been mentioned in reference to buying and selling activities in different societies. It should be apparent therefore that genre, as described by Martin, has a much broader application than the traditional literary genres. Consulting a doctor is a genre, as is making an appointment or applying for a job. All of these are social, goal-oriented language activities.

As native speakers we have some sense of a text having a beginning, middle, and end stage. As a consequence we have an awareness of whether a text is complete or incomplete. This knowledge is something teachers often use in helping students to develop their writing. They frequently spend some time with students in working on effective introductions and conclusions, thus indicating quite explicitly that a text has distinctive stages. The knowledge is also used in assessing a student's piece of writing. Teachers are usually right when they make a comment like: ''Your essay lacks a conclusion.'' It is this aspect of text, its organization into distinct stages, which is the other main factor contributing to its semantic unity. In other words, the goal or purpose of the language is not achieved unless the necessary stages have been gone through. In a previous section of this chapter, buying and selling transactions in different cultures were mentioned. Ventola (1983) identifies the stages of a buying and selling genre in a Western society thus:

Greeting
Turn allocation (selection of next customer: ''Who's next?'')
Service bid (offer of service: ''Can I help you?'')
Service (statement of needs and their provision: ''Yes, I'm looking for . . .'')
Resolution (decision to buy or not to buy: ''Yes, I'll have those.'')

Pay (exchange of payment)
Goods handover (exchange of goods)

The goal of purchasing goods or selling goods is realized as the speakers move through the appropriate stages. As mentioned previously, not all cultures achieve buying and selling goals in the same way. Some engage in bartering in order to achieve their goals. As a consequence the distinctive stages of their texts will differ from those described above.

One of the goals we pursue through language is entertaining and amusing our companions. One way we achieve this in our society is through the genre Narrative. Narrative deals with experience that is problematic in some respect and hence attracts our interest about the outcome. Labov and Waletzky (1967) identify these stages in oral Narrative: *Abstract, Orientation, Complication, Evaluation, Resolution, Coda.* The stages are well exemplified in the following Narrative elicited by a colleague in the course of a sociolinguistic interview.

Abstract	There is one story where I was a bit surprised. Because I've always wanted a dog that'd just be my dog. You know, and that's the way Cleo is, she's just my dog; she obeys me and nobody else. And a dog who would protect me, you know, and I didn't think Cleo lived up to that because she seemed to be more of a softy type of dog, affectionate but soft, you know.
Orientation	Anyway, this one day I was walking along the street. I had two hands full of bags 'n' clothes and I had just come back from the laundromat: like I told you before how Cleo goes for the smaller dogs?
Complication	Well, I didn't have her on the lead because I had my hands full and she took off after this dog. And anyway she ran up to it and she hit it, ran into it but didn't knock it over, she didn't bite it or nothin'. Then she just started sniffin' around and that.
Evaluation	And the guy who owned it was, say, in his thirties and he got very very stroppy towards me, you know, and he wanted to fight me about it, you know. And you know, naturally I got very defensive because he started saying, you know, he'd hit Cleo with his lead and I immediately dropped my bags and put my fists up, you know and go, ''Mate, come on,'' you know, ''have your go.''
Resolution	And then as soon as he put his fist up and took a step towards me Cleo immediately stepped in between the two

of us and stood at my feet and just growled and showed her teeth at this guy and he just took off. You know, he just said, ''Yeah, well, the next time I see you without your dog mate you're gone,'' and he took off.

Coda   .   And that is, you know, very pleasing to me because I realised that Cleo would stick up for me and she was the dog that I wanted.

The *Abstract* signals a Narrative is coming: It points to some problematic experience. It may also indicate something about the point of the story, the reason for the narrator telling it. In this case, the narrator indicates that the events he is about to narrate were a surprise to him; they ran counter to his expectations about the dog's behavior. In telling his listener this he also presents a picture of what he sees as the ''ideal'' relationship between dog and owner. The Abstract also gives some idea of what the Narrative will be about: In this instance, the dog protecting or not protecting the owner emerges as a focus for the Narrative.

The *Orientation* provides a setting of some kind; it may also introduce the main characters. Here the Orientation gives a place setting, together with some foreshadowing of what is to come by reminding the listener that Cleo, a very large dog by the way, has a tendency to pick on dogs much smaller than herself. Notice how the place setting is established through the circumstantial roles *along the street* and *from the laundromat*. The nature of the action that is about to come is suggested in the following transitivity structure:

Cleo	goes for	the smaller dog
Actor	Material Process	Goal

Already we can see some things about the nature of Narrative. Cleo has been introduced in the Abstract as a main character in the text. The nature of her role is made clear in the transitivity structure described above, where Cleo is Actor in the Material Process and ''smaller dogs'' is Goal. Narratives are about actions and about ''heroes'' and ''heroines.'' The main characters, who take on the roles of heros and heroines, are usually the ''doers'' in respect of most of the actions of the Narrative. This means that they hold the participant role of Actor in Material Processes. Those whom they are in some sense opposed to tend to occupy the participant role of Goal in this process type.

The *Complication* stage is about a problem of some kind; something goes wrong. In this case, Cleo, true to form, picks on a smaller dog. Once again in the Material and Behavioral Processes Cleo is Actor or

Behaver while the smaller dog is Goal. Consider the transitivity structures in the following clauses from the point where Cleo runs away from her owner and initiates the action that leads to the development of the conflict between the dogs and their owners. (Note that the conjunctions linking clauses have not been included in the analysis as they are not part of the transitivity structure.)

she	took off	after this dog
Actor	Material Process	Circumstance of Place

she	ran up	to it
Actor	Material Process	Circumstance of Place

she	hit	it
Actor	Material Process	Goal

ran into	it
Material Process	Goal

didn't knock	it	over
Material Process	Goal	Circumstance of Manner

she	didn't bite	it	or nothin'
Actor	Material Process	Goal	

she	just started sniffin' around	and that
Behaver	Behavioral Process	

The pattern that clearly emerges here is that Cleo is the "doer" or Actor or Behaver in the Material and behavioral Processes and the other dog is the "receiver" or Goal. Notice too, *the sequence of actions* in these clauses:

took off after
ran up to
ran into
didn't knock over
didn't bite
started sniffin'

This sequence reveals the nature of the problem that developed with the dogs. *Took off after, ran up to, ran into* indicate a mild skirmish of some kind. It is put into perspective by the negation of the Material Processes that follow: *didn't knock, didn't bite,* followed by the uneventful *started sniffin'.*

The *Evaluation,* as the name suggests, gives an evaluation of the events, revealing why they are seen to be significant and how the main character, or characters, react to them. In this case both dog owners become emotionally involved in the events, so much so they are prepared to fight about them. Notice the lexical items, both of which are modified by the intensifier *very,* which expresses the owners' reactions to what happened: *very, very stroppy, very defensive.*

In the *Resolution* the problem is sorted out for better or worse. For a while it seemed as if the owner of the other dog might take action against Cleo and his owner. This possible change of direction is signaled in the following transitivity structure:

he	would hit	Cleo	with his lead
Actor	Material Process	Goal	Circumstances of Manner

In this structure "the other dog's owner" is Actor in the Material Process, Cleo is Goal, and Circumstances of Manner indicates the weapon to be used against Cleo. Cleo, however, takes the initiative and becomes the heroine, saving her owner from an attack! The transitivity structure in the following clauses reveals the picture clearly:

Cleo	immediately	stepped in	between the two of us
Actor	Circumstance of Time	Material Process	Circumstance of Place

stood	at my feet
Material Process	Circumstance of Place

just growled
Behavioral Process

showed	her teeth	at this guy
Behavioral Process	Range	Circumstance of Place

Cleo is the Actor in the Material Processes; her behavior is threatening but she doesn't take action against the other owner so he is not Goal in these Processes. But her behavior is sufficient to send him into flight, thus saving the day for her owner!

Coda also reiterates that the story was worth telling, making it clear to the listener why the Narrative was told. As in this instance, the Coda often picks up the Abstract, only now there is nothing problematic about Cleo's protective behavior. The narrator makes it clear that she has proved herself and that she is just the dog he always wanted.

Speakers and writers have some freedom in choosing and ordering generic stages. Some stages may be optional, others may be repeated a number of times. For example, in written Narratives the Abstract stage does not seem to occur as frequently as in spoken ones. Also, in written Narratives there is more likely to be a repetition of the Complication and Resolution stages before the final Resolution is achieved. One has only to think of Narratives for young children such as ''The Three Little Pigs'' to know this is a common Narrative strategy. The wolf makes a number of attempts to trap the little pigs before they finally succeed in defeating him. On other occasions certain stages may be omitted, some may be repeated, and various orderings may occur to achieve one's goal through language. Mastery of a genre involves being able to deploy its potential to achieve one's purpose in a particular context.

Genre influences choices in all three types of meaning that Halliday identifies as co-occurring in the clause: experiential, interpersonal, and textual meanings. Experiential meanings have been introduced in the discussion of transitivity and textual meanings in the discussion of Theme. Interpersonal meanings are realized largely through choices in the mood and modality systems. (These are not dealt with in this chapter, as they tend not to be as significant in written texts as when spoken.) The pattern of choices for these three types of meaning changes in different stages of the genre. The analysis of some of the experiential meanings in the Narrative about Cleo shows how transitivity choices differ in the Complication and Resolution stages of the text. It is important to stress that genre determines changing patterns of meaning at each stage of the text. Otherwise there is a danger it will be seen as a form or structure into which context is slotted. Nothing could be further from the truth. Genre exists through language and the identification of its distinct stages is a function of the changing pattern of linguistic choices from state to stage of a given text.

The scope of learning about language that has been presented in the first part of this chapter is much broader than learning about the structures of the clause that is associated with traditional school grammar. The scope is considerable: from the functional description of how texts are organized in stages to achieve culturally determined goals. Or, to put it more technically, learning about language involves learning about how language is structured to mean, and how language, the denotative semiotic, is related to the connotative semiotic of genre.

At present, language and context—and genre is the linguistic manifestation of cultural context—are not brought together satisfactorily in the classroom. Indeed, it is no exaggeration to say they are hardly brought together at all. Syllabus documents have not given any guidelines as to how context is to be interpreted for systematic teaching practice. This is true not only for the texts children are asked to produce but also for the texts teachers and children use to promote language development. As a result, developing language through use remains an unfulfilled ideal. The practical outcomes have already been mentioned: the lack of clear goals for language development programs and, consequently, the lack of any sense of stages in achieving and approximating goals. The inclusion of genre as one type of context enables purposes for language use to be described in terms of types of text with distinctive stages and patterns of language. In other words, genre is a means for wedding text and context in the classroom.

Understanding language use from the point of view of purpose enables us to make some important distinctions regarding goals for language development. First, it enables us to distinguish genres that are important in the daily life of the community and those which are crucial in educational contexts. Applications for jobs and inquiries for information from government and professional agencies are only a few of the genres that play an important part in the broader life of the community. Exposition and Narrative, on the other hand, are genres that are important in education. Of course there is an overlap between school and community genres. Report, for example, is a genre that is commonly required in many different occupations as well as in educational contexts. The point is that schools need to decide which community genres as well as educational ones will be included in school programs.

Second, the systemic functional model enables us to identify the distinctive stages of the genres we wish students to master and key aspects of their linguistic realization. For example, the kind of analysis given earlier of the stages of Narrative and some of its experiential meanings can be used to give students a positive model of what they are working toward.

Third, the model provides, through its functional description of language, linguistic tools for teachers and students to use in developing mastery of a range of genres. For students such tools will play an important part in learning to handle the written genres of education. For teachers they will be invaluable for developing insights into the nature of teaching genres, the patterns of classroom discourse which are crucial for successful teaching and learning.

BRINGING LANGUAGE INTO CONSCIOUSNESS

Thus far I have argued that learning about language in an educational context means that students learn both about the language system and about the semiotic systems of register and genre that lie outside language. I have also focused on the systemic functional model of language as one that is particularly appropriate for school language programs. Once this model is adopted for school use, it offers a great deal of flexibility and choice in the way it can be used. Learning about language can go in different directions, depending on the starting point: from language to register or genre, or from genre or register to language. I would suggest that in educational contexts where the emphasis is on students' learning to use language appropriately or effectively for different purposes, that genre, the stages passed through to achieve goals within a given culture, provides a more readily accessible starting point for learning about language. In dealing with genre we are dealing with texts, and text is the semantic unit of language in use. There is another reason for making this suggestion: Within the community generally, as well as the school, there is a strong awareness that there are varieties of texts. This is clearly indicated by the fact that Report, Narrative, Consultation, Instructions, Recipe, and so on, are commonly used in many different contexts. By beginning with genre, therefore, we begin where there is already some awareness of unique features as far as texts are concerned.

From genre teachers and students can proceed to some examination of the patterns of linguistic choices that embody the meanings of the genre and that are characteristic of different stages of the text. At this point it should be stressed that such learning would be directly related to the texts the students produced. For example, in the Narratives written by young writers there is often a need to work on the Orientation as the stage where time and place settings are established for the action that is to follow. This may lead to some work on transitivity structures with a particular emphasis on circumstantial roles as a means for building up these descriptions. The purpose of such teaching is to make explicit the *potential* of the system for meaning at a given point in the grammar. In other words, what is being argued for is learning about language so that it becomes a conscious resource for meaning.

Given that the focus in this chapter is an applied one, it is nevertheless true that over a period of years students who work with language in this way will build up a body of knowledge about language in its own right. They will be involved in an increasingly deeper and more comprehensive understanding of the language system and its relation to context as they make use of this knowledge for their own purposes in using language. What this means is that over the years of their schooling they will develop a mastery of language knowledge, which they will be able to draw on and adapt for purposes that are wide-ranging both in and out of school.

It is often said by educators that making children conscious of language by teaching them about it is likely to prove an inhibiting factor in the development of writing abilities. Successful writing, it is claimed, depends very much on an unconscious flow of language. There is some truth in this statement but it does not present the whole picture by any means. For anyone who has spent some time in an infants' school classroom it is apparent that becoming literate involves a consciousness of language that is not present with speech, or rather is no longer present by the time children start school. To read and write, children must develop a consciousness of the units of language, in particular words, sentences or clause complexes, and texts and how these are organized graphically. Good teachers spend a great deal of time with young children, developing their awareness of how the constituents of language are presented in writing. Children have to learn to perceive these different units as entities that are distinct and yet at the same time semantically related.

It is probably true that during the competent writer's flow of composition this awareness falls into the background, so to speak, and the focus on meaning is predominant. But it re-emerges when the writer pauses, reads back, and makes changes to the text already written. James Britton has reported on the importance of this reading-back procedure in composition. He and colleagues from the London Institute of Education conducted an experiment in which writers were asked to write a text using a ballpoint pen without ink but writing on paper with a carbon copy. It was found that under these circumstances, in which the writer could not stop and read back, the quality of the text deteriorated greatly even for writers who were generally regarded as competent (Britton, Burgess, Martin, McLeod, & Rosen, 1975).

No matter how proficient a writer becomes, writing always demands a different degree of consciousness from speaking. While successful writers may become less conscious of the language system they are working with, it is nevertheless likely that there remains a level of consciousness regarding written language which is different from that of spoken language. What would seem to happen is that there are shifts in the degree of awareness at different points in the composition. What this study suggests is that writers need regularly to bring into conscious focus, so to speak, what has been written, in order to develop their texts successfully. It may well be more accurate to characterize composition in terms of shifts in the degree of conscious awareness writers brings to bear on their language. At this stage of our understanding about the nature of written composition, more than this cannot even be speculated about.

Over time the writer becomes conscious that language can be manipulated in various ways to achieve meaning: Word order can be changed; words, phrases, or clauses can be added or substituted; sentence order can be altered and whole paragraphs reordered within a text. But even with successful writers this process remains largely intuitive. This "reading-back" point is one place where writers can make good use of conscious knowledge about language. For young writers, from the very beginning there is a conscious grappling with the text as they attempt to achieve their meaning. Given that this degree of consciousness of language seems to exist for everyone in the early stages, it seems sensible to take advantage of what is happening as part of their learning and build on it in a constructive way.

Teaching Writing: Applying Early Language Development Strategies in the Classroom

Successful teaching depends on interactional strategies in the classroom. The new English saw "drawing-out" strategies in which the teacher brought to light the child's language abilities by providing frequent opportunities for language use and giving constant encouragement to the child for his or her efforts. The child language studies of the systemic functional model present a different perspective on the adult caretaker's role in child language development. They highlight the adult's role as guide and leader in linguistic exchanges with young children. (See Butt and Painter in this volume, as well as Halliday, 1975; Painter, 1984). The nature of this interaction can best be summed up as guidance in the context of shared experience, leading to the learner's being able to develop texts, where appropriate, as a solo effort. The application of strategies of early child language development in educational settings will be developed more fully in the following sections.

Two practices emerge as important ones to make use of in the classroom. The first is modeling. Adults are constantly giving young children examples of the different genres that play a part in their everyday lives. They do this in conversation with children and in interaction with other members of the family and neighborhood. Children learn the ways in which goals are achieved through language in the course of daily life. The adult's role in this interaction is to lead the child toward the successful development of the text through questions and comments that guide the child into a particular genre. Applebee and Langer (1983), who also advocate this strategy for learning, use a term coined by the psychologist Jerome Bruner when they refer to it as "scaffolding." (The same term is used by the American educator Donald Graves in reference to the "drawing-out" questions which he suggests teachers ask. The use is quite different in this context, where it refers to the active role taken by the adult in *jointly* constructing texts with the child.) The term is an apt one for describing the adult's role in providing the linguistic framework for the child's development of meaning.

The texts Applebee and Langer refer to in their discussion of scaffolding as a strategy for language development are from Halliday's study of a young child developing language (Halliday, 1975). The first text was jointly constructed by father and child after a visit to the zoo, where an incident with a goat took the attention of the young child, Nigel. Nigel had patted a goat which then attempted to eat the small plastic lid he was holding. The keeper intervened to prevent the goat from consuming his newfound food.

Nigel	try eat lid
Father	What tried to eat the lid?
Nigel	try eat lid
Father	What tried to eat the lid?
Nigel	goat . . . man said no . . . goat try eat lid . . . man said no

(Halliday, 1975, p. 112)

In the text above, Nigel's father helped him to shape a text of a Narrative type. There is a problem, the goat tried to eat the lid, and the beginnings of a solution, in that Nigel says the man said the goat was not to do this. Presumably the keeper took the lid away from the goat but Nigel does not include this in his text. To begin with, Nigel uses a transitivity structure, *try eat lid*, which includes *eating*, a *Behavioral Process*, and *lid*, which has the participant function of *Range*. However, he does not include the function *Behaver* in his transitivity structure. In other words, there is no mention of one of the main protagonists, the goat, in this brief drama. The question asked by Nigel's father, who knows very well what was responsible for trying to eat the lid, aims to get Nigel to include the main character, the goat, in this scenario. The purpose of the question is to provide Nigel with the scaffolding for reconstructing experience along Narrative lines in a text with an embryonic Complication, Resolution shape. Finally Nigel gets to this point where, on his own, he states the problem, *goat . . . man said no . . . goat try eat lid . . . man said no*. What has happened here is that the interaction has not only been the means for developing a more complete text but has also been the precursor for the child developing a very short Narrative type text on his own.

The second text was constructed by Nigel and his mother a short time afterward on the basis of the same episode.

Nigel   goat try eat lid . . . man said no . . .
Mother   Why did the man say no?
Nigel   Goat shouldn't eat the lid . . . (shaking head) good for it
Mother   The goat shouldn't eat the lid; it's not good for it.
Nigel   goat try eat lid . . . man said no . . . goat shouldn't eat lid . . . (shaking head) good for it

(Halliday, 1975, p. 112)

Notice on this occasion Nigel started his text with what was his end point in the exchange with his father. His mother's question serves to focus on another important aspect of Narrative in the development of Complication and Resolution stages and that is the reason (or reasons) for a certain course of action. Nigel responds to the scaffolding provided by his mother to embark on part of a relational transitivity structure, *good for it*, together with a negative shake of the head. His mother responds to this by modeling the structures for him: *The goat shouldn't eat the lid; it's not good for it*. So once again Nigel embarks on his Narrative alone, only he has now a much better developed Complication: *goat try eat lid . . . man said no . . . goat shouldn't eat lid . . . (shaking head) good for it*.

It is also important to consider another aspect of this interaction and that is whether its purpose is to elicit from the child information that is new or unknown to the other participant. Clearly in this instance it is not. Nigel's mother and father are well aware of the goat's role in the proceedings. The function of this question is to help the child reconstruct experience in a particular genre. Painter (1987) gives many similar examples in exchanges with her young son in which she has shared the experience being reconstructed and helps him to reconstruct in it discourse. Educators are often critical of this type of discourse in the classroom; they tend to see it as having a testing function, finding out whether the child "knows the answer." As such, they see it as having an inhibiting effect on classroom discourse as children are seen to be involved in an exchange where the teacher has all the answers. There is no doubt classroom discourse can carry this message very clearly to students. But this depends very much on how the role is taken up by the teacher. It is possible for the teacher to take up a guiding role, as parents do, without giving the impression that he or she knows all the answers and is only concerned with getting "right" answers from the class. Certainly it is mistaken to believe that adult-child discourse outside the classroom is concerned only with eliciting information that is "new" to the adult. Adults are as much concerned with helping children to develop texts as they are with getting "new" information from them. Indeed, as young children and adults share a great deal of the experience that is the subject of discourse, the odds are that adults usually *do* know the information the child is giving them. In other words, there is a clear precedent for teachers taking up a similar role in the classroom where the emphasis is on developing well-formed texts in different genres.

There are occasions when adults instruct children quite explicitly about how to construct a particular genre. Ventola gives the following example of a young child learning to buy goods in a post office:

Post Official	Yes, love.
Child	Could I have . . . um . . . two different first . . . the Australian ones.
Mother	Two first-day covers, you wanna say. . . .
Child	Could I have two . . . first-day covers
Post Official	Yes
Mother	Please
Child	Please (whispering)

(Ventola, 1984a, p. 1)

The direct teaching strategy of the adult also merits some comment. Educators are inclined to present early child language development as a process of indirect teaching strategies. What is being learned, as in the scaffolding process, is left implicit. But this is not always the case. The example above is not an isolated one. Adults do give direct instructions to children about what to say in order to construct a text in a particular genre. This seems to be particularly the case with what we might call procedural genres where there is a physical "doing" involved as well as language. Once again there is a precedent from early child language for a teaching strategy that tends to be downgraded in current teacher practice for language development.

By making use of modeling and jointly negotiated texts for teaching writing, we are making use of "natural" strategies for language development. These are part of the child's experience and hence "fit" the child's implicit understanding of how language use can proceed. What we have added, however, is an additional dimension, that of making explicit some aspects of the text the child is learning to produce, in terms of both its stages and some of the patterns of language that are important in developing the meanings of the genre. We would argue that by doing this the child is given a clear picture of what he or she is working toward and of what tools to use in developing control or mastery of a particular genre. There is evidence emerging from other sources that the method is a satisfactory one for working with children from different socioeconomic and ethnic backgrounds. Brian Gray has been working in this way for some years with aboriginal children in the Northern Territory of Australia. In his experience it has proved a most successful method for helping children who prior to its introduction were having considerable difficulty in learning to read and write (Gray, 1984). In addition to the program reported on in this chapter, the writer used the method extensively in teaching students in the junior secondary school who had varied socioeconomic and ethnic backgrounds. There are educators who acknowledge the value of turning to child language studies as a source for teaching strategies in schools. However, their adaptation of natural strategies still leaves what is being learned implicit, as it often is in oral language development. But it must be borne in mind that oral language development occurs daily over years before a child comes to school. In terms of hours of talk it may well be years before the writer catches up. Almost certainly the writer never does.

Teaching Grade Two How to Achieve Purposes Through Language: Modeling the Stages of Genres.

The work reported on here was part of a program of writing development undertaken at a Sydney primary school in 1985 by the Writing Project, a research project of the Department of Linguistics at the University of Sydney. Two classes were involved in the program, which was genre-and language-based. The class teachers made decisions about which purposes for writing they wanted their students to engage in and which genres they wanted the children to gain control over in order to achieve these purposes. The researcher's role was both a teaching and a consultancy one. It was her task to give the teachers knowledge about genres and their distinctive stages and about some of the patterns of linguistic choices which were commonly found in each. The researcher also suggested some strategies that could be used for teaching genres. In other words, she provided a theoretical framework for the work on writing development, but the choice regarding which genres to teach and how to teach them was the teachers'. In fact, the two teachers varied considerably in how they made use of the information the researcher gave them. In no sense were the teachers provided with a formula or routine for teaching writing. What they were given was a theoretical basis on which to ground and develop their teaching practice.

In the remainder of this chapter, learning about language will be discussed in relation to the writing program of the grade-two class involved in the research program. The children were 7 to 8 years old and were in their third year of schooling. The grade-two teacher decided to concentrate particularly on developing the abilities of her class in writing Narrative and Report throughout the year. These were by no means the only genres the children wrote; they also wrote Invitations, Instructions, and Rules for classroom behavior. But Narrative and Report were the ones given the most attention as the teacher saw these to be genres that were important in the educational context. The children were certainly familiar with Narratives, as these had been read to them many times. However, it was apparent from the children's writing before they commenced this program that they were not writing Narratives even though they were read a text of this genre as a stimulus for writing.

The teacher's strategies for introducing the genres to the children were modeling ones. That is to say, she was concerned first with presenting the class with examples of the genre through reading texts to them. With older children, their own reading would be an important source of modeling. This type of modeling can be described as implicit; it is what young children are exposed to daily in listening to the discourse of adults around them. As far as Narrative is concerned this kind of implicit modeling is likely to have been going on for years, as adults tend to choose Narratives to read to children long before they start school. This pattern is continued in the classroom as teachers, too, choose this genre for reading aloud to children. The other important factor here is that because Narrative is so highly valued in schools there are many fine examples of the genre in school libraries. Educators and publishers look for a high standard of writing in this type of text for children. In other words, children have easy access to very good Narratives as models for their own writing.

The situation is quite different for implicit modeling of Report writing. Factual writing is rarely read to children either at home or at school, so one important source of modeling is almost completely missing. Moreover, the models for children are not numerous and are often quite poorly written. (One exception is the Macdonald Starter series, which is excellent for children in the early stages of literacy.) There is often a deliberate strategy of writing down to children in factual writing which has no counterpart in Narrative writing for young readers. In addition there is frequently a strange mix of genres to be found within one text: Instructions are often blended with Reports or tagged onto the end, as if children are not going to be interested in a straight factual piece. So, for example, a Report about cats may include Instructions for caring for them. There seems no reason to assume such a lack of interest. Children reveal a constant fascination with finding out about their environment. The point is that just when children need a great deal of implicit experience of a genre it is difficult to give it to them in a satisfactory way.

Implicit modeling is not enough to ensure that students will take up the genre under focus in their own writing. This was evident from the grade-two class where the researcher was working. The children had been read innumerable Narratives during their first years at school but they were not writing Narratives, even though this reading was often intended as a stimulus for the students' own writing. The other kind of modeling used with the grade-two class was quite explicit: The stages of the genre were pointed out to them and named. This was done by working with examples of Report and Narrative. The stages of Report, General Classification, and Description that were introduced to the class were those identified by Martin and Rothery in an earlier investigation of generic structure in children's writing. (Martin & Rothery, 1981). They are exemplified in the following text by a grade-two writer:

> Budgerigars
> A budgerigar is a type of bird. Its colours are green and yellow and black and blue. It has a tail. It eats seed and drinks water. It has a beak.

The first sentence, *A budgerigar is a type of bird*, is the *General Classification*, and the remainder of the text is *Description*. The stage Description in a longer Report is likely to be subclassified so that a number of subtitles may be included.

The generic description of Narrative introduced to the teacher was adapted from that of Labov and Waletzky (1967). The stages they identify provide a basic description of Narrative in our culture. As the stages of Abstract and Coda are not common in written Narrative, these were not included in the description introduced to the children; nor was the Evaluation, which may not always appear as a distinct stage but as evaluative meanings spread throughout other stages of the text (Labov, 1972). Because the children already had a great deal of experience of implicit modeling of Narrative texts, the teacher decided to move quickly into an explicit description of the stages of Narrative. She did this by reading them the fairy tale "Little Red Riding Hood" and discussing with them the stages of the text and the part played by these in the overall development of the Narrative. Let her describe how she went about this:

> I read to the class a well-known story, "Little Red Riding Hood." I chose this story because it is so well-known to the class and therefore easy to recall.

We summarized the story in note form on the chalkboard. I then labeled the parts of the Narrative in terms of Start, Complication, Resolution. The children immediately "took" to these labels. They discussed how a Start to the story gave it direction, a Complication was something that went wrong, and a Resolution was how the problem got sorted out.

From there we discovered the necessity of each portion to the flow and interest of the story. We began the story at the Complication without being introduced to Red Riding Hood or knowing where she was going. I then asked the class to leave out the Complication. As the children accepted the labels so quickly and easily they were well able to tell me that Red Riding Hood would just walk around the woods, go to Granny's, and have afternoon tea. "Was this interesting?" "No" was the overwhelming response, although quickly the children came up with other Complications. They wanted the wolf to appear during afternoon tea or on the walk home!

When asked to omit the Resolution the children expressed displeasure because they wished for an ending, for something to happen to the wolf.

The children were very quickly able to appreciate the role of all three parts, although in hindsight I would have given them the term Orientation from the beginning. They also quickly applied this knowledge to other stories that they knew, noting how some had many Complications.

The children responded very positively to learning the stages of these two genres. This was not surprising because they were not learning anything that was completely new or outside their experience, particularly as far as Narrative was concerned. They had an implicit familarity with the genres under focus. What they knew implicitly was being made explicit in order to show how the stages in a text achieve a particular goal in their sociocultural context. What was most interesting and significant was to see the various ways in which the children started to make use of this information of their own accord. Educators have long considered the mark of successful learning to be the application of knowledge in new contexts, and this is exactly what occurred. The first and most obvious application was that the children started to use their knowledge of generic stages as a means for developing their own texts. This is not to say that every child immediately wrote well-formed Narratives and Reports. But there was clear evidence from the writing that almost every child in the class was attempting to shape his or her text to achieve particular purposes. In Narrative writing, for example, almost half of the class wrote short but well-formed texts; others handled the Orientation and Complication stages but had difficulty in going further of their own accord. The following texts exemplify some of these differences. The first is a good example of a complete Narrative:

The Magic Ring
by Ruanne

Orientation   Once upon a time there was a little girl called Melissa. She was a princess. Her mother and father had always kept a magic ring for her.

Complication   One day she went into the wood to find a Prince. When she came to the middle of the wood she saw a witch's house. She went through the gate. She knocked on the door but there was no answer. So she pushed open the door and went inside. When she got inside she saw a witch. The witch grabbed her and she gave a BIG scream of fright and she turned into stone.

Resolution   Then Magic Powers came to her and she got STRONGER and STRONGER and killed the witch. On the way home she saw the most beautiful Prince. When she got home she got married. She was so very happy. After the wedding she rushed home and packed all her clothes up.

Ruanne's text is complete in that it has the stages of Complication and Resolution as well as Orientation. It also provides a good example of the influence of modeling in more ways than one. Ruanne has obviously drawn on fairy tales as a model for her Narrative. At this stage of her writing development these are readily accessible models, as they have been read to her on many occasions. She has also made use of a Narrative that was jointly composed by the class and the teacher. In that text a budgerigar escaped from the clutches of a tiger by acquiring magical powers, another fairy-tale ploy, to escape certain death. Ruanne has introduced this into her Narrative as a very neat means for solving her main character's problems. Moving from Complication to Resolution is what young writers find hard. They have little difficulty in placing their main characters in all sort of predicaments but have much more trouble in sorting these out, as the following text reveals:

> Once upon a time there was a fish and his name was Timmy. That day a shark came and chased Timmy. Then a diver came and got Timmy and then the shark chased . . .

Emma, the writer of the text above, had no difficulty in composing Complication after Complication but, despite many helpful suggestions from the teacher, she could not resolve the Narrative to her satisfaction. Finally she did achieve a Resolution that was to her liking:

> Once upon a time there was a fish and his name was Timmy. That day a shark came and chased Timmy. Then a diver came and got Timmy.

Then the shark chased the diver. The diver got away but the shark followed the diver. The shark got tired and the shark went away. Then another shark came. The diver had a spear, he stabbed him and Timmy was saved.

The teacher and the researcher had no false expectations about miracles occurring as far as the children's writing was concerned. As stated before, the writing program was one that enabled teachers to formulate clear goals in terms of purposes and how these were achieved through language. Development was expected over time with teaching practice that aimed to take the child just that little bit further in achieving goals with each text the child wrote. In the long term this involved individual and small group work as well as whole class teaching.

As far as Report writing was concerned, the General Classification stage was the one some children needed help with. They tended to launch straight into the Description stage, as the texts below illustrate. Gathering information for the genre could also be a problem. The lack of good models of Reports was a problem not only from the point of view of learning the stages of the text but also as far as gaining information on a topic was concerned. The following Reports were written by one girl, Molly, shortly after the class had been introduced to Reports:

The octopus does not hurt but it might look dangerous but it isn't. It lives in the water. It does have gills but you can't see them. They have eight legs.

Fish have gills too. Some are very colourful and some are not. Some live in the Barrier Reef and some live in the sea. Little fish have to be careful because sharks can eat them and some big fish eat them.

The children's first efforts at writing Narratives and Reports were encouraging. The point is that none of the children had written Narratives or Reports before they were taught the stages of the genres and all were now in various stages of developing mastery of them. Nor did we have any evidence from our earlier data of a grade-two class writing complete Narratives.

By learning the generic stages of Narrative and Report, the children gained a metalanguage, which they proceeded to use of their own accord in talking about their own writing and the texts they read or that were read to them. In the course of their work the children frequently referred to their writing in terms of the stage they were at in writing the text. It was not unusual to hear children say casually they were writing the Complication or they had "a really good Resolution." On one occasion one boy asked another who was reading his Narrative to the class whether a certain part of the text was Complication or Resolution. This came out of the blue, so to speak, as the teacher had not, at this point, provided a focus of that kind. The teacher reported too, that the children, again of their own initiative, frequently drew attention to texts that were being read to them in terms of their stages. On another occasion when the researcher was working with one little girl in helping her to develop the Complication, Resolution stages of her Narrative, she rejected her own suggestion for a conclusion to her text by saying, "That can't be. It didn't get sorted out." Once again this seemed to point to her making use of knowledge of the stages of Narrative in shaping her own text.

Yet another time when the children were about to compose a Report in conjunction with the teacher, they engaged in a discussion with her about the differences between Narrative and Report. The class decided that the purpose of Reports was to give the reader information. Reports, they decided, were factual. Narratives, they suggested, were not true in the way Reports were; some Narratives, such as fairy tales, were not factual at all. This discussion seemed to indicate that the children were developing a good sense of different purposes for writing and that different types of texts or genres were the means for achieving these purposes through language. Overall, the children's spontaneous and very appropriate use of their new knowledge seemed to the teacher and the researcher to be evidence that the knowledge about texts was understood and it was seen to be useful, as they used it both as a guide in their own work and as a tool for working on the language they encountered in the classroom.

JOINTLY COMPOSING A TEXT: LEARNING HOW TO USE LANGUAGE TO DEVELOP A GENRE

Learning the stages of a genre is only one aspect of learning to develop a text in that genre. Children must learn to use the patterns of linguistic choices that convey its meaning. This is where the grade-two teacher made use of another strategy of early child language, that of the joint construction of a text between adult and child in which the adult leads the child into the development of a particular genre through appropriate questions and comments. This strategy was adapted inasmuch as the interaction was not on a one-to-one basis at this stage but involved all the class. The teacher provided the scaffolding for the development of the text by asking questions that pointed toward the stages and meanings of the genre under focus. A jointly negotiated text provides an active modeling of genre for children. The text produced is a model for their own writing; they have participated in its creation and so they have learned something about the way the potential of the linguistic system is drawn on in the development of the genre.

In the following sections of this chapter, parts of a transcript of a lesson in which grade-two children and their teacher constructed a Report about cats will be examined. The segments illustrate well both the negotiation of meanings between teacher and pupils and the children learning about how language is used to mean in this genre. What the pattern of interaction between teacher and children shows throughout this lesson is a shift back and forth in the negotiation of the text between the stages of the genre and the linguistic choices to mean in different parts of the text. The teacher focuses the attention of the class on the title and the stages of the text, but in composing the text the children's attention is drawn very closely indeed to the lexicogrammatical patterns for meaning. The teacher's role is crucial: Through her comments and questions she is responsible for guiding the children in the shift of focus from generic stages to linguistic choices in the development of the text. (The letter C. has been used to indicate one child speaking. ''Children'' is used where more than one child gives a response.)

T	All right, let's go with our Report. Can anyone suggest a name for our Report?
C	Cats?
C	Cats?
T	Cats. As simple as that? Do you want it simple?
C	A Cat Report
T	A Cat Report?
C	Cat Family
T	Cat Family
C	The Cats
C	Many Cats
T	Many Cats
C	We could have one on domestic cats and then there could be other ones.
T	Right, there could be different titles under the main title.
C	Yes
T	Okay. Let's get a main title up.
T	Right. Many Cats or Cat Report? (Different responses from children.) Hands up Many Cats. Cat Report? Cat Report. The Cat Report? (Children agree on ''The Cat Report.'')
T	Okay. How will we start? Would you like to take up Gordon's suggestion about making two different sections or a couple of different sections?
Children	Yes, a couple.

T	Remember when we wrote that Report about ships we had to start if off with something. Who remembers what we had to start if off with?
C	Orientation?
T	Like an Orientation. It was a sort of a General . . . ?
C	General . . .
T	It was a while ago. It was a General Statement. If you remember we wrote about the model ships and we wrote, "There are many different types of ships." We started it off with a General Statement. What sort of General Statement could we make to start off this Report? Caroline?
C	There are many different types of cats.
T	(laughing) There are many different types of cats. Okay. Right. (writing on overhead transparency) There . . . are . . . many . . . different . . . kinds . . . of . . . cats. Next section? Well, come on, what are we going to write next?

To begin with, the teacher took up her scaffolding or guiding role by pointing to the need for a title, but the decision about what the title should be was negotiated by the class until finally "The Cat Report" was decided on. Notice how the children decided the name of the genre should be included in the title. The teacher nudged them toward this by accepting the offer of "Cats" but suggesting they might want to add more to it. What they revealed during this discussion was that they were aware that Reports usually generalize about classes of things. The suggestion of "Cats" for the title demonstrates this clearly. In the structure of the nominal group the absence of a Deictic element means the nominal group is nonspecific and, within that, nonsingular (Halliday, 1985a; p. 162). The children made other suggestions for the title which carried a similar meaning: "Cat Family," where *Cat* is the Classifier, indicating the subclass of things under focus, and *Family* is the Thing in the nominal group structure. Family has a technical meaning in this context; where it refers to a biological classification of living creatures. Another suggestion, "Many Cats," is less successful as the Numerative, *many*, has a quantitative meaning which does not capture the generalization required for a Report.

The other issue at stakes is the deictic meaning in the nominal group where Report is Thing. The children suggested both a nonspecific Deictic, *a*, and a specific one, *the*. The nonspecific Deictic introduces new participants, apart from generic ones, into texts. *The*, on the other hand, is a specific Deictic, which means the identity of the participant is recoverable, either from the text or the context. For grade two, understandably, the identity of Report is recoverable from the context of situation in the classroom where the children are composing the text; hence their choice of the specific Deictic.

Modeling in language development takes place at other levels as well as genre. Young children make use of the lexicogrammatical patterns they hear and read in developing their own texts. In getting the children started on the jointly constructed text the teacher suggested a model for their opening, the General Classification Stage of the Report. She did this by referring to the opening of a previous Report about ships that she and the class had jointly negotiated. The opening for that Report was *There are many different kinds of ships.* Immediately one of the children made use of this to suggest the same lexicogrammatical pattern, *There are many different types of cats,* which the teacher laughingly accepted. The point is an important one, as teachers are often inclined to reject such direct modeling in children's work on a number of grounds: It is unoriginal; it is copying; the child is not putting it in his or her own words. All these reasons are educationally unsound. Modeling is a major source of learning for children from the earliest stage of language development. They have no sense of ''originality'' or ''copying''; they simply make use of the language available to them, whether it be spoken or written. Caroline in this instance showed just how modeling proceeds. She made use of the same experiential pattern of the clause the teacher gave but she inserted another lexical item, *cats,* as Thing in the nominal group *many different types of cats.* The transitivity structure of the clause is an existential one, and an important one for the class to become familiar with, as it is one of the transitivity structures for making generalizations. Caroline very sensibly took up the model provided by the teacher and used it for her own purposes in the genre under construction.

After composing the General Classification stage of the Report the teacher directed the attention of the class to the following stages, but one of the children objected to some meanings in the opening part and drew the attention of the class to several lexical items. The children then became involved in a serious discussion about the meanings they wanted to include in this part of the Report. The following section of the transcript is about this:

T   Right, could we start now? Gordon, your two subheadings, your two headings?

G   Yes, but wait a minute. In the first part, there are wild cats, there are savage cats. Wild cats and savage cats mean the same thing because wild cats have to be savage.

T   Who suggested savage? Savage? John, what did you mean by savage, John?

J	Um you know how a kind of, not the kind of cat you could have for a pet.
T	Savage to whom?
J	People?
T	To people. That's what I thought he was meaning, Gordon. Do you think we should have a better word there?
G	Wild cats are savage to people.
T	Not all wild cats.
G	They can be.
T	Remember we read about—what was that small wild cat that only went for little rabbits and rats and things?
C	Bobcat.
T	Bobcat. (Discussion among children) So do you think we should change that word "savage"? There are wild cats, there are—
Children	Domestic cats.
T	No, we want one like one . . . John wants one, one to hurt people.
Children	Powerful cats, vicious cats. (Other suggestions inaudible)
T	Powerful cats, vicious cats. (Takes up suggestion from class) There are man-eating cats.
C	Dangerous cats.
T	Dangerous cats. Beg pardon, I can't hear, John.
C	Dangerous cats would be ones that could just make a teeth mark or . . .
T	Yes, Guy was saying that dangerous could just mean even a little kitten that could scratch you. It could be dangerous to a baby, couldn't it? So will we change "savage," John, to your suggestion. Will we change that to "man-eating"? Right. We'll do an edit on that. We'll do it in red so that we know we're going to change it. So Gordon are you happy now to go on with subheadings? Right?

During this exchange the children focused very carefully on the meanings they were wanting to include in the Report. Of course in doing this they were learning about language. They were learning how to make fine distinctions of meaning through lexis, the most delicate choice in the grammar. These distinctions are important ones when the writer is aiming to convey accurate meanings about the subject matter of the Report. Later in the same lesson the meaning of *savage* was again disputed and the teacher asked a child to find it in the dictionary. According to the dictionary entry *wild* and *savage* were synonymous.

It is clear from the teacher's question at the end of the previous section of the transcript that she was now shifting the attention of the class back to the stages of the text. As mentioned earlier, this was typical of the pattern of text negotiation, a movement back and forth in focus from the stages of the text to the lexicogrammatical meanings that realized the stages. What needs to be emphasized at this point is that the pattern of shift from generic stages to linguistic choices is a consequence of the teacher having an explicit understanding of the nature of the genre and its linguistic realization. Without her negotiating role being informed in this way, the exchange may become a rather haphazard interaction which is likely to miss completely the key issues of the negotiating procedure, namely genre and the patterns of linguistic choices that constitute the text. The teacher next returned to the notion of subtitles suggested earlier and explained these to the children. Once again, the choice of subtitle is left to the children.

> T   Right, hang on, will we go to domestic cats first or will we go to wild cats?
> (Some children say domestic, some say wild cats.)
> Right, so we're going to make a little heading or a subheading that we're calling "Domestic Cats." So it's like an extra heading. The main heading was "The Cat Report by Poseidon" and the next subheading is "Domestic Cats." Okay. Let's have some information about domestic cats. Ruanne?

Most teachers would recognize the section of the text negotiation about the meanings of lexical items that was referred to earlier as having clearly to do with learning about language mainly because the focus was on what are commonly called vocabulary items. But the following segment of the lesson is as much about learning about language as the earlier one.

T	Okay. Let's have some information about domestic cats. Ruanne?
C	Some domestic cats are dangerous.
T	Some domestic cats are dangerous. Which domestic cats are dangerous?
C	A panther.
T	Is a panther a domestic cat?
Children	No, no.
T	No. Or should we tell people what domestic cats are?
Children	Yes.
T	Right oh. Come on.
C	Domestic cats can be house cats.
T	HmHm
Children	Not can be, are.
T	Can be or are, Gordon?
	(Children reply, "are.")
T	Domestic cats are house cats. Come on. Bridie? What else do we know about domestic cats? Nicholas? Samantha?

One of the linguistic features of the Report is the choice of the experiential meanings of existential and relational clauses. Both transitivity structures can be the means for generalizing. The existential clause states that something exists. A typical pattern is that which occurred many times in the joint negotiation of the Cat Report, *There are . . .* The first message of the Report has the following existential structure:

There	are	many different types of cats.
	Existential Process	Existent

It is a generalization about some aspect of existence. Similarly, relational clauses can make generalizations as, for example, in the clause *Koalas are a gray-brown color.* The transitivity analysis of this clause is as follows:

Koalas	are	a gray-brown color.
Carrier	Relational Process	Attribute

The experiential structure is such that the nominal group, *koalas*, is the Carrier and the group, *a gray-brown color*, is the Attribute. The quality depicted in the Attribute is attributed to the Carrier through the Relational Process *are*. In the discussion above, when the teacher asked for an elaboration of the meaning of domestic cats one child responded, *Domestic cats can be house cats.* This choice for meaning is not a generalization; it asserts through the modal, *can*, the possibility for domestic cats to be house cats. The rest of the class responded to this quickly without any prompting from the teacher and by stating *are* changed the meaning from one of possibility to one of generalization.

The Report proceeded in this manner until the section concerning domestic cats was complete. The final Report is as follows:

The Cat Report
by Poseidon (the name given the grade-two class)
There are many different kinds of cats. There are wild cats, there are man-eating cats and there are domestic cats.

Domestic Cats
Domestic cats are house cats. Some are playful, some are friendly, some are cute. They are tame. Cats were first kept to catch all the rats and mice in the larder. There are 36 kinds of domestic cats. There are fluffy cats, ginger cats, black cats, white cats. A cat has four legs, it has whiskers. It

has two eyes with slits for pupils. They purr when they are happy and they miaow when they want something.

At this stage it is worth comparing the joint negotiation of text that proceeded in this writing lesson with the one described and analyzed in some detail by Frances Christie (Chapter 4 of this volume). As Christie pointed out, the contribution of the children to the discourse of the lesson was minimal and the writing-task set did not extend the children's language development in any significant way. The discourse of the grade-two lesson proceeded very differently. First, the task was a demanding one in that it aimed to move the children into a genre they had virtually no experience of in their own composition. It was also a genre that played an important part in learning across the curriculum. Second, the teacher took up a scaffolding role in which her questions and comments guided the children toward the stages of the genre and its meanings but the particular shape the text took and its patterns of meanings were very much in the control of the children. Third, the children were engaged in language use in which they were learning about the potential of the language system to mean. In other words, they were engaged in an activity that promoted language development.

Choices for Meaning in the Report: The Potential of the Nominal Group

There were some aspects of the Report that the teacher was unhappy about. She commented on the difficulty of getting the children to give factual information about the appearance and behavior of the cats rather than descriptions such as *Cats are friendly, cute;* and so on. (It is significant to note that these descriptions were volunteered by girls.) It seemed to the researcher that this was a point of need both for the teacher and the students as far as some more explicit description of the structure of the language system was concerned. The purpose of such teaching would be to make explicit the potential for meaning of a part of the lexico-grammatical structure, in this case the nominal group, that played an important part in the realization of the genre. Making the structure explicit gave the children a conscious resource for meaning. In Reports where classes of things are described, the nominal group can be identified as one of the language structures with the potential for carrying much of the information load.

It has already been noted in the earlier discussion of the structure of the nominal group that its range of functions enables varying degrees of specification to be made about whatever is under focus as Thing in the structure. Consider for example the following description taken from a Report about whales and dolphins by the Australian naturalist and conservationist Vincent Serventy:

> *Toothless whales* have *horny plates called baleen on the upper jaw*. *These plates* have *bristles on the edge which strain out shrimps and other small sea creatures*. *Grey whales* can eat *about three tonnes of food* a day. (Serventy, 1984, italics mine)

In the short passage above there are seven nominal groups, some of which have quite complex structures. For example, in the group *horny plates called baleen on the upper jaw*, *plates* is Thing. Preceding the function Thing is an Epithet, *horny*. Following Thing are two Qualifiers. The first, *called baleen* is a phrase in which there is a nominal group, *baleen*. The other Qualifier is *on the upper jaw*, in which there is a nominal group, *the upper jaw*. This, in turn, has the functions Deictic, *the*; Classifier, *upper*; and Thing, *jaw*. The analysis can be presented as follows:

horny	plates	called [baleen]	on [the upper jaw]
Epithet	Thing	Qualifier	
		[Nominal group]	[Nominal Group]
		Thing	Deictic Classifier Thing

So, embedded within the nominal group *horny plates called baleen on the upper jaw* are two more nominal group structures. (The square brackets signal an embedded structure.) This brief analysis gives some idea of the potential of the nominal group structure for carrying a great deal of information.

Another common choice for meaning in the nominal group in Reports is that of the function Classifier, as this is the function that enables the most precise specification of whatever is Thing. It also occurs in this passage. One occurrence, *upper*, in the nominal group *the upper jaw*, has already been noted. *Toothless*, in the first nominal group, is a Classifier in that it marks a class of whales. The analysis is as follows:

Toothless	whales
Classifier	Thing

Grey, in the nominal group, *grey whales*, has a similar function. (Note however, that *grey* can be an Epithet as in the group *a grey bag*.)

grey	whales
Classifier	Thing

All of these aspects of nominal group structure are important ones for children to become familiar with over time if they are to become competent Report writers.

Learning About Language: Teaching Grade Two the Structure of the Nominal Group

The procedure followed in this part of the writing program was similar to that described in teaching genre. The researcher gave the teacher the theoretical framework, in this case the description of nominal group structure, but did not provide ready-made solutions for teaching it to the class. In this instance the class teacher was completely responsible for the classroom strategy used to teach grade two the structure of the nominal group.

The first step was to teach the class teacher the nominal group functions: *Deictic, Numerative, Epithet, Classifier, Thing* and *Qualifier*. Once she had an understanding of this structure she was able to identify much more precisely some of the problems in the jointly negotiated Report. For example, she realized that Epithets such as *friendly* and *cute* that she had been uneasy about were in fact additutional ones carrying a strong interpersonal meaning rather than experiential ones, which she had intuitively thought more appropriate. She also saw the need to include the function of Classifier, which subclassifies classes of Things and which plays an important role in mature Report writing. In addition there was the function Qualifier, which did not feature in the children's writing at all. She realized the children's attention could be drawn to the possibility of extending their description of whatever was under focus through this function which followed Thing in the nominal group structure.

The next step was to decide on more appropriate names for young children to use in labeling the functions of the nominal group. Martin suggested *Pointer* as the label for the Deictic function, *Short Describer* for the Epithet, and *Long Describer* for the Qualifier. It was decided to retain Classifier and Thing while Numerative was changed to *Number*. The teacher and the classroom researcher thought these labels were appropriate and so the teacher started to devise her strategies for teaching the functions to the children.

The structure of the nominal group was introduced in a lesson to the whole class. The children were told that they were going to learn about the different ways we can describe things. The teacher chose a nominal group that was adapted from a song the children were familiar with about a purple people-eater. The nominal group under focus was *a large flying purple people eater*. The class was given a stenciled picture of this creature in full flight. To teach the functions the teacher had prepared large cardboard labels, of a kind commonly found in infants' school classrooms, which bore the names Pointer, Number, Short Describer, Classifier, Thing, and Long Describer. Her strategy was to get the children to focus on Thing as the obligatory function of the nominal group. She did this by asking them whether it made sense to say the following things:

1. a——
2. a large——
3. a large flying——
4. a large flying purple——
5. a large flying purple people——
6. a large flying purple people eater

The children confidently rejected each of these suggestions until they reached the final one. They also agreed with no hesitation that all of these items served to give information about *eater*. The teacher then introduced the terms *Pointer* and *Short Describer* as the function names for the lexical items *a*, and *large*, *flying*, and *purple*, respectively. She pointed out to them from the structure of this group that it was possible to include more than one Short Describer. The children agreed, however, that there could only be one Pointer in the group.

The teacher then introduced the function *Thing* to the class as the central function about which the others gave more information. In this particular group, *eater* was *Thing*. The final function in the group under focus was that of *Classifier*, which the teacher introduced by asking the children what type of eater was being described. The children agreed it was a people eater and suggested other types of eaters, the principal one being a rock eater.

The teacher drew the children's attention to the paradigmatic aspect of language by asking them what other item could occur in the same slot as *a* in the nominal group. The class immediately suggested *the*. This enabled the teacher to draw attention to the fact that we often talk or write about more than one creature, thing, person, and so on. The children had no hesitation in suggesting where the function *Number* should occur in the group structure.

The final task in describing the group's structure was to draw the attention of the class to the possibility of extending the description in a place that occurred after Thing in the group structure. The children

Picture of purple people eater used in nominal group instruction.

were asked to look at their picture of the large flying purple people eater and suggest what else was important about his appearance. The teacher started them off by giving them the preposition *with* as the first word in the Long Describer. The children came up with the following suggestions: *with no hair, with feathers, with no beak*. The absence of a Long Describer in the original nominal group structure enabled the teacher to point out to the children that the choice of functions, apart from Thing, was optional. The more detailed you wanted your description to be, the more likely it was that all the functions would be included in the structure; some might be repeated, as was the case with the function Short Describer in the nominal group under focus.

At this point the teacher drew the children's attention back to where this type of description might be used. The children had no hesitation in dealing with this; they suggested that it would be important in Reports in which one had to give "a lot of information about things." They also said that descriptions of this kind were important in Narratives when one was describing characters and places. The class had already done some work on the importance of descriptions of characters and settings in the Orientation stage, so it was interesting to see how, once again, of their own accord, they related the explicit language description to a purpose with which they already had some familiarity. And again the teacher's role was crucial in opening up possibilities for the application of learning about language. Her knowledge pointed the way, so to speak, but the children were quick to follow the lead given and see the potential for its use.

The researcher noted that a focus on the function Classifier in the structure of nominal groups in Reports was one piece of language knowledge that emerged from this piece of teaching about language. The teacher would draw the children's attention to the need for this function in some of their descriptions. So, for example, when, in the course of developing a Report about the Australian bird the kookaburra the children composed the sentence *The kookaburra lives in the bush*, the teacher suggested the need for a Classifier before *bush*. The children immediately inserted *Australian*. One can well imagine the kind of guessing game that could have gone on if this explicit knowledge had not been shared between teacher and class. The teacher would have a notion of a more precise description, but how would she convey this to the children? Probably only by urging them to make more and more suggestions as to what could precede *bush* in the sentence until someone hit upon the right word. But this would not give the children any systematic view of why one description was considered more appropriate than another. Similar situations occurred in one-to-one situations with the children. In talking about the writing, teacher and children had a shared knowledge about text and context which provided the framework for their discussion.

No pressure was placed on the children immediately to write nominal groups in which there was an occurrence of every function. This was not the point of the teaching, which aimed to make clear to the children the potential for meaning at this point in the grammar, which they could take up according to their purposes in a given piece of writing. There was another important gain, however, that needs to be commented on: Teacher and class now had a metalanguage which both could use in discussing nominal group structure in whatever texts the children were working on. The teacher, for example, could now identify quite precisely strengths and weaknesses in this aspect of the children's writing and draw these to the writer's attention in a positive way. The shared meanings of the metalanguage enabled a precision in discussion that is sadly lacking in most discussions about school writing. This, after all, is one of the principal reasons for developing technical descriptions in a field: to enable meanings to be shared in as exact a way as possible.

LEARNING ABOUT LANGUAGE:
A SOCIOCULTURAL PERSPECTIVE

When children fail to write well in school contexts the judgment made about their work is often couched in cognitive terms. Such a focus misses the point. The critical factor is not cognitive but social. Children and adults master genres in social contexts. From early childhood adults and children work together to develop texts to achieve purposes in particular contexts. The crucial factor is interaction, with the adult playing a key role in guiding the development of the text in stages. At present, because the demands of writing in respect of genre and language remain hidden, the differences that emerge in children's language development can easily be attributed to cognitive factors. In fact, children are largely left to find for themselves the distinctive ways of organizing different texts. Those who read widely and proficiently are at an advantage as they are likely to internalize from their reading the stages of different genres. Children who are read to frequently are also benefiting from exposure to models of genres. There is no certainty about this, however. Many enthusiastic and proficient readers still have difficulty with writing. At most all we can say at present is that some children master genres mainly on the basis of exposure to them; others do not proceed in this way and hence flounder. But until we take steps to *teach* all children to write in ways that are challenging and interesting, and make clear to them the demands of the task, we can make no assumptions about differences in ability.

The seriousness of this situation is sometimes discounted by educators on two grounds. First, some maintain that writing plays only a small part in the work life of most individuals, if indeed it plays any part at all. While it is true that technology has freed many writers from the task of composing by hand, there is no evidence to suggest that written language is declining in importance in the work life of the community. Educators tend to ignore the role of reports, for example, in a wide variety of jobs: foremen reporting on the state of machinery and equipment on the factory floor; servers of law court documents who must give an account of how their documents were served; nurses who must write up reports of their patients' progress. These types of occupations do not fall within the realm of traditional professional occupations, but writing plays an important part in them. Indeed, when it comes to advancement in these jobs it often plays a crucial role.

The other argument employed to discount the importance of literacy is closely related to the previous one; it is claimed that traditionally writing is the province of the middle-class professional and that writing in educational institutions is geared only toward students moving into such an occupational level. It is claimed that as a consequence of this focus writing does not meet the needs of minority groups and may even be damaging in preventing them from forging their own path both politically and socially. This argument was dealt with to some extent in discussing the sociocultural importance of literacy; giving students access to the mainstream meanings of the society through literacy does not mean that these are necessarily adopted by all students in the same way. The other point stated was that by making what was learned explicit, students were given a clear understanding of what they were learning and the purposes for which it could be used. Some evidence to support the view that speakers and writers use literacy for their own social purposes emerged from a national economic conference held in Australia two years ago. There, industry and trade union leaders addressed the conference about the direction of the Australian economy. The sessions were televised and widely reported on in the print media. The journalists covering this event reported, somewhat to their own surprise, that the quality of the submissions written by the trade union representatives was superior to the quality of those from the employer groups. For any representatives from minority groups there is a strong awareness of the need to be able to use language appropriately to negotiate their concerns.

In conclusion, it can only be reiterated that matters of cognitive development are not at stake here, but rather issues of teaching are. If the curriculum remains hidden both in terms of goals and the way a subject is taught—or, more accurately, not taught—many students are likely to find learning difficult and/or irrelevant. The central issue is making what has to be learned explicit and teaching it to all students so that access to new knowledge is genuinely possible.

LEARNING ABOUT LANGUAGE: THE BASIS OF THE ENGLISH CURRICULUM

This chapter has dealt with teaching strategies that have focused on whole-class teaching. It would be wrong to think that all the language work in the classroom proceeded in this way. Once purposes for writing and some lexicogrammatical descriptions had been introduced to the class observed, there was a movement to small-group and one-to-one work, according to the children's needs. For some writers the class sessions were enough to get them under way and they needed minimal assistance from then on. Most children, however, required some small-group work and quite a lot of individual consultation. Just what course of action was taken depended on the assessment of the child's writing and what help the children themselves sought.

As this chapter made clear in the beginning, explicit knowledge about language has had no role in the English curriculum in Australian schools. In abandoning explicit knowledge about the language system, educators have unwittingly placed themselves in a position where they have lost all contact with a base for application in curriculum development and classroom practice. They have lost touch with a field where there is a rapid increase in understanding such matters as how texts are forged through language and how they are related to contexts. In the past educators have criticized linguistic approaches that were not compatible with educational aims, but in abandoning language knowledge completely these educators have lost the ability to make competent assessments of new developments in linguistics. As a result, a great deal of educational debate about language development has become trivialized and has focused on classroom strategies that have no sound language basis, particularly regarding how language is learned and how it is used in context.

Learning about language within the systemic functional model can inform every aspect of a language development program. First, it provides a basis for planning a program for language development that takes account of how language is used for different purposes in different contexts of situation. It does so in two ways: through a description of language that is functional and oriented to choice, and through the relationship established between text and context that enables us to see how the contexts of situation and culture influence choices in the language system. It thus offers a model for a program that aims to develop students' abilities to use language in a wide range of situational contexts. Second, it provides a foundation for developing strategies that aim to promote language through use. The strategy that has been focused on in this chapter is that of guidance in the context of shared experience: a strategy drawn from the evidence of child language studies regarding the adult's role in helping children to develop their language abilities. The guiding, negotiating role for classroom interaction can be adopted successfully only if teachers understand how language is used to achieve goals, both in respect of their own interaction with the class and in respect of the genres they and their students are producing. Third, learning about language provides the means for assessing students' development in using language so that teachers and students have some objective and relevant measure for evaluating progress. Fourth, and perhaps most important, learning about language gives students explicit knowledge they can apply in developing literacy as well as oracy. What use they make of the meanings rendered accessible by literacy is very much in their own hands.

CHAPTER 6

SYSTEMIC-FUNCTIONAL LINGUISTICS AND ITS APPLICATION TO THE TESOL CURRICULUM

Janet Jones
Sandra Gollin
Helen Drury
Dorothy Economou

University of Sydney
New South Wales, Australia

1. INTRODUCTION

As teachers of adults whose mother tongue is not English, we are constantly reminded of the language problems our students face when learning to function in different social contexts in Australia. These problems may have to do with the language needed to interact socially and maintain social relations at work or with the language demands on the student at university. In order to help students overcome some of their problems, the language teacher needs a thorough understanding of these social contexts. Although the four contributors to this chapter come from different teaching situations—three of us are concerned with overseas and migrant students at all stages of their university study, and one with adult migrants who are not pursuing a university career—we all share the conviction that there is an urgent need for language teachers to be equipped with a model of language that relates text and context and provides insights into the language, both spoken and written. We also agree that the "authentic" models of text found in many ELT teaching materials are inadequate and that a more systematic linguistic framework is needed to describe the "real" language learners have to cope with.

The Systemic-Functional (SF) model as developed by Halliday provides teachers with such a linguistic framework. Language, here, is seen as "social semiotic" (Halliday, 1978a), "as one among a number of

257

SITUATION: Feature of the context	(realized by)	TEXT: Functional component of semantic system
Field of discourse (what is going on)		Experiential meanings (transitivity, naming, etc.)
Tenor of discourse (who is taking part)		Interpersonal meanings (mood, modality, person, etc.)
Mode of discourse (role assigned to language)		Textual meanings (theme, information, cohesive relations)

Figure 1. Relation of the text to the context of situation

systems that taken all together constitute human culture'' (Halliday & Hasan, 1985, p. 4). Thus language is seen as it relates to social structure and as it is used in social contexts. By knowing the variables of the contexts of situation we can predict how the meanings appropriate to the context could be realized linguistically. This context of situation is described in terms of the three situational variables of *field, tenor,* and *mode* which together determine the register. These are related to the ideational, interpersonal, and textual metafunctional components of the semantic system. Figure 1 from Halliday and Hasan (1985, p. 26) represents the relationship between the text and the context of situation.

FIELD   refers to the social activity that is taking place as well as the institutional setting in which a piece of language occurs;

TENOR   refers to the nature of the relationship between the participants and includes an understanding of their roles and statuses within the social and linguistic context;

MODE   refers to what part the language is playing in the situation and includes the channel selected—spoken or written. Two important variables here are the distance between participants in the interaction (e.g., face to face vs. letter writing) and the distance of the speaker or the writer from the events that the language is talking about, that is, language in action versus language as reflection (e.g., TV commentary vs. newspaper report).

The situational variables of field, tenor and mode predict a particular text variety or register, which is defined as ''the configuration of semantic resources that the member of a culture typically associates with a situation type.'' ''It is a set of foregrounded options from the total meaning potential which define the variety of which a text is an instance'' (Halliday, 1978a, pp. 111, 145).

The concept of genre as used in this chapter is based on that of

Martin (1984a, p. 25, 1987), who sets up genre as a separate semiotic system underlying register and language. ''A genre is a staged, goal-oriented, purposeful activity in which speakers (and writers) engage as members of our culture.'' Thus, spoken and written texts can be characterized as showing distinct beginning-middle-end structures or schematic structures through which the speaker/writer moves to accomplish different social purposes. Of relevance in this chapter are the expository or factual written genres that tertiary students are required to read and write at tertiary level, such as textbooks, journal articles, essays, reports, and so on, or the genre of casual conversation discussed in Part B.

Within such a linguistic framework it is possible as language teachers to analyze spoken and written discourse in terms of its overall purpose and social context. With the insights gained from an analysis of the genres and registers, the language teacher can make these more accessible to the students.

What follows is a discussion of some of the contributions made by the SF model to the teaching of adult second language learners in Australia. Part A will focus on the application of the SF model to the teaching of reading and writing to ESL students at the tertiary level. First, an analysis of students' written texts will point to the problems they face when learning to control the factual written genres at the tertiary level. Second, the insights gained from analysis will be applied to two different teaching situations which will outline the approaches used and some of the techniques that help students overcome some of these problems. Part B will focus on the application of the SF model for making migrant adult second language learners sensitive to the nature of casual conversation.

PART A
2. AVAILABLE TEACHING TEXTS

The recent shift to language teaching that recognizes the need to teach ''communicative competence'' (Hymes, 1967) stresses that learning a language involves more than being grammatically competent. It involves the notion that an utterance must be appropriate on many different levels to the communicative situation. This shifts the focus from sentence-level to text-level discourse where the concern is to help students by means of communicative methods and procedures to understand and produce discourse appropriate to situations of use outside the classroom. These functional and communicative approaches to language teaching have been influenced by inputs from linguistics (e.g., semantically based grammars), sociolinguistics (e.g., Hymes's notion of communicative competence), applied linguistics (e.g., Wilkins, 1976; cf. notional syllabuses), philosophy (especially arising from speech act theory). At the same time other inputs from register analysis and discourse analysis influenced the content and materials of courses designed for specific needs—English for Special Purposes (ESP), English for Academic Purposes (EAP), English for Science and Technology (EST), and so on. (See, for example, Cooper, 1979; Jordan, 1980; Mackay & Rosenthal, 1980; Moore, 1974; Ross & Gasser, 1983, among others.)

The materials for these courses, particularly those designed to teach academic reading and writing to university-level ESL students, while addressing some of the needs of these students, appear to lack a consistent linguistic framework in the selection and analysis of their content. Many of these textbooks are organized in terms of the "rhetorical functions" of academic discourse (e.g., describing, defining, classifying, comparing). While it may be useful to practice individual functions at paragraph level, the student will need to go beyond this to understand how a text will display a range of functions such as defining, classifying, comparing, and how these integrate in the text.

Some of these materials integrate reading and writing, using analysis of the reading text as a basis for the writing tasks that practice these functions and associated grammatical structures. Many use "authentic" texts or those adapted from authentic sources such as science textbooks, journal articles, and reports, and most take into account the importance of coherence and provide exercises on cohesion. Students using these materials may be made aware of certain aspects of cohesion such as reference and conjunction or how to "describe a process" or define a certain topic or how to write a "well-organised" paragraph. This is certainly an advance on previous sentence-based teaching materials; even so, these tasks are of limited use to students who need to understand and produce lengthy texts. Also, they do not communicate to the student *why* certain choices in their writing will be inappropriate or *why* a text has a certain structure and *how* the features of cohesion practiced in exercises integrate to contribute to textual unity.

3. PROBLEMS: DISCUSSION OF STUDENT TEXTS

Analysis of student texts helps the teacher understand the problems the students have in learning to write at the university level. The benefits of such an analysis are in direct proportion to the framework for analysis. We have found the insights provided by the SF model invaluable in this respect. It enables us to analyze these texts not in terms of any stage theory of language development or language acquisition order but in terms of where the students are in relation to the native-speaker texts they aim to approximate. The analysis of a student text can be undertaken from different points of view. But if the interest is in how texts are produced and understood, then the most relevant considerations would be those that are directly related to schematic structure and to texture, namely, grammatical and lexical cohesion, as well as theme and conjunction. This does not mean that structures internal to the clause (e.g., those of mood and transitivity) are irrelevant; rather, it is a claim that those patterns of language are more relevant which are the output of the textual metafunction (Halliday, 1978a, 1985b). In other words, we are more concerned here with how the student constructs discourse above the clause rank, that is, at text level.

Below we present a discussion of student texts that illustrate some of the problems at text level. These text samples were taken from a wide range of student texts from both science and humanities disciplines. These examples can be regarded as "practice" texts; they are not the actual texts written for submission to various faculties for assessment purposes, but rather elicited as practice exercises done at home or in class. Of course not all texts will display the range of problems to be discussed here, but the following extracts point to general areas of difficulty that we have isolated in our analysis of student texts at different stages of university study. For example, postgraduate students who have completed their graduate study in their home country may have fewer problems related to the technical lexis of their field than does the undergraduate who is learning the field-specific lexis. On the other hand, the undergraduate may have completed all or part of his/her secondary schooling in Australia and may be more familiar with the whole cultural context of education in Australia and therefore with the factual genres such as essays and scientific reports required at the secondary level. All excerpts from student texts are labeled "Extract"; thus "Extract 1" means "example 1, an extract from a student text." In each case, our focus in its discussion is limited to just one point, at any one occasion. We do not examine every feature of language that appears infelicitous or even incorrect. The problems will be discussed as they relate to the following:

1. REGISTER (3.1)
   FIELD (3.1.1)
   TENOR (3.1.2)
   MODE (3.1.3)
2. SCHEMATIC STRUCTURE (3.2)
3. THEME (3.3)
4. COHESION (3.2)

REFERENCE (3.4.1)
LEXICAL COHESION (3.4.2)
CONJUNCTION (3.4.3)

3.1 Register

The importance of register in learning a language was described as early as 1964 by Halliday:

> The choice of items from the wrong register and the mixing of items from different registers, are among the most frequent mistakes made by non-native speakers of a language. (Halliday, McIntosh, & Stevens, 1964, p. 88)

Understanding the registers students need to produce involves not only an analysis of the linguistic features of the texts but also an analysis of the combination of the contextual variables of the situation and how the former relate to the latter. These contextual variables of field, tenor, and mode have been outlined above.

3.1.1 Field. Since field indicates the institutional focus of the text, the student here needs to be able to control technical lexis. This means first building up a reservoir of field-specific technical lexis, that is, those items which are indexical markers of the field. Benson and Greaves (1981, p. 49) distinguish (a) the indexical signals of field which alone indicate the field; (b) sets of lexical items "which being common to the general lexicon do not individually signal field, but their clustering does"; and (c) sets of lexical items "which do not particularly signal field" but which cut across fields such as *represent, influence, provide, efficient.* It is often this third group that creates difficulties for students in their writing. Students may have varying degrees of control of the field-specific technical terms but may not be able to use the "peripheral" lexis appropriately, though this is vital for expressing the relations between the technical concepts. The italicized lexis in the following extracts shows this lack of control of the non-field-specific lexis. The student has used the technical lexis of the field (*socialisation, norms, values, statuses,* etc.) but an inappropriate use of peripheral lexis hinders the expressions of his meanings.

Extract 1
Education influences socialisation of an individual. Socialisation of a child *is* that he learns to function correctly in the society. Socialisation *needs* three requirements. . . . The socialisation *points of view* are norms and values, statuses and roles. Institutions in a society such as families,

churches and parliaments *bring* many activities *contained* many statuses and roles which judge by norms and values.

If we rewrite the above, changing the italicized lexis in the following way, the meanings become more easily accessible:

Education *has an effect on* the socialisation of an individual. Socialisation *implies* that the child learns to function correctly in society. Socialisation *has* three requirements. . . . Socialisation *can be considered from several points of view*. These are norms and values, statuses and roles. Institutions in a society such as families, churches and parliaments *create* many activities which *reflect* many statuses and which are judged by norms and values.

Non-field-specific lexis does not belong to any one specific class. It may belong to the category **relational verbs,** for example, **indicate, reflect, show.** Of particular importance, in this class, are such lexical verbs as *influence, affect, cause, lead to.* For a similar reason, a subset of **nouns,** such as *reason, problem, argument, point of view, question,* are important, for, when such a noun is modified by a reference device like *this/the/such,* it permits reference to a foregoing or a following part of the text. Again, a certain subset of **adjectives,** such as *significant, effective, essential,* are important, as they permit evaluation of opinions and arguments expressed in the text. Thus a student will need to build up a resource of such lexis, in addition to the field-specific lexis, or technical terms.

Learning to control technicality involves the ability to define terms and concepts accurately. To do this effectively the student has to learn how to manipulate the linguistic resources that realize definitions. Martin (1987) has isolated some of these, all of which have to do with the semantic notion of *elaboration* (=). The following are some of the ways in which definitions are realized:

1. Apposition (elaboration in a nominal group complex—Halliday, 1985b, pp. 252–253)

Extract 2
The specific strain which lives with the root of cassava is called
VAM = the vassicular arbuscular mycorrhiza.
1 = 2

The above shows the student has control of this resource for expanding technical terms. Other ways of defining are not so easy.

2. Identifying relational clause (Halliday, 1985b, pp. 112–118), in which a relational verb such as *be, mean, define, represent, constitute* identifies the term and its definition

Extract 3
(a) According to the theory of cognitive development, there is a certain stage when the child's language is "completely develop."

By *"completely develop"* I mean *its the time when a child has acquired a language and has set his own rules of a language.*

TERM   DEFINITION

(b) By this essay, the word "bilingual" can be defined into two ways: normative and descriptive.

By *normative description,* it means *a person can be equally competent in two languages.*

· TERM   DEFINITION

In (a) and (b) above, the student has used a mental process *(I mean, it means)* instead of the identifying relational verb *mean.* Also, the student needs to clarify the expressions *completely develop, set his own rules* in (a), and *equally competent in two languages* in (b) to make these extracts more convincing.

3. Defining relative clause (embedding in Qualifier in nominal group, Halliday, 1985b, pp. 219–225)

Extract 4
Communicative Approach in language teaching is one way of teaching a language [[*which is based on communicative*]].

It is not clear in this extract if the student meant *communication* or something like *communicative methods and procedures.*

4. Elaborating clause complex (nondefining relative clauses) (Halliday, 1985b, pp. 203–206)

Extract 5
(a) This fungi can help cassava by absorbing a nutrient from the soil, *it* is Phosphorus or P.
(b) The relationship between cassava and mycorrhiza is a simple relationship. *It* was just found out about ten years ago.
(c) Second, dialect depends on social class, background, *what features of his background he works.*

In samples (a) and (b) *it* could have been replaced by *which* to form a nondefining clause. In (c) it is not clear what information the student wants to include on *background.* Note that replacing *it* by *which* would involve other changes. For example, in 5(a), the structure of the nominal group *a nutrient from the soil* may need to be changed to *a soil nutrient*, in order to avoid ambiguity. Such manipulation is a part of knowing how to produce a textually appropriate nondefining relative clause.

Students need to be able to define technical terms clearly and to use a variety of linguistic resources to do this; they also have to learn how to condense technical information into the nominal group, since in factual written genres it is at this point that the complex bringing together of experiential meanings tends to be expressed and this is the motivation for structural complexity and lexical density in the nominal group, in such writing.

3.1.2 Tenor. Since tenor has to do with the interpersonal distance of a text, we are concerned here with the student's ability to use appropriately these linguistic resources which express the "level of personality" (Martin, 1987). Although students are usually aware of the need to impersonalize their writing, certain aspects of tenor are easier to control than others. Making a text more impersonal involves at least 1–4 discussed below.

1. Removing the "person" (I, you, everyone, etc.) from subject/theme position. This might entail the use of passives.

Extract 6
(a) Before beginning a purification, *everybody* must read carefully the manuals on the tables because accidents and damages *can be happened* from carelessness.
(b) Here it will be trying to introduce some of the problem and the solution *you* have to do.
(c) *My* topic is coeducation is a good thing. First of all, *I* had better say a few words about the meaning of coeducation.

6(a) would sound more impersonal and appropriate if it were rewritten as

Before beginning a purification, *the manuals on the table must be read* carefully because accidents and damages can *happen* from carelessness.

In 6(b) the student is aware of the need to sound impersonal—*it will be trying to introduce*—but is not consistent ("that *you* have to do"). We could rewrite 6(c) as

Coeducation has many advantages. Before discussing these, it is necessary to define what is meant by coeducation.

Students typically face these difficulties when introducing their topic, that is, in the introduction stage of an essay or scientific report.

2. Using modal Adjuncts such as *possibly, certainly, supposedly* (Halliday, 1985b, pp. 50, 82–83); and interpersonal metaphors of modality and modulation. These metaphors are of two kinds, the **subjective** and the **objective**. Using the terminology here, a subjective interpersonal metaphor is personal, as in *I think/imagine/guess/suppose . . . that) . . .*, while an objective interpersonal metaphor is impersonal; it is the latter that is frequently used in the genres under focus. Examples would be *it is likely/possible/probable/usual/certain/necessary . . . (that) . . .* Compare for example:

> *I suppose* certain plants might grow better under these conditions. (subjective metaphor)
> *It is possible* that certain plants might grow better under these conditions. (objective metaphor)

The expression of impersonal tenor can also be achieved by using an appropriate modal Adjunct (i.e., by a congruent, nonmetaphorical choice), as below:

> Certain plants could *possibly* grow better under these conditions. (Adjunct: modal).

3. The use of mental processes of affection, perception, and cognition—processes of feeling, seeing, or thinking (Halliday, 1985b, p. 111); these are also needed when expressing opinions or attitudes and are normally made impersonal, as in: *It is thought that . . .* or *It was felt that . . .*, rather than *I think that . . .* or *I feel that . . .*

4. *Verbal processes* of saying (Halliday, 1985b, pp 227–251). Here the students may have problems in making assertions, claims, statements so that these appear impersonal. eg: *Smith states that . . . , It is claimed that . . . It can be said that . . .* To do this, students will need a pool of these verbs and their nominalized equivalents. All of this involves being able to control different kinds of projection—reports, ideas, and facts (Halliday, 1985b, pp. 227–251).

Extract 7
And *do you know* why we don't stop at only one children? Because two children are for replacement of their parents; two die and two are born.

Now *I daresay you agree* with me that no family should be allowed to have more than two children.

The above passage of the student's essay had adverse evaluation; and at least two of the reasons have to do with the way mental and verbal Processes (italicized) are used by the student. A possible rewrite of 7 would be:

The fact that two children constitute a replacement of their parents *can be seen* as an *argument* for not stopping at only one child. From this point of view, *the claim* would be that no family should be allowed to have more than two children.

Different aspects of tenor can be highlighted by getting students to re-write a text or part of a text using personal pronouns in Subject/Theme position, mental verbs, such as *think, see,* and verbal processes, as in *I agree, we claim,* and so on, to note the effect this has on the tenor.

In addition to the above difficulties (cf. examples above) there may also be shifts in tenor from one stage of the text to another, as, for example, between the Introduction stage and the Methods and Materials stage of a scientific paper. The student has to learn to adjust the tenor values accordingly.

3.1.3 Mode. Since our interest is in essay writing, we are concerned here with the nature of the written channel and how to control the "degree of distance between a text and what it describes" (Martin, 1987). This means controlling the level of abstraction of the text. Writing achieves this through different kinds of complexity from those in speech (Halliday, 1985a, p. 331). In written discourse one kind of complexity derives from its high lexical density—the high proportion of content words per clause. Often student texts have a low lexical density closer to that of speech (3.5–5.0), whereas the texts students have to read may have a lexical density of over 7.0. For example, extract 6(c) above is from a 250-word essay with a lexical density of 5.0, which was based on a reading passage of similar length and subject matter with a lexical density of 7.5. The reading passage was an extract from a university textbook on ecology. Expository texts generally tend to support their generalizations with concrete evidence and examples, and thus there may be shifts from abstract to concrete throughout the text (Martin & Peters, 1985, p. 85). A student may have difficulty controlling these shifts by giving either too many concrete examples or not enough to support the arguments in the text.

Extract 8
It is the common view that children should be controlled before they are taught. *How can a teacher teach while the students are yelling at other or taking no notice of the teacher?*

The italicized sentence above shows an unsuccessful shift from abstract to concrete, although this may not be so evident in isolation from the preceding text. It could be rewritten to sound more "abstract" as follows:

How can a teacher be effective in a class where the students are paying no attention because of the noise level?

Lexical density in written language is accompanied by less "grammatical intricacy" (Halliday, 1985a), which implies that in written texts there are fewer dependent clauses. Much of the complexity in writing occurs in the nominal group which may have a complex structure of Head noun, Premodifier, and Postmodifier—embedded clauses or phrases that can contain further nominal groups. This resource of embedding enables the nominal group to package the information tightly and "take over the main burden of the lexical content of the discourse" (Halliday, 1985a, p. 25).

The high proportion of nominal groups and high lexical density in written expository genres is often accompanied by a higher instance of grammatical metaphor (Halliday, 1985b, pp. 319–345; Martin, 1986a). The two most important kinds of grammatical metaphor that students might encounter in such writing and might themselves require for their own work are as follows. One may need to nominalize a verb (e.g., *behavior* for *behave*) or an adjective (e.g., *importance* for *important*) or a conjunction (e.g., *the cause* for *because; consequence* for *therefore*). Of course, some of the logical relations can also be expressed by such verbs as *(to), cause, lead to, result in,* and so on. The following examples show low lexical density and low levels of grammatical metaphor selection.

Extract 9
(a) They [teachers] should know some of these students are misbehaving because they have problems coping with the life they lead in school. Because they can't solve it themselves they behave in ways that are totally foreign to them. (lexical density of whole text: 3.5)

If we rewrite this sample to include nominalizations (italicized) and replace conjunctions (*because*) with causal verbs *cause* and *lead to*, the lexical density is increased to 7.0.

Student *misbehavior* may be caused by problems with life at school. Their *inability* to solve these problems may lead to kinds of *behavior* that are totally foreign to them.

(b) On the other hand, however, they (plants) may smell or taste terribly good to some insects or plants which help this plant grow. The insects are attracted and help disperse pollen of the plant and the other plants will get along with this plant. They all grow very well. They make use of each other or don't disturb each other much. (lexical density: 3.0)

A rewritten version shows nominalizations (italicized) and a higher lexical density (5.7).

On the other hand, however, a plant's *growth* may be influenced by other plants and animals being attracted by its *smell* and *taste*. Insects help in the *pollination* of this plant and other plants form a symbiotic relationship with it.

Sounding abstract, objective, and even obscure has to do with the features of mode discussed above, and it is therefore critical for the student to have control of complex nominal groups and nominalizations (see section 5, exercises 7 and 8 for examples of exercises on nominalizations). They are also an important resource for creating themes and organizing information (Halliday, 1985a, pp. 34–35).

3.2 Schematic Structure

It is important for students to know about the schematic structure of different genres, that is, the characteristic beginning-middle-end structure through which a text moves to achieve its purpose. In written texts the stages are often signaled overtly through titles and headings, internal conjunction (*first, next, moreover*), text reference (*this, these*), or lexical items that refer to sections of the text (*problem, reason, advantage*). An understanding of the schematic structures of different types of exposition is essential for successful writing at tertiary level. Martin and Peters (1985) and Peters (1985) distinguish two types of exposition—moral and factual. There are also subcategories of these two basic types. Within moral exposition, at least three subtypes can be recognized: (a) interpretive; (b) evaluative; and (c) argumentative. Factual exposition has at least two subtypes: (a) explanatory A, explaining what; and (b) explanatory B, explaining how/why. Texts may combine one or more of these types or use a different type for different stages of the text. Students can be made explicitly aware of the stages of an essay (Thesis ∧

Argument ∧ Conclusion) or a scientific report (Introduction ∧ Methods and Materials ∧ Discussion and Conclusion ∧ References ∧ [Abstract]); if they have only an implicit "feel" for it, they would be unable to manipulate the linguistic resources needed to signal these stages. Extract 10 is from an essay written in response to the instructions "No family should be allowed to have more than two children. Discuss." The extract is taken from the introductory paragraph and from the one following it. The essay could be classified as a type of moral argumentative exposition which tries to persuade the reader to accept the thesis through a series of arguments. In this extract, the opinion of the writer is clear (sentence 6) but it was not clear if this was to be taken as the thesis (see sentences 3 and 7–8).

Extract 10
(1) Children are the chain of human beings (2) If there is no child, the world of humans will stop at the end. (3) However, there are still problems whether we have few children or many. (4) Some custom appreciate a family with many children, especially in the ancient time. (5) But nowadays everything changes, a family tends to have only a few children. (6) On my opinion, a family should stop at only two children.

(7) There are both disadvantages and advantages from having only two. (8) First of all I would like to talk about disadvantages.

Extract 11 below is another example of an introductory paragraph that does not meet the expectation of the reader for this type of exposition, namely, factual (explanatory type B, explaining how and why). It is the introduction from an essay on ecology in which students were asked to write about specific interrelationships between plants and animals. The schematic structure for this type of exposition is set out below.

INTRODUCTION   [indicate phenomenon to be accounted for]
BODY   [analyse contingent relationships in data]
CONCLUSION   [restate]   (Martin & Peters, 1985, p. 87)

Extract 11
(1) Mangrove area is the swampy area where certain kinds of the tropical trees are prefer to grow. (2) Because oxygen, food and energy exchanging are met in equilibrium, on the other word, the ecosystems in mangrove area are quite suitable, it has been said to be a nursery ground for small marine animals. (3) In term of ecological point of view, the living creatures in this area are not only interrelated among themselves but also greatly depend on other physical factors. (4) To understand the overall ecosystems, general relations between mass and energy of living things and its surrounding are needed to discuss.

In this sample the writer does not make it clear that the mangrove area *is* a nursery ground for small marine animals and that the essay intends to discuss this relationship (sentence 4).

To master the schematic structure of the required academic genres the students need to be aware of more than just the overall beginning-middle-end structure of a text. They need to understand how each stage may have its own schematic structure and how this is accomplished linguistically. For example, the introduction stage of a scientific paper may have a distinct schematic structure of three stages (Problem ∧ Interpretation ∧ Hypothesis) (Murison, 1985). Further analysis reveals how these stages are realized through the language. Students can be taught how to recognize these elements of schematic structure through an understanding of authentic texts and can be given practice exercises to transfer this understanding to their writing. (For exercises on schematic structure see section 5, exercise 4.) Being aware of the overall purpose of the genres and the purpose of each stage of the text helps the student make the appropriate choices in the genre, register, and lexicogrammar.

3.3 Theme

Theme is realized by those elements which come in first position in the clause, paragraph, or text "which serve as the point of departure of the message" (Halliday, 1985b, pp. 38–67). The choice of theme is crucial to the control of the organization of the paragraph or text and contributes to their method of development (Fries, 1983). In learning to control the organization of information in a text the student must be made aware of the importance of the introductory paragraph which is thematic to the text and of paragraph themes or topic sentences which are thematic to a paragraph. Also, if there is no clear progression of themes between clauses in a paragraph, the text will appear disjointed and lacking in unity. In exposition, the argument may be built up by expanding the preceding ideas such that the Theme of one sentence depends on information from the Rheme of some previous sentence (Fries, 1983, p. 124). The argument will seem faulty or undeveloped if there is unmotivated interruption to this flow. For an exercise to make students aware of textual patterns of Theme selection, see exercise 3 in section 4 below.

3.4 Cohesion

The cohesion systems of reference, lexical cohesion, and conjunction contribute to the quality of "texture" and coherence of a text (Halliday & Hasan, 1976, 1985). Here the student needs to understand the different aspects of cohesion and, more important, how their interaction contributes to produce a coherent text.

3.4.1 Reference. Reference is the system whereby participants (people, places, things) are introduced into a text and, once introduced, can be referred to again through the systems of personal pronouns, demonstratives, and comparatives. The basic oppositions in the system are those between generic and specific reference and between new participants—**presenting reference,** for example, *a mangrove area*—and known participants—**presuming reference,** for example, *the mangrove area* (Martin, 1984a). Those items whose identity can be retrived from the verbal context are **endophoric.**

When such identity is retrieved from a preceding part of the text, the relation is known as **anaphoric,** as for *these* below:

A mangrove area is a swampy area where certain kinds of tropical trees prefer to grow. *These* areas are suitable . . .

Here the presence of *these* will be interpreted as indicating that the areas in question are the very same areas mentioned in the preceding sentence.

The identity of a reference item could, alternatively, be retrieved from a following part of the text; in this case the relation is known as **cataphoric,** as in the example below:

An animal is bound to depend on *other* living organisms for its food supply.

Here *other* will be interpreted as referring to organisms that are not the previously mentioned *an animal.*

Reference items can be **esophoric;** when the identity of the items can be retrieved from the same nominal group in which the items occur, as in the following:

The population of different competing species exists in a state of delicate balance.

Those reference items whose identity can be retrieved from outside the text are **exophoric,** as below:

We see then, that other plants and animals, through their effects, both direct and indirect, form an integral part of the environment of every living organism.

Reference is important because students need to identify and keep track of participants in a text in such a way as to avoid ambiguity; further, they need to know when the reference is presenting rather than presuming.

Extract 12
(a) Mangrove area is *the* swampy area where certain kinds of *the* tropical trees are prefer to grow.

(b) In the field of animal embryo transfer there are two methods to obtain the embryos from the reproductive organs of a female animal. They are (*) surgical method and (*) non-surgical method. (*) Surgical method is that embryos are got from the oviduct with a surgical method. To do that is cutting the lower abdomen of the female animal.

12(a) is the opening sentence of an essay. The student has used *the* instead of *a swampy area* and *the tropical trees* instead of *tropical trees*, or a presuming reference instead of a presenting reference. The identity of the two nominal groups cannot be retrieved either from the text or extralinguistically, so the reader is left uncertain as to which swampy area or which tropical trees are intended. In 12(b) the problem is in reverse. The student needs to say *the* before *surgical method* and *non-surgical method*, or a presuming reference anaphoric to "two methods." Also, there may be confusion between generic and specific use of *the* as in sample (a) above. The student could have used "*the* mangrove area" (generic). As the student learns to control the complex nominal groups required of the genre, problems with esophoric reference emerge.

Extract 13
The principle in discovery learning lies on (—) student's mastery of (—) rules or principles or concepts of (—) general ideas of what is learnt without emphasis much on (—) facts and details which requires only memorization.

Here, at points indicated by (—), the student has omitted *the* to refer to the head noun of each nominal group. The result is a nominal group which is hard to follow. A rewrite inserting *the* and punctuation helps to make the meaning clearer:

The principle in discovery learning lies in *the* student's mastery of *the* rules, principles, and concepts of *the* general ideas of what is learnt, without emphasis much on facts and details, which require only memorization.

In learning to control the features of the reference system appropriate to academic genres, students, in addition to the above problems, need to realize that in exposition, reference chains are short and participants are reintroduced to a text through repetition of the noun or nominal group or through text reference (e.g., *this problem, these processes*, etc.). Section 4, in exercises 1 and 2 on reference below, outlines some of the ways in which students can be made aware of the features of reference in their reading and writing.

3.4.2 Lexical cohesion. As discussed under Mode (3.1.3), exposition is characterized by high lexical density resulting in complex patterns of lexical cohesion. Lexical strings show relations of synonymy and repetition and, important for this genre, the taxonomic relations of hyponomy and meronymy (Halliday & Hasan, 1985; Hasan, 1984b). Students here may have problems with overuse of repetition as a cohesive device, poor or imprecise understanding of the taxonomic relations of the field-specific lexis, for instance, in explaining relationships between concepts or phenomena or in defining terms. One way of pointing to these relations in a text is to draw a tree diagram of the lexis in the text, showing the hierarchies of concepts (cf. Morris & Stewart-Dore, 1984). Students could also do this for their own texts either at the planning stage or after the first draft (see exercise 8).

Extract 14
(a) Language may be defined as a system of communication. There are two basic type of language variation.

    First, register deals with the style of the language. It describes the way people speak in linguistic point of view, and in the way language work.

    Second, dialect depends on social class background, what features of his background he speaks.

(b) I'd like to explain the relationships between Phytoplankton and Zooplankton. Plankton is the floating organism, in the seas and oceans. Plankton can be divided into two main parts, which was Phytoplankton and Zooplankton. Phyto means plant and plankton means floating, which has the complete meaning of plant which is floating in the seas. In Phytoplankton, two types of dinoflagellates and diatom can be classified. The both organism are unicellular, but different in their floating types.

The following tree diagrams may have helped the student make the lexical relations of 14(a) and 14(b) above more explicit.

Students need also to be aware of how lexical strings run through a text and interact with schematic structure and theme to contribute to unity in their writing. So, for example, some lexical strings may occur at the Intro-

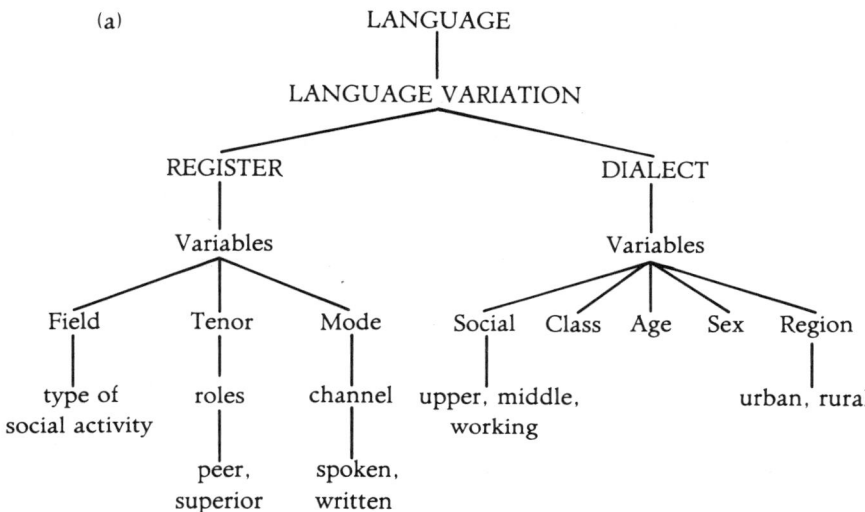

Figure 2. Simple lexical taxonomy for 14(a)

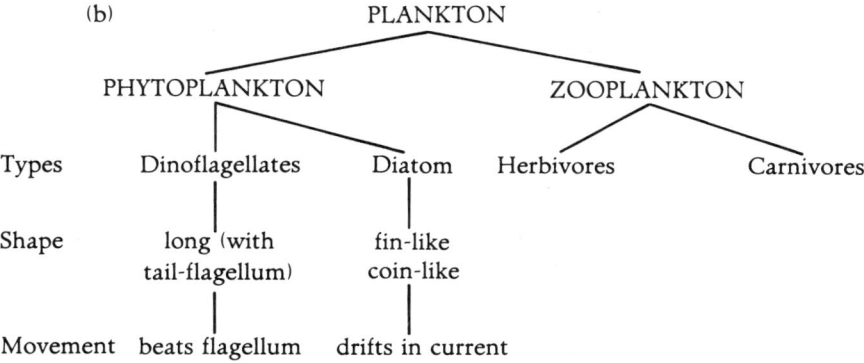

Figure 3. Simple lexical taxonomy for 14(b)

duction stage of a text, whereas others may run throughout the text as major participants and occur predominantly in thematic position. Students may have problems maintaining these patterns of interaction.

3.4.3 Conjunction. Conjunction is the discourse system used to express logical relations in a text either between clauses (external conjunction) or between sections of the text (rhetorical or internal conjunction). Important here is the use of internal conjunction to connect arguments of the text and give it rhetorical structure. While students may be aware of this device they may overuse it—especially temporal internal conjunction (Halliday & Hasan, 1976; Martin, 1983), as in 15 below—or may make an inappropriate choice. This may indicate that the student is learning to use this device and the overuse of a certain feature is part of the learning process. The following student text sample is from an essay on "how people learn." Here the student sets forth the important factors for a teacher to consider in order to promote successful learning in her students. The student has already set out her first three points, using "Firstly," "Secondly," and "Thirdly." The text continues:

Extract 15
Fourthly the teacher should encourage learning by activity. *In this case*, students will be active participants when they take part in the activities. *Moreover*, they should be allowed to work at their own pace. *Fifthly*, the lessons should be suitable for the students' competence so that they can succeed in their study. *However*, the task should be complex enough to arouse interest and curiosity. *Sixthly*, the students should receive some feedback. *In other words* they should have the result of their study *for example* the teacher comments on their written or spoken work. *Lastly*, the learners should be put in a situation where they have enough practice and reinforcement.

There is also this problem in reverse—a complete absence of any internal conjunction to structure the text. This is often accompanied by an overuse of external conjunction, linking clauses paratactically or hypotactically in clause complexes and may be a result of being taught conjunction at clause level and not discourse level. Thus the student can make the appropriate logical links between clauses but fails to make explicit the links between stages of the text or points in the argument. The result is a text that is closer to spoken language, which typically has "complex dependency structures" (Halliday, 1985b, p. 330), that is, dependent relations in clause complexes.

Extract 16
Mycorrhiza is a tiny organism *so* it can build many tiny hyphae, *which* can penetrate between the tiny space of soil particle *and* absorb phosphorous from the soil. Mychorrhiza can also absorb phosphorous more intensive than cassava roots *because* phosphorous is carried directly to the cassava roots *so* it is quicker than the roots do.

One final problem that students have in expressing logical relations in academic discourse and one which is related to the overuse of explicit external conjunction, is how to use the grammar to code these relationships incongruently. The use of grammatical metaphor to express cause appears to be the hallmark of an abstract discourse. The student has to learn to manipulate both congruent and incongruent realizations of reasoning according to the degree of abstraction required. The following extract shows only congruent realizations of cause.

Extract 17
They [teachers] should know that some of these students are misbehaving *because* they have problems coping with the life they lead at school. *Because* they can't solve it themselves they act out behaviors that are foreign to them. Teachers should be sensitive to these kind of students. They must know that they act out this way probably *because* they have problems at home and at school.

This sample has been partly rewritten (see extract 9(a)), replacing the conjunctions *because* with *caused by* and *lead to* (3.1.3 above).

With the insights gained from analysis of the problems in student texts it is possible to design an appropriate program for reading and writing at the university level which will help solve some of these problems. Sections 4 and 5 which follow outline the approaches used and some of the exercises we have designed for our students at this level.

4. AN APPROACH TO TEACHING ACADEMIC WRITING IN A PRE-SESSION COURSE AT THE EPC

The English Preparation Centre (EPC) in Sydney provides pre-session courses in EAP/EST for postgraduates, mostly from Asia, who will study at Australian universities under Australia's foreign aid program. Students attend classes for periods of one to seven months, depending on preselection test results.

Classes are usually composed of about eight students grouped broadly according to field of academic interest, and to some extent on levels of proficiency in English. This allows a good deal of flexibility and individualized attention. The aim is to develop language proficiency to a level where students can communicate effectively in the spoken and written genres of postgraduate study. Language learning is combined with study skills to accustom students to accepted patterns of learning in Western universities, and the students are encouraged to be as self-directed and independent as possible.

In learning to write academic genres and theses, EPC students display the typical problems of foreign university students described in section 3 above. Figure 4 is an outline of one approach used at the EPC for

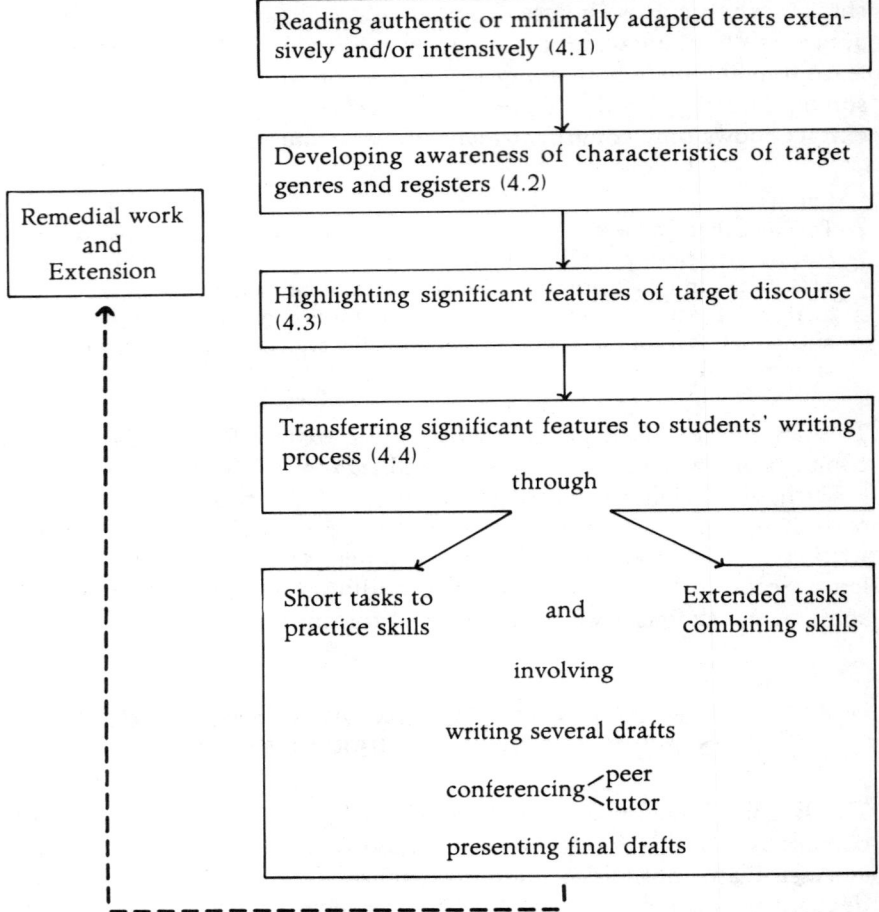

Figure 4.   An approach to teaching academic writing at advanced level

teaching academic writing in science disciplines. The theoretical frame-work is based on the systemic-functional model, placing prime impor-tance on the use of authentic texts as models for writing and always taking into account genre and register. Selected systems such as those concerned with cohesion and theme are explored for the contributions they make to texture, then seen again from the point of view of the whole. Methodologically, the communicative approach is adopted, stu-dents taking as much responsibility as possible for their own texts and actively negotiating meaning with other students or groups and relating it to its overall purpose and content.

4.1 Reading Authentic or Minimally Adapted Texts

The basis of this approach is the students' own reading materials in their academic fields. Apart from being authentic models, the texts also provide excellent motivation. Foreign postgraduates are under considerable time constraints and are usually anxious to begin reading in their field before university courses commence. Their supervisors have often already supplied lists of recommended reading. These textbooks, journals, and reports provide not only a guaranteed source of interest, but also a realistic basis for English practice. Thus learners are encouraged to read as extensively as possible in their fields, both in class and at home.

From the range of texts students have read extensively, certain texts are chosen for intensive reading by the class for the purpose of developing awareness of the characteristics of a certain genre, for example, the field report. If only part of a text is read intensively it is placed in context so that learners can appreciate how it contributes to the whole text. The same text, or part of it, is later used for highlighting significant features of discourse, for example the use of anaphoric reference. Thus the students are working intensively on familiar material.

Although students' own reading materials are preferred for these purposes it is not always feasible to start with these if a class contains a wide range of specialized interests. An "agriculture" class, for example, may contain soil scientists, plant breeders, and epidemiologists, and their reading lists would not overlap. Rather than impose the unnecessary strain of a large number of unfamiliar scientific concepts and technical lexis, a less specialized text in the target genre and register, such as the one quoted in exercise 1, is used as the basis for intensive study. Later, students are directed to look for more examples in their own reading.

If a class has great difficulty with authentic texts, minimally adapted ones may be used initially. However, even the smallest adaptations can alter the register or skew the cohesion of a text, and the result is not always an appropriate model of the kind of text the student wants to write. If possible, minimally adapted texts should be compared with the originals and the effects of changes discussed.

4.2 Developing Awareness of Characteristics of Genres and Registers

Through their extensive reading, learners are exposed to a wide range of the genres and registers they will have to reproduce in their own writing. In addition, they read articles from popular scientific journals such as *New Scientist*, or practical newsletters such as the *Rural Notes* for farmers from the New South Wales Department of Agriculture. In this way, the differences between academic and nonacademic genres are more easily seen.

It is particularly useful to compare texts on the same topic, for example the effects of certain pests on crops, one written for an academic journal, another for farmers, to see how lexical and grammatical choices affect register. Again, different genres can be compared, for example, instructions for carrying out field work and the completed report on that work.

As a follow-up, students write a similar text in their own field, keeping in mind a specific purpose and intended reader. The completed drafts are discussed in groups and changes are suggested by students. By experimenting with changing parts of the text, students gain awareness of the factors affecting genre and register. For example, changing explicit conjunctions to nominal groups or verbs can make a text sound much less congruent and closer to the academic genres (see extract 9(a) in 3.1.3).

Genre and register are always taken into account when reading and writing; a passage, no matter how small, is always considered in the light of the whole text. Many textbooks for developing academic writing skills, for example, the English in Focus series (Allen & Widdowson, 1975–1980), give insufficient indication to students of the wider context in which each sample text or piece of practice writing may be placed. In addition the range of registers covered is very limited.

4.3 Highlighting Significant Features of Target Discourse

While students are developing awareness of genres and registers through reading, they are also being introduced to the more significant aspects of the textual metafunction; notably, cohesion and Theme are discussed so that the students can transfer this learning to their own writing.

Two areas students find difficult are the use of reference and the development of Theme. The suggestions and exercises below are samples of a wider range that have been found to be effective. Note, for convenience, all exercises here are based on one text (Lawrie & Nott, 1984). In the classroom different texts may be chosen as best illustrating certain features. However, from time to time, all significant aspects were superimposed on one text (using OHP transparencies) to show how they contribute to a cohesive and coherent whole.

4.3.1 Reference. Scientific exposition characteristically contains a great deal of generic and exophoric reference. Much of the endophoric reference is cataphoric, particularly of the esophoric variety. Thus, the long cohesive anaphoric chains of demonstrative and personal reference characteristic of narrative genres are not usually found. Nevertheless, it is important to understand the difference between generic and nongeneric reference and to trace through reference to participants where this relation exists (see 3.4.1).

In differentiating between generic and nongeneric specific reference, particularly where the definite article is concerned, students are invariably confused about the function of the definite articles. *Cohesion in English* (Halliday & Hasan, 1976) contains a clear and comprehensive description (see also Hasan, 1984b). Halliday and Hasan (1976) has been used as the basis for Figure 5.

Once students are aware that *the* identifies a participant either inside or outside the text (ignoring here the special generic use), it is a simple matter to make them aware of the kind of relations, especially endophoric ones, that may exist in a text passage. One can first check out the nominal groups, asking (a) "Does this group have a specific determiner?" (in exposition, usually *the, this, that, these, those* occur); and if so, then (b) "Where can we find information about its identity?" If the answer to this is some part of the text, the reference is endophoric.

This exercise is important in developing students' own self-monitoring skills in writing. If they can develop the habit of asking the same questions about nominal groups in their own rough drafts, the use of demonstrative reference improves, which means that less reader guesswork is needed in interpreting their essays, reports, and so forth.

By tracing reference to participants through a text, students see how chains contribute to cohesion. OHP transparencies can be used to show by means of boxes and arrows how the participants link up. By superimposing different chains over the text, the whole reference system can be seen. This is a dramatic way of demonstrating a rather complex aspect of cohesion.

Exercise 1 shows how the anaphoric use of the demonstratives *this* and *these* may be highlighted. It is important to note that the exercises as presented here are not exactly in the form in which students encounter them. With our students, we use OHP to display at once both the text under focus and the instructions. This face-to-face layout has been abandoned in this chapter for convenience but it cannot be emphasized enough that the original method of exposure with arrows pointing to the part of the passage under discussion, with instructions and explanations fully visible at all times, is highly desirable, as we have found in our work. Another respect in which the exercises here differ is the exclusion of some parts of the text under discussion. In presentation to our students, we attempt to keep the whole text in perspective; especially with reference exercises, we

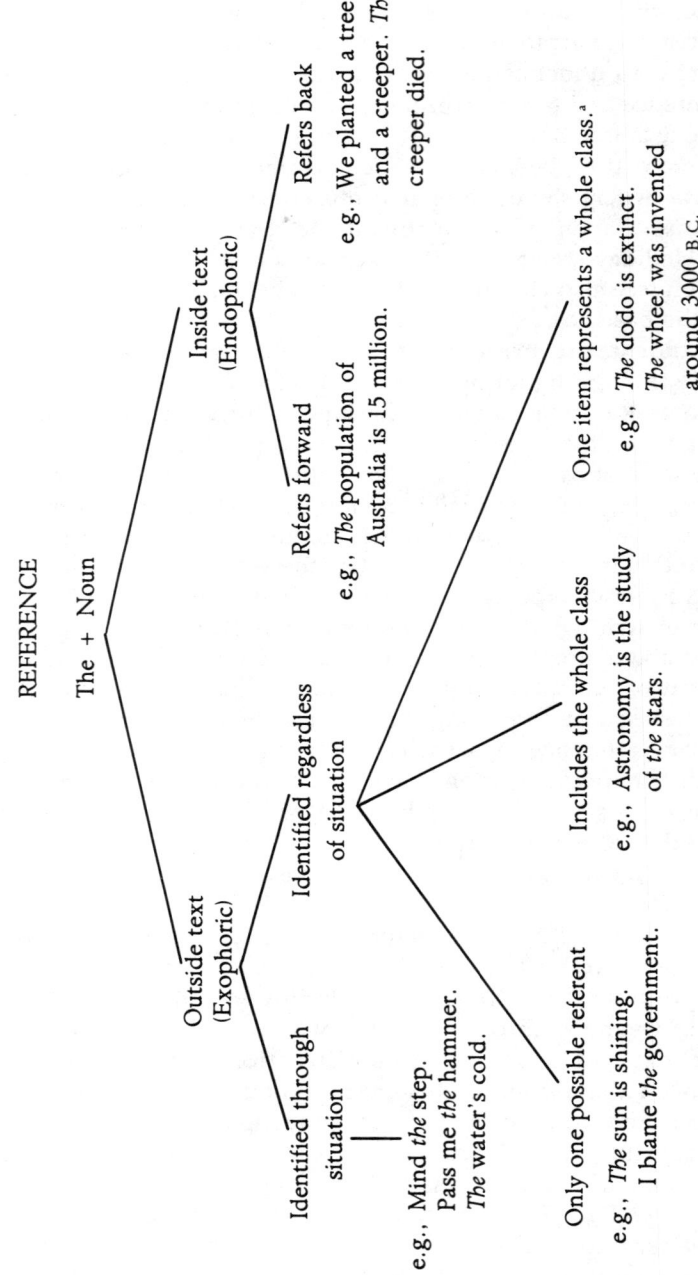

ᵃThis is a generic use of *the*, all others are specific.

Figure 5.   The uses of reference

would avoid plunging students into the middle as this can cause them great confusion.

Exercise 1

REFERENCE

The words *this* and *these* are often used to refer back to a fact or idea mentioned before (a noun group, a clause or a clause complex).

(With your tutor)   (a)   Look at the way *this* and *these* refer back in paragraphs 1, 2.

Many cities, of course, originated around areas with good agricultural lands. This historic association is now accentuating pressures on these lands. In Canada, for example, it has been estimated that over half the farm land lost to urbanisation is coming from the best 5% of agricultural farm land. In Europe it is reported that West Germany is losing 1% of its farm land every four years through urbanisation. On a world-wide scale, urbanisation in the period 1980–2000 will require 54 million hectares of land. If only 40% of this area is crop land the growth of cities will be equivalent to removing from the world the cultivated agricultural output of a nation the size of France (Brown 1981). The significance of this can be appreciated when it is realised that France produces about the same amount of beef and veal as Australia and somewhat more wheat. (See Section 2.)

As the above information indicates, the underlining pressure on the world's agricultural resources is the rapid growth of population. During the present decade, population will increase by 860 million. During the 1990s, population will increase by 94 million per year. (This is more than the population of a nation the size of Bangladesh.)

(Pair work)   (b)   Have a look at the underlined examples of *this* and *these* in paragraphs 3 and 4.

In historic terms 130 years were needed for world population to increase by 1 billion after 1800. This reduced to 15 years after 1960 with only approximately a decade being required in these times. A world population in 1980 of 4.4 billion will expand to 6.2 billion by the year 2000. Even without making any serious attempt to address pressing problems of distribution, resource access and persistent undernourishment in many parts of the world, agricultural output will be required to increase by 50% to 60% over a 20 year period to simply meet the food and fibre needs of this population growth (FAO 1981).

Such demands in aggregate terms are difficult to contemplate yet FAO research (1981) indicates that these needs can be met. It is important however, that existing productive resources are effectively utilised and that other measures are taken to increase production and improve distribution. This and other major reports such as *Global Future: Time to Act* (a report to President Reagan on global resources, environment and population, United States Department of State 1981) indicate that developed nations with export capacity, technology and associated infrastructure will have an increasingly important role to play in meeting the world's future food and fibre needs. This role is, in fact, an acceleration of an already well established trend.

On your copy of the text circle the parts *this* and *these* refer to.

(On your own,   (c)   Now try to find more examples of *this* and *these*
then discuss with   in the rest of the text.
your group.)   Circle what they refer back to on your text.
                         Did you find any examples of *this* and *these* which
                         do *not* refer back? What do they refer to?

Esophoric reference is confined to the nominal group; however, it is so common in academic exposition that it cannot be ignored in teaching reference. Practice is usefully combined with exercises on nominalization (see section 5, exercise 7) and grammatical metaphor.

The following exercise shows how esophora may be highlighted using OHP overlays on a text.

Exercise 2

REFERENCE

(With your tutor)   Read paragraph 1 and study the nominal groups underlined. Notice that all the underlined groups begin with 'the.' 'The' signals that we can identify the noun after it by reading on. (That is, we can say precisely which 'need' or which 'conversion' is referred to, by reading the phrase marked by a dotted line.)

The need for effective planning of rural lands is now recognised throughout the western world. Examples of countries introducing programmes in recent years to protect agricultural lands include the U.S.A., Japan, U.K., Germany and Canada. It is particularly relevant that the world's dominant food producer, the United States, has now introduced a broad range of measures to curb the conversion of agricultural land to other uses. These measures are in recognition of the fact that agricultural land in that nation is being lost at the rate of 1.2 million hectares per year (United States Department of Agriculture 1981). If existing trends continued, all the prime farm land of Florida, presently producing 50% of the world's grapefruit and 25% of the world's oranges, would be lost by the year 2000. By the same time the States of Virginia and California would lose about one-fifth of the best of their agricultural lands (Brown 1978).

These kinds of expression are common in academic texts and are sometimes difficult to understand because of grammatical metaphor. You can 'unravel' them by starting at the end and working back. For example, 'the need for effective planning of rural lands' could be unraveled as 'rural lands need to be planned effectively.' Notice that 'need' and 'planning' become verbs.

(In pairs)   (a)   Try to unravel the other underlined nominalisations. (Note, you may have to add verbs like 'have' or 'be.'

> Many cities, of course, originated around areas with good agricultural lands. This historic association is now accentuating pressures on these lands. In Canada, for example, it has been estimated that over half of the farm land lost to urbanisation is coming from the best 5% of agricultural farm land. In Europe it is reported that West Germany is losing 1% of its farm land every four years through urbanisation. On a world-wide scale, urbanisation in the period 1980–2000 will require 54 million hectares of land. If only 40% of this area is crop land <u>the growth</u> of cities will be equivalent to removing from the world <u>the cultivated agricultural output</u> of a nation the size of France (Brown 1981). <u>The significance</u> of this can be appreciated when it is realised that France produces about <u>the same amount</u> of beef and veal as Australia and somewhat more wheat. (See Section 2.)

(b)   Now look at paragraph 2. Put a dotted line under the phrases which identify the underlined nouns. Try to unravel the nominal groups.

(c)   In your own reading materials, find more examples like these and try to unravel them.

4.3.2 Theme. Thematic development can be presented to learners in a fairly generalized way, which enables them to improve the coherence of their own writing.

Theme and Information are two structural expressions of the textual metafunction (Halliday, 1985b). Space does not permit a more detailed account of these here (see Fries, 1983; Halliday, 1985b, pp. 38–64). The importance of Theme for successful exposition means that students have to be made aware of the part it plays in such writing. The position is made more complex by the fact that in any paragraph usually the first sentence is thematically important; it is the Theme of that paragraph. At the same time, as the text develops there are definite semantic relations between the Theme and Rheme of the successive clauses. This relation is definitely not of only one kind (see exercise 3 below), but very often in exposition, we would find that some experiential meaning expressed in Rheme is picked up in Theme. In other words, the unmarked position is that Theme and Given (Information) usually combine. In the exercise below, the focus is simply on unmarked Theme selections. The first sentence of each segment is underlined in its capacity as the paragraph-initiating sentence, the Theme of the paragraph.

Exercise 3

THEME

(With your tutor)   Successful writers link ideas from one sentence to the next within paragraphs.

If you look at the main clause of a sentence you can divide it in two parts. Roughly speaking, the part before the verb contains the theme (i.e. what the sentence is about). The rest of the clause is called the rheme (i.e. it contains some new information that the writer wants to give the reader).

All or part of this *new information* is usually carried on to the next sentence, where it becomes the theme. This old or *given* information is often expressed in different words, but the *meaning* is carried on.

(a)   If you look at paragraphs 1 and 2 you will see a zig-zag pattern of information like this:

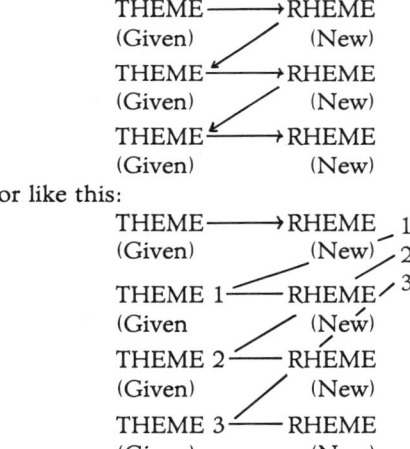

or like this:

where the new information in one sentence is spread out over several following sentences.

1. The need for effective planning of rural lands is now recognised throughout the Western world.

2. Examples of countries introducing programmes in recent years to protect agricultural lands include the USA, Japan, UK, Germany and Canada.

3. It is particularly relevant that the world's dominant food producer, the United States has now introduced a broad range of measures to curb the conversion of agricultural land to other uses.

4. These measures are in recognition of the fact that agricultural land in that nation is being lost at the rate of 1.2 million hectares per year (United States Department of Agriculture 1981).

5. If existing trends continued, all the prime farm land of Florida, presently producing 50% of the world's grapefruit and 25% of the world's oranges, would be lost by the year 2000.

6. By the same time the States of Virginia and California would lose about one-fifth of the best of their agricultural lands (Brown 1978).

7. Many cities, of course, originated around areas with good agricultural lands.

8. This historic association is now accentuating pressures on these lands.

9. In Canada, for example, it has been estimated that over half the farm land lost to urbanisation is coming from the best 5% of agricultural farm land.

10. In Europe it is reported that West Germany is losing 1% of its farm land every four years through urbanisation.

11. On a world-wide scale, urbanisation in the period 1980–2000 will require 54 million hectares of land.

12. If only 40% of this area is crop land the growth of cities will be equivalent to removing from the world the cultivated agricultural output of a nation the size of France (Brown 1981).

13. The significance of this can be appreciated when it is realised that France produces about the same amount of beef and veal as Australia and somewhat more wheat. (See Section 2.)

(Pair work)   (b) Now look at the last two paragraphs of your text. Try to outline this pattern for yourselves. Don't worry if some sentences do not fit this pattern. This is a rough guide, not a fixed rule.

(With your tutor)   Another thing successful writers do is to link each paragraph back to the one before, or to several preceding paragraphs.

Notice the beginning of paragraph 3: *As the above information indicates*. This refers back to the whole of paragraphs 1 and 2.

(c) Try to find other examples of this kind in your text. What do they refer back to?

4.4 Transferring Significant Features to Students' Writing Process

Once learners have been sensitized to a particular cohesive feature, they are asked to do some writing of their own, in a genre with which they are already familiar from reading and discussion. Topics are related to their own field and for practical purposes are kept short (say, 200–300 words) and written in class.

As an example, agriculture students may be asked to describe the causes and effects of a certain disease on a crop, imagining their text to be part of a longer report. They are not told to concentrate on any particular cohesive feature, but rather to concentrate on conveying meaning. After first drafts are completed they are photocopied and students form small groups to discuss them.

They may be asked to consider the way causal relationships have been coded, or to look at the development of theme, or to see how reference has been used. After much discussion, even argument, suggestions on alternative expressions are given. Sometimes the tutor is asked to settle disputes or give advice. At this point, areas needing further teacher exposition or remedial work can also be identified. However, it is vital for students to build confidence in their own intuitions about language, so that they can be as self-sufficient as possible. After discussion, second drafts are written, and rediscussed if time permits. Final drafts are kept by students for future reference.

Having worked on a number of small tasks students then apply what they have learned of genre, register, and cohesion to an authentic writing task. Each student chooses a topic related to his field and writes a short paper or report (2,000–3,000 words) suitable for presentation at a seminar. The task involves extensive and intensive reading around the topic, note-taking, planning, and synthesizing factual data into a cohesive and coherent text. Rough drafts are worked on in groups and in consultation with the tutor. The final product is typed up and presented to the class or another group in a seminar.

We have found this approach successful at the EPC, where students have time to read and write extensively. However, there are many students on campus who for one reason or another have not had the benefit of a pre-session course. The following program is designed for them.

5. AN APPROACH TO TEACHING WRITING IN THE SERVICE ENGLISH PROGRAM AT THE UNIVERSITY OF SYDNEY

5.1 Background

The provision of help in written English for students of non-English-speaking backgrounds is part of the overall service English program offered to students undertaking degree courses or research programs at the University of Sydney. The need to improve writing performance is perceived by the majority of students as the most urgent. The students come from all faculties of the university, either as undergraduate or postgraduate students or as research staff or visiting scholars; their writing needs and levels are thus diverse. In addition, their backgrounds differ: approximately 50 percent are migrants while the remainder are overseas students. Clearly, they have been exposed to different forms of writing practice in English and different teaching methods, some of which have provided them with a good basis for university study. Moreover, they are literate in their own language and many already have a strong concept of how certain academic writing tasks are achieved in their first language. This, however, may conflict with accepted academic genres in an Australian university.

The written tasks demanded by their area of study may range from essays to scientific reports, from journal articles to theses. They will often receive little or no direction from teaching departments as to how to produce these written papers, apart from some advice on layout and presentation, such as how to provide citations or footnotes. What little advice there is about writing essays and reports is sometimes misleading and ambiguous, since adequate descriptions of the generic requirements according to subject discipline do not yet exist.

5.2 The Writing Program

Unlike a pre-session program (see section 4 above), in which students follow an intensive full-time course, the service English program has the task of providing help in written academic English, which is further complicated by the demands on student time from their degree studies or research. Our program is organized at different levels, both in terms of content and course duration. In general there is a progression from a macro level to a micro level, from the whole to the parts. In the process of constructing a text, a great deal of input comes to the student from discussions with peers and tutors. This conferencing helps to assess, evaluate, and redraft written choices. In this way the final meaning is a negotiation which focuses on the process of constructing a text. The insights gained from the SF model are used to identify errors in the student texts. Typical errors have been described in section 3. This way of assessing student texts forms a basis for further written work and course development. The structure of the program is illustrated in Figure 6. The courses comprising the program will be described in the following section. Space does not allow for exemplification of exercises used in every course but, where possible, typical exercise types have been included with the course description.

5.3 The Content of the Courses

5.3.1 Intensive courses. These are offered in the first half of the university year in essay writing for the humanities and social sciences and in writing scientific papers. They usually comprise a course of 2½ hours per week over a 4- or 5-week period. Within these courses the emphasis is on the overall structure of an essay or paper and how this fulfills the purpose for which it is written. Students are exposed to different genres and registers, with authentic or minimally adapted texts as models, and they compare these to their own texts. Schematic structure is made explicit not only in terms of the whole essay or paper but also within each stage. The following exercise illustrates one way of increasing student awareness of the schematic structure in the introduction to a scientific paper. First, students are presented with an authentic model of the introduction to a scientific paper and the three general stages in the structure of the introduction are identified and discussed. Then, another text is examined in which the sentences composing the introduction are jumbled up. Students must use their knowledge of schematic structure to reorder the sentences correctly. A key part of the exercise is a comparison of the two texts (in class more texts would be

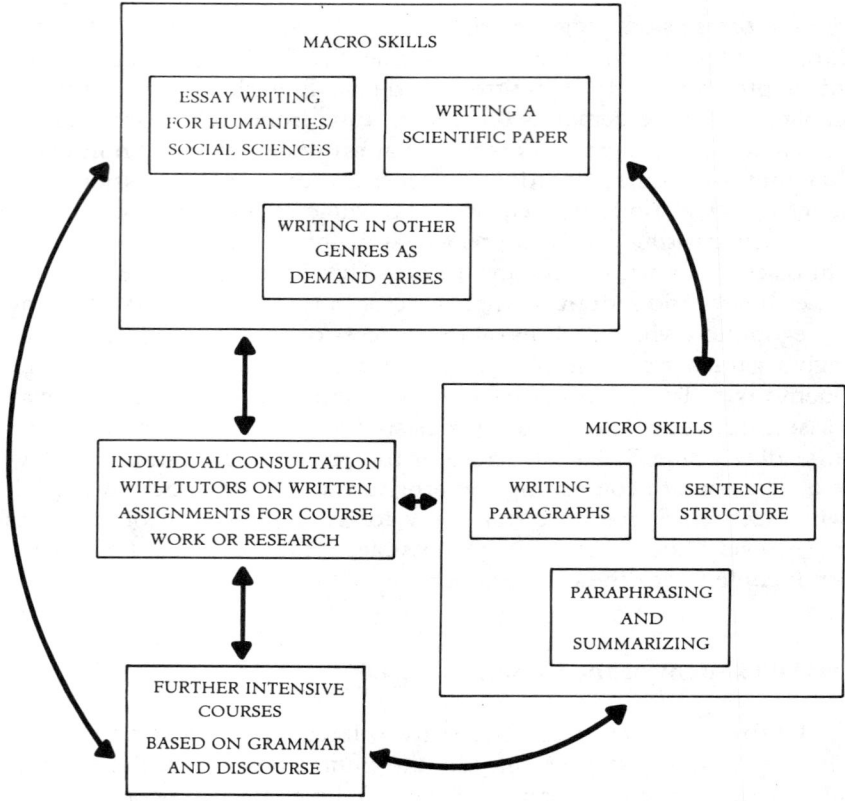

Figure 6.   Structure of program for teaching writing at an advanced level

examined) and an assessment of how well they fit in to the generalized schematic structure model for the introduction to a scientific paper.

Exercise 4
Structure of the Introduction to a Scientific Paper
The following diagram represents the structure of an introduction. There are usually three stages and the text develops from the general to the particular. While there may be exceptions to this pattern, it is generally applicable. Each stage in the structure is illustrated by an example from the introduction to the paper 'Reclamation of Saline Land in the Murray Basin' (Coad, A.R., 1981 *Water* Vol. 8, No. 4).

GENERAL INTRODUCTION

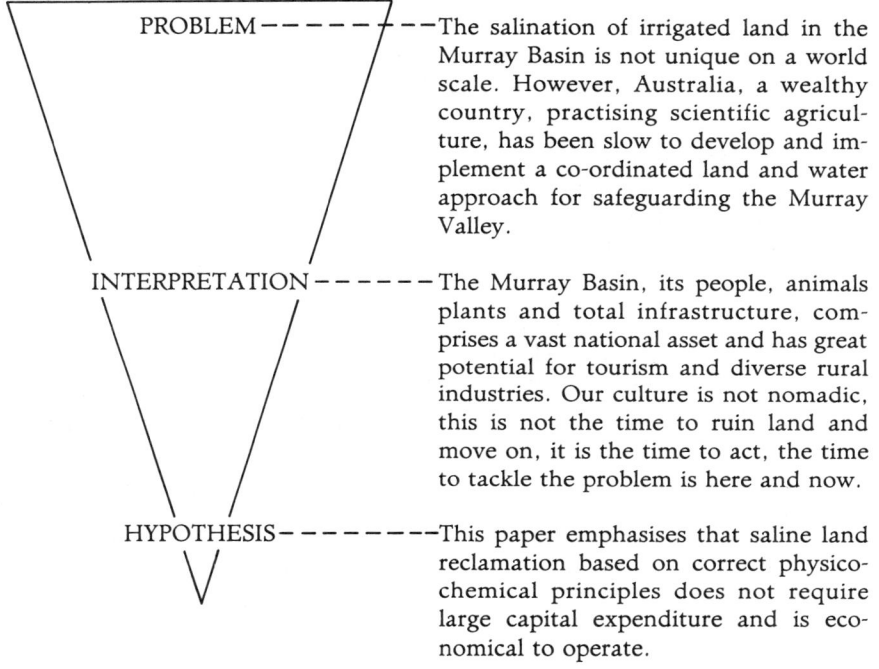

PROBLEM– – – – – – – –The salination of irrigated land in the Murray Basin is not unique on a world scale. However, Australia, a wealthy country, practising scientific agriculture, has been slow to develop and implement a co-ordinated land and water approach for safeguarding the Murray Valley.

INTERPRETATION– – – – – –The Murray Basin, its people, animals plants and total infrastructure, comprises a vast national asset and has great potential for tourism and diverse rural industries. Our culture is not nomadic, this is not the time to ruin land and move on, it is the time to act, the time to tackle the problem is here and now.

HYPOTHESIS– – – – – – – –This paper emphasises that saline land reclamation based on correct physico-chemical principles does not require large capital expenditure and is economical to operate.

The following introduction is from a paper on rice (Willis, R., Palipane, K., and Greenfield, H., 1985 *Composition of Australian Foods, 13 Rice*). There are four sentences in the introduction but they are not in the correct order. Using the above diagram and example, put the sentences in a correct order and identify the three stages in the introduction. Discuss how this example differs from or is similar to the above example.

A. This paper reports on a laboratory investigation of the nutrient composition of seven brands of Australian commerically-produced rice, including white, parboiled and brown rice, available in retail outlets and the changes in the levels of some B-vitamins and minerals during cooking.

B. The rice industry in Australia began in the 1920s in irrigation areas along the Murrumbidgee and Murray Rivers, and these areas currently produce > 95% of the total Australian crop of about 500,000t/year, with the remainder being produced in Queensland in the Burdekin Valley and Atherton Tablelands areas (about 15,000t/year) and the Ord River area of Western Australia (< 2,000t/year); while about 90% of the Australian crop is exported, the 10% consumed locally constitutes the bulk of rice available in Australia (M. Goldring, Ricegrowers Co-operative Mills, Ltd., pers. commun.)

C. Rice (Oryza sativa L.) is traditionally grown in tropical regions of the world, but the availability of irrigation has led to the establishment of rice growing areas in temperate regions, such as Spain, Italy and California.

D. Rice is available in Australia in three forms; as white or polished rice that has had the bran layer removed by abrasive milling, as brown or unpolished rice that has the bran layer retained and as parboiled rice that has been partially cooked with the bran layer on the grain and after drying, the bran layer removed by milling.

Subsequently, specific cohesive features that help to realize the schematic structure, such as reference and/or conjunction, are highlighted. For example, in the above exercise, in order to put the jumbled sentences in the text on rice in their correct order, it is necessary for students to recognize the cohesive links between the lexical items in the Rheme of sentence B in the rice text:

constitutes the bulk of *rice available* in Australia

and the following Theme/Rheme in sentence D:

Rice is available in Australia

When students have worked through exercises to make them familiar with the lexicogrammatical characteristics at each stage, they will be given appropriate writing tasks to practice the skills they have learned. Some exercises will concentrate on specific skills while others will integrate a number of skills. By comparing their own texts through the conferencing technique, students become more aware of areas where they may be failing. Tutor examination of student writing will further reveal their individual problem areas and, depending on these, they will be advised to attend weekly class(es) of 1 to 1½ hours in a micro skill area, either in paragraph writing/summarizing and paraphrasing or in sentence structure.

5.4 Micro Skills Courses

5.4.1 Paragraph writing. The paragraph-writing course aims to give students extensive writing practice within the framework of a structured paragraph. Topics chosen can be general in nature, for example, leisure, overpopulation, or from the students' own area of study. Students must choose an area of focus within the general content domain. In writing their paragraph they must make this area of focus clear, that is, form a thesis statement. When students have written a fully structured paragraph, they conference with each other and the tutor. Often student texts or authentic models may be chosen for group discussion; the stages in the schematic structure can be revealed step by step on the OHP; predictions about how the text may develop can be made and the writer's method of development evaluated. For example, the thesis statement of the following paragraph, taken from Cosgrove and Jackson (1972), makes its purpose clear, that is, to explore definitions of leisure:

THESIS   Various attempts have been made to define leisure.

EXPLANATION   The one adopted by the International Study Group on
                  leisure and Social Sciences states that 'leisure consists of
                  a number of occupations in which the individual may in-
                  dulge of his own free will—either to rest, to amuse him-
                  self, to add to his knowledge and improve his skills
                  disinterestingly and to increase his voluntary participa-
                  tion in the life of the community after discharging his
                  professional, family and social duties'. The inclusion of
                  phrases like 'of his own free will' and 'disinterestedly' are
                  vaguely discomforting, and the difficulties involved in dif-
                  ferentiating between social duties and voluntary partici-
                  pation in the life of the community are considerable.

CONCLUSION   This definition, like many others, is not saying more than
                  that we are at leisure when we have time free from the
                  necessity to work, and it may not be possible to be more
                  precise. It should be emphasised, however, that these def-
                  initions are likely to be interpreted in different and even
                  conflicting ways.

However, the orientation of the following paragraph, a student text, is
not so clear from the first sentence only, although it is obviously different from the above:

People really need to have leisure time to enjoy themselves.

Students can suggest possible developments and then assess the writer's
choice:

But how much and how often they need leisure time depends on what
they do.

EXPLANATION   For some people who are working very hard with their
                  mind they do need leisure time and it should be a part of
                  their daily activity. This does not mean that other people
                  who are doing physical work do not need leisure.

Here the second sentence together with the first makes the thesis of the
paragraph much clearer. In this way students are not only exposed to
different realizations of schematic structure within the paragraph but
also to different methods of development, some of which are more successful than others. Specific discourse features, such as Theme/Rheme
or reference, may be focused on in the discussion. Authentic models

from introductory textbooks, as in the first example above, or from journals of a more popular nature are also used to exemplify schematic structure and text development (for more details see Drury & Gollin, 1987).

5.4.2 Paraphrasing and summarizing. Paraphrasing and summarizing are skills that students need in all disciplines. Recognition of schematic structure and the relationship between ideas in a text is an important first step in manipulating these skills. Authentic and minimally adapted texts are discussed to make explicit what the schematic structures are like. Students suggest the area of focus or topic of the text, as well as other ideas that should be included in a summary. Model summaries of the text in question are examined and related to the original. Differences between the original and the summary are particularly noted, as are the language forms used in the summary to express the topic and other key points. Model paraphrases are also examined and compared to the original. A number of different summaries and/or paraphrases of the same text can be compared, and students can suggest which is the most successful and why. Students also have the opportunity to write their own summaries and paraphrases and confer with their peers or tutor to improve their drafts.

5.4.3 Sentence structure. A frequent complaint from students is that they have difficulty writing a "good English sentence" and they perceive that many of their problems lie at this level. In fact, traditional grammar courses have usually equipped students with the ability to write a correct sentence and the grammatical concepts that students bring to the course are expanded and built on. However, often the sentences practiced in traditional courses are without context or purpose and therefore students may have difficulty transferring these skills to the text level. Functional grammar, as a text-based grammar, emphasizes the role each sentence plays in realizing the overall meaning. Thus any examination of sentence structure must always keep in focus the relationship of that sentence to the others as part of the same text. Initially, students are introduced to the idea of the clause as a representation of reality. Halliday points out that we interpret reality as consisting of "goings on": "of doing, happening, feeling, being" (Halliday, 1985b, p.101). So the role of transitivity structures in conveying meanings is emphasized.

Within this framework, students focus on verb meanings and make their own verb classification. A variety of different verb lists can be used and students usually come up with categories such as, "doing," "happening," "sensing," "feeling," "thinking," "saying," "being," "having." In class discussion, students often suggest contexts for the verbs—usually of sentence length—to support their categorization. Also, this grouping of verbal processes requires students to discuss how verbs differ from each other in function, for example, how ''sensing'' verbs differ from ''doing'' verbs. Rules that students might have previously learned without realizing their significance—for example, that ''sensing'' verbs are not used in continuous tenses (Thomson & Martinet, 1969, pp. 95, 164)—can be reinterpreted and new insights into how language really works can be gained.

In a clause the verbal process is usually found with other elements, namely, the participants in the process and the circumstances associated with the process. ''These provide the frame of reference for interpreting our experience of what goes on'' (Halliday, 1985b). To help students to develop their concept of the clause, it is useful to go through a text and identify participants and circumstances and the processes to which they belong. For this purpose, it is particularly useful to make students aware of the kinds of Participants and/or Circumstances a particular Process normally requires. For example, *the article claimed that* . . . appears unremarkable while *the article thought/felt/heard that* . . . is, in some sense, extraordinary. The explanation lies in the difference between Verbal and Mental Processes. For lack of space we are not able to include an example exercise here, such as is used with our students.

For successful text development, students must be able to control and manipulate the relationships between clauses. By examining authentic texts in exercises such as 5 below, students are able to identify how clauses are related to each other, whether as equally or unequally (paratactically or hypotactically) and what logical relationship is being expressed between the ideas in the clauses (expansion or projection) (Halliday, 1985b). This type of exercise, since it is based on authentic texts, allows for the discussion of indeterminate structures in the language (for example, *according to*) so that students are made aware of the dangers of a rigid rule-based approach. It also facilitates the exemplification of defining relative clauses and their role as part of the nominal group. The exercise below follows one in which transitivity structures have been discussed with the students. We generally use the same passage for the exercise for relations between clauses, since with this device the students are able to build up information about the meanings of the text cumulatively while also being made aware of the lexicogrammatical patterns that made these meanings. The passage in question is this:

BOOZE NEWS
The World Turns to Drink

The use of illegal drugs such as heroin and cocaine may hog all the media attention but, according to the World Health Organization (WHO), all its member states have expressed profound concern over the dramatic increase that has occurred in alcohol-related problems. This is particularly so in developing countries, where alcohol consumption has now become a feature of everyday life. (*New Internationalist*, July 1983)

Exercise 5

Well, you've just divided the first paragraph into clauses. We can think of a clause as a verb or part of a verb plus all the words which are attached to it. All these words together form a unit which expresses an idea which has meaning. Some of these ideas are complete on their own and they form independent clauses; others depend on another clause for their full meaning and they are called dependent clauses. Try to decide which of the clauses you have identified are dependent.

When we develop our ideas into a paragraph, we help the reader to follow them by relating one idea to the next in a logical way. Sometimes we show this relationship clearly by using a conjunction like *and*, *but*, *because*, *if*, *when*, or a relative pronoun like *that*, *who*, or *which*. But sometimes we don't use a conjunction, for example:

Having studied hard, she took a holiday.

So you must think about the meaning of both clauses to see how they're related. If we expand the above example to make the relationship clearer, we could write:

After she studied hard, she took a holiday.

or

Because she studied hard, she took a holiday.

So you see that the relationship could be either one of cause or time and we must look at the context of the sentence in order to decide which meaning is appropriate. Now look again at the first paragraph in "Booze News." How are the clauses related? Are there any special words which show this relationship clearly?

Teachers' Notes

The use of illegal drugs such as heroin and cocaine may hog all the media attention but,

independent clause, related to the next clause with "but" signalling contrast/concession.

according to the World Health Organization (WHO),

"according" certainly has the form of non-finite verb—the present participle. So this word group could be a clause because it contains part of a verb. But the verb "accord" is rather rare in English and it has a different meaning from the one expressed here. In fact, we always use the "according to" form in this context. So this word group is closer in meaning to a prepositional phrase where "according to" is a kind of verbal preposition. Let's try to rewrite this sentence as
1. a true clause:
WHO said that . . .
2. a prepositional phrase:
in a WHO report, . . .

all its members states have expressed profound concern over the dramatic increase

independent clause, in a relationship of contrast/concession to the first clause

that has occurred in alcohol-related problems.

dependent clause which explains what the "dramatic increase" is. Note: In fact, this clause "defines" what the "dramatic increase" is and therefore it is an essential part of the noun group containing "dramatic increase." So although it is a clause it is contained in the noun group.

This is particularly so in developing countries,

independent clause

where alcohol consumption has now become a feature of everyday life

dependent clause, related to the last clause by "where," a spatial relationship

Context-based practice in linking together independent clauses to form clause complexes is also useful in developing student skills in text construction. In the following exercise part of the paragraph has been rewritten in the form of independent clauses. Students would be shown by bracketing which clauses should be joined together to form clause complexes, and since the context of the clauses is given, they can choose the logical relationships that they think join together the ideas in the independent clauses in the most appropriate way.

Exercise 6

(a) Here is the first sentence of the second paragraph of the text:

Between 1965 and 1980 the worldwide production of beer for commercial purposes more than doubled.

The rest of the paragraph has been partly rewritten so that now there are more independent clauses than in the original text:

⌈North America and Europe maintained their traditional position.
|They produce and consume the most beer.
⌊The developing nations consumed a remarkable amount.
⌈Indeed, consumption increased to a very high degree.
|This means that by the end of the century, per capita consumption
|levels could be comparable to Europe.
⌊This depends on the present consumption trend continuing.
⌈At the same time, production of spirits rose by 67%.
⌊Per capita consumption of spirits went up by one third.

Even though this part of the paragraph has been rewritten, the content is the same. Try to form one sentence from the sentences that have been grouped together in brackets and use a variety of ways to combine these ideas.

(b) Compare your sentences with those of a partner.

(c) Now compare your paragraph with the original.

The traditional brewing areas of North America and Europe maintained their place as largest producers and highest per capita consumers but the developing nations showed a remarkable rate of increased consumption. Indeed, the rate was so high that, if continued, it would lead to per capita consumption levels comparable to Europe's by the end of the century. Meanwhile the production of spirits rose by 67 percent, with per capita consumption going up by one third.

Grammatical structures that cause particular difficulty and that are required for academic writing are focused on in the course. For example, exercises that aim to show students how relational processes are used to present whole clauses as facts rather than opinions. This is a typical area of difficulty as discussed previously in section 3.1.2: *Tenor*. Once again an authentic model is used to exemplify these relationships, and students are asked to try to rewrite the original text using more congruent/projecting verbal processes. By rewriting and careful questioning, students are directed toward making their own insights about why the writer used relational processes (*be*) rather than projecting processes (*feel, think, fear*). Obviously, this exercise in particular requires much discussion and exemplification so that students can come to understand the nature of the choice system for presenting ideas either as facts in an impersonal way or as opinions in a personal way. Because of its length the exercise is not included here. Many of the points can be based on the same text; this means there are many ways in which one text can be exploited so that students can learn about and practice sentence structure in the context of an authentic text. A start for such work could be exercises 1 and 2 in section 4.3.1.

Structures below the clause are also studied, in particular nominal group structure. Students are given practice in unraveling metaphorical nominal groups, expressing them in a more congruent way, and noting how the nominal group structure can be expanded and contracted. After examining how nominal groups can be unraveled in the first part of an authentic text, students are encouraged to try to do the same in the second part, and then finally, in the last part of the text, students attempt to change more congruent forms back into their original less congruent forms and then compare their texts with the original. This exercise is admittedly very challenging and students need considerable teacher guidance and explanation, but the discussion arising from exercises like this one is extremely valuable in identifying and practicing structures that students need to use in their writing.

Exercise 7

NOMINALIZATIONS

Normally, verbs refer to actions or processes, conjunctions to relations between clauses, adjectives to qualities. But if you look at the following text, which is an example of academic writing, you will find some examples of actions and qualities expressed as nouns. This process is called nominalization and it is very common in academic writing. If you don't understand an academic text even though you know all the words in the text, it may help to unravel the nominalizations. This text comes from the Results and Discussion section of a scientific paper on the changes in composition of different brands of rice using different cooking methods.

Notice the way that the nominalizations underlined in the original text (Text A) have been changed in Text B:

Text A
Changes in the mineral composition during cooking in distilled water and tap water are given in Table 5; the data are expressed on a dry weight basis. It could be expected that cooking in distilled water by the absorption method would have little effect on mineral composition as no water is discarded,

Text B
Table 5 shows the ways in which the minerals of which rice is composed change when the rice is cooked in distilled water or tap water; the data are expressed on a dry weight basis. It could be expected that when rice is cooked in distilled water using a method which absorbs the water, the minerals of which rice is composed are hardly affected because no water is discarded.

Now try to rewrite the underlined nominalizations in the next section of Text A:

and the data for sodium, calcium, iron, magnesium and zinc showed no change. Potassium, however, showed a decrease after cooking, suggesting that some potassium had moved from the grain into the fluid that remained on the surface of the glass cooking vessel. Rice cooked in tap water showed increases in sodium, calcium, iron and zinc.

_____
_____
_____
_____
_____

To complete the last part of the paragraph, change the underlined words back into nouns. You may need to rearrange the sentences and use different forms of the words. In the last line, change the underlined noun into a process.

_____
_____
_____
_____
_____

These minerals increased. This shows that minerals dissolved in the water were absorbed and this would vary with different sources of water. While minerals in the rice increased very little, with the possible exception of zinc, this could be important nutritionally where the water supplied to the towns had more minerals in it than [the water in] Sydney.

Here is the original text to compare with your version:

These increases reflect absorption of minerals dissolved in the water and would vary with different sources of water. While most of the increases, with the possible exception of zinc, were small, they could be important nutritionally in towns serviced by a more highly mineralised town water supply than [that of] Sydney.

5.5 Further Courses

Further intensive courses are offered later in the year. These cater to students' expressed needs after their first intensive course and attempt to give students access to higher skills which will enable them to make their writing more prestigious. Since this involves discussion of grammatical metaphor and incongruence, courses have been largely experimental up till now. The following exercise illustrates how students' awareness of different ways of reasoning can be extended. First, part of an authentic text that exemplifies different ways of reasoning is presented. The clauses are rewritten with different verbs, nouns, conjunctions, and prepositions to express cause/effect relationships. Students are then asked to rewrite causal relationships in the rest of the text in a number of different ways, on the basis of the examples they have been given. More abstract ways of expressing cause and effect are pointed out in the text and students are asked to identify all the cause/effect relationships used by the writer in a subsequent section of the text. Finally, after pair and class discussion, students are asked to express a diagrammatic representation of a cause/effect chain in written terms. This type of exercise is extremely valuable in once again sensitizing students to the language choice system available to them and, in particular, to the choices made by writers of authentic academic genres.

Exercise 8

REASONING

You are probably familiar with the use of conjunctions, such as *and, because, although, when,* to link together ideas in clauses in a logical way. However, ideas can be linked together in other ways using *verbs, prepositions* and *nouns.*

The following excerpt from a paragraph, titled "Exercise," taken from a paper on asthma ("Asthma," McFadden, Jr., and Austen, K. F.) discusses some of the causes of this condition. In the first part of the paragraph, which you can see below, the words used by the writer to imply the cause/effect relationship have been underlined.

Asthma can also be <u>induced</u> or made worse <u>by</u> physical exertion. Provocation of bronchospasm <u>by</u> exercise is probably operative to some extent in every asthmatic patient.

"Induced" is a verb and "by" is a preposition. We can rewrite the clauses in a number of different ways to express the cause/effect relationship. Look at the examples below.

VERBS

Here we've used other verbs to express the relationship in the first clause.

EFFECT		CAUSE
Asthma can also	be caused by	or made worse by physical exertion. or be made worse by physical exertion.
Asthma can also	result from	or be made worse by physical exertion.

We can turn the clause around and put the CAUSE in first position.

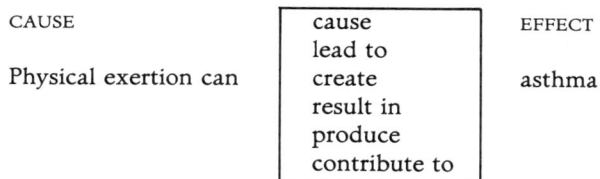

CAUSE		EFFECT
Physical exertion can	cause lead to create result in produce contribute to	asthma.

Notice how using these other verbs makes it difficult to add on the idea that 'asthma can be made worse by physical exertion.' Even in the first two sentences, where we added on this idea, the result was rather clumsy. So this may be one reason why the writer chose the verb "induce." He also wanted to give not only the meaning of 'cause' but also the extra meaning of physical exertion 'starting' the asthma.

NOUNS
In these examples we've replaced the verb "induce" with nouns.

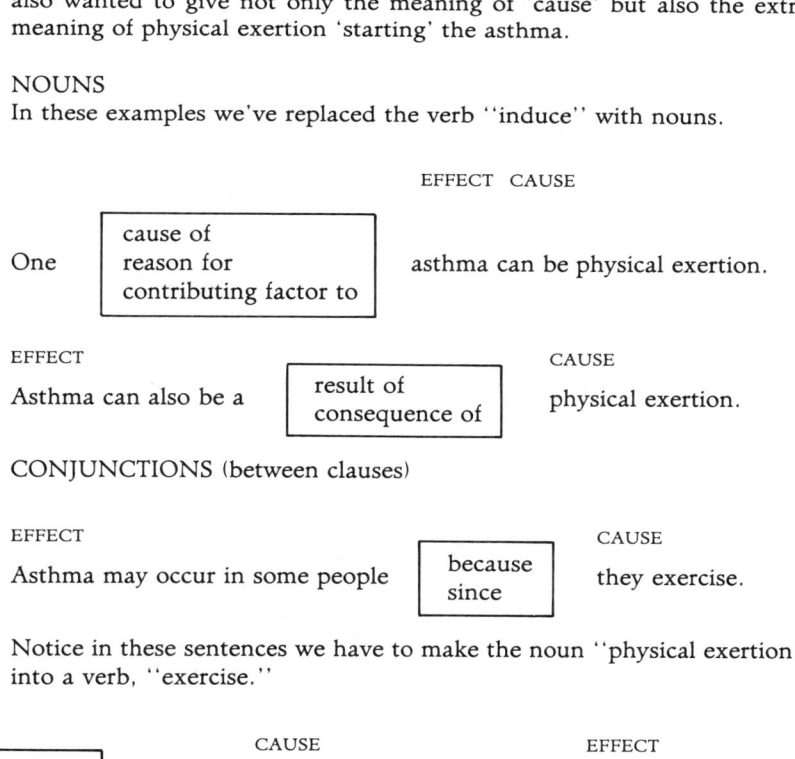

	EFFECT	CAUSE
One	cause of reason for contributing factor to	asthma can be physical exertion.

EFFECT		CAUSE
Asthma can also be a	result of consequence of	physical exertion.

CONJUNCTIONS (between clauses)

EFFECT		CAUSE
Asthma may occur in some people	because since	they exercise.

Notice in these sentences we have to make the noun "physical exertion" into a verb, "exercise."

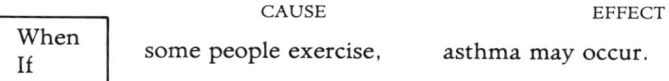

	CAUSE	EFFECT
When If	some people exercise,	asthma may occur.

CONJUNCTIONS (between sentences)

CAUSE   EFFECT

Some people exercise.
| Consequently |
| Therefore |
| Because of this |
| For this reason |
| Hence |
asthma occurs.

PREPOSITIONS

EFFECT   CAUSE

Asthma can be induced or made worse
| because of |
| through |
| due to |
physical exercise.

Provocation of bronchospasm
| because of |
| through |
| due to |
exercise.

In the rest of the text try to express the underlined casual relationships in an alternative way.

Exercise. Asthma can also be induced or made worse by physical exertion. Provocation of bronchospasm by exercise is probably operative to some extent in every asthmatic patient, and in some it may be the only trigger mechanism that will produce symptoms. In the latter circumstance, when such patients are followed for sufficient periods of time, one can often observe the development of recurring episodes of airway obstruction independent of exercise: thus, the onset of this problem can frequently serve as the first manifestation of the full-blown asthmatic syndrome. Exercise-induced asthma is particularly troublesome in children because of their usual high level of physical activity. There is a significant interaction between the climatic environment in which the exercise is performed and the magnitude of the postexertional obstruction. For example, the inhalation of cold air during physical exertion markedly enhances the response, while warm, humid air can blunt or abolish it. Consequently, activities such as ice hockey, skiing, or ice skating are more provocative than is swimming in an indoor heated pool.

The mechanism by which exercise produces acute exacerbations of asthma has not been conclusively determined, but strong evidence is accumulating that indicates that it is related to the degree of cooling of intrathoracic airways that develops as heat and water are transferred to the inspired air to bring the latter to body conditions before it reaches the alveoli.

Cause/effect relationships can also be expressed in a more abstract way than in the underlined words above. Let us look at some examples from the text.

CAUSE	CAUSE/EFFECT RELATIONSHIP
It (physical exertion)	may be the only trigger mechanism.

CAUSE/EFFECT RELATIONSHIP	CAUSE	EFFECT
There is a signifi-cant interaction be-tween	the climatic environ-ment in which the ex-ercise is performed	and the magnitude of the postexertional obstruc-tion.

CAUSE	CAUSE/EFFECT RELATIONSHIP	EFFECT
The inhalation of cold air during physical exercise	markedly enhances	the response.

In the next paragraph, entitled ''Environmental Factors'' underline all the ways in which cause and effect are expressed.

   Environmental factors. An additional group of persons will become symptomatic when confronted with environmental conditions which promote the concentration of airborne pollutants and antigens. This type of asthma, the so-called ''Tokyo-Yokohama'' or ''New Orleans asthma,'' tends to occur in individuals living in heavy industrial or dense urban areas during thermal inversions, or in other situations associated with stagnant air masses. Such atmospheric conditions gen-erally make all types of asthma worse, but they also cause the de novo development of symptoms in some individuals who are not otherwise troubled. The reaction may be idiosyncratic, but it may also be toxic, resulting from exposure to chemicals like SO_2 that depress lung func-tion in anyone if inhaled in sufficient concentration. Alternatively, in-halation of polluted air could alter the threshold of the irritant receptors in the airways of a latent asthmatic so as to create a response to other less noxious stimuli.

Now it's your turn to write your own paragraph. The following diagram illustrates the factors that lead to a heart attack or stroke. Try to [put] the diagram in written form using a variety of ways of expressing the cause/effect relationships.

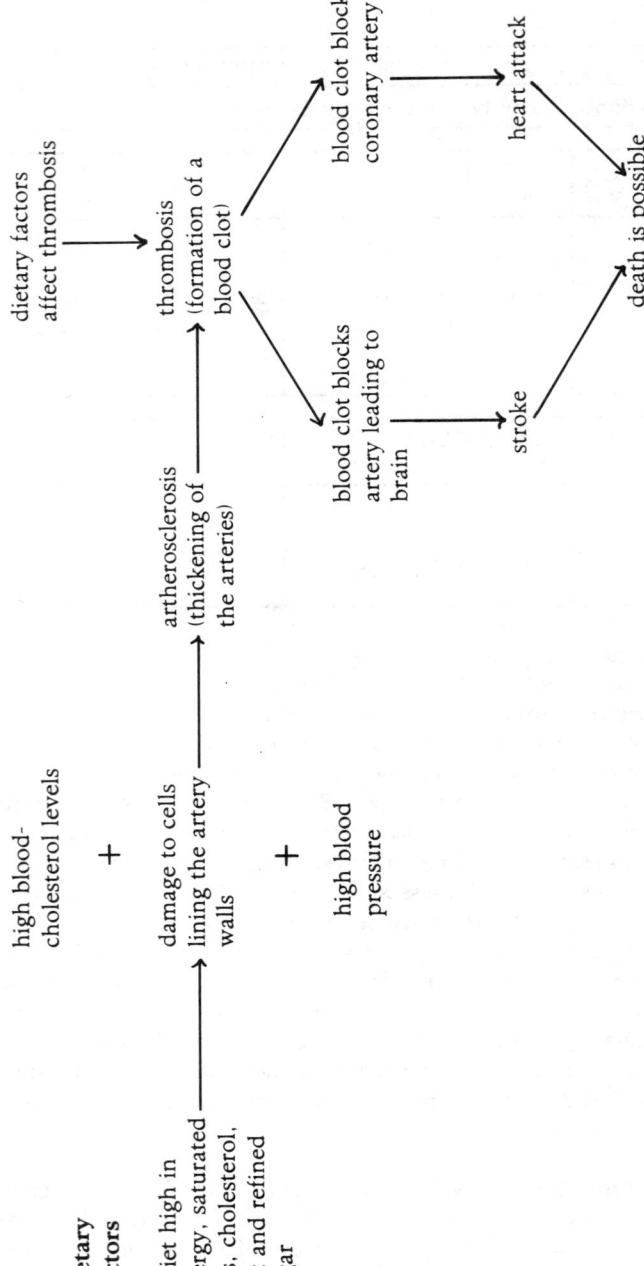

Factors That Lead to a Heart Attack or Stroke (based on A. & J. Borushek, *The Complete Australian Heart Disease Prevention Manual*, 1981, p. 38)

5.6 Individual Instruction

At all stages of the course students also have the opportunity to consult tutors on an individual basis for help with specific written tasks from their own discipline. This is an essential part of the program not only because it is often the only help available to some students who cannot attend courses but also because it is often the most efficient way of meeting students' specific needs.

The role of spoken communication in the construction of written text has been referred to in this course description. The ability to express and assess ideas and concepts orally often aids written expression. However, authentic oral texts are not as easily obtainable as written texts and their generic description has hardly begun. The final part of this chapter, which represents an initial step in this direction, will focus on the difficulties encountered in collecting and analyzing authentic spoken texts as the basis for courses that aim to improve listening and speaking skills in English.

PART B
6. CASUAL CONVERSATION AND THE MIGRANT ADULT IN AUSTRALIA

6.1 Learner Needs

Many migrants, even those whose proficiency level in English is high, report experiencing great difficulties in their attempts to understand, and so to participate in, sustained Australian casual conversation—namely, conversations with Australian workmates or fellow Australian students during break times. Many migrants' problems at work or in courses are related to their inability to integrate socially into their new environment.

Most migrant second language learners are aware of the importance of learning to understand and participate in casual conversations with their colleagues or workmates. They specifically request help in this area and often return to language classes even after they have succeeded in getting a job or placement in a course of study, in order to improve their skills. They realize that it is through such conversations that social relationships are developed and maintained. Further, they realize that life in Australia, and their success and their understanding of the society they are living in, would be influenced positively by the development of such relationships.

However, unlike language skills required for execution of jobs or achievement of educational qualifications, casual conversation of the sort that occurs during coffee breaks or lunch breaks is not compulsory. Learners may never even attempt in their places of learning or work to participate in casual conversations. Often what happens is that such conversations are so difficult for learners to follow or understand that they often cannot attempt to enter into them. When braver students do make an attempt, the response of Australian speakers to their participation sometimes makes even these students give up.

6.2 Authentic Texts

Unlike written forms of language, which were the focus of the teaching concerns described in Part A of this chapter, very few texts of spoken language, particularly of casual conversation, are available for reference. This means that very little commercially produced language-teaching material contains authentic texts of casual conversation and no material contains an adequate description of such language based on authentic texts. Thus, language teachers often have very few resources to turn to and comparatively little knowledge of such language beyond their own observations and intuitions.

The difficulties of recording and transcribing spontaneous, naturally occurring speech (Halliday 1985c) are compounded by the difficulties of reading and analyzing transcripts of such language. Moreover, as spoken language has only relatively recently become an object of linguistic study, the variety of different types of authentic data collected by linguists is limited. The SF model seems to be, based as it is on analysis of authentic data, the only one that provides the necessary coherent and comprehensive framework within which to interpret such data. However, even with this model, data relevant to this teaching situation is limited.

The relevant data, taking sociocultural factors revealed by learner needs into account, would be authentic, complete conversations displaying the following characteristics.

Participants in the conversation:
1. At least three or four speakers should be involved in the one conversation. (This was a typical situation mentioned by learners.)
2. Speakers should be Australian native speakers of English (To fulfill our need for authentic native speaker texts to analyze.)
3. Speakers should include at least one from a different background and life-style. (Approximately the cultural difference a migrant would display.)
4. Speakers should not be friends outside the workplace. (This was usually the case with migrants entering a workplace.)
5. Speakers should include at least one newcomer to the workplace. (This was the typical situation our students were in.)

The conversation itself:

6. The subject or topic of conversation should not be related to what the speakers are working on together.
7. The conversation should be "a goodwill exchange" (Ventola, 1979, 1984a), not an information or goods and services exchange; that is, the purpose of the exchange should be an abstract one, not a concrete one such as exchanging information, competing, asking for favors, and so on.

The last two points have been referred to by students as characteristics of the conversations they have most difficulty with.

6.3 Available Student Texts

Most commercially produced language-teaching materials purporting to give the students information and examples of casual conversations in which social relationships may be formed usually include only parts of conversations, and these are scripted and performed by actors. Moreover, many of these concentrate on specific functions that realize service encounters or discussions, not casual conversations of the sort referred to above. An example of this is provided by Jones (1977).

There are texts in which the sections that seem to deal with true casual conversation present examples and general characteristics of casual conversation which are usually based on the writer's intuitions. Sometimes linguistic theories or models are referred to but usually only superficially and often only as the inspirational source for the material. An example of this is Boardman (1979).

Some materials do include authentic data consisting of the same type of language. One of these is a 1975 book-and-cassette course which consists entirely of a series of casual conversations including scripts and some analysis by Crystal and Davy (1975). Unfortunately, the conversations are among close friends, not colleagues, and all the speakers have similar lifestyles and backgrounds; they are all middle-class and English.

As so little authentic casual conversation is included or referred to in language-teaching materials, linguistic studies have been relied upon for more relevant texts.

Some studies taking a sociocultural perspective, carried out by the National Council of Industrial Language Training in London, have concentrated on analyses of conversations collected between native and nonnative speakers of English; these studies deal with the cultural causes of misunderstandings and breakdowns (see Gumpertz, 1982a, 1982b). These, however, do not include all native speaker texts.

The work found most useful has been a study of Australian conversation using the SF model which includes some casual conversations of the type referred to as chat or goodwill exchanges (Ventola, 1984a). Unfortunately, the chats studied are very brief exchanges between strangers.

6.4 Collection of Authentic Texts

In a research and materials development project for the Adult Migrant Education Service in Sydney, texts were collected such as those described that were needed for teaching the nature of Australian casual conversation.

The notion of register was used to decide which social context to collect data in. The question asked was this: What combination of situational variables would yield data that would be most generally useful and relevant? The clients for whom the research was carried out were migrant second language learners of English in Australia. However, the data collected seem to be useful for the needs of foreign students as well.

The data were collected during coffee breaks of the staff of a medical records office in a large Sydney public hospital. This situation seemed suitable because there were over 50 workers in the one large workplace who did not necessarily work very closely together. There was a clearly defined 15-minute time period and a place for coffee breaks. As they took coffee breaks in shifts, they could not necessarily choose whom they had coffee with.

Most workers were native English speakers, though not all were from Australia or Sydney. Two groups of four people were recorded each day for a week. One group was very mixed, with speakers of different sex, age, socioeconomic and educational background, marital status, and lifestyle. None were friends and two were very new to the workplace. This was the group whose conversations were analyzed more closely.

Recording was carried out carefully, so as not to disturb the authenticity of the conversations even by the presence of an outsider recording. The recording equipment was thus set up before people arrived for their coffee break. Each of the speakers was interviewed and photographed after the conversations were collected. The recorded conversations seem therefore more authentic than many used in linguistic research, where often the situation, participants, and conversation are set up by the researcher.

6.5 Analysis of the Data

The most noticeable feature of the 14 conversations was that very little of each conversation (if any at all) referred in any way to the workplace context. For the major part of the conversations, in terms of Field, there was no topic that related to their work, and in terms of Tenor, there were no expressions of the quite marked differences in their status at work. One of the speakers was in a highly responsible position and in fact had trained all the others when they started their jobs.

Where the conversation was like this, that is, *not* a realization of the work context, it will be referred to as a chat or a chat component. None of the conversations consists of less than 60% chat and most consist completely of chat. The context of situation (i.e., the three main Register variables) of the chats is described below.

CONTEXT OF SITUATION

FIELD   Personal experience in the following four basic domains or institutions of Australian society (basic in that they are common to all the speakers in the group and also to the great majority of members of the society).

1. Work, study, money (not including their present occupations, studies, salaries)
2. Home and family
3. Leisure and entertainment
4. Health and illness

Domains that are more controversial and less common to a large majority of people in the society are avoided. These include religion, politics, sex, and ethics.

The activity or activity sequences referred to are those which are known by most members of the society to occur typically in the above mentioned basic domains of life. The participants in the activities, besides the speakers themselves, are people, places, and objects familiar to most speakers (particularly all urban Sydney-siders).

The social activity going on in this context is in fact "taking a break" from the work situation. The only social goal to be achieved is to make sure everyone feels comfortable; this is achieved by confirming and sharing their social likenesses or equal "belongingness" in the society.

TENOR   All participants behave as equals. Despite their different positions in the hierarchy at work, ages, and sex, no power relationships are expressed. The chats are marked for solidarity. Attitudes to the various topics, activities, and participants are expressed frequently.

However, the social distance is not minimal; it is medium and the affect range is strongly influenced by the need to maintain cooperative relationships for conflict-free daily work contact. Therefore, attitudes expressed are those believed to be shared by all participants. If a difference in attitude is held by a participant it is either not expressed or, if expressed, not developed.

MODE   Face-to-face and spoken, but the language is almost completely of the type referred to as Reflection. It is easily understood without visual information from the context. It is characterized by cycles of different and individual complete texts of the genres referred to in the SF model as Observation/Comment and Personal Narrative (Martin & Rothery, 1980). Most of these texts are produced by individual speakers but some are jointly created by all the participants.

6.6 Text Analysis

This section will deal with aspects of the data that considerations of Field, Tenor, and Mode allowed to be clarified and that were found valuable in preparing materials and methodologies for teaching. A number of excerpts from one coffee-break conversation will be presented and discussed below.

The coffee-break conversation that the excerpts are taken from was held on a Friday afternoon. Approximately 60% of this conversation is what is referred to as chat. The entire chat component is in the general topic area of Leisure and Entertainment. Overall, in the seven coffee-break conversations of this group of four clerical workers, the topic of Leisure and Entertainment took up approximately 25% of chat time. It made up 60% of the Friday-afternoon conversation and about 85% of the Monday-morning conversation. On both Tuesday and Thursday a small section of each chat was also in this general topic area.

Below, in excerpt 1, the last section of the Friday-afternoon chat is presented. The topic of this section could be described as Outdoor Cinemas or more precisely "Aren't outdoor cinemas funny?"

This section is described as a Cycle of Texts. Later the notions of Cycle, and in particular of Text, employed here, will be expanded. Briefly, the elements present in this section leading to such a description of it are, first, that all the participants have a turn at contributing to the section and, second, that *all* and *only* these turns are on the particular aspect of the chat topic that I have described as "Aren't Outdoor Cinemas Funny?"

Excerpt 1

A Cycle of Texts

Bronwyn	oh, I can remember when I used to go to the movies	1
	in the country had this beautiful entrance—right?	2
Gary	yeah	3
Bronwyn	then you went outside—yes, into a paddock no	4
	roof and canvas deckchairs	5
Pauline	well, I went to the movies two years ago in in Towns-	6
	ville and you had ah—my aunt said, ''I'll drive you	7
	there''—my girlfriend and I were staying with her—	8
	''you can take some cushions with you'' and we said,	9
	''what for? you don't take cushions with you in Syd-	10
	ney to the pictures''—''no, you have to take cush-	11
	ions''—so she drove us there and she come—and she'd	12
	come back at whatever time, you know—and we went	13
	in and it was all deckchairs and so so we s— no won-	14
	der we had to have cushions because it was so un-	15
	comfortable watching this thing all night	16
Gary	deckchairs	17
Bronwyn	we used—we used	18
Pauline	it was inside though with our deckchairs	19
Bronwyn	no, we we used to turn up with our cushion and our	20
	blanket and a brolly in case it rained not too	21
	many people used to go to the movies because if it	22
	rained you'd have your brolly up	23
Gary	oh, I I don't know if this was—but there was a first	24
	indoor picture theatre in Queensland's Maj—Majes-	25
	tic—and that's at Pamona—and it's really really old	26
	but the roof is just still all there but originally it was	27
	just like what you see—they built up round it but it's	28
	sort of the ⌈inside	29
Pauline	⌊mmm	30
Pat	I hate it at the drive-in when you've got to have wind-	31
	screen wipers on	32
Gary	but no deckchairs	33
Pauline	well, I went to the drive-in in New Guinea in Port	34
	Moresby and what you do there is—you take a picnic	35
	with you—you know, food and everything and you	36
	get out of the car and you take little s— fold-up seats	37
	and sit in front of the car—or blankets and p— pillows	38
	and put them on the bonnet of the ⌈car and sit on	39
	it with your back on the windscreen	40
Gary, Pat	⌊ mmm	41
	and sit on it	42
Pauline	and everybody does that you see—so it's no good sit-	43

Text labels (right margin): Text 1 (lines 1–5), Text 2 (lines 6–17), Text 1 (line 18), Text 2 (line 19), Text 1 (lines 20–23), Text 3 (lines 24–30), Text 4 (lines 31–33), Text 5 (lines 34–43)

	ting in the car because you can't see because there's	44	
	people sitting on it because it's so hot up there that	45	
	you don't sit in the car	46	
Pat	yeah— when Mark used to have his station wag-	47	Text 4
	on he used to always	48	
Pauline	you know people sitting—a little table and chairs and	49	Text 5
	wine and everything	50	
Pat	reverse in and um	51	

END OF BREAK (knocking sound)

Pauline	it's time to go	52	
Pat	and ah and we'd be sitting in the back of the station	53	
	wagon and watch it—take—pillows and blankets	54	
Bronwyn	what were you doing in the back of a station	55	
	wagon I want to know!	56	Text 4
Pat	at the drive-in we used to lie on our stomachs that	57	
	far apart and watch it like that because I always like	58	
	watching the film—I'd always have to scream "bug-	59	
	ger off now—I want to watch the film"	60	
Bronwyn	go to the drive-in	61	

6.7 A Cycle of Texts

The term *text* is used here as in the SF model to refer to a unit of language in use. It refers to a meaning unit which is structured so that it coheres and functions as a unity with respect to its environment (Halliday & Hasan, 1976).

Thus, the earlier mention of the turns taken by participants in excerpt 1 refer only to what can be described now as text production turns. Throughout the chats it seems to be the case that each participant individually or a number of them jointly produce complete texts.

If a text is not complete before someone begins a new one, it is invariably the case that the new text is not allowed to proceed or that it is immediately followed by the completion of the first text. An example of each of these can be seen in excerpt 1. Text 1 is completed after text 2 is produced and completed. Text 4 is not allowed to proceed in lines 47 and 48 until Text 5 has been completed.

The term *cycle* refers to the fact that a number of complete texts are produced in turn by the participants in the conversation. A cycle is characterized as such by the fact that each text within it deals with the same specific aspect of the general topic. In the cycle of excerpt 1, each text is a personal observation made by each of the participants on the subject of "Aren't Outdoor Cinemas Funny?"

> *Text 1*, based on Bronwyn's experience of country cinemas, points out that because they have no roof one needs an umbrella.

Text 2, based on Pauline's experience of a Townsville cinema, points out that because they have deck chairs, one needs a cushion.

Text 3, based on Gary's experience of a country town cinema, points out that indoor cinemas can be built up around outdoor ones.

Text 4, based on Pat's experience of drive-ins in Australia, points out that windshield wipers are needed if it rains and blankets and cushions are needed to lie on if one has a station wagon.

Text 5, based on Pauline's experience of drive-ins in New Guinea, points out that tables and chairs or blankets and cushions are needed because it is too hot to sit in the car.

These texts are all descriptions of places and activities observed and experienced by each participant, all of which belong to the general categories of "Outdoor Cinemas" and "Funny Activities."

This organization of the chats into cycles, each dealing with one aspect of the broader subject of the chat, seems to be an expression of two features in particular of the context of the situation. These are first, the equality of status of the particpants—a feature of the Tenor; and second, the sharing of social likenesses—a feature of the Field.

In an examination of all the chats the following were observed:

1. Over the chats, though not necessarily within one chat, the number of text production turns taken is shared equally by the four participants.
2. Although it is not always the case that each of the four participants produces a text in any one cycle, it is always the case that more than one participant does. Sometimes a cycle may consist of only two or three texts, and sometimes, although it may consist of five or six, these may be produced by only two or three participants. In excerpt 1, all four participants contributed a text, though one participant contributed two. This is quite a typical cycle.

It seems clear that such cyclical organization of texts in a way that "gives everyone a go" is functional in that it realizes the equal status of the participants. This feature has been described as the principle of reciprocity, expressing equality of status (Poynton, 1984, 1985).

Also, the requirements that any text produced must be within the same specific domain that other texts in the cycle deal with is quite obviously functional. By contributing to or initiating the cycle, the participants prove that they have experienced or observed something that is familiar to the others and, more important, that they hold the same attitude toward it. This can be seen as a way of expressing the higher level of contact demanded by the tenor feature of solidarity. Without such real social contact the participants can still achieve contact by their participation in the cycles.

6.8 Texts and Text Types

As mentioned earlier, the two genres or text types identified as the most common in the chats are Observation/Comment and Personal Narrative. There are more Observation/Comment texts than there are Narrative. There are a number of different types of Narratives.

Some of the reasons for the selection and frequent use of the Observation/Comment genre could be the following, all of which are functional in respect to the context of situation.

First, Observation/Comment is a very flexible and relatively simple genre in terms of structure. There seem to be only two obligatory elements, the observation and the comment. The order in which these elements occur is optional and the number of times each element can occur is not restricted. The complexity of each element may vary—particularly the Comment, which may be expressed in many different ways.

Second, it is also a genre that could be described as an elaboration of the Observation genre, which can itself stand alone as a text type. This allows for even greater flexibility in text production such that the joint or sequential texts can be produced by a number of participants.

Below, in excerpt 2, is a typical example of this genre.

Excerpt 2: Observation/Comment Text

Gary	but	Observation
	in the s— I usually wear jeans and sandshoes to the pictures, you know, no matter where it is	
Pauline	yes	
Gary	but if I go the State I usually put on something a little better because you can't outdo the place	Comment
Pauline	no	
Bronwyn	exactly	

In terms of context of situation such a genre is clearly very functional. Besides its relative simplicity of structure and flexibility in terms of length and complexity of each element, it is also a simple and direct means of expressing solidarity. One major expression of solidarity is in the sharing of attitudes. The function of the Comment element is just this. Moreover, the Observation/Comment is the most direct way to describe typical activities and familiar entities that make up the society common to the participants. This is therefore a direct realization of the confirming of social likenesses described earlier as the social activity going on in this context.

Excerpt 2 is a text that initiates a cycle described as ''Clothes Worn to Go to the Cinema.'' It follows the cycle ''Nice Cinemas in Downtown

Sydney.'' In this earlier cycle one comment repeated by all the participants is that the State Theatre is a magnificent cinema. In excerpt 2 Gary's text leads to a synonymous comment in *you can't outdo the place*. Gary has chosen to make a comment he knows the others agree with and he has chosen to describe an activity sequence that he believes is seen by all as a typical one. He has judged correctly, it seems, from their responses. The participation of those not producing a text is usually limited to back-channeling responses including ''mm'' (not seen in excerpt 2) as well as others such as *yes, no,* and *exactly* (all seen in excerpt 2). Other contributions are short cooperative statements usually synonymous with the comment made by the text producer.

Therefore the usual text production turn flows freely with the other participants' contributions not really affecting the development of the text (i.e., not interrupting it).

It is rare in these chats that a participant expresses a contrary attitude to that expressed by the text producer. In the interviews conducted after the data collection it was discovered that when one of the participants disagreed with an attitude expressed, the typical response was to pretend to agree. The participants all said this did not happen often—indicating that they usually selected appropriate comments for the most part.

It is interesting therefore to note where and how disagreement with an attitude is in fact expressed. Below, in excerpt 3, is a rare case in which this happened.

Excerpt 3: Observation/Comment Text

Pauline	mm see	
	I quite liked the Hoyt's Entertainment Centre before they put in all those stupid pinball machines—	Comment 1
	it was quite nice when it first opened	Comment 1
Gary	they're good pinball machines (LAUGHING)	Comment 2
Bronwyn	oh no	
Pauline	no	
	now you've got all these young teenagers doing that and the whole place's just full of them	Observation 1
	now	
	and you can't walk through	
Pat	bing! ting!	
Pauline	you've got kids everywhere	Observation 1
	but	
	when it first opened it was quite nice, you know, nice place	Comment 1 repeated
Gary	yes	

Gary makes his comment with a laugh. Both Bronwyn and Pauline dismiss it with cries of "no" and Pat does not contribute. Pauline goes on to provide a detailed observation element before repeating her original comment. Gary's response to this is finally "yes" and he takes up the next text production turn after Pauline. Here we see a comment expressing a known-to-be shared attitude. This is the text in excerpt 2. Gary is clearly looking for the way back into shared social sentiments.

From what we see in excerpt 3 it seems that in this context disagreement or a nonshared attitude can be expressed only briefly and lightheartedly. It is also unlikely to be taken up by others.

As such Observation/Comment texts are often about activities and/or entities familiar to most participants and as they express attitudes usually shared by all of the participants, these texts are sometimes jointly created. In excerpt 4 below, one participant, Pat, is not familiar with the subject and her only contribution is a question. This kind of information-seeking question is very seldom seen in these chats, but Pat's only alternative is noncontribution.

Excerpt 4: Jointly Created Observation/Comment Text

Pauline	have you ever been to the State since—oh, you ought to—since it's been renovated because it looks really nice	Comment 1
Bronwyn	all the paintings have been restored	Observation 1
Pauline	oh, good	
Bronwyn	and all the gilt's been redone the	
Pauline	yes	
Bronwyn	the chandeliers have been cleaned	
Gary	and the organ guy's there now too	
Bronwyn	yes	
Gary	he plays there now	
Pat	the organ grinder with the monkey?	
Bronwyn	an organ comes up	
Gary	out of the ceiling	
Bronwyn	out of the floor	
Pauline	it's beautiful you'll have to go	Comment 1
Gary	but that wasn't working for years and they fixed all that up as well	Observation 1 continued
Pauline	yes, yes it's lovely	Comment 1

The other text type that typically occurs in these chats is that of Personal Narrative.

As these are reflections of personal experience and the participants are not friends outside their work situation, it is less likely that these texts or even parts of these texts can be jointly created. However, in some cases, they are—to some extent because of the relative emphasis placed in the Narrative—found in the chats, on certain components of the Narrative Schematic Structure.

The essential components of the Narrative Schematic Structure, as it will be referred to, are Orientation, Complication, and Resolution. In the Narratives found in these chats the longest and most complex component is the orientation. It is here that observations and even comments can occur, as this is the setting of the story in space and time and the entities in the story are presented here. The other components of the narratives are usually short. Thus, the kinds of narratives that occur in these chats are much closer to the Observation/Comment genre than to Personal Narratives found in other data. They have the same goal as all naturally occurring narratives, to relate a story in which something out of the ordinary or unexpected happens in the normal course of events. This is easily reconizable as another way of sharing social likeness, for only by knowing what the normal course of events is can one select the incident in which something unusual occurs. However, it seems that because the main aim of the social activity is to confirm social likeness, the orientation component rather than the resolution or complication is given most time and emphasis in these narratives.

In excerpt 5 below, Pat is unable to contribute to the jointly created Observation/Comment text about the State Theatre. But Pat can, however, contribute to the cycle "Clothes Worn to the Cinema," initiated by Gary.

Excerpt 5: Personal Narrative Text

Pauline	no, I remember once I went to a film and I'd just bought this new outfit and it was long, silky black pants that came up all in one and	Abstract Orientation
Pauline	mm	
Pat	then it was an overlay with splits right up to here and that was in silk and I didn't think anything of it till I had to go to the toilet.	
	I had to take the whole lot off and pull the whole lot down so I missed half of the film	Complication Resolution

The long description of her outfit can almost be seen as an observation provided to follow Gary's comment that for some cinemas you need to dress up.

As can be seen from the above analyses of texts, the SF concepts of Context, Text, Genre, and Schematic Structure have been of value in providing an approach to the analysis of these chats, which has allowed for a global view. The work described in this chapter is just a beginning, but it seems clear that the approach taken may lead to more definitive generalizations about the nature of chat. It is hoped that the relationship between and within cycles of one chat will become clearer. Also, when more work is done at the level of text by further analysis of not only schematic structure, but discourse systems as well, the statements made in this chapter can be further substantiated. Finally, a detailed description of the language at the clause level, that is, of the lexicogrammatical and phonological systems begun here, needs to be completed.

Once such analysis becomes available, it will perhaps be possible to have a description of the nature of casual conversation in as much detail as that which exists for the more static and finite written texts used in academic study. Only a detailed description such as this can serve as a reference for diagnosing specific learner difficulties at all these levels of language—as has been carried out in the work described in Part A of this chapter, in respect to academic writing.

However, this is not to say that there can be no application made of the analysis of chat carried out so far. An application is described in the next section.

6.9 Application of Text Collection and Analysis to Teaching Situation

The problem of lack of authentic texts and therefore knowledge about the nature of casual conversation on the teacher's part has been to a great degree addressed by the collection and analysis of the series of authentic Australian coffee-break chats described above. The way this can affect and change approaches to the teaching of the understanding and production of casual conversation by students is outlined below in the sections entitled "Methodology" and "Materials."

However, the analysis of conversations also revealed that the problem of lack of knowledge on the student's part about the society and culture forming the context and content of such conversations among Australians is unfortunately not so easily addressed. It at first seems that the students may find out and experience enough of what they need to know to chat to Australian colleagues only if they are here a lifetime! Not only must they know what are considered the noncontroversial domains of Australian society and also, within those, the range of typical activities, well-known people, places, and objects, but they must also know what the commonly held attitudes to all these are!

But the SF approach to the analysis of the chats has allowed for an important insight into the tasks language learners face in mastering such chats. These tasks have been revealed as two distinct though related ones. The first is that of following, understanding, and, perhaps after much exposure, participating in chats with Anglo-Australian speakers. This process cannot be a short one. First, learners need access to such chat (not easy for outsiders), and second, it needs to be reinforced by the knowledge gained by living in and experiencing the society and culture. It is no accident that even a fluent English speaker from another society may have difficulties participating in such chats.

One concrete step that can be taken now, using this data, is that of providing access or exposure to such chats—something very difficult, if not impossible, for the learners to get in real life. A nonparticipating listener does not last long in a real-life chat. Someone who does not know the rules or the demands of the context will probably be quickly "expelled," in some sense, from a chat.

So the authentic conversations can provide a large accessible source of such knowledge and experience for the students. A beginning has been made to aid students in "understanding" or "following" Australian casual conversations. These are described, and sample pages included, in the section below entitled "Materials."

The second task learners face in their attempts to master casual conversations of this sort is one that may take a lot less time and effort: learning how to participate in chats in English but with other non-English speakers. Many non-English speakers are in such a situation more often, even during their full-time language courses and particularly in their first jobs in this country. It would entail giving some information about the context-of-situation variables operating in Anglo-Australian chats, and if students are willing to operate with the same sociocultural demands, they may learn to participate in such chats without needing to know all about the basic institutions in Australian society and the typical attitudes to these. Students may be able to operate to some extent within their own social context and shared knowledge and attitudes.

6.9.1 Methodology. Before the authentic data were available and after many experiments, a decision was made to teach casual conversation skills without help of any textbooks or reference sources. This was done by recording the students' own conversations, among themselves in their own break times. In follow-up sessions transcripts of parts of these conversations were used to diagnose and improve on the aspects that caused difficulties. This system was more useful since here, as is not the case with most commercial texts, we were working with a real, known, and in many ways constant context of situation. We were thus to deal with the relationship between the situational variables and the lexicogrammar and phonology, to some extent. However, when assessments were made of the students' language or the demands of the context we were ultimately relying on our own intuitions and experience as native speakers.

The coffee-break data have led to changes in our approach to teaching such conversational skills. The major change is in the expanded program that can be offered to students. Sessions are still run in which learners' coffee-break conversations are recorded and analyzed. They are fewer but more valuable now that there are some authentic texts to refer to and now that there is more knowledge of the nature of such conversation. More important, however, this knowledge has also allowed for guided "production" sessions as well as the above diagnostic sessions. These are usually a series of lessons on each of the genres now seen as typical in chat: Observation/Comment and Narrative.

Using a communicative methodology that allows students to create texts that are real, from their own personal or shared experience, teachers can provide the guidance and "scaffolding" (Applebee & Langer, 1983), that learners require when they are learning to produce a new text type. References can easily be made to the "model" structure—the schematic structure of the relevant genre.

Once students can produce adequate individual texts of this type, sessions aimed at production of *cycles* of such texts in groups can be conducted. The last refinement is then to present and practice the interaction between participants in each individual text.

The final step in the sessions devoted to a particular genre would be to identify and analyze texts of this type in listening material developed from the authentic data collected, particularly for work at the clause level as well as for the overall interaction. Students are thus helped to participate in chats among themselves, and they are also being prepared for eventual participation in chats with Australians.

Below is an elaboration of how some of this data has been developed into listening material for intermediate- to advanced-level learners with the aim of exposing students to authentic speech as well as to a typical chat topic and typical attitudes to it.

6.9.2 Materials.

After trials and experiments with the data, the listening course finally developed consists of a book and two 90-minute cassettes (Economou, 1985). The aim of these materials was primarily to provide access to authentic Australian conversation. Thus, the materials do not include rules, generalizations, or prescriptions for the production of casual conversation. They do, however, include in simple language much information (visual as well as verbal) that students may need in order to understand the conversations on the cassette.

The format of each section of the course is the following:

1. Background information about the speakers and the workplace context, including photos (at the beginning of each unit).
2. Sociocultural information assumed, by the speakers of any section presented, to be known by the listeners (page 1 of every section).
3. A clearly presented transcript of the section (page 2 of every section).
4. Notes on language that may be needed by the students, including elaborations of compacted or elided speech, explanations of idioms or complex interaction and of phonological features (pages 3 and 4 of every section).
5. A comprehension check provided at the end of the book and cassette as a means of review.

The excerpts below are from the final unit, unit 5. This unit contains six sections taken in sequence from a coffee-break chat on the topic of children working and earning money. The sample shows excerpts from each of the four pages that make up section 4 of Unit 5.

COFFEE-BREAK CHAT 4

Notes on Society and Culture

- Children in large families can help their families if they earn money when they are still young and at school. They can buy things that they need—clothes or school things.

  (lines 1–4)

- Many people also believe that it is good for all children to earn money when they are young. It is good because they can learn about the value of money and about how to manage money.

  (lines 1–10)

COFFEE-BREAK CHAT 4

Script

Everyone is talking about how good it is
for children to work part-time.

Bronwyn	and that was really good because then the kids bought	1
	things that they wanted for themselves—Tony was at the	2
	stage where he was buying all his own clothes, paying	3
	everything he wanted for school	4
Gary	good on him	5
Pauline	good—yes, good	6
Bronwyn	and banking it—he's got things in—invested here and in-	7
	vested there and in short and long-term deposits	8
Pauline	mm good	9

COFFEE-BREAK CHAT 4

Notes on Language

Words			
1	and that was really good	=	and the fact that my sons liked their jobs was really good
1	because then	=	because when they worked
1	the kids	=	the children
		:	casual speech
2	Tony was at the stage where he was buying	=	Tony was earning enough money to buy
5	good on him	=	bravo
		:	shows admiration and respect–idiom

Sounds			
2	for themselves	=	''fərthəmselves''
2	Tony was at	=	''Tonywəzət''
		:	sounds like one word; very fast
3	all	:	extra stress to show it is unusual
5	good on him	=	''goodonim''
		:	sounds like one word and the *h* in *him* is not pronounced

The first four units, do not contain sections from other coffee-break chats but sections from the interviews conducted. In the first unit, ''Interview with Bronwyn.'' Bronwyn is talking about her previous job.

INTERVIEW WITH BRONWYN 1

Notes on Society and Culture

• Family usually means parents and their children only; a large family usually means more than four children.

(lines 2–3)

- Many people believe that if a woman has a large family of young children she should not work full-time—but some women believe that they need the satisfaction of work outside the home.

(lines 1–8)

INTERVIEW WITH BRONWYN 2

Script

Bronwyn is talking about her attitude to work.

Bronwyn	well for me to start at the beginning, work is very im-	1
	portant—I have a large family of young children	2
Interviewer	oh yes	3
Bronwyn	and um people tell me that that should be enough	4
Interviewer	mm	5
Bronwyn	but it never has been	6
Bronwyn	um	7
Interviewer	so you've worked most of the time?	8
Bronwyn	yes	9

INTERVIEW WITH BRONWYN 1

Notes on Language

Words

1	*well*	:	introduces Bronwyn's answer to the Interviewer's questions
1	*for me to start at the be-ginning*	=	I'll start with the first thing you asked me
		:	the interviewer asked Bronwyn to talk about many things—the first thing was her attitude to work
1.2	*work is very important*	=	work is very important to me
4	*people tell me that* that *should be enough*	=	people tell me that having a large family should be enough satisfaction and enough work for me
6	it *never has been*	=	having a large family has never been enough satisfaction or work for me

Sounds

1	*for to at*	=	''fə'' ''tə'' ''ət''
		:	the vowel sounds in these words are the same—the short neutral vowel ə
6	*but*	=	''bət''
9	*yes*	=	''yeah''
		:	often pronounced like this in casual conversation

4.7 *um*	= I'm going to continue
	: this is not a word but it is a sound which has a meaning

The rationale for devoting only the final unit to chat is based on the great difficulty students had (even with all the supplementary information provided) in understanding the coffee-break chats. There seemed to be three reasons for this difficulty.

First, the lack of visual context—a video cassette would have been easier to understand. Second, the brief information given in the notes on society and culture for each section does not provide enough background information for the students on the topic of the chat, particularly on commonly held attitudes toward aspects of it. Finally, if students have very little or no experience with listening to any kind of authentic speech recordings in the classroom, they need a period of familiarization. They need to become used to the accent, typical intonation and stress patterns, assimilations, elisions, and contractions of authentic casual speech. Of course they also have to have practice in identifying the voices, in coping with the speed of the speech, and with overlapping voices.

In "Coffee Break," there is an attempt to address both areas of difficulty by including four units containing only sections from the interviews conducted with each of the four speakers who participate in the coffee-break chat in unit 5.

In working through these units, students become familiar with all the features of authentic speech mentioned above, within the simpler dialogue structure of the interview text. Also, because the topic of all the interviews was about the speakers' experiences and attitudes to work, the students are also exposed in units 1–4 to many aspects of the field of the coffee-break chat in unit 5.

After completing this course students are able to listen to more coffee-break chats on other topics without preparatory work in simpler spoken texts. Background information on the topic area still needs to be provided for them, though this can be in written or visual form. If one can judge by the enthusiastic response to the course, it may be that more of such data can be developed into such listening material.

The final step, one hopes, will be to develop a reference book for both students and teachers to provide a thorough analysis of the nature of casual conversation using examples from the authentic text students can refer to in the listening materials. This will be possible as the more detailed linguistic analysis nears completion.

CHAPTER 7

THE PROGRAMME IN LINGUISTICS AND ENGLISH TEACHING, UNIVERSITY COLLEGE LONDON, 1964–1971

1. INTRODUCTION

John Pearce, Geoffrey Thornton,
and David Mackay

The first significant phase of curriculum development began in England and Wales in the 1950s, led notably by the Primary French scheme and, not long after the shock of the first Sputnik, by the earliest Nuffield projects in science. At the time when Michael Halliday was securing the Nuffield Foundation's support for a program in English, the prevailing model of curriculum development relied on a full-time project team whose task was to generate new classroom materials. Conscious that his background gave him little direct knowledge of schools, Halliday was nevertheless convinced that linguistics could provide insights and procedures which would be of great value to English teaching. When the Programme began in September 1964, it naturally followed the prevailing project model, putting academic scholars and experienced schoolteachers side by side. The chosen territory, however, apart from being unexplored, was already contentious, while the intellectual gulf between linguists and English teachers (whose subjects and routes of development were and are different) was much greater than in the case of, say, Nuffield science, as we shall see.

The opening phase of the Programme adopted the developing work of David Mackay and his colleagues, described below, and gathered a small group of others, teachers and linguists, whose first task was to clear the ground. The teachers faced a considerable task of academic study of what was to them a little-known discipline, formulated in a highly abstract fashion and itself liable to dramatic intellectual upheavals. For their part, the linguists were called upon to address a school subject of the first importance which had no agreed body of theory and no accepted rationale to account for the differences between its university-level and its school-level realizations. Moreover, English was becoming the battleground for stridently argumentative factions. The Programme's first three-year period, however, led to a consolidating series of papers. In his preface to them, Halliday explained the purpose of the work thus:

"Its purpose was to look into the teaching of English from the standpoint of modern developments in linguistics, to make a study of the contemporary English language that would be helpful to English teachers, and to offer recommendations about aims and methods, while carrying out such experimentation as proved possible in the time available" (Doughty, 1968, p. i).

The reason for the Programme's existence, Halliday wrote, was the "widespread conviction that the teaching of English often falls far short of meeting the demands now facing it. Someone, some time, has to translate ideas into classroom practices. . . . This translation process must and can only remain the responsibility of the teacher." This was by no means a scheme for producing the sort of total program for English from the age of 8 to 18 that some voices were to suggest, but the carefully low-key explanation of the Programme's aims did not always protect it from the asperities of those who wished to insist that its purposes were ominous.

Those unfamiliar with the English school system may not know that its practice has always tried to avoid centrally or locally designed curriculum specifications. No agency, other than Examinations Boards, has ever, until the 1980s, sought to suggest either the content or the objectives of any school subject, apart from the special case of religious knowledge. That fact underlies the constant anxiety, voiced in every curriculum debate in England, that some prescription might eventually be attempted. By extension, any body seeking to make useful suggestions is liable to be characterized as usurping the teacher's freedom in the matter. A program funded by Schools Council, however exploratory its nature, could be viewed as seeking to prescribe in a domain where teachers had wrestled with intractable problems and had much capital and pride invested in the solutions they had evolved. This situation lends a particular coloring to Halliday's preface of 1968, which goes on to say that the Programme's endeavor did not "require our arguing for or against a particular methodology or attempting to specify the content of an English syllabus." The recommendations offered in the first batch of papers were "such as could be carried out in the context of wide varieties of subject matter and in conjunction with widely different pedagogical practices. They relate to the handling of pupils' linguistic experience rather than to the specific content of a series of lessons," and the imputation of offering a "new grammar" for school use "as a source of handy exercises and testing points" was specifically repudiated. Indeed, a bridge to other views about the purposes of English teaching was offered in the insistence upon the need to increase pupils' ability to meet the linguistic demands of school and life after school.

The Programme papers of 1968, ten in all, fell into three groups: those offering linguistic descriptions of language; those discussing the relevance of such descriptions to the work of classroom teachers; and one that dealt with the first classroom material to be published by the Programme, discussed in the following section. This grouping was to underly the whole of the Programme's work, providing a framework which tied together the disciplined study of language with classroom material based, however distantly, on that discipline.

From September 1967, the Programme was greatly expanded and was thenceforward funded by Schools Council. Primary and secondary teachers were recruited, and the need to equip these newcomers with the essentials of linguistic science occupied much of their first year. From then on, the Programme worked in comparatively separate blocs: the Breakthrough to Literacy unit was heavily engaged in field trials, while the embryonic Language in Use unit was at a much earlier stage of its work. As these units developed, they and the linguists in the Programme tended to pursue their separate concerns, with less cross-participation than had occurred in other such projects, partly because Halliday himself had left University College, and partly because the teachers' concerns had become pedagogical to a degree that frustrated the linguists, who did not themselves form a functioning group.

Another reason why the Programme tended to divide into separate units lay in the differences between the Schools Council approach and that of projects elsewhere. In these, the academic participants were seen as full-time participants who usually took part personally in classroom trials, whether they were senior professors or research assistants. In early Schools Council projects, however, the role of the academics was nearer that of consultant. They provided the specialist instruction of the teacher members, acted as a check on the intellectual rigor and competence of the output, and undertook their own research work as well as a modicum of normal university teaching.

The council's method of working, at that time, left it to the projects to select trial schools and to make approaches to local education authorities. The teaching material produced would be published commercially, with royalties going not to the authors but to the council. The concerns of publishers sometimes constrained the work, although the council is rarely given credit for supporting striking innovations, of which the loose-leaf format of *Language in Use* is an example that was

332 PEARCE, ET AL.

to become influential. One effect was to put the material, in any subject, into the commercial context of competing material. In the case of Breakthrough, the departure from conventional reading schemes was at first a commercial handicap, and it was to be some years before commercial initial-literacy schemes emerged that accepted the implications of a linguistic perspective. In the case of *Language in Use*, the material was competitive with nothing comparable, but teachers did not find it easy, for various reasons to be explored in succeeding sections, to employ it in a *systematic* way within the context of mainstream English courses.

As we have noted, in order that they would have common ground with the linguists, the teachers all spent their first year in the full-time study of linguistics and this applied to all the teachers who joined the project later. However, ensuring a corresponding sharing of the teachers' educational know-how with linguists proved to be difficult, largely because of the difference in the two disciplines and their resulting practices.

M. A. K. Halliday, director of the Programme, whose writing during this period revealed an understanding of a wide range of major educational issues, was the exception. From the seminars that he led in the first year of the Programme, as well as from *The Linguistic Sciences and Language Teaching* (Halliday et al., 1964) and the papers that were subsequently collected in *Explorations in the Functions of Language* (Halliday, 1973), the linguistic elements at the root of many an inappropriate English lesson, as well as those at the center of young children's early language learning, were given a startling clarity. For some of us this immersion in linguistics was both illuminating and perplexing, taking us into academic areas our training had never considered relevant, extending our awareness of the nature of language and the use we all make of it. We listened to Halliday lecture on systemic grammar and attended regular sessions with skilled phoneticians. At weekly meetings we met with the director and staff of the Institute of Education Sociological Research Unit, read Firth's papers, studied the work of Whorf, and were invited to attend occasional meetings with educationalists who introduced us to the work of Vygotsky and added to our knowledge of Bruner and Piaget; and we had our first encounter with grammatical cohesion. Added to this program were the reading and reflection we were able to undertake, and the discussions we had with members of the team. We counted ourselves lucky indeed to have the time to reconsider crucial issues concerning language and education, to search for a clearer understanding of the gains and losses in the way school curricula had been made to respond to fashions and changes of emphasis in educational practices.

For some of those who joined the project later, this experience was less satisfying because it seemed too closely geared to the needs of students fresh from school. Bearing in mind that the teachers had all come straight from active classroom involvement, some felt that they might have had greater profit from a more reciprocal approach with more discussion and less lecturing. However, in the end everyone had at the very least an interesting grounding in the basic linguistic concepts and this, tempered by the common sense engendered by active classrooms, was put to practical use.

2. THE BREAKTHROUGH CONNECTION: "BREAKING THROUGH THE SOUND BARRIER INTO THE WRITTEN LANGUAGE"

David Mackay, Pamela Schaub, and Brian Thompson

The Initial Literacy Project was set up as part of the Programme in Linguistics and English Teaching in 1965. In that year Brian Thompson was appointed to the staff of the Programme in Linguistics and English Teaching so that work with class teachers could be extended. But even before this happened, while we (Thompson and Mackay) had been exploring the many possible ways of applying some linguistics to the work of the primary classroom, a number of issues constantly intruded themselves into our thinking.

We were aware of an oppressive educational conundrum which, for all the changes and all the switches to and fro of fashionable educational ideas, remained a stumbling block. There were a number of causes we had begun to identify. Although the use of written language received high priority in schools, much of the time this was concerned with teaching reading and with using comprehension and English exercises. Thus, much language work was controlled and shaped by the textbooks used to prepare children for the now discredited 11 + secondary = school selection examination. (In the course of time there had been increasing pressure, from the 11 + class down the age groups, to involve younger and younger children in preparation for this exam.)

From such practices it was well nigh impossible to compose a coherent theory as a basis for the formulation of a relevant and linguistically adequate curriculum. Indeed, one seldom heard words such as *language* and *literacy* used in educational circles. Teachers had had no training in how children might be encouraged to use spoken language in the classroom to realize some of what Halliday referred to as its "limitless potential." "Language is, for the child, a rich and adaptable instrument for the realisation of his intentions; there is hardly any limit to what he can do with it" (Halliday 1973, p. 10). Today there are still many children much of whose linguistic potential has been poorly developed. In her book *Children's Minds*, Margaret Donaldson (1978, 1983, p. 13–14) writes: "In the first few years at school all appears to go very well. The children seem eager, lively, happy. There is commonly an atmosphere of spontaneity in which they are encouraged to explore and discover and create. There is much concern, on the part of teachers, with high educational ideals. These things tend to be true even in parts of the community which are far from being socially privileged in other ways. However, when we consider what has happened by the time the children reach adolescence, we are forced to recognize that the promise of the early years frequently remains unfulfilled. Large numbers leave school with the bitter taste of defeat in them, not having mastered even moderately well those basic skills which society demands, much less having become people who rejoice in the exercise of creative intelligence."

In several local education authorities there was a good deal of concern on the part of primary school inspectors and advisers to persuade teachers away from a devotion to instructional English exercises, toward a range of imaginative and everyday language activities. Teachers were encouraged to ease up on correctness as the major classroom priority and leave children free, for instance, to write about anything they liked. The teachers were to be concerned with the content of children's work and were urged to leave the development of handwriting and spelling skills to be picked up by the children themselves, in the process of carrying out varied writing activities. As a result of such advice, classroom practice went from one extreme to another: from an exclusive concentration on skills to their almost total neglect by the teacher. Later, Halliday aptly described this pedagogical approach as "benevolent inertia." "Teaching," he wrote, "is neither filling holes nor benevolent inertia, but guidance; the provision of environments in which learning can take place, in which there is order, progression and guidance" (Halliday, 1968, p. 105). When in due course we came to consider the needs of nonliterate five-year-olds, we were to remember these words.

Traditionally, children's introduction to written language has been through the teaching of reading. This has been approached in either of two ways. One led to letters and sounds, with a concentration on learning the alphabet and the spelling patterns enshrined in the "Cat sat on the mat" phonic approach; the other to the "whole-word" recognition method associated with large labels (flash cards) on which were written words carrying clear and easily understood meanings, such as *aeroplane*, *dog, kitten, ball, Spot,* but also with banal, repetitive texts made up of sentences like *Look. Look. See the kitty.* Inevitably this led to children spending a long time with linguistic fragments and with meanings that were nothing like those they encountered in everyday life. In these special beginners' texts, grammar and semantics were relegated to minor roles, and thus resulted in abnormal, unfamiliar language. To quote Halliday again: "Children have a very broad concept of the meaningfulness of language, in addition to their immense tolerance of inexplicable tasks; but they are not accustomed to being faced with language which, in their own functional terms, has no meaning at all, and the old-style reader was not seen by them as language. It made no connexion with language in use" (Halliday, 1973, p. 10).

We found much of the professional literature of the time assertive about how and what children should be taught but with little to say about how children learn. There were few references to children as learners and seldom any mention of written composition as an activity for five- and six-year-olds. Our intention was to find a way to ensure that the grammar of their mother tongue and the semantic systems they encountered in their daily lives would be at the center of their transition to written language. To do this we had to put the means of production into their own hands from the beginning. They would learn to compose texts in language that reflected home and school, they would approach reading through writing that they had themselves produced, and they would share their writing with others just as they did their talk.

2.1 The Search for New Materials

At the start of the new school year (1965), we were given permission to work daily in an inner-city London infants' school with a teacher and 40 five-year-olds (and later with two such classes). We started off well primed with ideas that had grown out of our past experience of working with children, work that was now infused with ideas that owed much to the work of Halliday, Bruner, Piaget, and Vygotsky. We were also influenced by some remarkable teachers, among them Sylvia Ashton-Warner (1963–1980), whose work with Maori children strengthened our resolve that children everywhere should be helped "to make the connexion with language in use", and another, remembered for the way she made sentences with her children by pegging word cards to a clothesline stretched across her classroom—a good idea, but a better one had it been the children who had done the pegging. We were concerned to see children's acquisition of reading and writing as a continuation of the active involvements that had accompanied their linguistic development and not as activities controlled by inappropriate texts unrelated to their experience of language and life.

Instead of viewing children negatively—as "not knowing their sounds," for instance—we were anxious for children to be seen as resourceful language users and learners. Our starting point was to acknowledge their nearly complete command of the phonology of the family accent and of their advancing grasp of the grammar of their community's dialect, helped along by parents and friends. We ourselves were aware of their growing vocabularies, growing in two senses: first, by adding words to their internal word stores; and second, by the way in which words, some more than others, were gradually gathering a range of meanings and associations, and how these same words were being linked together and sorted into categories. Then, through their ability to make sentences and respond to those of the people around them, they were able, *in their own way*, to make sense of their thoughts, feelings, and actions and to interpret those of other people—in short, to turn complex information about people, places, and things, real and imagined, *into a sense of reality*.

About this Margaret Donaldson writes: "Here is the heart of the matter. By the time they come to school, all normal children can show skill as thinkers and language-users to a degree which must compel our respect, so long as they are dealing with "real-life" meaningful situations in which they have purposes and intentions and in which they can recognise and respond to similar purposes and intentions in others. These human intentions are the matrix in which the child's thinking is embedded. They sustain and direct his thoughts and his speech, just as they sustain and direct the thoughts and speech of adults—even intellectually sophisticated adults—most of the time" (1978, p. 21).

Our concern with children as learners was with the strength of their desire to learn about everything going on around them; their need to be independent, to do things for themselves, in their own way; their need to practice and to be able to make mistakes among people who provide feedback from which they are able to correct themselves; their need to be at least within reach of enjoyment and success in what they are learning. To succeed at home or at school, children need to be active learners in benign social settings. For the teacher, knowing about children as learners is indispensable if teaching skills are to be applied effectively.

Our search was for simple, practical ways to enable children to draw on their own resources, on their own experiences and their own environment, and to reflect their own lives in how they were going to handle written language. After hearing them talk about themselves we were more conscious than ever of the linguistic inadequacy, the poverty of ideas, and the general misrepresentation of life in the ubiquitous reading primers. We were now mindful of Vygotsky's warning that "in learning to write, the child must disengage himself from the sensory aspect of speech and replace words by images of words. Speech that is merely imaged and that requires symbolization of the sound image in written signs (i.e., a second degree of symbolization) naturally must be as much harder than oral speech for the child as algebra is than arithmetic" (1962, pp. 98–99).

Our most immediate task was to invent materials that would place learners in continuous control of the written language they were producing in becoming both readers and writers. Now the teacher's role was to respond to the needs that children made manifest in their speech and writing, and to base her guidance and instruction of what this revealed to her, rather than to hand this crucial responsibility over to the authors of workbooks. Above all we wanted to ensure that when composing texts, children would be free to use their own language and their own interpretations of life. And provided they were not forced into contact with the conflicting language of reading primers, they would be saved from assuming that such language was what the school expected them to use. As far as we knew there was no precedent for the materials we wanted.

Of the time allocated every day to our experimental work in the classroom, an important part was spent in getting to know the children; observing them as they worked with their teachers; listening to them talk about themselves and the things that interested them; noting the ways in which the teachers responded to these and how they introduced them to new, stimulating ideas. Part of the time we were also concerned to find how well they were able to manage the little word cards that we made for them. Prompted by the findings Jessie Reid reported in her paper "Learning to Think About Reading" (1966), we encouraged them to talk about what this meant to them. They talked of drawing letters, numbers, and names (and indeed, sometimes children included a sprinkling of these in their drawings and paintings). Whenever we worked with them, whether making sentences with the word cards or reading to them or telling them stories, we discussed what was going on and encouraged them to do the same. It was an important part of such talk that the new, unfamiliar *technical* meanings of words (such as speaking, listening, reading, writing, sentence, word space, direction, left to right, reading aloud, reading silently, speech tunes, sounds, letters, numbers) and the ideas associated with them were made clear from their context. It was also important to provide many examples of each so that they could accumulate the evidence they needed to understand the underlying concepts.

When this *fusion of doing and discussion* took place under careful teacher guidance, starting with children's interests and extending them, children's awareness of what they could do with spoken and written language grew. So too did their ability to talk about what they were doing. We became increasingly conscious of how these children were coming to grips with the language of education as they experienced it in the classroom and of the way in which they were accustoming themselves to the difference between spoken and written language.

This called on teachers for a greater level of awareness of what children were doing and thinking as they got to grips with written language. It required teachers to know more about language than is called for when reading texts are the main learning medium. Indeed, until children start writing, few of these issues are brought to the surface: The books tend to obscure what it is that children are doing.

Despite the inadequacy of the original word-cards with which we had introduced the children to this way of composing written sentences (the cards were loose and had to be sorted out), they did well enough to set us on the way to making some important discoveries before we removed them. We found that when children were freed from the need to handwrite and spell, they were able to give all their attention to managing the writing system, to meeting the demands of English word order, and to remembering the shape of the words they used. To a significant degree what Vygotsky refers to as the "abstract quality of written language" was made concrete by the children's active involvement in making the words of their own sentences *move into place*.

2.2 Inventing the Word Folder

We now knew that the materials for which we were searching had to be in the form of a retrievable word store. Experiments with manila cardboard gave us the idea for a simple folder that could stand up on a child's desk, with a holder for words rather like a printer's composing stick. We arranged the words grammatically, not alphabetically: nouns, adjectives, definite and indefinite articles, pronouns, verbs, noun and verb endings, punctuation marks, prepositions, *wh-* words, conjunctions. Later, when the folder became the Sentence Maker, it had a blank third page added for personal words. And so that the final vocabulary selection would faithfully reflect children's writing, uncontaminated by reading-primer sentences, all our trial schools sent us their children's writing done during one week. This material was then fed into a computer which gave us information about the frequency with which each word had been used, and we based the final version of the Sentence Maker on that information.

Long before this, the children in our first experimental class had shown us that they needed to be carefully trained to use the Sentence Maker and to do so the teacher had to have a large version for use with a group of children. This Teacher's Sentence Maker became a most important apparatus because it enabled sentence making to be shared, demonstrated, discussed. These group activities depended for their success on the teacher's ability to get the children to talk about themselves and their families and then to lead them to choose a particular spoken sentence to turn into a written sentence; it also enabled her to carefully monitor individual children's progress and to introduce each of them to an individual Sentence Maker at the right time.

However, it was equally important for the Teacher's Sentence Maker to be used regularly for two further purposes: first, when there were new things for the children to learn, for instance, how to add inflectional endings to words; and second, to revise what children had found difficult or what they had forgotten. Only when children are left to learn on their own by a teacher who is not herself sufficiently aware of their constant need for guidance do they grow fearful, falter, and begin to fail. This is more likely to happen with a teacher who is used to only correcting and grading children's work instead of finding explanations for errors and demonstrating what it is children need to know in order to correct themselves.

Until we did this ourselves, we were not fully aware of how much there was for children to learn that remains hidden in traditional approaches to the teaching of reading. Using the Sentence Maker enabled us to see the problems with which children were struggling. We were often surprised by the variety of issues that arose in the course of quite brief group sessions and by the children's responses during the discussions which arose from sentence making. We were not alone in this; when, during her evaluation of Breakthrough, Reid (1974) observed a child making a sentence, the boy sitting behind her tapped her on the shoulder and said, pointing to the Sentence Maker: "You know, with this you can make any sentence in the whole world."

Very quickly, children showed us that they were better able to compose interesting written texts—even those that consisted of one sentence—when they had first had the chance to talk freely about what they were going to write. Although children needed plenty of guidance from us, we discovered that they also learned a great deal from one another and that satisfying their curiosity concerning other children's work was a considerable source of help and encouragement to them.

We took great care to see that our responses motivated children toward personal achievement and to an awareness of their growing competence, while also encouraging them to compete with themselves rather than with others. Indeed, when children were working together rather than alone, talking and discussing rather than having to work silently and learning from one another rather than always being told what to do by the teacher, and when their writing recalled both personal and shared experiences, these were the sources of their enjoyment and their understanding.

2.3 Working in a Project Classroom

Throughout all the linguistic activity that soon had children and teacher making books, there were many opportunities that this "concrete," manipulative approach provided for talking about and making manifest the otherwise mysterious business of reading and writing.

On visiting one of our trial classrooms at the beginning of the school year, we were informed by the teacher that although the children had been in school only a week, she had a group who were longing to have a go with the Teacher's Sentence Maker and she invited us to accompany them in their first Breakthrough session. When we were all comfortably settled, she asked them what they thought they were going to do. "These are words," said a girl, "and we must be going to do something with them." "Are we going to read?" asked a boy. "Can you read any of the words?" asked the teacher. They could recognize *school, children, television, birthday party, teacher,* and so on. "What do you think we could do with the words?" "Perhaps we're going to write them." "It has something to do with reading and writing," said one of the girls. It was clear that these were children whose introduction to reading and writing had already gotten under way at home. "If you will tell me something about yourselves," explained the teacher, "then I'll help you to turn the words that you speak into writing. To do that you'll have to use some of these words. Tell me how you like school." "Well, you feel quite new to start with," said one of the boys. "But it's nice. We do a lot of nice things." "You could make a book about all the things you do at school," the teacher suggested. They liked the idea. "How would it be if we started with how you feel about starting school?" They happily agreed to make the sentence *We are the new children.*

The teacher repeated it while they counted the words. She separated each spoken word with a pause to mark the word spaces they would make sure were present in their sentence. Then they began searching for the words in the Teacher's Sentence Maker and each of five children in turn placed one in the sentence stand. (Later we sometimes found that it was by no means easy for some teachers to resist doing all this themselves.) When they could not find a word, the teacher showed them where it was, let them examine it and notice its place in the store, and then take it from its pocket and slip it into position in the sentence. They measured each word space with a finger, and when the sentence was finished they smiled at the teacher and at one another. She responded by asking them to show it and read it to the rest of the class. The children were all aware of being on the edge of something important and when the teacher suggested that they would probably like to paint a picture of themselves to go with the sentence, all the children in the class felt involved.

Later that day the portraits were ready. Before leaving we asked the sentence makers: "What sentence will you make tomorrow?" Several children said they could think of one. One of the girls said she was going to write the new sentence for her mother and father, a suggestion which was taken up with great enthusiasm by the whole group. The next day a fine collection of 30 or more signed portraits gazed from a great sheet of paper that had been fixed on a wall outside the classroom. Under it the teacher had written:

We are the new children.

From the start these children were very clear about what they had to do. The teacher made certain of this in each short lesson and the moment she suggested to the children that they might like to make a book about all the things they did at school, she opened up a real use for the children's writing. Indeed, in so doing she was ensuring that the classroom as a learning environment would generate the contexts from which the stimulus to write would arise.

Central to this approach is the difference between two very different ways of eliciting classroom writing: first, one that is enclosed in a tight little circuit—the child's writing is addressed to the teacher; the teacher being an examiner returns the notebook and so ignores the need for an audience; and second, one that is a direct result of the personal involvement of the writers in what is going on in and out of the classroom, in what has first been talked about before it is made into a "published" (public) document and used to communicate to an audience. For this to succeed, it is crucial that children are aware that their work is valued appropriately and prepared with care for this purpose. The most telling way for this to happen is to use children's writings to make books to which they may have added pictures and drawings. This then creates the possibility of obtaining valuable feedback not from one person but from many, from a readership, and from the teacher's comments and commendations. At this time ('1968) it was not common for this to happen.

No sooner were Sentence Makers in daily use than we saw that it was necessary to provide new materials to support children in their need to learn about the relationship among sounds, letters, and words. It was the children's demands for personal words (words that were not included in the Sentence Maker's printed pages) that led us to provide Word Makers—the first with one page each of consonants and vowels; the second with three pages, one of initial consonants, one of simple and complex vowels, and one of final consonants, thus making it possible for children to make discoveries about written syllables.

Thus, when Robert came to his teacher and requested the word *fighting*, she said to him, "Look in your Sentence Maker for *night* and get a Word Maker and make *night*. Then, because *night* and *fight* have the same spelling pattern, change *night* into *fight*. I think you know how to do that." When he needed *game*, Robert found *came* and worked out the changes needed in the same way. His sentence read: *I play fighting games with my dad.* Later the teacher followed this up by asking Robert to explain to the rest of the class how he made *fighting games* for himself.

About this time (1966) Charles Read was investigating the spelling system for English created by some preschool children. His work was reported in 1970 and published in 1971 and 1975. Had we known about this during our work, we would have taken account of it. Later, we found children inventing their own spelling system when they had to have a word that Breakthrough did not provide. It was clear that children can live comfortably with two divergent spelling systems—their own and standard spelling. And in Patrick's case, how well the former prepares children for handling the latter, provided they are not made to be scared of making mistakes. Instead, if the ingenuity of their efforts is acknowledged and at some convenient time set beside the ingenuity of standard spelling, they will prosper. Patrick's story of Roy the Boy (Mackay & Simo, 1976) is an example of a piece of writing of some considerable length, composed entirely in invented spelling by a boy who bears this out incontrovertibly.

Charles Read's work has been developed more widely in the United States than in the United Kingdom, and by no one more expertly and with greater clarity than Edmund Henderson (1981, 1985), whose work has now influenced many education departments and spread to teacher education colleges and to schools themselves.

2.4 An Early Research Report from Australia

In 1973 a research report from the Education Department, Victoria, Australia (Cullen & Turnbull, 1973) set "some of the better sentences from the Breakthrough Grades" beside "some of the better sentences from the Non-Breakthrough Grades."

Some Breakthrough sentences:
    I might be going to Vicki's house or I might be going to Karen's house
    after school.
    My cat and our other cat were chasing each other down the hall this
    morning.
    My mum is working at the hotel.
    I like Tania Heather Andrea Margaret and Helena very much.

Some Non-Breakthrough sentences:
    The dog is big and the dog can jump.
    I like the dog. Here is the cat.
    run Betty jump run John jump   Betty has a doll John has a drum

In the Breakthrough sentences it is clear that the children are writing
"from life." The variety of content and sentence structure they reveal
are valid samples of the normal language of children and of its relative
richness, compared to the linguistic stereotyping that children have to
suffer when they read from schoolbooks. The writers of the first set of
sentences are not influenced and restricted by molding their writing on
their reading primers. In the second group of sentences the influence of
reading primers and the lack of personal involvement are very marked.
The form and subject matter of the sentences are borrowed. These are
typical examples of the remarkably different effects on children of these
disparate language environments

2.5 Language in Everything the Children Do

Of course, in the early stages, work with a small group around the teacher's Sentence Maker only took up a small part of the children's day, in
which there was likely to be time for a variety of activities—time for
stories and nursery rhymes, mathematics and science, music and movement, painting and modeling with clay and junk materials, cutting and
pasting, dramatic play, outdoor visits, occasional parties and concerts,
and, in the most favored classrooms, a great deal of talk and discussion.
    We were concerned that the children's use of spoken and written
language should reflect the new perspectives that experiences at home
and school were opening up for them and that their work with Sentence
Makers should enable them to record a goodly portion of this in books
made in school for all the children to read. If, as we claimed, the Sentence Makers (both the child's and the teacher's) were the heart of
Breakthrough, then the writing produced in this way and the associated
learning were also at the heart of the process by which these children
were becoming literate.
    During our first year's experimental work, when handmade Sentence

Makers were in use, we collaborated closely with our two reception-class teachers in creating a literacy program. This brought together diverse ingredients, which included the children's accounts of real and make-believe episodes from their lives; stories told or read by the teacher; singing and speaking rhymes and verses; contrasting silent reading and reading aloud by having children reading the books made in class to themselves and to one another; teaching children strategies to deal with problems that arise in making sense of what is being read; continuing work with Sentence Makers and Word Makers; helping children talk about the relationships between *their* speech sounds and letters; introducing them to the idea of spelling; playing word games; talking about letter shapes and practicing handwriting. Two "behind-the-scenes" ingredients were crucial to running the program successfully: first, the talk, discussion, and explanation relating to everything the children were doing, and second, the care and consistency with which all parts of the program were attended to throughout the year.

2.6 Preparing for National Trials

Planning the first phase of the Breakthrough trials began as soon as it was clear that the children in our two experimental classes were making good progress in reading and writing. The extra attention they had received while Breakthrough was being developed was offset to quite an extent by the rather poor quality of our handmade materials and by the absence of a teacher's manual and of printed books for the children.

Two further infants' school reception classes accepted to join the Initial Literacy Programme, one with middle-class and the other with mixed middle-class/working-class intakes. Our aim was to invite the new teachers to collaborate with us in preparing for a country-wide trial. For this we had to be reasonably clear about the kind of guidance future teachers would need, to help them understand the principals and practice underlying this work. We would require a teacher's manual which took account of the classroom experiences of our four teachers, and a number of children's book which took account of the present writing as well as the further writing needs of the five-to six-year-olds in the project classrooms.

2.7 National Trials of Prototype Materials

This work brought to an end the Nuffield Foundation's funding of the Programme in Linguistics and English Teaching and ushered that of the Schools Council in its place. With the Programme as a whole entering its final phase, five new teachers were added to the team. Pamela

Schaub, who had already helped us in making the handmade materials with which we started, was appointed to the Initial Literacy team. Plans for a major trial were finalized and negotiations were begun to obtain the services of Jessie Reid of the Centre for Research in Educational Sciences, University of Edinburgh, to provide us with an independent evaluation of our work.

Trial schools were chosen to be as representative as possible of social and environmental conditions throughout England. Twelve local education authorities, from Newcastle-upon-Tyne in the northeast to Cornwall in the southwest, selected 43 schools willing to take part. It says much for those who chose the schools that as few as five were reluctant to take part in the project. At the beginning of the next school year our expanded team visited each of the designated areas to brief the teachers involved and to deliver the new materials: new Sentence makers and stands for both teachers and pupils; pupils' Word Makers; a magnet board; figurines and magnets; 24 books with black-and-white illustrations; and the first version of the teacher's manual. Much of the year was spent in monitoring and recording the progress of teachers and children and visiting project schools to sort out difficulties and to learn from the teachers about the new ways in which they had decided to organize the classroom.

By far the most irritating and persistent problem was due to the faulty gluing of the word folder (now known as the Sentence Maker) and the Word Makers and the inadequacy of the cardboard sentence stand. While the manufacturers searched for a robust synthetic glue that could be guaranteed to bond the card for the word pockets to the cover of the Sentence Maker, a design student, Philip Kay, came up with excellent solutions to our problems. Not only did he redesign the two former items but he also created the model for an extruded plastic stand which has been manufactured according to his design ever since.

2.8 Evaluation and Preparations for Publication

The following year was our most demanding. We had twice the number of classrooms to visit; arrangements for the evaluation of the project had to be completed to ensure that Miss Reid could issue her first questionnaire to all the participating schools in December 1969; and we had to have all the materials revised and finalized in the light of teachers' comments and criticisms, and ready for publication in spring 1970. With much to accomplish, we needed another pair of experienced hands. We invited Frances Knowles, the headmistress of one of our trial schools, with whom we had worked for two years, to join the team. She was seconded to the project for its final year and her special knowledge of

Breakthrough in the classroom made an important contribution to the work of this complicated year.

For some time we had felt the need for a title to take the place of the cumbersome, impersonal "Initial Literacy Project Materials," and the pressure of preparing for publication made this a matter of some urgency. The eventual choice of *The Breakthrough to Literacy* was made from suggestions many teachers had sent us. Its aptness is commented on by Halliday in his introduction to the second edition of the teacher's manual: "*Breakthrough* is designed to provide the means whereby a child can create new resources for meaning through interaction with his teacher (and with other children) in school, as a natural extension of what he has been doing all along through interaction with family and friends in home and neighbourhood. *Breakthrough* does this by helping him to break through the sound barrier into the written language, thereby adding a new dimension to his capabilities for language use" (Halliday, 1978b, p. 3).

2.9 "Breakthrough" in Scottish Gaelic and Other Languages

As far as we know, the first use of Breakthrough in a language other than English occurred in the classroom of Catherine Morrison, an infants' teacher in a small village school in the Western Isles of Scotland. Soon after the publication of Breakthrough, she used the Sentence Maker with her class of bilingual (Gaelic-English) children and quickly saw that it would be possible to make a Gaelic adaptation of it for them. During the following five years she used the spoken and written modes of both languages for all the children's work.

Then, in 1975 the newly created Local Council established a bilingual policy for the Western Isles and, with some funding from the Scottish Education Department, set up the Bilingual Education Project. This gave Gaelic-speaking children in project primary schools the opportunity to speak, read, and write their mother tongue. In 1980, after careful trials, a Gaelic Sentence Maker was published, and since then, children have used both languages for all their schoolwork. For the first time in the history of the Gaels, young children have been writing in Gaelic about themselves and their island environment. The best of this has been used in making a series of 24 stories with the illustrations as well as the texts by primary school children.

Like Miss Morrison, other teachers with children in similar linguistic situations saw that Breakthrough opened up the opportunity for their non-English-speakers to become literate in their mother tongue first, or alongside English as their second language. In this way Breakthrough has been adapted for use in Bengali, Greek, Italian, Spanish, and Irish

Gaelic. In Western Australia, it is in use in one of the aboriginal languages of the people of the outback. In 1986 news came from Singapore of a Chinese Sentence Maker, and one in Welsh is being prepared for publication.

About ten years ago, the Molteno Project of the Institute for the Study of English in Africa (Rhodes University, Grahamstown, 6140 South Africa) began to experiment with the Sentence Maker adapted for use in the Bantu languages of Xhosa and Setswana. The teachers who took part in this work were all given careful guidance and continuing support until they were both competent and confident. As soon as it became clear that the materials worked as well under southern African conditions, where classes had around 50 students, as they worked in the United Kingdom, with classes half this size, the Molteno Project extended its involvement to include the following languages: Zulu, Northern Sotho, Southern Sotho, Venda, and Tsonga. Of Breakthrough the project staff write: "It is relevant to children. They create sentences about their own life experiences in a vocabulary that they themselves use. The best of their writing becomes reading material for the class" (Rodseth, Ngambu, Mgetyana, and Nama, 1985, p. 97).

2.10 The Teacher Is Still the Kingpin

The success of this project was secured by the faith and enthusiasm its leaders derived from their understanding of the conditions in which Breakthrough can flourish, and by the form and quality of its in-service provision. They saw the danger of leaving teachers to work in isolation. The Project team secured the support of the head teachers; provided regular workshops at which teachers could pool their experiences and learn from one another; and set up a teacher network that made sure no teacher was left to her own devices. In contemporary Britain, despite all the support provided by teachers' centers, we have nothing to compare with the continuing care teachers need whenever they make a break with outmoded attitudes and traditions.

However good, relevant, and appropriate pedagogical materials are, the teacher is still the kingpin. Materials work well only if children are led by an informed and well-prepared guide. Teaching and learning can flourish only when decisions about the educational needs of children are made by teachers and not by textbooks behind which are faceless people who know nothing about the condition of the children in a particular classroom. The best of the project teachers with whom we collaborated revealed how imaginative classroom programs can, if need be, absorb primers without distorting valid pedagogical goals. They also showed how children respond to courteous, caring, and stimulating people who value them and the culture from which they come, and who provide the thoughtful, consistent guidance from which confidence and success grow.

But, as Reid (1974, pp. 97-98) observes in her evaluation of Breakthrough:

> Some teachers did not, in the end, like working with Breakthrough. Though they mostly had specific objections to make, usually about its limitations, they may have been rationalizing a more general feeling of incongeniality. Even if they were, their opinions are no less valid as indications that they did not share their colleagues' enthusiasm. But of the genuineness of that enthusiasm, and of its origin in some degree of sympathy with the theoretical basis and the aims of the method, and in satisfaction with its results, rather than merely in a sense of novelty, there can be no doubt.
>
> Whitehead saw all education as taking place in cycles of exploration, precision, and synthesis. 'Breakthrough' begins for the child in the exploration and discovery of new linguistic experience; properly used and built on, it can lead him in time to encounter and master the elements of precision of the writing system, and thus achieve the synthesis that allows him to moved easily between words on paper and words in the mind. The present study has by no means given an exhaustive account of all the factors which influence this progress, but it has revealed something of the way the system works, something of its potential weaknesses, and something of its particular power in informed and intelligent hands.

3. *LANGUAGE IN USE*—AND AFTER

Geoffrey Thornton

The material that eventually became *Language in Use* (Doughty, Pearce, & Thornton, 1971) was originally developed with sixth-form (students 16-18 years of age) teaching in mind. The first version was tried out in the spring term of 1969 in a dozen schools and colleges. It proved in practice to be so flexible that the main trial, using a much enlarged and rewritten version, was tried out by some 200 teachers in schools and colleges in many parts of England and northern Ireland during the academic year 1969–1970. This trial version was then completely rewritten for publication in the light of teachers' experiences and comments, while the explanatory papers written by the team to accompany the material were expanded into a paperback, *Exploring Language* (Doughty, Pearce, & Thornton), published in 1972.

Although the material was extensively reshaped during the course of these rewritings, the approach, and the design which reflected that approach, were not fundamentally altered. It was described by Peter Doughty in *Language, English and the Curriculum* (Arnold, 1974, p. 11):

> It seemed to us that there was no sense in which we could consider preparing materials which required for their successful use a long period of training prior to their being taken into the classroom. The teacher had to feel able to pick up what we offered and start using it right away in the context of his ordinary day-to day practice. As far as the pupil was concerned, we did not want to demand a particular analytic technique for the discussion of language. It did not seem consonant with current educational thinking for us to expect pupils to acquire an explicit technique of linguistic analysis before they could begin to explore their own language. Moreover, the acquisition of the kind of meta-language such a technique would make necessary was irrelevant to the needs of the majority of pupils, given our educational objectives.

It followed from this that any material produced had to be for the teacher, not the pupil. There was no question of writing anything like a coursebook. If the material was to have built-in flexibility of use, relevant to a wide variety of teaching situations, there would need to be a large corpus of material, presented in such a way as to offer teachers the possibility of designing courses, or course elements, to meet their own requirements.

It was from considerations like this that the key feature of *Language in Use* emerged—the *unit*. The unit was a plan for a sequence of lessons, occupying notionally between 1½ hours and 4 hours of class time. This enabled teachers to adapt the way in which they used a unit, or sequence of units, to their own situation—how long their lessons were, what sort of class, at what level, and what they wished their pupils to derive from the experiences suggested by the unit. Eighty units were written for the first trial. The titles of the themes in which they were grouped give some indication of the thinking behind them. They included "Variety in English," "Language as Social Behavior," "Precision and Interpretation," "Choice and Constraint," "Observing Speech in Action," "Spoken and Written," "Language and Information." The next version was expanded to 138 units, grouped again in much the same themes.

It was hoped that these units, as well as providing suggestions for teachers, would also provide them with insights into the linguistic perspective from which they derived—in other words, have an educative effect on teachers as well as their pupils. Their use was intended to inspire and enable pupils to explore their own implicit knowledge of language as derived from their experience of using it themselves, and of the use made by other people in the environment in which they were growing up. This meant in effect requiring pupils to provide their own raw material for a sequence of activities intended to make them more aware of the nature and function of language, and of the part that language plays in their own lives and in that of those in their communities. In so doing, they would—so the theory went—develop their ability to use spoken and written language more effectively in an ever-widening variety of situations.

It also meant asking teachers, many of them, to base their ''language teaching'' on a quite different premise from that with which they were familiar. Instead of basing their teaching on bodies of knowledge—for instance, Parts of Speech as traditionally defined—which had to be *taught*, they would have to regard their pupils' learning processes as founded upon a combination of exploration and activities.

The 10 themes into which the units were grouped were themselves set out under three headings:

> Language—its nature and function
> Language and individual man
> Language and social man

In this way, it was hoped to lay emphasis on three aspects of language as a phenomenon: the characteristics of its realization in sound, or as marks on paper; the part that it plays in the lives of individuals; and its functions in social life. In the first section, two themes (Using language to convey information, and Using language expressively) explore some of the ways in which language is used to pass on information, and two others (Sound and symbol, and Pattern in language) look at ways in which we draw upon the resources of language to communicate what we want to say. The three themes in the second group were concerned with aspects of the part language plays in enabling individuals to relate to the world around them. They were Language and reality, Language and culture, Language and experience. The introduction to the group defines the different emphases: ''While theme E, Language and reality, is concerned with the determining effect of the actual structure of language upon the way that we interpret our experience of the world, theme F, Language and culture, shifts the focus onto the effects of custom and habit as they act upon us through language. . . . Theme G, Language and experience, deals with our deliberate and conscious use of language to give meaning to our experience of the world.''

In the third group the focus of the themes, and of the units in them, shifted from the individual's use of language to bring order and meaning to his or her own experience, to the use of language intended to bring order and meaning into relationships with others. These included relationships at the individual level, as with members of the family, and at the social level, in the context of group interaction, and also the part language plays in the creation of social organizations like schools and companies. The Themes were the following: Language in individual relationships, Language in social relationships, and Language in social organizations. The latter, incidentally, draws attention to the fact that there is no single word in the English language to cover places like schools, colleges, factories, firms, businesses, hospitals, and so on, where large assemblies of people work together.

Below are two examples of units, demonstrating how they were set out on the page, how the area to be investigated was defined, and how procedures and activities were suggested to teachers. All 110 of them were the result of their forerunners' being used in the classroom and commented upon by teachers taking part in the trial.

JUDGING YOUR AUDIENCE

This unit considers an aspect of language which is fundamental to writing: it must be directed toward a specific context if it is to convey the information successfully. It explores the degree to which the writer's view of his audience must strongly determine his way of writing. When the object is to convey a body of information, this aspect of the writer's task is so important that the success of his efforts depends to a large extent on his success in judging the needs of the reader for whom he is writing.

(1) In this session, the class works out for each of three texts in turn its intended audience. It is best done with the class working in pairs or small groups. When they have done this, they should select a topic, well-known to them, and each write three pieces, each one for a different audience. The texts should be short, about 150 words in all, and the audiences well differentiated. The following suggestions may be useful:

(a)	feature in a mass daily	lead article in a *Sunday Review*	*New Society*
(b)	Penguin Special	school text-book	academic article
(c)	a review in mass daily	in serious weekly	in specialist journal
(d)	record sleeve	*Melody Maker*	*The Gramophone*

(2) This session uses the texts written by the class. These should be circulated and the class, working pairs or groups, should assess how successfully they meet the needs of the audiences for which they are intended. Points to look for include:

(a) inappropriate use of technical language for the level of the audience chosen

(b) assumption of too much or too little background knowledge in the reader

(c) condescension towards a non-specialist reader

(d) choice of a style which of too formal or too relaxed for the audience concerned.

(3) Select a text intended for an educated adult reader, dealing with a topic in the area of a school subject like history or geography, and ask the class to re-write it for eleven-year-olds. Circulate the results and ask the class to discuss them in the terms which were used for the texts in (2). If it is possible to secure the comments of eleven-year-olds they can be the basis for an additional session.

(4) The aim of this session is to apply the class's new understanding of audience to the needs of the public examiner as an audience. Place questions from different examination levels, internal and external, side by side, for discussion, so that the class can explore what is appropriate to the examiner as an audience.

MAN'S JOB/WOMAN'S WORK

The goal of this unit is to show how a very familiar pattern in our vocabulary can reveal much about the attitude of our culture to what those words classify. It takes as its starting point that certain tasks are traditionally thought to be the prerogative of one sex or the other, and goes on to explore how the patterns of the vocabulary we use perpetuate these assumptions.

(1) The aim of this session is to discover which tasks in the household are regarded as the man's job, and which the woman's. In discussion, consider such jobs as cooking, washing, washing-up, shopping, decorating, gardening, driving or washing the car, changing nappies, pushing the pram or mending fuses. The discussion should look at the position of brothers and sisters, as well as fathers and mothers, and consider to what extent tensions arise where there is uncertainty as to who should do what within the family.

(2/3) The aim of these sessions is to show that a number of words in the language carry with them the suggestion that particular jobs are properly performed by one sex or the other, and thereby show that such additional meanings are an essential part of the way language determines how we behave. This may be done in three ways:

(a) by writing up the words *Manager* and *Manageress*, and asking the class to supply a list of organisations or institutions they may be found in charge of

(b) by asking for examples of words which name jobs traditionally reserved for one sex, such as *matron, au pair, jockey*—or *disc jockey*. A variation of this is to write up a list of terms like 'con woman', 'charman' or nightwatchwoman' where the normal indications have been reversed

(c) by asking for words like *mayor* which usually connote one sex, but may be the other, and exploring the linguistic difficulties that follow.

(4) For this session, each member of the class should compile a list of names for jobs. By attempting to sort them into two simple lists, one clearly male, the other female, the class will discover that

(a)   one term or the other has to be specially marked, as in *doctor/ lady doctor* or *nurse/male nurse*

(b)   a similar job has different labels, as in *Air Steward/Air Hostess*

(c)   some pairs have a missing term, as in—*/fishwife,—/tomboy,* or *wide boy—*

(d)   in some related jobs, as in *bus conductor/bus conductress* and *bus driver—,*

a missing term may be significant.

The discussion will show how the resources of the language are exploited for this kind of labelling and consequently where the culture reveals itself in the gaps and special cases that occur.

The subject matter of F2, man's job/woman's work, had a certain novelty at the time *Language in Use* (Doughty et al., 1971) was published. The points it was making can now largely be taken for granted, but the contemporary use of, for example, the gender neutral term *chair* to replace *chairman* or chairman illustrates the way in which units may continue, with suitable emendation, to be topical.

The publication of *Language in Use* was not without its problems. The project team was adamant that the published version, like the two trial versions, should be loose-leaf in order to emphasize the flexible nature of the material being offered to teachers. The format assumed a symbolic significance. It was therefore fortunate that when Bryan Bennett, then education director of Edward Arnold, saw the manuscript and accompanying notes and Schools Council was seeking a publisher, he recognized not only the potential of the material but also the importance of the format. He saw to it that the technical problems were solved, and the "Red Book," as it came to be called, came out in autumn of 1971. It has remained on Arnold's list for fifteen years, has sold 55,000 copies all over the world, and has been translated into Italian and Dutch.

It was followed by *Exploring Language* (Doughty et al., 1972) a paperback based on the series of study papers written to accompany the trial versions of *Language in Use*. In these papers the members of the team had sought to expand and make explicit the linguistic ideas on which the material was based. The intention was explained thus in the foreword:

This book is written for teachers, and those training to become teachers, because the authors believe that it is part of every teacher's job to think about the part played by language in teaching and learning. It is not an analysis of English grammar, nor an introduction to Linguistic Science, nor a test-book on how to study language in the classroom, but an account of how human beings 'use language to live'. Its point of departure is the individual's own understanding of the nature and function of language which he has acquired in the process of learning a language, and it proceeds by asking him to review this understanding in the light of an objectively linguistic approach to language. Its aim is to convince a reader that understanding language is important to anyone involved in teaching and learning; and that exploring language need be neither arid nor technically formidable for the layman.

The chapter headings give some idea of the scope of the book: "Language, Teaching and Learning"; "Understanding, Exploration and Awareness"; "The Language We Acquire; "Language and Experience"; "Language and Relationships"; "Language and Society; "Command of a Language"; "Speech and Talk"; "Spoken and Written"; "Accent and Dialect; "Diversity in Written English."

The book was not essentially, however, an attempt to define some of the areas with which teachers professionally concerned with the linguistic development of their pupils should be acquainted. It was, rather, an exploration of the connection, as the team saw it after their experience of developing *Language in Use*, between the insights afforded by a linguistics-based study of those areas and the capacity of the teacher in the classroom *actively and productively* to promote pupils' ability to cope with the linguistic demands made upon them, in and out of school. It must not be forgotten that the origins of the Programme lay in a recognition that traditional work "in language" did not succeed in doing this for a substantial proportion of students in schools and colleges.

Historically, the Programme closed when the Schools Council terminated its funding in August 1971. At that time, only the initial portion of the *Breakthrough* material had been published, while *Language in Use* and *Exploring Language* were in press. However, members of the Programme were to continue working together for a long time.

One development was a series of paperbacks, also published by Edward Arnold, called EXPLORATIONS IN LANGUAGE STUDY (see appendix C for a complete list of titles in the series) in which each volume would constitute an "exploration focused upon a meeting point between the insights of Linguistic Science, often in conjunction with other social sciences, and the linguistic questions raised by the study of a particular aspect of individual behaviour or human society." The title of the first volume, *Language Study, the Teacher and the Learner*, emphasized the centrality of the particular confluence, and the 18 titles so far published examine the interaction from different perspectives and at different levels.

The two volumes by Professor Halliday himself, *Explorations in the Functions of Language* (1973) and *Learning How to Mean* (1975) provide detailed extension of the model of language that he has developed. That language exists at all is due to the nature of the human brain, and in *Language, Brain and Interactive Processes* Roger Gurney offered an account of the way in which the processes of the brain give us, as human beings, the capacity to learn, develop, and use language. Factors that bear on the kind of language developed by children growing up in different societies, or in different areas of one society, have been explored in a number of volumes such as *Language and Community*, *English as a Second and Foreign Language*, and *Language in Bilingual Communities*. One of the most influential has been Peter Trudgill's *Accent, Dialect and the School* (1975), which asked what the possession of certain accents and dialects might mean for the chances of success—or failure—in school. It was a theme taken up again in *They Don't Speak Our Language*.

Aspects of organization in schools, and of the teaching that goes on in them, were discussed in *Language in the Junior School* and *Language, Learning and Remedial Teaching*, while classroom practice was the concern of two books on writing, *Teaching Writing* and *Assessing Writing*. It is still the case that chances of success within the school system rest ultimately upon a pupil's ability to write. For too long it has been assumed that teachers can do little for those not, as it were, "born to write." The two columns on writing seek to convince teachers that effective help can be given, and suggest ways of doing so.

Ian Forsyth and Kathleen Wood (1980) worked in the Programme on the language education needs of pupils in the lower and middle forms of secondary schools, and gradually evolved a set of textbooks published by Longman under the title *Language and Communication*. These volumes constitute a study of language, its origins, its structure, its rules, its scope, its present uses, like a conventional textbook, but with language itself as the focus of study.

Another publication to be noted is *Themes for Language Learning*, a book for use by primary teachers by Frank Skitt (published by A & C Black), which owes much to the concept of *Language in Use*.

The final publication of the Programme itself was the second series of Papers in Linguistics and English Teaching, which came out in 1974. Professor Halliday's own contribution, *Language and Social Man*, contained a postscript in which he summed up the work of the Programme as he saw it. He begins by asserting, incontrovertibly, that,

Language has for a long time been a depressed area in our educational system; and only a serious concern with language on the part of teachers, a concern that is enlightened, imaginative and human, can restore it to the central place which it ought to occupy if we are tackling the problem of educational failure at its deepest level. (Halliday, 1974, p. 86)

He then refers to *Breakthrough to Literacy* as being, apart from the breakthrough of the title, a breakthrough in "the whole concept of language in the primary school," and to *Language in Use* (Doughty et al., 1971) as another breakthrough in concept, this time for the secondary school. He continues:

There is another breakthrough still to come, in the training of teachers, who have so far been left to fend almost entirely for themselves as far as language is concerned. Perhaps we may look forward to a time when language study has some place in the professional training of all teachers, and the central place in the relevant specialist courses, especially those relating to English and to literacy ('teaching or reading'). 'Language study' is not meant to imply a diluted version of academic linguistics—a subject which has often been defined much too rigidly in the university context; but, rather, a serious exploration of language from different angles, ignoring the artificial boundaries which universities (like schools) tend to interpose between one discipline and another. The exploration of language cannot be neatly classified as natural science, social science, humanity or fine art; it takes something from each of these world views. If we claim that language has a key place in the process of education, this is not only for the obvious reason that it is the primary channel for the transmission of knowledge, but much more because it reflects, as nothing else does, the multi-level personality of man. (Halliday, 1974, p. 81-88)

Professor Halliday, whose idea the Programme was, and who provided the inspiration for all those who worked in and for it, thus expresses his own concern to tackle "the problem of educational failure at its deepest level"—that of language—and his conviction that, if we are successfully to do this, then theory and practice must be brought into fruitful relationship. We have recorded here something of what the Programme did during, its existence and have noted some of the writings that came after. It remains to ask what the impact on the educational scene of those endeavors has been.

4. WHAT DIFFERENCE HAS IT MADE?

John Pearce

Someone, some time, has to translate ideas into classroom practice.

It has to be conceded at once that *Language in Use* (Doughty et al., 1971) has not had anything like the direct effect on classroom teaching that it aspired to, or that *Breakthrough to Literacy* (Halliday, 1978b) has achieved in primary schools. During the development of the material, the *Language in Use* team encountered much willingness to listen and experiment, at all levels in the system. It also encountered resistance. Some of it, inevitably if not always voiced openly, reflected an attachment to a Nesfield-type grammar and clause analysis, which at the time had not been long dropped from public examination syllabuses for English at age 16. Much more of it came from a belief in literature as the only serious element in English teaching, expressed in terms like this in a letter received during the life of the project: "Language is *not* separate from us, but part of us; not our Meccano, but the pulsing of our blood." It was usually possible to meet such objections persuasively, but they are evidence of the resistance to the aims, objectives, and recommended teaching practices of the project that have persisted in some quarters. Nevertheless, if the impact on routine classroom practice has not been as great as was hoped, it can fairly be claimed that the work of the Programme has continued to exert influence on professional opinion and research during the last 15 years. That the issues the Programme faced are still pressing makes it all the more important to try to answer the question "What difference has it made?" In so doing, light may be shed on such subquestions as What is it like to bring linguists and teachers into joint action on English teaching? What are the possibilities and pitfalls? What is the relationship between such work and prevailing ideologies among teachers? What bearing do changes in educational system have on the work?

We have to begin with the structure of the Programme itself, conceived as it was in the light of a prevailing model of a curriculum project, usually known as the Research/Development/Diffusion model (RD&D). Under this model, a team of scholars and teachers collaborate to investigate the problems of relating leading-edge scholarship to school instruction, develop practical materials that embody their solutions, and disseminate them to schools. It is, in many respects, a simplistic model, but it originated in projects in several countries where the provenance of team members became less and less significant in the face of their common developmental task. In most curriculum projects in England, this merging did not happen. In the case of the Programme in Linguistics and English Teaching, the research was largely confined to the academic members, while the development was left to the teacher members, and serious dissemination was not at that time part of the brief of Schools Council projects. These features can be found in many such projects in England. Where the Programme differed, however, from most curriculum projects was its concern with an age range that spanned the life of the pupil from initial literacy to A level. At the same time, there was no possibility of engaging the public examination system during the three years in which the whole Programme was funded by Schools Council.

4.1 The Primary Sector

English local education authorities do not prescribe the reading schemes and methods their schools are to use, and in the late 1960s many head teachers were content to allow their teachers to make their own individual choices. The emphasis on a school-wide policy and coherence has developed more recently and is now usual. The dissemination of *Breakthrough*, therefore, depended not on convincing a handful of influential officers but on changing the climate of teaching opinion and practice. Until the mid-1970s, moreover, only a small minority of newly qualified primary teachers remained in the profession beyond the age of 25, so that the teachers who had to be reached and enthused were not those undergoing initial training but those returning from raising families and those in charge of often small schools. There is no way of estimating the take-up statistically, even in a single education authority, let alone in 104 very diverse authorities. However, in 1977 it was reported orally to an inspectors' conference that in three contrasted authorities the proportions of primary schools basing their initial literacy work on *Breakthrough* were, respectively, 40%, 32%, and 11%. The average of these three rates would probably give a rather inflated impression of the take-up for full and systematic use over the country as a whole, and the proportions have declined sharply in many areas with the arrival of newer, highly professional schemes from competing publishers.

To leave it at that, however, would be to undervalue the overall impact of the *Breakthrough* materials. The proportion of teachers in primary schools exposed to it at one time or another in their careers remains high, and a substantial proportion of schools employ the materials as one element in a wider initial literacy policy. They have not become professionally tagged as "remedial" in intent, and every teacher who has used them will have absorbed some important linguistic principles about the relationship between spoken and written language, the nature of the orthography, and the ways in which children learn language.

This is more than can be said for many of the relevant institutions in higher education. Until the restructuring of colleges in the mid-1970s, primary teachers were trained largely in separate establishments, many of which underwent closure or a severe reduction in size between 1974 and 1980. One consequence of this upheaval was the loss of many lecturers competent to provide the basic training in language and literacy that everyone insisted the students needed. The newly qualified primary teacher who has had even an adequate grounding in these matters remains rare in England. The reason lies in the way higher education classifies knowledge: "literacy" is categorized not under "language" but under "education." Since in much of teacher training in England the function of "Education" departments is to conduct such instruction as has not already been preempted by more academic and powerful departments, and while linguistics departments are uncommon and English departments regard literacy as outside their remit, this critical area of training continues to resist every pressure to improve it. Whether *Breakthrough* forms part of the work is thereby relegated to a secondary issue.

4.2 The Secondary Sector to Age 16

Every recognized study of English teaching in English secondary schools, including the Bullock Report in 1975 and the Survey by Her Majesty's Inspectors in 1979, has emphasized the scale of the reliance on teachers with qualifications other than in English. It is far from unusual to find English departments of 10 or 12 teachers where only 3 or 4 are qualified English specialists. These specialists are usually weighed down by the burden of teaching the all-important examination courses for pupils aged 14 to 16. Time is not provided for departmental planning or training on an adequate scale, and even if it were, the specialists have a natural attachment to the courses that legitimize their seniority and status within the school. Hence, the changing of examination syllabuses calls for a substantial shift of opinion and a widely shared body of discontent, as well as a considerable time-scale. It is hardly surprising, therefore, that the essentials of age 16+ English examinations remain, at the time of writing, very similar to those specified for the earliest formal written examinations at school level in the 1860s—essay on unseen topics, summary, and written questions on the comprehension of a written text.

One thrust of development over the past 30 years has been toward a way of formulating the demand on the pupil's writing so as to make it more personal (in the jargon, "expressive"). The search has been for ways of eliciting writing which allows the individual to use a task to order experience. Such emphasis is closely related to the stress on the educative nature of literature stemming directly from the writing of F. R. Leavis, whose view is often represented to students as a suggestion that pupils should be encouraged to do with their own experience what great authors (so the argument runs) are thought to have done with theirs. This ideology has prevailed in a majority of English departments engaged in teacher training, and in almost all those doing so through the postgraduate certificate route. Given the prevalence of this way of thinking, it is not to be wondered at that approaches deriving from a linguistic perspective have received scant support and much misrepresentation.

There have been contrary influences. Many leading members of Her Majesty's Inspectorate have acknowledged a considerable debt to *Language in Use*, a fact which has played some part in the new examination requirements operative from 1986. There has been a slow but steady increase in the number and standing of lecturers in education whose formative discipline has been linguistics or sociolinguistics. While initial training too often remains linguistically naive, in-service training at higher-degree level has incorporated extensive study in those fields. Courses from the Open University (such as PE 232 Language Development) have steadily increased the linguistic element, if not always going as far as some academic linguists would wish. Linguists who have themselves drawn upon school outputs and processes for their own research data remain few, with the Perera (1986) and Mercer (1981) notable exceptions.

Conscious of some shift in opinion, at least at authoritative levels, educational publishers have at last begun to abandon the old grammar and slot-filler exercises: the best of the coursebooks now include the serious attention to language called for by those who have understood the implications of the Programme's work. Making material available in coursebooks offers no guarantee that teachers will actually use it. Publishers have therefore, been assiduous in the "language-awareness" market, which ranges from contemporary versions of the time-honored content of comparative philology to serious attempts to alert pupils to speech variety, the nature of dialect, and the peculiar status, forms, and constraints of written text. The broadcasting media, in television and radio, have also developed a number of series based, sometimes explicitly, on the topics and approach of *Language in Use*.

England and Wales constituted a multiethnic society by 1971, but the general recognition of this fact, and the educational industry that was to arise in response, lay in the future. The informed specialists in the field enjoy no more general acceptance than their linguist colleagues. Moreover, many educationists in England still believe, at root, that the proper role of the immigrant is to assimilate to the host culture and language. In this domain, as in that of the native language and its educational treatment, English society remains deeply divided.

4.3 The Age 16-19 Sector

The proportion of students in full-time education after the age of 16 in England and Wales is lower than in any other major advanced economy, whether for academic courses or for vocational training. One reason is the split between the sixth forms in schools and the colleges of further education, a split reinforced by sharp differences in perceived status. The original target of *Language in Use* was the minority time of sixth forms, a curriculum zone created by the pursuit of three major specialist subjects for examination at age 18+, each of which specialized sixth-form colleges in a handful of areas, minority-time studies have fallen victim to the demand from students for courses offering some formal certification. The same has happened in further education, but in schools the effect has been to push *Language in Use* into the position of a teacher's resource demanding a degree of adaptation that heavily pressed teachers find difficult. Its influence has thus tended to become increasingly oblique, although it continues to enlist the enthusiasm of a minority of teachers who discover it on departmental shelves in schools. We know of no course of initial training of teachers in which it is brought formally to the student's attention in the context of school practice.

The major subject courses to age 18+ led to examinations at Advanced Level of the General Certificate of Education, and the first widespread discussion of linguistic studies and their relevance to school English arose in this context. The official body responsible for policy at the time, the Secondary School Examinations Council, issued in 1964 a report entitled *The Examining of English Language*. It included an appendix by Professor Randolph Quirk proposing an optional alternative test of the candidate's insight into language studied from a linguistic perspective. Quirk's argument, which the relevant committee endorsed, was that without some such treatment the prospective teacher of English would never gain the necessary insight into language in general or the English language in particular. The furor that this appendix created deterred the authorities from even offering such an option, and to this day professional and lay opinion remains frustrated by the absence of any agreement on the matter. Partly as a result, facile nostrums like restoring instruction in traditional grammar gain adherents in political quarters. In the meantime, a few experimental courses in schools are developing, but they tend to show that linguists underestimate the scale and depth of the technical knowledge that such courses demand of the teachers conducting them.

The position in the further education part of the post-age-16 sector has developed quite differently. Until the early 1970s many vocational courses had a compulsory element of English language, usually realized as formal essay-writing and summarizing, with a variety of minor tasks derived from models of tests long abandoned by the schools. There was a substantial group of courses, however, in which minority time was provided and its effective use protected. Overall, these contexts provided an opportunity for experimental classroom work on a larger scale than in the schools, and *Language in Use* was seized on with enthusiasm. The most influential adaptation was conducted by a small group of examiners in the main national course in public administration, who instigated the development that became known as the assignment method. This was adopted by the new Business Education Council in 1977 as its basic teaching-and-learning strategy for all its course modules. In the council's program, the student is provided with a concrete and specific situational context in which he or she must make decisions, legal or financial or managerial, and convey them, or matters relating to them, to a variety of specified audiences. The development was led by a mix of systematic in-service training, policy advice from the council, and the publication of textbooks, in all of which leading parts were played by former members of the Programme. The widespread adoption of *Language in Use* in the period prior to this development was without doubt a significant facilitating factor, and when the Business Education Council issued its guidelines on the design of assignments in 1981 they read as a direct application of the principles behind the Programme's material.

The past decade has seen far greater change in further education curricula, however, than just that in business studies. The work stimulated by the Further Education Unit (originally set up within the Department of Education and Science) has affected every aspect of further education except courses leading to prestigious paper qualifications such as Advanced Level or those of professional bodies. The scale of vocational and prevocational preparation has been greatly increased, and a massive program has taken place to equip teachers to lead students, effectively, whose capacity for formal learning was inherently limited or had been undermined by their experience of school. In all of this, the influence of the Programme's work has been seminal, not least in lending legitimacy to areas of study obviously of great importance but not grounded in conventional degree subjects. For example, the very large scale of the Youth Training Scheme calls for numerous teachers and course tutors who have been set free from the conventional English middle-class belief that effective communication occurs only in RP (Received Pronunciation), and have thereby gained confidence in their own regional speech and have inculcated a similar confidence in their students. The only source of such insights, until very recently, was directly or indirectly mediated from linguistic studies by the work of the Programme.

4.4 What Was Possible?

It is fair to ask how much influence the Programme could have had and what it could have achieved, given the real world in which it had to work. The answer inevitably has to begin with the absence of formal curriculum specification or central modes of control and influence on schools. Given that fundamental feature, every attempt at curriculum change has to operate through individual teachers and their professional groups. Teachers in England, as elsewhere, tend to behave first socially and second academically: that is to say, they identify and associate with those who share and respond to their felt needs and aspirations or embody and revitalize their formative experiences—above all, the experiences that constitute their sense of identity. It is not surprising that the specialist English teacher, working as he or she does with a number of nonspecialists, committed to a belief in the civilizing and sensitizing power of the subject in an insensitive and often hostile environment, should associate with like-minded others and seek to reinforce the sense of missionary zeal that has been present in the teaching profession in England for over a century. In this climate, the advocacy of alternative aims or approaches is inherently likely to be labeled heretical.

That is very far from the whole story, of course. English teachers certainly betray a tendency to associate with those whom they can characterize as prophets. This happened with especially unfortunate results in the case of Bernstein (see "Class Codes and Control," vol. 1, 1971), whose very abstract perceptions were seized on as a simple political solution to a complex social problem. The misreading of Bernstein as postulating a simplistic equation between "restricted code" and "working-class speech" was not helpful to the *Language in Use* team. Relations with Bernstein and his unit were cordial and productive, but the educational community displayed a serious inability to grasp his real substance. The misreading that prevailed not only distracted from an understanding of the Programmes' material, but in some colleges was regarded for a time as being of more significance.

A rather similar pattern of identification with a professional leader whose writing may not be fully understood occurred with James Britton ("Language and Learning," 1970), and can be seen at work again in the more recent vogue for the writing of Donald Graves (1983). But whatever the susceptibility of the English teaching community to such gurus, a linguistically oriented view of its collective task cannot hope for widespread adoption as long as the majority of English teachers lack the central perceptions and knowledge necessary for applying it. What these are remains disputed in detail, but the experience of the Programme suggests that they include the following:

1. the priority of spoken over written language, and the relationships between them, preferably informed by phonetic understanding;
2. the nature and scope of linguistic variety, and its implications for text and genre;
3. the relationships between reality and its linguistic representation;
4. a sufficient knowledge of the grammar of modern English to permit both some textual analysis with students *and* a grasp of the limitations of traditional school grammar.

In relation to the normal academic concerns of many linguists, this list will appear modest and perhaps very "applied" in the limited sense. It is important, however, for linguists to avoid the mistake of supposing that the teacher at school level is qualified only by the mastery required of the future academic researcher. It is also important to protect teachers from the (to them) largely irrelevant scholastic disputes that have inevitably marked the formative stages of what is, after all, a newly established academic discipline—of which those about transformational-generative grammar were merely the best known.

The other lesson of the Programme was that the original RD&D model of a curriculum project entails, for its successful working, a complete immersion of all members of the project in its agenda. This is not a symmetrical matter, in that the academic scholars are called upon for a greater degree of self-denial than are the teachers, because the agenda of such a project is focused on changing practice in schools. Since the learning behaviors of school-age pupils, and especially their range of ability, are maximally different from those encountered in universities, the scholars have at least as much to learn about schools as the teachers have about the academic discipline. Could the Programme itself, through its materials, have taken the course of building in the kind of linguistic knowledge cited above as necessary for teachers? At one level this is impraticable: There is no way of replicating in printed materials, even with audio backup, the ear training at the heart of phonetic understanding of text. More generally, it has become more possible since 1971 for curriculum projects to impose prerequisite studies on teachers aspiring to use new materials. But at the time of the Programme, this was in the future, and even now it remains at odds with a publisher's need to find, quickly, a viable market. While there are some units in *Language in Use* that seek to convey such knowledge in ways that teachers can grasp at their own level while pupils do so at theirs, there is little evidence that this strategy worked at anything beyond a piecemeal level. To do more than this, it would have been necessary to convert the package from a set of resources available for open choice into a planned sequence worked out on a much more elaborate scale, with no guarantee that it would be used.

The real answer is that all teachers of English need a sound grounding in language as well as in literature, and the links and balance between them need particular care in the professional phase of their training. At present, in England, such an outcome appears as unlikely as ever, with the obsession with microcomputing as a "resource" appearing to engage lecturers to an extent that continues to exclude the linguistic study of language.

APPENDIX

A: Nuffield Programme in Linguistics and English Teaching, 1964-1967

Papers published by Longman in 1968:

1. Doughty, P. S., *The Relevance of Linguistics for the Teacher of English*
2. Hasan, R., & Lushington, S., *The Subject-Matter of English*
3. Mackay, D, & Thompson, B., *The Initial Teaching of Reading and Writing*
4. Doughty, P. S., *Current Attitudes to Written English*
5. Doughty, P. S., *Linguistics and the Teaching of English*
6. Philp, A. M., *Attitudes to Correctness in English*
7. Hasan, R., *Grammatical Cohesion in Spoken and Written English*
8. Davies, E., *Aspects of General Linguistics*
9. Albrow, K. H., *The Rhythm and Intonation of Spoken English*
10. Davies, E., *Elements of English Clause Structure*

B: Schools Council Programme in Linguistics and English Teaching, 1967-1971

Second series of papers published by Longman in 1972, edited by Stephen Lushington:

1. *Language at Work*
   Thornton, G. M., "*The Individual and His Development of a Language*"

Birk, D, *"You Never Speak a Dead Language"*
Hudson, R., *"An Exercise in Linguistic Description"*
2. Albrow, K. H., *"The English Writing System"*
3. Halliday, M. A. K., *"Language and Social Man"*
4. *Language: Classrooms and Examinations*
    Forsyth, I., *"Language Studies for the Middle Years"*
    Pearce, J. J., *"English and Examinations"*
    Language and Social Man was subsequently reprinted in M. A. K. Halliday.
(1978). *Language and Social Semiotic: The Social Interpretation of Language and Meaning.* London: Edward Arnold.
    Language Studies for the Middle Years became the starting point for I. Forsyth & K. Wood. (1980). *Language and Communication 1, 2, 3.* London: Longman.

C: Explorations in Language Study

(Series published by Edward Arnold)
Ashworth, E. (1973). *Language in the Junior School.*
Carter, R., & Burton, D. (Eds.). (1982) *Literary Text and Language Study.*
Doughty, A., & Doughty, P. S. (1974). *Language and Community.*
Doughty, P. S., & Thornton, G. M. (1973). *Language Study, the Teacher and the Learner.*
Gannon, P. (1985). *Assessing Writing.*
Gurney, R. (1973). *Language, Brain and Interactive Processes.*
Gurney, R. (1976). *Language, Learning and Remedial Teaching.*
Halliday, M. A. K. (1973). *Explorations in the Functions of Language.*
Halliday, M. A. K. (1975). *Learning How to Mean.*
Harris, S., & Morgan, K. (1979). *Language Projects.*
Harrison, B. (1973). *English as a Second and Foreign Language.*
Richmond, J. (1982). *The Resources of Classroom Language.*
Rogers, S. (Ed.). (1976). *They Don't Speak Our Language.*
Sharp, D. (1973). *Language in Bilingual Communities.*
Thornton, G. M. (1974). *Language, Experience and School.*
Thornton, G. M. (1980) *Teaching Writing.*
Thornton, G. M. (1986). *Language, Ignorance and Education.*
Trudgill, P. (1985). *Accent, Dialect and the School.*

Translations:
Doughty, P. S., & Doughty, A. (1975). *Language and Community.* Tokyo: Burin.
Halliday, M. A. K. (1982) *Exploraciones sobre las funciones del lenguaje.* Barcelona: Editorial Medica y Tecnica.
Trudgill, P. (1979). *La varietà della lingua inglese.* Bergamo: Minerva Italica.

D: Breakthrough to Literacy

Besides the Breakthrough apparatus, the Teacher's Manual, The Breakthrough Dictionary and the Breakthrough Books, details of which will be found in the current Longman catalogue, the following references illustrate the scope and range of the material:

Ashworth, L. et al. (n.d.) *A Practical Guide to Breakthrough to Literacy.* Coventry, England: Elm Bank Teacher's Centre.

Johnston, M. R. (1979). *An Introduction to Breakthrough to Literacy.* Cape Town, South Africa: Longman Penguin Southern Africa.

Rodseth, V., Ngambu, S., Mgetyana, N., & Nama, A. (1985). *Breakthrough to Zulu.* Cape Town: Maskew Miller Longman.

Western Isles Bilingual Education Project:
Na facil (The Words). (1981). London: Longman for Schools Council.
Grian (Sun). (1980/1985). Stornoway, Isle of Lewis, Scotland: Acair.

A Welsh version is due to be published in 1987 as *ar y throthwy (on the threshold),* Gwasg Gomer, Llandysul, Wales, Uk: Gomer Press, on behalf of the School Curriculum Development Committee.

Notes:

The Breakthrough to Zulu teacher's manual (Rodseth et al., 1975) is used in southern African Schools in which Xhosa, Zulu, Tswana, Northern Sotho, Southern Sotho, Venda, and Tsonga are the mother tongues. *Breakthrough* was produced in these languages as part of the Molteno Project, by the Institute for the Study of English in Africa (ISEA) of Rhodes University, Grahamstown, South Africa. This work was initiated by Mr. Victor Rodseth.

Na Facil is the Scottish Gaelic version of the Sentence Maker.

Grian is the title of a series of 24 books in Gaelic for primary school children. The books are derived from the writings of children in the Western Isles Bilingual Project Schools.

E: Publications of the Language in Use Project

Doughty, P., Pearce, J. & Thornton, G. (1971). *Language in Use.* London: Edward Arnold.
Translations:
Taal gebruiken. (1978). Groningen, The Netherlands: Wolters-Noordhoff.
Il linguaggia educato. (1981). Milan: Franco Angeli Editore.

Doughty, P., Pearce, J., & Thornton, G. (1972). *Exploring Language.* London: Edward Arnold.
Translation:
Kielen tiet. (1976) Helsinki: Kustannusosakeyhtio Tammi.

Doughty, P. (1974). *Language, 'English' and the Curriculum*. London: Edward Arnold.

Doughty, A., & Doughty, P. (1974). *Using 'Language in Use'*. London: Edward Arnold.

REFERENCES

Adams, A., & Pearce, J. (1974). *Every English Teacher*. Oxford: Oxford University Press.

Allen, J. P. B. and Widdowson, H. G. (1973-1980) *English in Focus*. London: Oxford University Press.

Anglin, J. M. (1980). Acquiring linguistic skills: A study of sentence construction in preschool children. In D. R. Olson (Ed.).

Applebee, A. N., & Langer, J. (1983). Instructional scaffolding: Reading and writing as natural language activities. *Language Arts, 60*, (2), 168–175.

Ashton-Warner, S. (1980). *Teacher*. London: Virago. (Original work published 1963)

Barnes, D. (1977). The study of classroom communication in education. In M. Gill, & W. J. Crocker (Eds.), *English in Teacher Education*. Armidale, Australia: University of New England Press.

Barnes, D., & Barnes, D. (1984). *Versions of English*. London: Heinemann Educational.

Barnes, D., Britton, J., & Rosen, H. (1971). *Language, the learner and the school*. Harmondsworth, England: Penguin.

Bates, E., Camaioni, L., & Volterra, V. (1979). The acquisition of performatives prior to speech. In E. Ochs & B. B. Schieffelin (Eds.), *Developmental pragmatics* (pp. 111–130). New York: Academic.

Bateson, G. (1980). *Mind and nature: A necessary unity*. London: Fontana.

Bateson, M. C. (1975). Mother-infant exchanges: The epigenesis of the conversational interaction. In D. Aaronson & R. W. Reiber (Eds.), *Developmental psycholinguistics and communication disorders (Annals of the New York Academy of Sciences, 263*, pp. 101–113).

Benson, J. D., & Greaves, W. S. (1981). Field of discourse: Theory and application. *Applied Linguistics, 2*(1).

Berger, P. L., & Luckmann, T. (1966). *The social construction of reality*. Harmondsworth, England: Penguin.

Bernstein, B. (1971). *Class, codes and control: Vol. 1. Theoretical studies towards a sociology of language*. London: Routledge & Kegan Paul.

Bernstein, B. (Ed.). (1973). *Class, codes and control: Vol. 2. Applied studies toward a sociology of language*. London: Routledge & Kegan Paul.

Bernstein, B. (1979). The new pedagogy: Sequencing the new pedagogy: Underlying assumptions. In J. Maling-Keepes & B. D. Keepes (Eds.). Westport, CT:

Birdwhistell, R. L. (1970). *Kinesics and context*. Philadelphia: University of Pennsylvania Press.

Birns, B. (1976). The emergence and socialisation of sex differences in the earliest years. *Merrill-Palmer Quarterly, 22*(3), 229–254.

Bloom, B. S., Engelhart, M. D., Furst, E. J., Hill, W. H., & Krathwohl, D. R. (1956). *Taxonomy of educational objectives: The classification of educational goals: Handbook 1: Cognitive domain*. London: Longmans.

Bloom, L. (1970). *Language development: Form and function in emerging grammars*. Cambridge, MA: MIT Press.

Bloomfield, L. (1933). *Language*. London: Allen & Unwin.

Boardman, R. (1979). *Over to you*. London: Cambridge University Press.

Bower, T. G. R. (1971). The object world of the infant. *Scientific American, 225*(4), 30–38.

Brazelton, T. B., et al. (1974). The origins of reciprocity: The early mother-infant interaction. In M. Lewis & L. A. Rosenblum (Eds.), *The effect of the infant on its caregiver*. New York: Wiley.

Brazelton, T. B., & Tronick, E. (1980) Preverbal communication between mothers and infants. In D. R. Olson (Ed.).

Britton, J. (1970). *Language and learning*. Harmondsworth, England: Penguin.

Britton, J., Burgess, T., Martin, N., McLeod, A., & Rosen, H. (1975). *The development of writing abilities (11–16)*. London: Macmillan Education.

Brown, R., & Bullugi, U. (1964). Three processes in the child's acquisition of syntax. In E. H. Lenneberg (Ed.).

Brown, R. & Cazden, C. (1975). The early development of the mother tongue. In E. H. Lenneberg & E. Lenneberg (Eds.), *The foundations of language development* (Vol. 1 and 2). New York: Academic Press.

Bruner, J. S. (1975). The ontogenesis of speech acts. *Journal of Child Language, 2*, 1–19.

Bruner, J. S. (1977) Early social interaction and language acquisition. In H. R. Schaffer (Ed.), *Studies in mother-infant interaction*. New York: Academic Press.

Bruner, J. S. (1978). The role of dialogue in language acquisition. In A. Sinclair, R. J. Jarvelle, & W. J. M. Levelt. (Eds.), *The child's concept of language*. New York: Springer-Verlag.

Bruner, J. S. (1983). *In search of mind*. New York: Harper & Row.

Bullock Report: Department of Education and Science. Committee of Inquiry under the chairmanship of Sir Alan Bullock. (1975). *A language for life*. London: Her Majesty's Survey Office.

Bullowa, M. (Ed.). (1979). *Before speech*. Cambridge, England: Cambridge University Press.

Business Education Council. (1977). *BEC national awards: Course specification*. London: BEC, Portland Place.

Business Education Council. (1980). *Second annual review of standards*. London: BEC, Portland Place. (Mimeo)

Business Education Council. (1981). *Third annual review of standards*. London: BEC, Portland Place. (Mimeo)

Buss, A., & Plomin, R. (1984). *Temperament: Early developing personality traits*. Hillsdale, NJ: Erlbaum.

Butt, D. G. (1985). *Talking and thinking: The patterns of behaviour*. Geelong, Australia: Deakin University Press.

Cambourne, B. (1984). The origins of teachers' doubts about "naturalising" literacy education. In S. Bahr (Ed.), *Selected key papers of the 10th Australian Reading Conference* (Vol. 2).

Cameron, D. (1985). What has gender got to do with sex? *Language and Communication*, 5(1), 19–27.

Carter, A. L. (1978). The development of systematic vocalisations prior to words: A case study. In N. Waterson & C. Snow (Eds.).

Carter A. L. (1979). Prespeech meaning relations. In P. Fletcher & M. Garman (Eds.), *Language acquisition* Cambridge, England: Cambridge University Press.

Cazden, D. (1971). *Child language and education*. New York: Holt, Rinehart & Winston.

Chomsky, N. (1968). *Language and mind*. New York: Harcourt Brace Jovanovich.

Chomsky, N. (1972). *Problems of knowledge and freedom*. London: Fontana Collins.

Chomsky, N. (1975). *Reflections on language*. New York: Pantheon.

Christie, F. (1976). *The teaching of English in elementary schools in New South Wales 1848–1900: An enquiry into social conditions and pedagogical theories determining the teaching of English*. Unpublished master's thesis, University of Sydney.

Christie, F. (1981). *The 'received tradition' of English language study in school: The decline of rhetoric and the corruption of grammar*. Unpublished master's thesis, University of Sydney.

Christie, F. (1985a). In R. F. Walker, F. Christie, B. Horvath, J. Rothery, & M. MacCausland. A knock on the door: an analysis of classroom discourse. In R. Hasan (Ed.).

Christie, F. (1985b). *Language education*. Geelong, Australia: Deakin University Press.

Christie, F. (1985c, November). *Curriculum genres: Towards a description of the construction of knowledge in schools*. Paper presented at the Working Conference on Interaction of Spoken and Written Language in Educational Settings, held at the University of New England, Armidale, Australia.

Christie, F., & Rothery, J. (1979). English in Australia: An interpretation of role in the curriculum. In J. Maling-Keepes & B. D. Keepes (Ed.).

Clark, H., & Clark, E. (1977). *Psychology and language: An introduction to psycholinguistics*. New York: Harcourt Brace Jovanovich.

Clark, M. (Ed.). (1985). *New directions in the study of reading*. Lewes, England: The Falmer Press.

Condon, W. (1979). Neonatal entrainment and enculturation. In M. Bullowa (Ed.).

Connell, W. (1980). *A history of education in the twentieth century world*. Canberra: Curriculum Development Centre.

Cooper, J. (1979). *Think and link*. London: Edward Arnold.

Cosgrove, I. & Jackson, R. (1972). *The Geography of Recreation and Leisure*. London: Hutchinson & Co.

Crystal, D., & Davy D. (1975). *Advanced conversational English*. London: Longman.

Cullen, M., & Turnbull, K. (1973). *The quality of children's first writing: Some comments on an Aspect of Breakthrough to Literacy* (Research Rep. No. 1, 73). Melbourne: Victoria Education Department.

Currie, J. (n.d.-a). *The principles and practice of early and infant school educaiton*. London: Stewart.

Currie, J. (n.d.-b). *The principles and practice of common school education*. London: Stewart.

Dawes, R. (n.d.). *Suggestive hints toward improved instruction, making it bear upon practical life, intended for use of schoolmasters and teachers in our elementary schools and others taking an interest in national education* (3rd ed.). London: Greenbridge.

Department of Education, New South Wales. (1968). *Curriculum for primary schools: English*. Sydney: Government Printer.

Dixon, J. (1967). *Growth through English*. London: National Association for the Teaching of English and the Oxford University Press.

Donaldson, M. (1983) *Children's minds*. London: Fontana (Original work published 1978).

Dore, J. (1973). *The development of speech acts*. Doctoral dissertation, City University of New York.

Dore, J. (1978). Conditions for the acquisition of speech acts. In I. Markova (Ed.). *Language and social context*. Chichester, England: Wiley.

Doughty, P., Pearce, J., & Thornton, G. (1971). *Language in use*. Schools Council Publication. London: Edward Arnold.

Doughty, P., Pearce J., & Thornton, G. (1972). *Exploring language*. London: Edward Arnold.

Drury, H., & Gollin, S. (1987). The use of systemic functional linguistics in the analysis of ESL student writing and recommendations for the teaching situation. In C. Painter & J. R. Martin (Eds.).

Dunn, H. (1837). *Popular education, or, the normal school manual: Containing practical suggestions for daily and Sunday school teachers*. London: Sunday School Union.

Eco, U. (1973). Social life as a sign system. In *Structuralism: An introduction*. Oxford: Claredon.

Economou, D. (1985). *Coffee break: A course in understanding authentic Australian casual conversation*. Adelaide: National Curriculum Resources Centre.

Edelsky, C. (1976). The acquisition of communicative competence: Recognition of linguistic correlates of sex roles. *Merrill-Palmer Quarterly, 22* (1), 47–59.

Education Department of Victoria (1981). *Society in view handbook: A process approach to social competence*. Melbourne: Publications and Information Branch, Education Department of Victoria.

Ervin, S. (1964). Imitation and structural change in children's language. In E. H. Lenneberg (Ed.).

Evans, D. W. (1978). *People and communication*. London: Pitman.

Fawcett, R. P., Halliday, M. A. K., Lamb, S. M., & Makkai, A. (Eds.). (1984). *Semiotics of culture and language*. London: Pinter.

Ferrier, L. (1978). Word, context and imitation. In A. Lock (Ed.).

Firth, J. R. (1950). Personality and language in society. *Sociological Review, 42,* 37–52. Reprinted in J. R. Firth (1957). *Papers in linguistics 1934–1951*. London: Oxford University Press.

Fishman, P. (1978). Interaction: The work women do. *Social Problems, 25,* 397–416.

Fitch, J. (1880). *Lectures on education*. Cambridge, England. Cambridge University Press.

Forsyth, I., & Wood, K. (1980). *Language and communication, 1, 2, and 3*. London: Longman.

Friedl, E. (1975). *Women and men: An anthropologist's view*. New York: Holt, Rinehart & Winston.

Fries, P. (1983). On the status of Theme in English: Arguments from discourse. In J. S. Petofi & E. Sozer (Eds.).

Gibson, R. (1984). *Structuralism and education*. London: Hodder & Stoughton.

Gill, J. (1883). *Introductory text book to school education*. London: Longmans and Green.

Ginn and Company (   ). *Reading 360*. Aylesbury, England: Ginn and Company.

Ginsburg, H., & Opper, S. (1969). *Piaget's theory of intellectual development: An introduction*. Englewood Cliffs, NJ: Prentice-Hall.

Gladman, F. J. (n.d.). *School method*. (12th ed.). London: Jarrold.

Goffman, E. (1977). The arrangement between the sexes. *Theory and Society, 4,* 301-331.

Graves, D. H. (1983). *Writing: Teachers and children at work*. Portsmouth, NH: Heinemann Educational.

Gray, B. (1984). Helping children to become language learners in the classroom. In P. Kidston & D. Patullo (Eds.), *Reading and writing: Implications for teaching*. Meanjin Reading Council of the Australian Reading Association.

Greenfield, P. M., & Smith, J. H. (1976). *The structure of communication in early language development*. New York: Academic Press.

Gregory, M. (1967). Aspects of varieties differentiation. *Journal of Linguistics, 3.*

Guiora, A., Beit-Hallahmi, B., Fried, R., & Yoder, C. (1982). Language environment and gender identity attainment. *Language Learning, 32*(2), 289-304.

Gumpertz, J., & Hymes, D. (1972). *Directions in sociolinguistics*. New York: Holt, Rinehart & Winston.

Gumpertz, J. J. (1982a). *Discourse Strategies* (Studies in Interactional Sociolinguistics 1). London: Cambridge University Press.

Gumpettz, J. J. (1982b). *Language and Social Identity* (Studies in Interactional Sociolinguistics 2). London: Cambridge University Press.

Haas, A. (1979). Male and female spoken language differences: Stereotypes and evidence. *Psychological Bulletin, 86*(3), 616–626.

Haas, A. (1981). Partner influence on sex-associated spoken language of children. *Sex Roles*, 7(9), 925–935.

Halliday, M. A. K. (1967-1968). Language and experience. In A. Peel, A. Wilkinson, & W. Curr (Eds.), *The place of language. Educational Review*, 20(2). School of Education, University of Birmingham.

Halliday, M. A. K. (1971a). Introduction. In R. Doughty, J. Pearce, & G. Thornton (Eds.). *Language in use*. London: Edward Arnold.

Halliday, M. A. K. (1971b). Language in a social perspective. In *The context of language. Educational Review*, 23(3).

Halliday, M. A. K. (1973). *Explorations in the functions of language*. London: Edward Arnold.

Halliday, M. A. K. (1974). *Language and social man* (Schools Council Programme in Linguistics and English Teaching: Paper Series 11, Vol. 3). London: Longman.

Halliday, M. A. K. (1975). *Learning how to mean: Explorations in the development of language*. London: Edward Arnold.

Halliday, M. A. K. (1977). *Aims and Perspectives in Linguistics*. (Occasional Paper No. 1). Applied Linguistics Association of Australia.

Halliday, M. A. K. (1978a). *Language as social semiotic: The social interpretation of language and meaning*. London: Edward Arnold.

Halliday, M. A. K. (1978b). Foreword. In D. Mackay, B. Thompson, & P. Schaub. *Breakthrough to literacy: Teacher's manual*. London: Longman for the Schools Council.

Halliday, M. A. K. (1978c). Meaning and the construction of reality in early childhood. In H. L. Pick & E. Saltzman (Eds.). *Modes of perceiving and processing information*. Hillsdale, NJ: Erlbaum.

Halliday, M. A. K. (1979a). Development of texture in child language. In T. Myers (Ed.). *The development of conversation and discourse*. Edinburgh: Edinburgh University Press.

Halliday, M. A. K. (1979b). One child's protolanguage. In M. Bullowa (Ed.).

Halliday, M. A. K. (1980). Three aspects of children's language development: Learning language, learning through language, learning about language. In Y. M. Goodman (Ed.), *Oral and written language development: Impact on schools*. (Proceedings from the 1979–1980 Impact Conferences), International Reading Association and National Council of Teachers of English.

Halliday, M. A. K. (1983). On the transition from child tongue to mother tongue. *Australian Journal of Linguistics*.

Halliday, M. A. K. (1984a). Language as code and language as behaviour: A systemic functional interpretation of the nature and ontogenesis of dialogue. In R. P. Fawcett, M. A. K. Halliday, S. M. Lamb, & A. Makkai (Eds.).

Halliday, M. A. K. (1984b). *Listening to Nigel: Conversations of a very small child*. Department of Linguistics, University of Sydney. (Mimeo)

Halliday, M. A. K. (1985a). Spoken and written modes of meaning. In *Interaction of spoken and written language in educational settings*. Armidale College of Advanced Education, Australia. Reproduced with permission. To appear in R. Horowitz & S. Samuels (Eds.). (Forthcoming). *Comprehending oral and written language*. Academic Press.

Halliday, M. A. K. (1985b). *An introduction to functional grammar*. London: Edward Arnold.

Halliday, M. A. K. (1985c). 'On casual conversation'. In R. Hasan (Ed.). *Discourse on Discourse*. Occasional Paper No. 7, Applied Linguistics Association of Australia.

Halliday, M. A. K., & Hasan, R. (1976). *Cohesion in English*. London: Edward Arnold.

Halliday, M. A. K., & Hasan, R. (1985). *Language, context and text: A sociosemiotic perspective*. Geelong, Australia: Deakin University Press.

Halliday, M. A. K., McIntosh, A., & Strevens, P. (1964). *The linguistic sciences and language teaching*. London: Longmans.

Hasan, R. (1978). Text in the systemic functional model. In W. Dressler (Ed.). *Current trends in textlinguistics* Berlin: de Gruyter.

Hasan, R. (1979). On the notion of text. In J. S. Petofi (Ed.), *Text vs. sentence: Basic questions of textlinguistics*. Hamburg: Helmut Buske.

Hasan, R. (1983). A Fragment of Message Semantics. Macquarie University, Australia. (Mimeo)

Hasan, R. (1984a). What kind of resource is language? *Australian Review of Applied Linguistics*, 7(1), 57–85.

Hasan, R. (1984b). Coherence and cohesive harmony. In J. Flood (Ed.), *Understanding reading comprehension*. Newark, De: International Reading Association.

Hasan, R. (1984c). Ways of saying: Ways of meaning. In R. P. Fawcett, M. A. K. Halliday, S. M. Lamb, & A. Makkai (Eds.).

Hasan, R. (Ed.). (1985a). *Discourse on Discourse* (Occasional Paper No. 7, Applied Linguistics Association of Australia).

Hasan, R. (1985b). *Linguistics, language and verbal art*. Geelong, Australia: Deakin University.

Hasan, R. (1985c). 'The texture of a text'. In M. A. K. Halliday, & R. Hasan. *Language, context and text: a sociosemiotic perspective*. Geelong, Australia: Deakin University Press.

Hasan, R. (1986). The ontogenesis of ideology: An interpretation of mother-child talk. In T. Threadgold, E. A. Grosz, G. Kress, & M. A. K. Halliday, (Eds.).

Havighurst, R. J. (1953). *Human development and education*. New York: Longmans, Green & Company.

Heisenberg, W. (1958). *Physics and philosophy*. New York: Harper & Row.

Henderson, E. H. (1981). *Learning to read and write: The child's knowledge of words*. Dekalb, IL: Northern Illinois University Press.

Henderson, E. H. (1985). *Teaching spelling*. Boston: Houghton Mifflin.

Hjelmslev, L. (1961). *Prologomena to a theory of language*. (F. Whitefield, Trans.). Madison: University of Wisconsin Press.

Horvath, B. (1985). *Variation in Australian English*. London: Cambridge University Press.

Hoyt, F. S. (1906). Grammar in the elementary curriculum. *Teachers College Record, 7,* 473–494.

Huey, E. (1908). *The psychology and pedagogy of reading, with a review of the history of reading and writing and of methods texts, and hygiene in reading.* New York: Macmillan.

Hymes, D. (1967). Models of the interaction of language and social setting. *Journal of Social Issues, 23.*

Ibrahim, M. H. (1973. *Grammatical gender.* The Hague: Mouton.

Johnson, K. (1981). *Communication in writing.* London: Longman.

Jones, L. (1977). *Functions of English.* London: Cambridge University Press.

Jordan, R. R. (1980). *Academic writing course.* Sydney: Collins.

Kohlberg, L. A. (1966). A cognitive-developmental analysis of children's sex role concepts and attitudes. In E. E. Maccoby (Ed.), *The development of sex differences.* Stanford, CA: Stanford University Press.

Kolln, M. (1981). Closing the books on alchemy. *College Composition and Communication, 32*(5), 139–151.

Kramer, C. (1974). Stereotypes of women's speech: The word from cartoons. *Journal of Popular Culture, 8,* 624–630.

Kramer, C. (1978). Male and female perceptions of male and female speech. *Language and Speech, 20*(2), 151–161.

Krathwohl, D. R., Bloom, B. S., Masia, B. B. (1964). *Taxonomy of educational objectives: The classification of educational goals: Handbook 2. Affective domain.* London: Longmans, Green & Company.

Kress, G. (1982). *Learning to write.* London: Routledge & Kegan Paul.

Kress, G. & Hodge, R. (1979). *Language as ideology.* London: Routledge & Kegan Paul.

Labov, W. (1970). The study of language in its social context. *Stadium Generale, 23,* 66–84.

Labov, W. (1972). *Language in the inner city: Studies in the black English vernacular.* Philadelphia: University of Pennsylvania Press.

Labov, W. & Waletzky, H. (1967). Narrative analysis: Oral versions of personal experience. In J. Helm (Ed.), *Essays on the verbal and visual arts.* Seattle: University of Washington Press.

Lakoff, R. (1975). *Language and woman's place.* New York: Harper & Row.

Laurie, S. (1867). *On primary instruction in relation to education.* Edinburgh: Blackwood.

Lawrie, R. A. & Nott, M. J. (1984). *Agricultural Land Bulletin 3.* Bathurst City Agricultural Land Suitability Study. Department of Agriculture, New South Wales, Australia.

Lenneberg, E. H. (Ed.) (1964). *New directions in the study of language.* Cambridge, MA: MIT Press.

Lewis, M., & Weinraub, M. (1974). Sex of parent × sex of child: Socioemotional development. In R. C. Friedman, Riehart, R. M., & R. L. Vande Wiele (Eds.), *Sex differences in behaviour.* New York: Wiley.

Lock, A. (Ed.). (1978). *Action, gesture and symbol.* London: Academic Press.

Luria, A. R. (1975). *Cognitive development: Its cultural and social foundations.* Cambridge, MA: Harvard University Press.

Luria, A. R. & la Yudovich, F. (1971). *Speech and the development of mental processes in the child.* Harmondsworth, England: Penguin.

McNeil, D. (1970). *The acquisition of language.* New York: Harper & Row.

McShane, J. (1980). *Learning to talk.* Cambridge, England: Cambridge University Press.

McTear, M. (1985) *Children's conversation.* Oxford: Blackwell.

Maccoby, E. E, & Jacklin, C. N. (1974). *The psychology of sex differences.* Stanford, CA: Stanford University Press.

Mackay, D. & Simo, J. (1976). *Help your child to read and write, and more.* London: Penguin.

Mackay, D., Thompson, B., & Schaub, P. (1970). *Breakthrough to literacy.* London: Longman.

Mackay, S., & Rosenthal, L. (1980). *Writing for a specific purpose.* Englewood Cliffs, NJ: Prentice-Hall.

Maling-Keepes, J., & Keepes, B. D. (Eds.). (1979). *Language in education: Language Development Project, Phase 1.* Canberra: The Curriculum Development Centre.

Martin, J. R. (1983). Conjunction in English. In J. S. Petofi, & E. Sozer (Eds.).

Martin, J. R. (1984a). Language, register and genre. In F. Christie (Ed.), *Children writing: Reader.* Geelong, Australia: Deakin University Press.

Martin, J. R. (1984b). Types of writing in infants and primary school. In L. Unsworth (Ed.)., *Reading, writing and spelling: Proceedings of the Fifth Macarthur Reading Language Symposium.* Sydney: Macarthur Institute of Higher Education.

Martin, J. R. (1985a). Process and text: Two aspects of human semiosis. In W. S. Greaves & J. D. Benson (Eds.), *Systemic perspectives on discourse: Selected theoretical papers from the 9th International Systemic Workshop (Vol. 5)* Norwood, NJ: Ablex.

Martin, J. R. (1985b). *Factual writing: Exploring and challenging social reality.* Geelong, Australia: Deakin University Press.

Martin, J. R. (1986a). Systemic-functional linguistics and an understanding of written text (Writing Project Rep. 1986). *Working Papers in Linguistics No. 4.* Department of Linguistics, University of Sydney.

Martin, J. R. (1986b). Grammaticalising ecology: The politics of baby seals and kangaroos. In T. Threadgold, E. A. Grosz, G. Kress, & M. A. K. Halliday (Eds.). (pp.225–267).

Martin, J. R. (1987). Intervening in the process of writing development. In C. Painter & Martin J. R. (Eds.).

Martin, J. R. & Peters, P. (1985). On the analysis of exposition. In R. Hasan (Ed.).

Martin, J. R. & Rothery, J. (1980, 1981). Writing Project Rep. Nos. 1, 2. *Working Papers in Linguistics.* Linguistics Department, University of Sydney.

Menn, L. (1978). *Pattern, control and contrast in beginning speech.* Bloomington: Indiana University Linguistics Club.

Menyuk, P. (1969). *Sentences children use*. Cambridge, MA: MIT Press.

Mercer, N. (Ed.) (1981). *Language in school and community*. London: Edward Arnold.

Milroy, D. (1984). Urban dialects in the British Isles. In P. Trudgill (Ed.).

Milroy, J. (1984). The history of English in the British Isles. In P. Trudgill (Ed.).

Moffett, J. (1981). *Coming on center: English education in evolution*. Upper Montclair, NJ: Boynton/Cook.

Moore, J. (1979, 1980). *Reading and thinking in English*. Oxford: Oxford University Press.

Morris, A., & Stewart-Dore, N. (1984). *Learning to learn from text: Effective reading in the content areas*. Sydney: Addison-Wesley.

Murison, E. (1985). Writing a scientific paper. Materials for Language Study Centre, University of Sydney.

Murphy, G. (1938). *An historical introduction to modern psychology*. London: Kegan Paul, Trench Trubner.

Nelson, K. (1973). Structure and strategy in learning how to talk. *Monographs of the Society for Research in Child Development*, (Serial No. 149).

Newby, M. (1981ff). *Making language, 1, 2, 3*. Oxford: Oxford University Press.

Newson, J. (1979). The growth of shared understandings between infant and care giver. In M. Bullowa (Ed.).

Oldenburg, J. (1986). The transition phase of a second child—18 months to 2 years. *Australian Review of Applied Linguistics, 9*(1).

Olson, D. R. (Ed.). (1980). *The social foundations of language and thought*. New York: Norton.

Open University. (1971). *Reading development* (Course PE261). Milton Keynes: Open University Press.

Open University. (1972). *Language development* (Course PE233). Milton Keynes: Open University Press.

Painter, C. (1984). *Into the mother tongue: A case study of early language development*. London: Pinter.

Painter, C. (1985). *Learning the mother tongue*. Geelong, Australia: Deakin University Press.

Painter, C. (1987). The role of interaction in learning to speak and learning to write. In C. Painter & J. R. Martin (Eds.).

Painter, C. & Martin, J. R. (Eds.) (1987). *Writing to mean: Teaching genres across the curriculum* (Occasional Paper). The Applied Linguistics Association of Australia.

Parke, R. D., O'Leary, S. E. & West, S. (1972). Mother-father newborn interactions: Effects of maternal medication, labor and sex of the infant. *Proceedings of the American Psychological Association*, (Vol. 7).

Pearce, J. (1972). Literacy is not enough. In M. Clark (Ed.).

Pearce, J. (1978). The death of essay—English under BEC. *Journal of Further and Higher Education, 2*(1).

Pearce, J. (1985). *The heart of English 9 to 14*. Oxford: Oxford University Press.

Pearce, J., Cooper, A., Leggott, P., & Sprenger, C. (1978). *People in touch: Assignments in communication and human relations*. London: Edward Arnold.

Penman, T. (1981). *The web of language*. Oxford: Oxford University Press.

Perera, K. (1986). Grammatical differences between speech and writing in children aged 8 to 12. In A. Wilkinson (Ed.), *The Writing of Writing* (pp. 91-108). London: Open University Press.

Perera, K. (1984). *Children's Writing and Reading*. London: Blackwell.

Peters, P.. (1985) *Strategies for student writers*. Queensland, Australia: Wiley.

Petofi, J. S. & Sozer, E. (Eds.). (1983). *Micro and macro connexity: Papers in textlinguistics: Vol. 45*. Hamburg: Helmut Buske.

Popper, K. (1972). *Objective knowledge: An evolutionary approach*. Oxford: Clarendon Press.

Poynton, C. (1984). Names as vocatives: Forms and functions. In M. Berry, M. Stubbs, & R. Carter (Eds.), *Nottingham Linguistics Circular, 13, Special issue on Systemic Linguistics*.

Poynton, C. (1985). *Language and gender: Making the difference*. Geelong, Australia: Deakin University Press.

Qui, S. (1985). *Early language development in Chinese children*. Master's thesis, Department of Linguistics, University of Sydney.

Read, C. (1971). Pre-school children's knowledge of English phonology. *Harvard Educational Review, 41*, 1-34.

Read, C. (1975). *Children's categorization of speech sounds in English* (Research Rep. No. 17). Urbana, IL: National Council of Teachers of English.

Reid, J. F. (1966). Learning to think about reading. *Educational Review, 9(1)*, 56-62.

Reid, J. F. (1974). *Breakthrough in action: An independent evaluation of Breakthrough to Literacy*. London: Longman for the Schools Council.

Richards, M. M. (1982). Empiricism and learning to mean. In S. A. Kuczaj (Ed.), *Language development: Vol. 1. Syntax and semantics*. Hillsdale, NJ: Erlbaum.

Robinson, R. (1867). *Teacher's manual of method and organisation adapted to the primary schools of Great Britain, Ireland and the Colonies* (2nd ed.). London: Longmans, Green.

Rochester, S., & Martin, J. R. (1979). *crazy talk: A study of the discourse of schizophrenic speakers*. New York: Plenum.

Rodseth, V., Ngambu, S., Mgetyana, N., & Nama, A. (1985). *Breakthrough to Zulu* (Teacher's Manual). Cape Town, South Africa: Maskew Miller Longman.

Rogers, S. (1975). *Children and language*. Oxford: Oxford University Press.

Rosen, C. & Rosen, H. (1973). *The language of primary school children*. Harmondsworth, England: Penguin.

Ross, L. & Gasser, M. (1983). *Academic English*. Englewood Cliffs, NJ: Prentice-Hall.

Rothery, J. (1984). The development of genres—primary to junior secondary school. In F. Christie (Ed.), *Children writing: Study guide*. Geelong, Australia: Deakin University Press.

Rothery, J. (1986a). Teaching writing in the primary school: A genre-based approach to the development of writing abilities (Writing Project Rep.).

Working Papers in Linguistics, No. 4. Department of Linguistics, University of Sydney.

Rothery, J. (1986b). Writing to learn and learning to write. (Writing Project Rep.). *Working Papers in Linguistics, No. 4.* Department of Linguistics, University of Sydney.

Rothery, J. (1986c). Let's teach children to write (Writing Project Rep.) *Working Papers in Linguistics, No. 4.* Department of Linguistics, University of Sydney.

Rothery, J. & Martin, J. R. (1986). What a functional approach to the writing task can show teachers about good writing. In B. Couture (Ed.), *Functional approaches to writing.* London: Pinter.

Rubin, G. (1975). The traffic in women: Notes on the "political economy" of sex. In R. Reiter (Ed.), *Toward an anthropology of women.* New York: Monthly Review Press.

Rubin, J. Z., Provenzano, F. Y., & Luria, Z. (1974). The eye of the beholder: Parents' views on sex of newborns. *American Journal of Orthopsychiatry, 44*(4), 512–519.

Ruble, D., & Ruble, T. (1982). Sex stereotypes. In G. Miller (Ed.)., *In the eye of the beholder.* New York: Praeger.

Rummel, R. J. (1967). Understanding factor analysis. *Journal of Conflict Resolution, 11*(4), 444–480.

Sapir, E. (1949). In D. G. Mandelbaum (Ed.), *Selected writings of Edward Sapir in language, culture and personality.* Berkeley: University of California Press.

Seavey, C. A., Katz, P. A., & Zalk, S. R. (1975). Baby X: The effect of gender labels on adult responses to infants. *Sex Roles, 2,* 103–110.

Secondary Examinations Council in collaboration with the Open University. (1986). *GSCE: A guide for Teachers—English.* Milton Keynes: Open University Press.

Secondary School Examinations Council. (1964). *The examining of English.* London: Her Majesty's Survey Office.

Seely, J. (1982ff). *Oxford secondary English,* (3 vols.). Oxford: Oxford University Press.

Serventy, V. (1984). *Whale and dolphin.* Sydney: John Ferguson.

Siegler, D. M., & Siegler, R. S. (1976). Stereotypes of males' and females' speech. *Psychological Reports, 39,* 167–170.

Sinclair, J., & Coulthard, M. (1975). *Towards an analysis of discourse.* Oxford: Oxford University Press.

Singer, H. (1979). *Reading: Learning to read* (Coursebook in the Board of Education Course on Reading). Geelong, Australia: Deakin University Press.

Smith, F., & Miller, G. A. (Eds.). (1966). *The genesis of language.* Cambridge, MA: MIT Press.

Stenhouse, L. (1975). *An introduction to curriculum research and development* (An Open University Set Book). London: Heinemann Educational.

Strodbeck, F. L., & Mann, R. D. (1956). Sex role differentiation in jury deliberations. *Sociometry, 19,* 3-11.

Sylvester-Bradley, B., & Trevarthen, C. (1978). "Baby talk" as an adaptation to the infant's communication. In N. Waterson & C. Snow (Eds.).

Thomson, A. & Martinet, A. (1969). *A practical English grammar.* Oxford: Oxford University Press.

Thornton, G. (1980), *Teaching writing.* London: Edward Arnold.

Threadgold, T., Grosz, E. A., Kress, G., & Halliday, M. A. K. (Eds.). (1980). *Semiotics, ideology and language.* Sydney: Sydney Association for Studies in Society and Culture.

Thwaite, A. (1983). *Sexism in Three Mills and Boon romances.* Bachelor's thesis. Department of Linguistics, University of Sydney.

Trevarthen, C. (1974). Conversations with a two-month old. *New Scientist, 2,* 230–235.

Trevarthen, C. (1979). Communication and co-operation in early infancy: A description of primary intersubjectivity. In M. Bullowa (Ed.).

Trevarthen, C. (1980). The foundations of intersubjectivity: Development of interpersonal and cooperative understanding in infants. In D. R. Olson (Ed.)

Trevarthen, C., & Hubley, P. (1978). Secondary intersubjectivity: Confidence, confiding and acts of meaning in the first year. In A. Lock (Ed.)

Trudgill, P. (1975). *Accent, dialect and the school.* London Edward Arnold.

Trudgill, P. (Ed.). (1984). *Language in the British Isles.* Cambridge, England: Cambridge University Press.

Ure, J., & Ellis, J. (1977). Register in descriptive linguistics and linguistic sociology. In O. Uribe-Vileges (Ed.), *Issues in sociolinguistics.* The Hague: Mouton.

Ventola, E. (1979). The structure of casual conversation. *Journal of Pragmatics, 3(3/4).*

Ventola, E. (1983). Contrasting schematic structures in service encounters. *Applied Linguistics, 4(3),* 242–258.

Ventola, E. (1984a). *Can I help you?* Unpublished doctoral dissertation, Department of Linguistics, University of Sydney.

Ventola, E. (1984b). Orientation to social semiotics in foreign language teaching. *Applied Linguistics, 5.*

Vygotsky, L. S. (1962). *Thought and language.* Cambridge, MA: MIT; New York: Wiley.

Waterson, N., & Snow C. (Eds.). (1978). *The development of communication.* Chichester, England: Wiley.

Wells, C. G. (1981). *Learning through interaction: The study of language development.* Cambridge, England: Cambridge University Press.

Whorf, B. (1956). *Language, thought and reality* (J. Carroll, Ed.). Cambridge, MA: MIT Press.

Wilber, K. (1982). *The holographic paradigm and other paradoxes.* Boulder, CO: Shambhala.

Wilkins, D. (1976). *Notional syllabuses.* Oxford: Oxford University Press.

Wilkins, W. (1886). *The principles that underlie the art of teaching.* Sydney: Government Printer.

Wilkinson, A., Barnsley, G., Hanna, P., & Swan, M. (1980). *Assessing language development.* Oxford: Oxford University Press.

AUTHOR INDEX

383

Menn, L., 35, 36, 377
Menyuk, P., 201, 378
Mercer, N., 360, 378
Mgetyana, N., 347, 379
Miller, G.A., 201, 380
Milroy, D., 378
Milroy, J., 378
Moffett, J., 163, 378
Moore, J., 260, 378
Morris, A., 274, 378
Murison, E., 271, 378
Murphy, G., 378

N
Nama, A., 347, 379
Nelson, K., 35, 378
Newby, M., 378
Newson, J., 107, 108, 378
Ngambu, S., 347, 379
Nott, M.J., 280, 376

O
Oldenburg, J., 28, 36, 378
O'Leary, S.E., 378
Olson, D., 378
Opper, S., 200, 373

P
Painter, C., 18, 28, 57, 108, 200, 230, 232, 378
Parke, R.D., 378
Pearce, J., 203, 348, 353, 356, 357, 369, 372, 378
Penman, T., 379
Perera, K., 360, 379
Peters, P., 269, 270, 377, 379
Petofi, J.S., 379
Plomin, R., 115, 370
Popper, K., 104, 379
Poynton, C., 24, 113, 128, 317, 379
Provenzano, F.Y., 114, 380

Q
Qui, S., 28, 379

R
Read, C., 342, 379
Reid, J.F., 337, 339, 348, 379
Richards, M.M., 20, 379
Robinson, R., 157, 379

Rochester, S., 26, 168, 379
Rodseth, V., 347, 379
Rogers, S., 379
Rosen, C., 203, 204, 208, 379
Rosen, H., 202, 203, 204, 208, 229, 369, 370, 379
Rosenthal, L., 260, 377
Ross, L., 260, 379
Rothery, J., 64, 161, 204, 236, 371, 377, 379, 380
Rubin, G., 111, 150, 380
Rubin, J.Z., 114, 380
Ruble, D., 119, 125, 380
Ruble, T., 119, 125, 380
Rummel, R.J., 129, 380

S
Sapir, E., 113, 149, 380
Schaub, P., 203, 377
Seavey, C.A., 114, 380
Seely, J., 380
Serventy, V., 380
Siegler, D.M., 127, 380
Siegler, R.S., 127, 380
Simo, J., 342, 377
Sinclair, J., 70, 380
Singer, H., 166, 197, 380
Smith, F., 36, 380
Smith, J.H., 201, 373
Snow, C., 381
Sozer, E., 379
Sprenger, C., 378
Stenhouse, L., 162, 380
Stewart-Dore, N., 274, 378
Strevens, P., 202, 262, 375
Strodbeck, F.L., 127, 380
Swan, M., 162, 164, 381
Sylvester-Bradley, B., 27, 380

T
Thompson, B., 230, 377
Thomson, A., 297, 381
Thornton, G., 230, 348, 353, 356, 357, 372, 381
Threadgold, T., 381
Thwaite, A., 147, 381
Trevarthen, C., 26, 27, 106, 380, 381
Tronick, E., 27, 370
Trudgill, P., 355, 381
Turnbull, D., 342, 372

SUBJECT INDEX